# THE CHURCH IN THE STORMS

# THE
# CHURCH
# IN THE
# STORMS

## ROBERTO DE MATTEI

*Translated by*
Nicholas Reitzug

SOPHIA INSTITUTE PRESS
Manchester, New Hampshire

# Contents

## VOLUME I

### From the Early Church to the Crusades

Introduction. . . . . . . . . . . . . . . . . . . . . . . . . . . . . . . . . . . . . . 5

Chapter I: The First Three Centuries of the Church . . . . . . . . . . . . . . .19

    1.   Christianity and the Roman Empire . . . . . . . . . . . . . . . . . . 19

    2.   The Beginning of the Persecutions . . . . . . . . . . . . . . . . . . . 21

    3.   "Christianos esse non licet" . . . . . . . . . . . . . . . . . . . . . . . 25

    4.   The Witness of Martyrdom . . . . . . . . . . . . . . . . . . . . . . 29

    5.   Martyrdom and Christian Combat. . . . . . . . . . . . . . . . . . 31

Chapter II: The Crisis of the Fourth Century . . . . . . . . . . . . . . . . . .35

    1.   The "Constantinian Shift" . . . . . . . . . . . . . . . . . . . . . . . 35

    2.   The Heresy of Arius . . . . . . . . . . . . . . . . . . . . . . . . . . 37

    3.   The Council of Nicaea. . . . . . . . . . . . . . . . . . . . . . . . . . 39

    4.   The Battle of St. Athanasius . . . . . . . . . . . . . . . . . . . . . . 44

    5.   St. Hilary of Poitiers, the Athanasius of the West . . . . . . . . . . 47

Chapter III: Monks Conquer the World . . . . . . . . . . . . . . . . . . . .51

    1.   Monasticism as a Category of the Christian Spirit . . . . . . . . . . 51

    2.   Monasticism in the East. . . . . . . . . . . . . . . . . . . . . . . . . 53

    3.   Monasticism in the West . . . . . . . . . . . . . . . . . . . . . . . . 57

    4.   St. Benedict of Nursia . . . . . . . . . . . . . . . . . . . . . . . . . 59

    5.   The Spread of the Benedictine *Rule*. . . . . . . . . . . . . . . . . . 63

Chapter IV: Pagan Rome and Christian Rome. . . . . . . . . . . . . . . . . .67

    1.   The Barbarians at the End of the Fourth Century . . . . . . . . . . 67

    2.   St. Ambrose and Theodosius. . . . . . . . . . . . . . . . . . . . . . 70

    3.   Paganism and Christianity . . . . . . . . . . . . . . . . . . . . . . . 72

    4.   St. Augustine . . . . . . . . . . . . . . . . . . . . . . . . . . . . . . 76

    5.   St. Jerome . . . . . . . . . . . . . . . . . . . . . . . . . . . . . . . . 78

Chapter V: Why the Roman Empire Fell . . . . . . . . . . . . . . . .81
   1.  The Twilight of the Roman Empire. . . . . . . . . . . . . . . . . 81
   2.  A World of Gray Hair . . . . . . . . . . . . . . . . . . . . . . . . . 85
   3.  Salvian of Marseille . . . . . . . . . . . . . . . . . . . . . . . . 87
   4.  St. Leo the Great . . . . . . . . . . . . . . . . . . . . . . . . . . . 89

Chapter VI: The Conversion of the European Nations. . . . . . . . . . . . . . .93
   1.  The Conversion of Clovis. . . . . . . . . . . . . . . . . . . . . . . 93
   2.  Ireland, "the Island of Saints" . . . . . . . . . . . . . . . . . . .101
   3.  "Not Angles, but Angels". . . . . . . . . . . . . . . . . . . . . . .103
   4.  St. Gregory the Great and "His Women" . . . . . . . . . . . . .105
   5.  St. Boniface and Germany . . . . . . . . . . . . . . . . . . . . . .107

Chapter VII: The Youthfulness of Christian Europe . . . . . . . . . . . . . . .109
   1.  Charlemagne . . . . . . . . . . . . . . . . . . . . . . . . . . . . . .109
   2.  Britain under Alfred the Great. . . . . . . . . . . . . . . . . . . .113
   3.  The Feats of Covadonga. . . . . . . . . . . . . . . . . . . . . . . .115
   4.  Christendom at the Dawn of the Year 1000. . . . . . . . . . . . . .120

Chapter VIII: The Reform of the Church in the Year 1000 . . . . . . . . . . . 125
   1.  The Scourges of the Church in the Eleventh Century . . . . . . . .125
   2.  Italian Reformers. . . . . . . . . . . . . . . . . . . . . . . . . . .128
   3.  The Spirit of Cluny. . . . . . . . . . . . . . . . . . . . . . . . . .130
   4.  St. Gregory VII . . . . . . . . . . . . . . . . . . . . . . . . . . . .133
   5.  What Is the Reform of the Church? . . . . . . . . . . . . . . . . .136

Chapter IX: The Spirit of the Crusades . . . . . . . . . . . . . . . . . . . . 141
   1.  The Origins of the Crusades. . . . . . . . . . . . . . . . . . . . .141
   2.  Urban II and the Council of Clermont. . . . . . . . . . . . . . . .144
   3.  Toward Jerusalem . . . . . . . . . . . . . . . . . . . . . . . . . .148
   4.  The Liberation of the Holy City. . . . . . . . . . . . . . . . . . .152
   5.  The Crusades as a Category of the Spirit . . . . . . . . . . . . . .155

# VOLUME II
## From the Middle Ages to the French Revolution

Foreword. . . . . . . . . . . . . . . . . . . . . . . . . . . . . . . . .161

Chapter I: The Light of the Middle Ages . . . . . . . . . . . . . . . .165
   1.  When the Philosophy of the Gospel Governed States . . . . . . . .165
   2.  The Origins and Nature of the Middle Ages . . . . . . . . . . . . .167
   3.  The Age of Cathedrals. . . . . . . . . . . . . . . . . . . . . . .169
   4.  Areas of Darkness in the Middle Ages . . . . . . . . . . . . . . .173
   5.  Holiness in the Middle Ages: From Cluny to St. Bernard . . . . . .176
   6.  St. Dominic and St. Francis . . . . . . . . . . . . . . . . . . . .178
   7.  St. Louis, King of France . . . . . . . . . . . . . . . . . . . . .181

Chapter II: The Crisis of Medieval Christianity . . . . . . . . . . . . .185
   1.  The Fourteenth Century and the End of the Middle Ages. . . . . .185
   2.  The Slap of Anagni. . . . . . . . . . . . . . . . . . . . . . . . .187
   3.  The Avignon Captivity . . . . . . . . . . . . . . . . . . . . . .189
   4.  William of Ockham and Marsilius of Padua . . . . . . . . . . . .191
   5.  A Fame, Peste, et Bello Libera Nos, Domine . . . . . . . . . . . .193
   6.  St. Catherine and St. Bridget. . . . . . . . . . . . . . . . . . .196
   7.  Carthusians: Never Reformed, Never Deformed . . . . . . . . . .199

Chapter III: The Age of the Great Schism. . . . . . . . . . . . . . . . .201
   1.  The Conclave of 1378 . . . . . . . . . . . . . . . . . . . . . . .201
   2.  Material Schism and Formal Schism . . . . . . . . . . . . . . . .203
   3.  Schism and Conciliar Theories . . . . . . . . . . . . . . . . . .204
   4.  The Councils of Pisa and Constance . . . . . . . . . . . . . . . .206
   5.  The Condemnation of Conciliarism . . . . . . . . . . . . . . . .208
   6.  St. Vincent Ferrer and St. Bernardine of Siena . . . . . . . . . . .209
   7.  St. Joan of Arc. . . . . . . . . . . . . . . . . . . . . . . . . . .211

Chapter IV: The Popes between Humanism and Crusade. . . . . . . . . . . .215
    1.  The Jubilee of 1450 . . . . . . . . . . . . . . . . . . . . . .215
    2.  Between Humanism and Crusade . . . . . . . . . . . . . . . .216
    3.  The Project of a Crusade: Callistus III, Pius II, Paul II . . . . . . . .219
    4.  George Skanderbeg and Pomponius Laetus . . . . . . . . . . . . .221
    5.  The Popes of the Renaissance: From Sixtus IV to Innocent VIII. . .223
    6.  From Alexander VI to Leo X. . . . . . . . . . . . . . . . . . . .225
    7.  St. Francis of Paola. . . . . . . . . . . . . . . . . . . . . . . .228

Chapter V: Protestant Revolution and Catholic Reform. . . . . . . . . . . .231
    1.  The Origins of the Protestant Revolution. . . . . . . . . . . . . .231
    2.  Martin Luther's Rebellion . . . . . . . . . . . . . . . . . . . .232
    3.  John Calvin . . . . . . . . . . . . . . . . . . . . . . . . . . .236
    4.  Henry VIII and the Anglican Schism. . . . . . . . . . . . . . . .237
    5.  The True Catholic Reform . . . . . . . . . . . . . . . . . . . .240
    6.  The Council of Trent . . . . . . . . . . . . . . . . . . . . . .243
    7.  St. Pius V: A Model Pope. . . . . . . . . . . . . . . . . . . . .245

Chapter VI: The Missionary Church in the Sixteenth and Seventeenth
Centuries . . . . . . . . . . . . . . . . . . . . . . . . . . . . . . . .249
    1.  The Universality of the Church . . . . . . . . . . . . . . . . . .249
    2.  The Missionary Vocation of the Church. . . . . . . . . . . . . . .252
    3.  St. Francis Xavier. . . . . . . . . . . . . . . . . . . . . . . . .254
    4.  Send Me Wherever You Wish, Even to India . . . . . . . . . . . . .257
    5.  Outside the Church There Is No Salvation . . . . . . . . . . . . .258
    6.  Missionary Spirit and Crusader Spirit . . . . . . . . . . . . . . .260
    7.  The Canadian Martyrs . . . . . . . . . . . . . . . . . . . . . .262

Chapter VII: The European Crisis of Conscience . . . . . . . . . . . . . . .265
    1.  Between Fidelity and Apostasy . . . . . . . . . . . . . . . . . .265
    2.  The Saints of the Counter-Reformation . . . . . . . . . . . . . .267
    3.  The Thirty Years' War and the Peace of Westphalia . . . . . . . . .269
    4.  Jansenism . . . . . . . . . . . . . . . . . . . . . . . . . . . .271
    5.  Devotion to the Sacred Heart . . . . . . . . . . . . . . . . . . .272
    6.  Louis XIV and the Sacred Heart . . . . . . . . . . . . . . . . . .274
    7.  The Announcement of Punishments and the Kingdom of Mary. . .277

Chapter VIII: The Church against Internal and External Enemies. . . . . . .281

   1.   The Holy Leagues against the Turks . . . . . . . . . . . . . . . . . .281

   2.   The Birth of Freemasonry . . . . . . . . . . . . . . . . . . . . . . . .283

   3.   The Moral Crisis of the Eighteenth Century . . . . . . . . . . . . . .285

   4.   Voltaire and the Enlightenment Philosophers . . . . . . . . . . . .286

   5.   Jansenism and Gallicanism in the Seventeenth Century . . . . . . .288

   6.   From the Suppression of the Society of Jesus to the French
       Revolution. . . . . . . . . . . . . . . . . . . . . . . . . . . . . . . . .290

   7.   The Testament of Fr. Lorenzo Ricci . . . . . . . . . . . . . . . . . .293

Chapter IX: The French Revolution . . . . . . . . . . . . . . . . . . . . . .297

   1.   The Origins of the French Revolution . . . . . . . . . . . . . . . . .297

   2.   The Revolution of a Minority . . . . . . . . . . . . . . . . . . . . . .300

   3.   The Anti-Christian Nature of the Revolution . . . . . . . . . . . .303

   4.   The Reign of Terror . . . . . . . . . . . . . . . . . . . . . . . . . . .305

   5.   The Climax and End of the Revolution . . . . . . . . . . . . . . . .308

   6.   The Vendée . . . . . . . . . . . . . . . . . . . . . . . . . . . . . . . .309

   7.   The Essence of the French Revolution. . . . . . . . . . . . . . . . .312

Chapter X: The Birth of the Counter-Revolution . . . . . . . . . . . . . . .315

   1.   Reaction to the French Revolution. . . . . . . . . . . . . . . . . . .315

   2.   The Christian Friendships . . . . . . . . . . . . . . . . . . . . . . . .318

   3.   Fr. Pierre Picot de Clorivière. . . . . . . . . . . . . . . . . . . . . . .321

   4.   The Revolution Was Satanic in Its Essence . . . . . . . . . . . . . .323

   5.   Erratic Passions. . . . . . . . . . . . . . . . . . . . . . . . . . . . . .325

   6.   Intellectuals of the Restoration . . . . . . . . . . . . . . . . . . . . .326

   7.   The Popes and the Counter-Revolution . . . . . . . . . . . . . . . .328

About the Author . . . . . . . . . . . . . . . . . . . . . . . . . . . . . . . . .331

# THE CHURCH IN THE STORMS

# FROM THE EARLY CHURCH TO THE CRUSADES

# Introduction

## Orare et Pugnare

In the Gospels, Jesus makes use of many metaphors to describe the Church He founded. One of the most fitting is the image of the boat threatened by the tempest (Matt. 8:23–27; Mark 4:35–41; Luke 8:22–25). This image was often used by the Church Fathers and saints, who spoke of the Church as a little boat buffeted by the waves, which lives, one might say, amid tempests without ever allowing itself to be submerged by the waves.[1]

St. Catherine of Siena, for example, took a vow to visit St. Peter's Basilica every morning while in Rome to pray before Giotto's mosaic in the pediment of the old basilica, which portrayed the scene of the storm-tossed barque of Peter. One day, January 29, 1380, toward the hour of Vespers, Jesus leaped out of the mosaic, approached Catherine who was rapt in ecstasy, and placed on her weak shoulders the agitated little boat that was the Church. The saint, oppressed by the weight, fell to the ground in a faint. This would be Catherine's last visit to St. Peter's, she who had always exhorted the pope with these words: "Grab the barque of the holy Church."[2]

Benedict XVI, for his part, using the metaphor applied by St. Basil to the period after the Council of Nicaea,[3] compared our time to a nocturnal naval battle in a storm-wracked sea, and in his homily for the feast of Sts. Peter and

---

[1]  See St. Augustine, *Discourse* 75, 3.4 and 4.5.
[2]  See St. Catherine of Siena, *Letter* 373.
[3]  St. Basil, *De Spiritu Sancto* 30, 77.

Paul, June 29, 2006, described the barque of the Church as "jolted by the winds of ideology," though unsinkable and secure on her course.

Agitation and torment have accompanied the Church throughout her entire history and have assaulted the pontificate of Joseph Ratzinger in particular, against the backdrop of a twenty-first century thick with fears and unknowns for the Church. What are the tempests that threaten the barque of Peter today, just as they did yesterday?

There are fierce winds that blow from outside the Church, such as the massacre of Christians in the Middle East and secular persecutions in the West. But the worst storms are those that come from within the Church herself. Under the pontificate of Benedict XVI, various crises have erupted, emphasized by mass media well beyond their actual scope, like the pedophilia scandal among the clergy and the internal struggles in the Roman Curia.[4] But an even vaster hurricane looms on the horizon: the rebellion of the clergy in Central Europe, promoted by organizations such as We Are Church and theorized by the Swiss theologian Hans Küng, author of the pamphlet titled *Let Us Save the Church*,[5] in which he directly opposes Benedict XVI, with whom he shared the experience of being the youngest theologian at the Second Vatican Council.

In this defamatory pamphlet, which recalls the incendiary booklets of Luther, Küng expands on the themes of a letter addressed to the bishops of the world in 2010, in which he incited them to an open rebellion against Benedict XVI, saying, "He failed to adopt the spirit of the Second Vatican Council as the compass for orienting the Catholic Church, carrying out its reforms; he received into the Catholic Church, without any preconditions, the traditionalist bishops of the Fraternity of St. Pius X, ordained illegally outside of the Catholic Church, who rejected the Council in some of its essential points; he has promoted with every means at his disposal the medieval Tridentine Mass, and has occasionally celebrated the Eucharist in Latin, turning his back on the faithful; he has strengthened around the world the anti-conciliar forces within the Church through the nomination of anti-conciliar leaders in positions of responsibility and reactionary bishops."[6]

---

[4]    This volume was first published in 2012, during the pontificate of Pope Benedict XVI.—Editor's Note.

[5]    Hans Küng, *Let Us Save the Church*. The pamphlet, published in 2011 in various languages, has been reprinted numerous times.

[6]    H. Küng, "Why Benedict XVI Has Failed," *La Repubblica*, April 22, 2010.

This appeal by Küng to the bishops was meant to encourage them to make their voice heard publicly and to promote and support "reform initiatives" (revolutionary actions, in other words), inviting them to act, using their episcopal authority, not only individually, but collegially, "in unison with other bishops, with priests, with women and men who form the people of the Church."[7]

Disobedience, according to Küng, must be exercised on a "regional" basis, through forms of "heteropraxis." This is not a matter of producing documents, but of acting concretely in rupture with Rome, above all regarding the incandescent problem of priestly celibacy. "The Vatican," he writes, "often turns a deaf ear to the justified requests of the bishops, priests, and laity. One more reason for aiming at intelligent regional solutions. As you well know, a particularly delicate problem concerns the law on celibacy, a norm of medieval origins, which has now been rightly placed in discussion around the world in the context of the scandal raised by clerical abuse. A change in opposition to Rome seems nearly impossible, but this does not condemn us to passivity. A priest who after serious reflection has matured the intention to marry should not be forced to resign automatically from his role if he could only count on the support of his bishop and his community. Just one episcopal conference could open the path to a regional solution."[8] This itinerary has been delineated and abundantly followed in German-speaking countries. Priests are living *more uxorio*, with a serene conscience, and are asking for the support and solidarity of the faithful and their bishops, rebelling in effect against the authority of Rome.

"The often-dramatic situation in the Church today" was at the center of the homily given by the pontiff in the Chrism Mass on April 5, 2012. This was not a generic denunciation: the pope made explicit reference to the situation of the Church in Austria, where an appeal to disobedience was published by the movement Pfarrer-Initiative (Initiative of Parish Priests), which is part of the network We Are Church. This appeal, signed by four hundred Austrian priests, asks for female ordination and communion for the divorced and remarried — all matters upon which the Church has already expressed herself in an irrevocable manner.

The disobedience of exponents of the clergy denounced by the pope does not represent an episode of isolated disobedience, but organized adherence to error and heresy. It has presented itself as schism, at least potential schism. The

7   Ibid.
8   Ibid.

fundamental distinction between heresy and schism dates from the time of St. Jerome, who defined heresy as the perversion of dogma, while schism is separation from the Church.[9] Whereas in heresy there prevails a doctrinal or theological separation, in schism it is a disciplinary or ecclesial separation. Not all heresies are translated into schisms, but every schism generally presupposes a heresy.

The history of the Church, from the time of its origins, is the history of persecutions, but also of schisms and heresies, which, since the beginning, have undermined its unity. St. Paul's letters often refer to these deviations from the teachings of Christ and the Church, already being proposed to the faithful. Thus, in the Letter to the Ephesians, he admonishes them not to "live as the Gentiles do, in the futility of their minds; they are darkened in their understanding, alienated from the life of God because of the ignorance that is in them, due to their hardness of heart" (Eph. 4:17–18). The origin of this alienation from the life of God is man's lack of submission to Jesus Christ, the only Way, Truth, and Life.

The pope reminds us in his homily, "Jesus Christ carried out His commission through His obedience and humility unto the Cross, thus rendering credible His mission. Not my will, but your will: this is the word that reveals the Son, both His humility and His divinity, and points out the path to follow." The priest must always repeat the Gospel phrase, "My teaching is not mine" (John 7:16). "We do not announce private theories and opinions, but the faith of the Church of which we are servants.... But disobedience," the pope says, "is this truly a way? Can one perceive in this any sort of conformity to Christ, which is the presupposition of every true renewal, or rather only the desperate push to do something, to transform the Church according to our desires and our ideas?"

Those who, as Hans Küng, would like to transform the Church according to their own desires and ideas, have offloaded on Benedict XVI the accusation of disobedience. In his virulent writings, Küng has arrived at the point of defining the pope "schismatic" if he were ever to reach an agreement with the Fraternity of St. Pius X, to reintroduce it fully into the Church. This would be, according to the Swiss heretic, a return to the Tradition from which the Second Vatican Council definitively separated us.

With this scandalous decision, Pope Benedict, already surrounded by a halo of detachment that many do not care for, would further distance himself from the People of God. The classic doctrine on schisms ought to be a warning to

---

[9]  St. Jerome, in *Epistolam ad Titum*, PL III.737.

him, which says that there is schism in the Church when one separates from the pope, but also when one separates from the entire body of the Church. "The pope, too, could become a schismatic, if he does not intend to maintain the appropriate unity and harmony with the entire body of the Church" (Francisco Suarez, the authoritative Spanish theologian of the 1600s). A schismatic pope, according to canonical doctrine, forfeits his ministry. In any case, he cannot pretend obedience. Pope Benedict seems to favor in this way the movement of "disobedience," growing everywhere, with respect to a hierarchy that is disobedient to the Gospel. His would be the exclusive responsibility for the grave discord and enmity that he ushers into the Church in this way.[10]

Küng forewarns therefore the formalization in the Church of a schism that already exists, and which he himself foments. Benedict XVI is aware of this, and this helps to understand his ecclesiastical politics, which seem aimed at averting the official explosion of this fracture within the ecclesial body. The appeal to disobedience, amplified by the media, is widening every day, however. Küng's influence is profound, and the action of We Are Church is vast and capillary. Despite having his authorization revoked to teach as a Catholic theologian, Küng is still a priest, with full faculties to carry out all the functions of his ministry. His ideas are seen with sympathy by many bishops, even within the Roman Curia.

In Italy, Küng's theses are invoked more or less openly by the "Dioscuri" of progressivism: Enzo Bianchi, the prior of Bose, and Alberto Melloni, secretary of the Foundation for Religious Sciences John XXIII in Bologna. Bianchi and Melloni are among the signatories of the public manifestation of dissent toward John Paul II, signed in 1989 by sixty-three exponents of Catholic theology and culture, well ensconced in ecclesiastical institutions. They affirmed that the Second Vatican Council constituted a radical and irreversible "turning point" in the "understanding of ecclesial faith"; that the Holy See allows itself to be "conditioned by worldly logic" and by a "mentality of privilege," neglecting the "style of Christ"; that the function of the pontifical Magisterium "in the Early Church" was not "reducible to the function of leader of the community," and for this reason this function needs to be reconsidered, while the hierarchical nature of the visible Church ought to give way to a "conception of the Church as a communion of churches"; and finally, that it would "certainly be necessary to

---

[10] Hans Küng, "The Pope Is Provoking Disobedience," press release, *La Repubblica*, May 22, 2012.

examine closely" the legitimacy of the Magisterium's pronouncements in matters of ethics, with evident reference to sexual morality.[11]

It is important to emphasize how, in the requests of the innovators, the democratization of the Church is always tied to the widening of her morality. Getting married and laying claim to his affectivity, the dissenting parish priest elevates himself above Rome, seeking the support of the local structures on which he depends. This process, according to Küng and his disciples, to the extent to which it might involve an episcopal conference, like that in Germany or Austria, can lead to a definitive disintegration of the power of Rome and to the creation of a new conciliar church.

Those who would accuse the pope and the ecclesial hierarchy presume that the cause of the priestly sexual abuse crisis was in the institution of celibacy and in Catholic "repression" of sexuality, and they request, like Küng, that priests and bishops be allowed to marry.[12] But the facts before our eyes demonstrate the exact contrary: the moral decadence of the clergy has its origins in the years immediately after the Council, precisely when the "new theology" was rejecting traditional morality and espousing the theology of secularization. The theology of the innovators, urged by its ecumenical embrace of the world's values, sought an impossible dialogue between Christian morality and its dissipators. Using "pastoral sociology," they opened the door to the "sciences of the world," to sociology and psychoanalysis, finding teachers in the theoreticians of the sexual revolution: Wilhelm Reich, Herbert Marcuse, and Erich Fromm. The coryphaeus of the "new morality," defined by some as "porno-theologians,"[13] substituted the objectivity of natural law with individual liberty, freed of any normative obligation and immersed in the historical-cultural context — in other words, in "situational ethics." Given that sexuality constitutes an integral part of the person, they claim sexuality's positive role because, according to them, the Council teaches that only in a dialogical relationship with another person can the human being find fulfillment.

Among the values of the world that the Church must embrace, it was held, there is democracy, but also the sexual revolution, which substituted the Marxist

---

[11]   H. Küng, "Letters to Christians. Today in the Church ... ," *Il Regno-Attualità* 34, no. 10 (May 15, 1989): 244–45.

[12]   Küng, *Let Us Save the Church*, 249–51; Küng, "Ratzinger Gives His *Mea Culpa* for Pedophiles," *La Repubblica*, March 18, 2010.

[13]   Msgr. Domenico Celada, "The Porno-Theologians," *Il Tempo*, June 23, 1973.

categories of the bourgeoisie and the proletariat with repression and liberation. This implied the reduction of man to a set of physical needs and, in the end, to sexual energy. The family, founded on monogamous, indissoluble marriage between a man and a woman, was considered the repressive social institution par excellence: no sociological consideration could justify its continuation.

In his *Letter to the Catholics of Ireland* of March 19, 2010, Benedict XVI recalled how in the 1960s, "the tendency [was] decisive, even on the part of priests and religious, to adopt secular ways of thinking and judging reality without sufficient reference to the Gospel. The Vatican Council's program of renewal was at times misunderstood and there was a tendency, dictated by an honest yet erroneous intention, to avoid correctional approaches in irregular canonical situations." These situations are exploding today, along with the ideas that provoked them.

The "reforming" theses, expounded today by Hans Küng are shared by his admirers, unabashedly as well as hiddenly. The prior of Bose, Enzo Bianchi, rejoiced in the pages of *La Stampa* at rediscovering in bookshops a work such as *Being Christian* by Küng almost forty years after its first publication, characterizing it as follows:

> A dense and articulated analysis of Christianity beginning with the historical Jesus and his proclamation of the "good news," an investigation conducted with competence and great ecumenical sensibility by the then young Catholic theologian who participated in the Second Vatican Council as a *peritus*. Küng was and remains an enthusiast of Christ, a convinced believer that the Gospel can speak to the heart and mind of men and women of every age and every culture, a thinker who does not shrink before the challenges of dialogue with reason and with other religions. And the profound impact that this work of his has had on many Christians and on those outside the Church or who withdrew to the margins of it, are an unequivocal proof of its worth.[14]

Alberto Melloni, without naming Küng, often brings up his ecclesiological vision on the pages of *Corriere della Sera*, as he did on June 17, 2012, in a full-page article titled "The Council of Trent Is Finished after Five Centuries." Melloni and Marco Rizzi assert that the current crisis is that of the "model of Church elaborated by the Council of Trent in the mid-sixteenth century, which the Second Vatican

[14] *La Stampa*, March 11, 2012.

Council sought to bring up to date with the profound changes that have taken place in the centuries following it." The Tridentine model, according to these authors, had at its center an authoritarian and bureaucratic organism: the Roman Curia. Today this model is in crisis, and the Church must change "the form of ecclesiastical governance," following the royal road of "collegiality" indicated by Vatican II. "A permanent collegial organ," wrote Melloni for the same newspaper on June 4, "has been awaited since 1964, and it is not the synod of bishops convoked with an advisory function: to delay asking how to set in motion this aspect of communion means making the pope a target for those who 'help him' and to render the church the laughingstock of the media." These are the same ideas of Küng, according to whom "the power of the papacy has been transformed into an institution with a monarchical, absolutist imprint,"[15] who goes on to refer to the collegial dimension that he wanted to attribute to the Council.

We do well to remember that Melloni is consulted by the *Corriere della Sera* as an oracle for every problem that concerns the Catholic Church, while Enzo Bianchi is considered a "master of spirituality" by many Italian bishops and by Marco Tarquinio, the director of the Italian Episcopal Conference's newspaper *Avvenire*,[16] who defended him in its pages against the just and opportune criticism leveled against him by Msgr. Antonio Livi.[17]

The battle rages in the night, as St. John Bosco saw it in the famous dream of the "two columns in the sea."[18] The ship of Peter is assailed and the pope has been grievously wounded, once and then a second time; he falls and dies, but a new pope, overcoming all obstacles, anchors the ship to two columns that rise out of the sea: on top of one the Host radiates, on the other stands the Immaculate Conception. The enemy ships flee and are smashed, while the Church celebrates her triumph. Today, the little barque of Peter seems tossed by the storm, and those in it facing the turbulent waves look with trepidation at its captain who is the Vicar of Christ. The pope's primacy of governance, along with the infallibility of his teaching Magisterium, constitute the foundation upon which Jesus Christ instituted His Church and upon which she will remain firm until the end of time. This primacy was conferred to Peter, prince of the apostles, after the Resurrection (John 21:15–17), and was recognized by the

---

[15]  Küng, *Let Us Save the Church*, 10–11.
[16]  M. Tarquinio, "Those Malicious Deformations," *Avvenire*, March 23, 2012.
[17]  Msgr. Antonio Livi, "False Prophets," *La Bussola*, March 17, 2012.
[18]  Eugenio Pilla, *The Dreams of Don Bosco* (Cantagalli: Siena, 1979), 193–196.

primitive Church not as a personal or transitory privilege, but as a permanent and essential element of the divine constitution of the Church, to which Jesus gave a monarchical form precisely to ensure her indefectibility.

There is no collegial leadership of the barque of Peter, just as there is no license of customs within her. Yet conciliarism, condemned by Pope Eugene IV at the Council of Florence (1439) and by Blessed Pius IX at the First Vatican Council (1870), has never been eradicated from the Church. "Collegiality," in the postconciliar age, has been the order of an egalitarian and democratic vision that contrasts papal "centralism" with a structure of governance based on the role of one or more synods.

This is a type of parliament of the Church, with factions and parties fighting each other, as always happens, due to the centrifugal tendencies at work. In fact, the universality of the Church imposes the exercise of strong central authority, and if fragmentation and anarchy exist today, it is certainly not due to an excess of power, but if anything to the weakening of papal governance, to the advantage of the episcopal conferences and the peripheral and local realities. The crisis before us is the consequence also of this process of erosion of pontifical centrality. On the other hand, the great reformers of the Church, like St. Gregory the Great in the sixth century and St. Gregory VII in the eleventh, have always accompanied their work of renewal with a clear affirmation of the pontifical primacy. Whoever presumes to "reform" the papacy undermines the juridical foundation of the Church, and with it her moral law, while those who love the Church will accompany the defense of the natural and moral law with that of the pontifical primacy, against conciliarist and localist tendencies.

Nor does this suffice today. In his *Letter to the Catholics of Ireland*, Benedict XVI unites the call to an authentic reform of the Church to the appeal "to the ideal of sanctity, charity and transcendent wisdom," which in the past rendered Europe great and still has the power today to re-edify her (n. 3). The invitation to the Irish faithful "to aspire to high ideals of sanctity, of charity, and of truth and to draw inspiration from the wealth of a vast religious and cultural tradition" (n. 12) resounds as an appeal to all Catholics and men of good will to rediscover the only foundation for moral and social reconstruction in Jesus Christ, "who is the same yesterday and today and for ever" (Heb. 13:8). When the tempest rages and the barque is covered by waves, the disciples approach Jesus, who was sleeping, and, waking him, say, " 'Lord, save us, we are lost!' And he said to them, 'Why are you afraid, O men of little faith?' " Then the Gospel says, "Then he rose and rebuked the winds and the sea; and there was a great calm. And the men marveled, saying, 'What sort of man is this, that even the winds and sea obey him?'" (Matt. 8:25–27).

Only Jesus, and no one else, can save the Church, because He alone founded her and is her head. Men, beginning with the Vicar of Christ down to the last of the faithful, can only collaborate with Divine Grace that reaches us through the influence of the Holy Spirit and urges us to radical fidelity to Christ and His law.

We cannot save the Church, but we can love and serve her, imitating the example of all those who throughout history have given their lives for her. Whoever presumes to save the Church wants to build the Church according to his own opinions, rather than those of Christ. The Church instituted by Jesus Christ is monarchical because she is founded on the primacy of Peter, and she is hierarchical because the bishops, in union with the pope, exercise in her a supreme power to govern and sanctify. Neither the pope nor the bishops can change the law of the gospel handed down by Jesus Himself. This law, communicated by Jesus to the apostles, excludes access to sacred orders by women, subjugates the laity to the clergy, imposes celibacy on the clergy, and calls all men and women to continence and sacrifice.

The current crisis was not born from this model of doctrine and life that the Tradition hands down to us, but from distancing from it. All heresiarchs throughout the centuries have proposed a pseudoreform of the Church that disfigures her countenance. But the only true reform is that of rediscovering the Tradition, which is nothing other than the perennial teaching of Christ, and living it with integrity, as the saints have done.[19] In the difficult periods of Church history, it has been saints, not heretics, who have saved her.

Heretics always contrast the Church of antiquity with her medieval and Tridentine evolution, but the history of the Church in the first millennium teaches us something else. History, which is a teacher of life and Christian faith, teaches us through the example of martyrs how the truth is not negotiable and must be testified to — if necessary, with blood. The monks and hermits recall the rejection of the world and the need for constant union with the Lord, in silence and prayer. The action of the apologists shows us how the apostolate is exercised not only by explicating the faith in positive affirmations, but also confuting prejudice and

---

[19]    See Roberto de Mattei, *Apologia of the Tradition* (Turin: Lindau, 2011).

error with the arms of argumentation and controversy. In the first millennium of history, the foundations and roots of Christianity were set down, and the Christian sovereigns and princes who created European nations offer us the example of how the world can be Christianized, without belonging to the world.

The example of the Crusaders is the most generous of all, because they offered their lives for the Church, ignoring the trials they would have to endure to fulfill their vocation to the bitter end. The spirit with which they hurled themselves into the liberation of the Holy Sepulcher is the same that we must ask today to liberate the Church and Christian civilization from the evils that afflict them. No one should be scandalized. The beauty of the Church is in the variety of vocations expressed within her. The number of vocations is as large as the number of rational creatures, but all converge on just one end, which is the glory of God, first cause and final end of the created universe. There is a very famous page in St. Thérèse's *Story of a Soul* in which she describes the multiplicity of vocations that she would like to embrace. We do well to reread it and appreciate all the love for Jesus and the Church that filled her:

> To be your spouse, to be a Carmelite, and by my union with you to be the mother of souls, should this not suffice for me? And yet it is not so! No doubt, these three privileges sum up my true vocation: Carmelite, Spouse, Mother; and yet I feel within me other vocations. I feel the vocation of the Warrior, the Priest, the Apostle, the Doctor, the Martyr; finally, I feel the need, the desire to carry out the most heroic deeds for You, O Jesus.

> I feel within my soul the courage of the Crusader, the Papal Guard: I would want to die on the field of battle in defense of the Church. I feel in me the vocation of the Priest. With what love O Jesus, would I carry you in my hands when, at my voice, you would come down from Heaven. And with what love would I give you to souls! But alas, while desiring to be a Priest, I admire and envy the humility of St. Francis of Assisi and I feel the vocation of imitating him in refusing the sublime dignity of the Priesthood.

> O Jesus, my love, my life, how can I combine these contrasts? How can I realize the desires of my poor little soul?

> Ah, in spite of my littleness, I would like to enlighten souls as did the Prophets and the Doctors. I have the vocation of the Apostle. I would like to travel over the whole earth to preach your name and to plant your

glorious Cross on infidel soil! But, o my Beloved, one mission alone would not be sufficient for me: I would want to preach the Gospel on all five continents simultaneously and even to the most remote isles. I would be a missionary, not for a few years only but from the beginning of creation until the consummation of the ages. But above all, O my Beloved Savior, I would shed my blood for you even to the very last drop!

Martyrdom was the dream of my youth, and this dream has grown with me within Carmel's cloisters. But here again, I feel that my dream is a folly, for I cannot confine myself to desiring one kind of martyrdom. To satisfy me I need all! Like you my adorable Spouse, I would be scourged and crucified. I would die flayed like St. Bartholomew. I would be plunged into boiling oil like St. John. I would undergo all the tortures inflicted upon the martyrs. With St. Agnes and St. Cecilia, I would present my neck to the sword, and like Joan of Arc my dear sister, I would whisper your name at the stake, O Jesus! When thinking of the torments that will be the lot of Christians at the time of the antichrist, I feel my heart leap with joy and I would that these torments be reserved for me. Jesus, Jesus! If I wanted to write all my desires, I would have to borrow your book of life: for in it are reported all the actions of all the saints, and I would accomplish all of them for you.

O my Jesus, what is your answer to all my follies? Is there a soul more little, more powerless than mine? Nevertheless, even because of my weakness, it has pleased you, O Lord, to grant my little childish desires, and you desire, today, to grant other desires that are greater than the universe.[20]

The words of St. Thérèse constitute a manifesto of Catholic faith to be counterposed to the heterodox proclamations of Hans Küng and the rebels of We Are Church. This is the true freedom of the sons of God, never detached from the truth. Every man, every nation, but also every historical epoch has its vocation, which is the way in which it performs the will of God in the present moment. In the current tempest, God asks us to do what is lacking to our time and to the Church: to pray and to fight. The soul of every apostolate is the interior life, which is the impulse of the soul toward God, all the more important in a world busy with self-contemplation in the absence of God.

[20]   St. Thérèse of the Child Jesus, *Complete Works* (Libreria Editrice Vaticana: Vatican City, 1997), 221.

But prayer is not enough. The motto of Catholic Action was once, "Prayer, action, sacrifice." Action and sacrifice today can be summarized in the fight against the external and internal enemies of the Church. Her fight against evil has led the Church to be defined as "militant." Benedict XVI said, "The word *ecclesia militans* is a bit out of fashion, but in fact we can understand better than ever that it is true, that it bears truth. We can see how evil seeks to dominate in the world and that it is necessary to enter the fight against evil. We see how it does this in many ferocious ways with different forms of violence, but also masked as good and precisely in this way destroys the foundations of morality in society. St. Augustine said that all of history is a struggle between two loves: love of self to the point of despising God; love of God to the point of disregarding self in martyrdom."[21]

The one who loves me, said Jesus, observes my commandments (John 14:21). But today the law of God has been violated and mocked, and the one who loves God fights so that his commandments can be freely observed and publicly professed. We do not fight to impose the Faith, because nothing is freer than the act of faith. We fight to protect this Faith from evil and from error, because nothing is truer than the Christian Faith. The Lord desires that we pray and fight for Him, in a clash that has become global and has assumed a total and definitive character.

*Orare et pugnare*: may this motto gather Christian warriors from every corner of the world and unite them in defense of the divine law against the enemies of God and His Church, who, as the "Prayer for Missionaries" by St. Luis Maria Grignon de Monfort reminds us, have already raised the war cry: "*Sonuerunt, frenduerunt, fremuerunt, multiplicati sunt.*" But we repeat with the great French saint, "*Dirumpamus vincula eorum et projiciamus a nobis jugum ipsorum. Qui habitat in coelis irridebit eos*" (Ps. 2:3–4).

## CAVEAT

The following pages collect some of the conversations on Church history held by the author with Radio Maria for the program *Christian Roots*, from January 2011 to April 2012. Every chapter faithfully presents the text of the conversation, maintaining the spoken language. Given that this is not an academic text, it sometimes lacks citations and references to the works quoted. The author, wanting to

---

[21] Benedict XVI, Words at the End of Lunch with the Cardinals, May 21, 2012.

resonate the Catholic Tradition without any pretense of originality, has drawn upon many historical, theological, and spiritual works, including *The Liturgical Year* by Fr. Prosper Guéranger, the conversations on the *Saints of the Day* given by Plinio Corrêa de Oliveira until his death in 1995, Abbot Joseph Lemann's three-volume work *La Dame des Nations dans l'Europe catholique,* and the first two volumes of *History of the Church* by Henri Daniel Rops, of which some passages were presented verbatim, at times without indication.

CHAPTER I

# The First Three Centuries of the Church

## 1. CHRISTIANITY AND THE ROMAN EMPIRE

We live in an age of crisis in every sense: economic crisis, political crisis, and above all spiritual and moral crisis. [22] These latter crises are what here interest us most; they touch our lives, because we are not only bodies, as the majority of people believe and practice, but bodies ineluctably animated by *souls*. The soul is not only the more noble part of our being, but that which gives life to our being, the reason why we live and breathe. We have a soul, and so we have, or ought to have, a spiritual life. This spiritual life is born from the gift of faith infused in us at baptism and nourished by grace communicated through the sacraments of the Church. All that concerns the Church touches our faith, and what touches our faith has consequences for our soul and for those who are dear to us. For this reason, we must attentively consider the Church and its history, because understanding what happened yesterday helps us to live today.

When we speak of the Church, we must remember that there are actually three Churches that form a whole: the Church Militant formed by all the baptized who profess the same faith under the same pastors; the Church Suffering, composed of all the deceased being purified in Purgatory, awaiting their entrance into Paradise; and finally, the Church Triumphant, formed by the saints

---

[22] Radio Maria, conversation on September 21, 2011.

who already live in the eternal joy of the divine glory. Together, these three realities form the communion of saints, a dogma we profess in our creed.

To understand the history of the Church, not only yesterday or two thousand years ago, but also, and above all, today, we must keep our minds fixed on the word "militant." The Church Militant means a Church that is "fighting." St. Paul explains in many passages in his letters how the life of a Christian is a *bonum certamen*, a good fight that must be waged "as a good soldier of Jesus Christ" (2 Tim. 2:3). He says, "Let us cast off the works of darkness and put on the armor of light" (Rom. 13:12). The Church on earth suffers, certainly, but most of all it fights. It suffers both when it wages its warfare and because of it; however, for the Church and for Christians, the time of suffering is in Purgatory more than here on earth. We were not born to suffer, but to fight and to win, although suffering accompanies us our entire life. We must not, however, be satisfied with this suffering, because it is the consequence of sin. Life on earth is a struggle, a struggle between two cities, the City of God and that of the devil, between the Church and her enemies who, as St. Augustine says in the *City of God*, wage war until the end of time.

We would like, then, to recall the most important episodes of this combat that is renewed every day, and in which we must not be spectators but protagonists. We must imagine the world as a great theater, with the angels in Heaven as spectators and, in the gallery of honor, Jesus and Mary. Let us choose then to play our part, studying the script of history.

Let us begin by speaking of the early centuries of the Church, so far away, but also very near. Those centuries were a period of persecution and martyrdom and were also for this reason a period of fighting. The fight was first conducted by the apostles, and then by their successors, to carry out the mandate of Christ, which was to spread the gospel to the ends of the earth.

In that moment, Christianity stood before the Roman Empire, the largest empire history had ever known. Christianity and the Roman Empire were the same age, so to speak, because while the history of Rome began 753 years before Christ with the foundation of the city by Romulus and Remus, the birth of the empire was the work of Augustus, under whose reign Jesus was born in Palestine.

The Roman Empire and nascent Christianity stood in opposition, engaging in a relentless conflict devoid of all agreement or compromise. This war was not declared by Christianity but by the empire, which did not tolerate the presumption of absolute truth on the part of Christianity, nor its message of radical and integral salvation.

The first great clash was the trial of Jesus, promoted by the Jews in their Sanhedrin, and brought before Pilate, who represented the Roman Empire and who surrendered Christ to his executioners. This is not the place to discuss whether he bore greater responsibility than those who betrayed Jesus to him, fomenting him. What is important to emphasize is that Jesus wanted to show from the very beginning that, between the Church and the world, there exists a radical incompatibility. The Passion and death of Jesus were to be the model of all physical pain and suffering, but especially spiritual and moral suffering, which Christians would have to endure throughout their history.

The Roman Empire not only condemned Jesus through the hand of Pilate; after Pilate was removed from Palestine, the empire continued to condemn Christ, refusing to give Christianity the status of *religio licita*, a legal religion in the empire.

The persecution against Christians began in Palestine with the lapidation of Stephen, desired by Caiaphas in 34, then with the death of James of Zebedee, the first martyr among the apostles, sent to his death by King Herod Agrippa I. The apologists speak of a report that the emperor Tiberius (14–37) requested of the procurator in Galilee, Pontius Pilate, after these events. According to Tertullian, Pilate's report would have pushed Tiberius to propose that the Senate recognize the divinity of Jesus and grant Christianity the status of *religio licita*, but the Roman Senate rejected it. The Roman senatorial aristocracy, from the very beginning, displayed its aversion toward Christianity by fomenting persecutions against it, especially in the highest spheres of society, while popular antipathy was stoked by the Jews, as the Acts of the Apostles recalls (19:33ff.).

## 2. THE BEGINNING OF THE PERSECUTIONS

*The beginning of large-scale persecutions against*
*Christians happens only in the year 64.*

On the night of July 18 of that year, the trumpets of the guards rang out in Rome, sounding the fire alarm. A violent blaze was spreading through the lower-class neighborhood around the Circus Maximus, in the apothecaries and the cloth merchants' shops. Fueled by the stocks of oil and combustible materials, the fire suddenly reached the entire area around the Palatine and the Caelian Hill. All attempts to extinguish it were in vain. For six days and six nights, the flames engulfed Rome. Four of its fourteen neighborhoods were razed completely; six others were left only with parts of walls and clusters of uninhabitable blackened houses. Only four neighborhoods remained intact. The French historian Daniel Rops reconstructs this event with admirable clarity.

The emperor at the time was Nero (54–68), who had succeeded his adoptive father Claudio (41–54). Today there is an effort to rehabilitate his memory. But Nero was the man who had his mother, Agrippina, murdered, the woman who had set him on the throne by means of a crime. Nero was the man who repudiated his legitimate wife, Octavia, slandering her in an abject manner before having her executed. He was the man who, for his ferocity, was now being accused by the vox populi of having started the fire. It is said that his slaves were seen running through the poorer neighborhoods of the city carrying torches. Suetonius passes on the claim that, during the blaze, Nero was seen on top of a tower, dressed in theatrical costume with lyre in hand, singing a poem he had composed about the capture of Troy and the fire set off by Agamemnon's warriors.

What is certain is that Nero vented his fury on Christians, accusing them of being the authors of the destruction of Rome. From one day to the next, by his order, the prisons were filled, which Tacitus described as a "vast multitude" of arrested Christians — words that offer us a precious indication of the growth of the new faith in Rome, less than thirty-five years after the death of Christ.

A terrible destiny awaited the Christians of Rome. The torture, decapitation, and crucifixion of the victims in the Circus of Nero (the same place where St. Peter's Basilica stands today) was not enough. They made Christians the hunted prey of ferocious Mastiff dogs in the imperial parks, having the skins of beasts sown to their bodies. They reproduced the most barbarous and obscene mythological scenes in which Christians were forced to appear and suffer outrages of every sort. In the evening, along the lanes populated by demented groups of thugs, Nero drove through the streets, his chariot illuminated by living beings burned as torches in the pitch and resin with which they had been covered.

The future Pope St. Clement of Rome (d. 97), perhaps an eyewitness to this gruesome scene, preserved an unforgettable memory of horror of that night of August 15, 64. Tacitus, as well, confessed that such an excess of atrocity aroused, in good consciences, compassion toward Christians.

Saints Peter and Paul died in the course of this terrible persecution, along with thousands of other Christians. Today, above the tomb of Peter, stands the mother basilica of Christianity, dedicated to him; and in the same place where

Nero tried to suffocate forever the voice of Peter, the words of his successors continue to be addressed to the peoples of the earth.

After the death of Nero, there was a period of peace until the arrival of the emperor Domitian (81–96). By around the year 90, the Christian faith had grown, extending even to the top of the social ladder.

This time, the first to be struck were those belonging to the aristocracy: Flavio Clemente, suspected for a long time due to his lack of collaboration with the emperor in matters concerning official worship, and who, according to Suetonius, was sent to his death "for a slight suspicion." His wife, Domitilla, was sent to the prison island of Pandataria. Today, one of the most impressive catacombs of the Roman underground bears her name. Domitilla and her husband belonged to the *gens Flavia*, the most noble family of Rome, cousins to the emperor Domitian. This did not spare them persecution. Nor was one of the most illustrious exponents of the Roman aristocracy spared: the consul Acilius Glabrio, known for his rectitude and valor, and whose family cemetery on the Via Salaria is considered the oldest Christian necropolis.

Manius Acilius Glabrio was a Roman senator and consul in the year 91. He was suspected by Domitian of being a Christian and executed. Eusebius writes that the emperor harbored an invidious grudge toward him, especially since the time he had called him to the *Juvenalia* on Monte Albano and forced him to fight a great lion. Glabrio not only came out unscathed, but even struck the beast a mortal blow. These were the Christians, slaves and aristocrats, helpless women and men, yet capable of killing a lion with their bare hands.

It was Domitian, moreover, who sent the evangelist John into exile on the island of Patmos, and who had the descendants of the one who had called himself "king of the Jews" hunted down in Palestine, sending the sons of Jude the Apostle to Rome for an interrogation that led to nothing.

Hatred, fueled by circles of Jews and pagans, surrounded Christians. It was hatred without a precise motive, but when the vox populi cries out, observes Daniel Rops, it is not always God's voice, and neither that of reason nor good sense. Christian rites, poorly understood, were intentionally interpreted in the worst of ways. The accusations against Christians, already raised by the Jews who had persecuted and crucified Jesus, were quite varied and are listed by Minucius Felix in his *Octavius*, by Tertullian in the *Apologeticum*, and by Athenagoras in his *Supplication for Christians*. The accusation of atheism arose from their refusal to sacrifice to the Roman gods; that of incest, because of the

familiarity that existed among them, because they called each other brothers
and sisters, and because of the kiss of peace they offered in the Christian assemblies, all of which led Romans to consider their relations as blameworthy.
Christians were accused of adoring the head of a donkey; of adoring the geni-
tals of their priests; of cutting the throats of children and drinking their blood
in rites of Christian initiation; of not having altars, temples, or simulacra; of
gathering in secret; and of being the cause of calamities throughout the empire. The eucharistic sacrifice, with its formulas such as, "This is my Body, this
is my Blood," surely reminded Romans of cannibalistic practices.

The apologists demolished these absurd accusations in vain. The slander
continued to circulate and to spread. Tertullian tells us how in Carthage,
shortly before the composition of the *Apologeticum*, a portrait representing
the Christian God with donkey ears, goat's hooves, a book in hand, and wearing a toga was displayed in public. The apologist writes, "If the Tiber were to
flood its banks, if the Nile were not to inundate the fields, if the heavens were
to close, and the earth to shake, or famine to strike, or war, or the plague, the
shout would immediately ring out: 'To the lions with the Christians! Death to
Christians!'" And he adds:

> Most men had dedicated to the name "Christian" a hatred so blind
> that they were not able to speak favorably of a Christian without add-
> ing a rebuke for bearing this name. One says, "That Caius Seius is an
> honest man, too bad he's a Christian!" Another adds, "For my part, I
> find it strange that Lucius Titius, such an enlightened man, immedi-
> ately became a Christian." No one asks if Caius is honest and Lucius
> enlightened precisely because they became Christians, or if they be-
> came Christians due to the fact that one is honest and the other
> enlightened.

The Jews were among the first accusers of Christians. They too venerated one
God, but although the simulacrum of their God was portrayed in the Pantheon,
they were accepted because they represented a nation toward which Rome had
promulgated laws of tolerance. Christians did not constitute a nation; they
were only subjects of Rome. Most of them were not even Roman citizens, at
least until the edict of Caracalla in 212 declared all subjects of the empire to
be Roman citizens.

## 3. "CHRISTIANOS ESSE NON LICET"

All these accusations had an extrajuridical nature. They did not exert an influence on the juridical mentality of the Romans. They needed to provide a foundation for their slander, and this was summarized in a simple formula, the *Institutum Neronianum,* of which Tertullian speaks and which is summarized in the juridical aphorism: *Christianos esse non licet,* meaning, "It is forbidden to be a Christian."

Many scholars have attempted to demonstrate that Christians were persecuted for civil reasons based on the laws sanctioned against crimes of lese-majesty, or for reasons regarding social harmony (resistance or *coercitio,* considered a remedy for public order). In truth, the underlying reason was religious, and the juridical foundation of the persecutions remained such. "The motive that explains both the beginning as well as the continuation of the persecutions is hatred against Christians," writes Ludwig von Hertling, recalling Tertullian's statement: "The moment the truth entered the world, it aroused hatred and aversion by its mere existence."

We must remember that Roman religion was an essentially political religion; as the text of the *Twelve Tables* reads, "No one on his own behalf may have gods either new or foreign that have not been recognized by the state." The Roman imperium was above all a political power, but the veneration of the gods was one of the duties of the state and constituted an important element in Roman law. The task of the state was that of regulating the public worship of the gods, independently of the private religion of citizens. Yet Christianity was accused of atheism because it refused the religion of the "goddess Rome" incarnated in the divine emperor. Each could adore his own gods, provided he adored Rome and Caesar — otherwise he committed the crime of sacrilege.

Already in 42 BC, Augustus (27 BC–AD 14) had his adoptive father, Caesar, divinized by decree of the Senate. Divine veneration for himself was then demanded by the emperors Caligula (37–41) and Domitian (81–96). From the third century onward, the cult of the emperor was imposed as an expression of political and religious loyalty on the part of his subjects. Christianity never opposed the constituted power that claimed — and still claims — that it derives from God, but it opposed those powers when they became a dominion usurping the rights of God. Christian loyalty toward Rome had its foundation in chapter 13 of St. Paul's Letter to the Romans and in the second chapter of the First Letter of St. Peter. It is expressed in the evangelical formula "Give to Caesar what is Caesar's, and to God what is God's," spoken by Jesus Himself (Mark 12:17).

In 112, the juridical position of Christianity in the empire was defined for the first time, by means of an exchange of correspondence between the imperial legate, Pliny the Younger, and his superior, the emperor Trajan (98–117). The question that Pliny posed the emperor can be summarized thus: "Is it the very name of Christian that one must punish?" In this case, must one send to their death not only those who profess its doctrine, but also those who renounce it? Pliny suggests that a policy of clemency, leading them to apostasy, could have better results, as far as the social and religious peace of the provinces is concerned. In his response, Trajan defined the line of conduct the functionary must follow: "One must not seek out Christians, but if they are denounced and they confess to being Christian, they must be castigated. If someone, however, denies they are Christian and proves it by supplicating our gods, he shall obtain pardon." The rescript of Trajan imposed, therefore, as a measure of clemency, not to promote the search for Christians, but once they were denounced or recognized as such, to put them on trial and condemn them — offering pardon to the apostate, however.

Beyond the greater level of clemency demonstrated by Trajan with respect to his predecessors, it remains clear that the juridical foundation of the persecutions lay in the mere fact of calling themselves Christians — not in being one, but in proclaiming to be one, because it was enough to deny being a Christian, sacrifice to the emperor, and obtain pardon. As Tertullian rightly observed in an ironic moment, "The Christian must be punished not because he is guilty, but because he has been discovered, although he should not have been sought out."

But given that they condemned the *nomen*, and not the crimes attributable to that *nomen*, it sufficed to renounce the *nomen* of "Christian" to obtain pardon, something not covered by the code of Roman penal law for one who had committed other crimes.

The policy of Trajan guided that of his successors for the following 150 years. It was not licit to be (or to *say* you were) a Christian. Every Christian was a candidate for martyrdom. It depended on the emperor, however, to apply the law with greater or lesser severity. This explains how the first three centuries were not a period of systematic persecutions. There were periods of bloody persecutions, but also periods of greater tranquility in which the Roman authorities left Christians free to conduct their lives in peace.

Christians, on the other hand, accepted Roman institutions (Rom. 13:1–7; Titus 3; 1 Pet. 2:13–15), prayed for the established powers (1 Tim. 2:1–2), paid taxes, and respected the laws of the state. The Church of the early centuries, therefore, was not a hidden or clandestine Church; Christians were recognized as such, their figures of authority (bishops, priests, deacons) were known, the general outline of their ideas was in part evident. The Christian philosopher Justin (c. 100–165), for example, opened a public school in Rome, published his writings, and could address his *Apologia* to Marcus Aurelius, Antoninus Pius, and Lucius Verus, before being arrested for his faith.

Christians lived in their own families, exercising professions like any other citizen, and for their religious functions met in modest places of worship within the walls of the city. They practiced their own rites of inhumation and did not cremate their deceased. In fact, they had underground cemeteries that later came to be called "catacombs" (from the Greek *katacumbas*).

The catacombs were not secret places where Christians hid, but burial grounds where the dead were buried. Roman law conceded to all without distinction the *Jus sepulcri*, even to those condemned to death, whose remains a judge could grant to whomever might ask to bury them.

The period of persecutions inaugurated under Nero was marked by a crescendo over the course of three centuries, albeit at alternating moments. After Domitian and Trajan, the African Septimius Severus (193–211) issued for the first time, at the start of the third century, a decree prohibiting conversion to Christianity. The famous School of Alexandria was closed, and many Christians were martyred (among whom were Perpetua and Felicity, along with many others in Carthage). The edict of Severus was enforced under his son Caracalla (211–217) as well, especially in Africa. More tolerant was Alexander Severus (217–235), whose mother, Julia Mamea, converted to Christianity and was in contact with Origen and Hippolytus.

Maximinus Thrax (235–238), the first of a long line of soldier-emperors, presumed he could destroy the Church by condemning its bishops, presbyters, and doctors to death with an edict. In 249, a coup d'état hatched by anti-Christian forces against the Christian Phillip the Arab (244–249) brought Decius (249–251) to power. Origen underlines the shift that occurred under Decius, who decided to wipe out every trace of Christianity. He instituted in every city an ad hoc commission and issued an edict in 250, ordering all citizens of the empire to burn incense before the pagan divinities and to participate in the sacred banquets under the supervision of public authorities. Those who refused were imprisoned and subjected to every type of torture unto death. What Decius wanted to achieve at all costs was the apostasy of Christians, their renunciation of the faith. Many evaded the order by fleeing, others apostatized. Thus began the problem of the *lapsi* — namely, those Christians who, to escape death, had offered incense to idols, but then repented for having done so. Among the many martyrs, there was Pope Fabian (236–250) in Rome. Origen wrote, "From this moment, the persecutions were no longer carried out in a sporadic manner as before, but in a common and generalized form." Decius's successor Gallo (251–253) did not persecute the Church, but ordered that all citizens sacrifice to the god Apollo. Popes Cornelius and Lucius died in exile.

The emperor Valerian (253–261) sought to strike at the leaders of the Church, convinced that once the head was severed, the body too would be dissolved. Thus, he issued a new edict (258) by which he imposed capital punishment on the leaders of the Church and Christian nobility and prohibited all meetings of worship of any type and in any place. Another pope, St. Sixtus II (260–261), ambushed while presiding over a liturgical ceremony in the catacombs of St. Calixtus, was decapitated along with four deacons who were assisting him. The deacon Lawrence was killed on August 10, 258, and buried in the Verano cemetery along the Via Tiburtina.

In the second half of the third century, there was a truce of about forty years. The son of Valerian, Gallienus (261–268), revoked the edict against Christians, and there began under his rule and that of his successor Aureliano (270–275), the Sun worshiper, a period of peace. But by the end of the century, the emperor Diocletian (284–305) from Dalmatia unleashed the last and most violent of the persecutions. In 297, he determined to purge the military of all Christians. Between 303 and 304, Diocletian issued a total of four decrees by which he sought the annihilation of Christianity. In 303, a first edict ordered the destruction of churches, and Christian nobility were deprived of their social rank and the plebians of their freedom. In the summer of 303, the second and third edicts followed, ordering the arrest of the clergy and mandatory sacrifice to the Roman gods. Not all of these orders were carried out, but in 304, a fourth edict ruled that the entire population of the empire was to offer sacrifice to the pagan divinities under pain of death. Most of the martyrs who were later included in the Church's liturgy belong to this persecution: Sebastian, Pancras, Agnes, Sotero, Protus, Giacinto, Peter, Marcellinus, and many others.

## 4. The Witness of Martyrdom

The reports of Christian origin on the persecutions are usually divided into three groups: *Acta*, which are the official minutes of the trial; *Martyria* and *Passio*, which are documents of a private character; and *Gesta*, the historical narrations that arose after the end of the persecutions. The first literary reports among pagan sources of the persecution of Christians date to Tacitus (*Annales*, around 115) and Suetonius (*Vita Neronis*, around 122).

The martyrs offered their witness to Christ in two ways: with their words and with their blood. We recall a considerable number of arrested Christians who took advantage of the occasion of their trial to profess their faith publicly. At times it was a very simple affirmation, like that on the lips of the African martyrs, "I am a Christian!" Or again, responding to the request to identify themselves, "What is your name? — Christian! That suffices!" At times it was a more explicit act of faith, such as that of St. Justin in Rome in 163: "We worship the God of the Christians. We believe He is the one God, the Creator from the beginning, and has ordained every creature visible and invisible. We believe in the Lord Jesus Christ, the Son of God, announced by the Prophets, sent to save men, the Messiah Redeemer, Teacher of sublime lessons."

St. Ignatius of Antioch was among the most renowned martyrs, thanks to the significance he was able to give to his martyrdom. Condemned in Antioch with his two companions Rufus and Zosimus, Ignatius was sent to Rome to be devoured by the lions. Aware of the destiny that awaited him, he showed an enthusiasm that can only be called supernatural. He writes to the Christians of Smyrna, "Under the blade of the executioner or among the ferocious beasts, it is near to God that I will always remain." In the face of the most terrifying destiny imaginable, his only fear is that of being spared. And he cries out, "For the altar is ready, allow me to carry out my sacrifice! Let me be the prey to the wild beasts! It is through them that I shall reach God. I am the wheat of God: to become the white bread of Christ, it must be ground by the teeth of the beasts."

The *Golden Legend*, a most popular book in the Middle Ages, affirms that, based on an interpretation of the moniker "Theophorous" that Ignatius used during his life, when his heart was removed after death, the name of Christ was found there written in letters of gold.

Half a century later, under the reign of the emperor Antoninus, another great saint and bishop of the East, Polycarp, met the same fate. He had known Ignatius in life, and after his death collected his letters and meditated on his example. We have an abundance of information about his trial and death, thanks to a letter that the community of Smyrna sent to the brethren in Phrygia, in response to their request to tell them about these events right as they were happening. Polycarp was an elderly man, nearly ninety years old, but there is no age limit for giving witness to the Spirit, and often God gives to the weakest the strength to fight.

The Proconsul presses him:

> "Recant! Swear and I will let you go free. Insult Christ."

> "I have served him for eighty-four years and he has never done me harm. Why then should I blaspheme my King and my Savior?"

> "Swear for the good fortune of Caesar!"

> "You flatter yourself hoping to persuade me. I tell you in all truth: I am a Christian."

> "I have wild animals at my beck and call."

> "Give your orders. We, when we change, do not change from better to worse; it is beautiful to pass from evil to justice."

> "If you do not repent, I'll have you perish at the stake, seeing that you scorn the beasts."

> "You threaten me with fire that burns for an hour and then goes out. But do you know the fire of justice that is coming? Do you know the punishment that will devour the impious? Go, do not delay! Decide as you wish."

Between 178 and 180 there occurred another famous martyrdom, that of St. Cecilia.

Cecilia belonged to one of the most noble and ancient families of Rome, that of the *gens Caecilia,* who for centuries had made their name illustrious by episodes of glory. Before her executioner she proclaims:

> *Non possumus!* This is impossible for us. Rather than live in pain and abandonment, we prefer to die in supreme freedom. And this truth that we proclaim is what torments you, you who go to such extents to have us lie.

When Perpetua, a young woman of noble birth, was arrested on the accusation of being Christian, she still had her father and mother, her two brothers — one of whom was a catechumen — and a little unweaned child. Her elderly father was a convinced pagan who exerted great effort to bring his daughter back to the traditional religion. When he finds out that she is summoned to appear before the judge, he hastens from his villa in Tunisia. Her father says to her:

> My daughter, have mercy on my gray hair, have mercy on your father, if I am still worthy of being called your father. If it is true that these hands have raised you to the blossom of maturity, if among all my children you are my favorite, do not consign me to the derision of the world. Think about your brothers, your mother, your aunt, your child that cannot survive without you. Turn back on your decision and do not lose your entire family. None of us will have the right to speak as a free man, if you are condemned.

Perpetua responds:

> See what my father has said in his affection. At the same time he was kissing my hands, he threw himself at my feet, no longer calling me daughter but lady. And it hurts me to see my father in this state. He alone in the whole family did not rejoice in my passion. I sought to console him, saying, "What God wills shall come to pass in the trial, know that. We are not masters of our lives; we belong to God."

Another day, the poor father came to the court with Perpetua's child in his arms: "Have mercy on the gray hair of your father and on the youth of your child. Offer the sacrifice for the salvation of the emperor." Perpetua refuses and declares herself a Christian. But seeing that her father remained by her side, Ilarianus pushes him away and has him struck with a staff. "This blow you have inflicted upon my father," the martyr adds, "wounds me as if I had been struck, so much is my suffering for this father so old and disgraced." Finally, the day of her agony approaches. One last time the old father comes to see his daughter. Perpetua: "Pain wracked him and, in his suffering, he pulled out his beard, fell to the ground, prostrated himself on the ground face down. He cursed his years and found words that would have upset anyone. And I cried over the disgraces of his old age" (*Passio of Perpetua and Felicity* V/VI).

## 5. MARTYRDOM AND CHRISTIAN COMBAT

According to the Christian vision, martyrdom is the most perfect act of charity, because it makes one a perfect imitator of Jesus according to the words of the

Gospel. Jesus, the Son of God, has demonstrated his charity, giving for us his life. "Greater love has no man than this, that a man lay down his life for his friends" (John 15:13).

The concept of martyrdom is inherent to the life of the Christian. Jesus, in his great discourse on the mission of the apostles (Matt. 10), says, "I send you out as sheep in the midst of wolves" (v. 16) and announces, "Beware of men, for they will deliver you up to councils, and flog you in their synagogues," (v. 17) "and you will be dragged before governors and kings for my sake, to bear testimony before them and the gentiles" (v. 18).

The specific meaning of the term "martyrdom" is connected with "giving witness," which reaches its peak in the profession of the phrase *christianus sum*. Witness is the essence of martyrdom, and it must be made publicly to the point of shedding blood. The witness of the martyr presupposes and confirms the witness of Him who "was born and came into the world to bear witness to the truth" (John 18:37).

What makes the martyr is not a violent death, but the fact that death was inflicted out of hatred for Christian truth: this final element distinguishes the Christian holocaust from any other sacrifice. The martyr must be put to death because of his fidelity to a principal of faith and morality of which the Church is the infallible teacher. It is not death that makes the martyr, says St. Augustine, but the fact that his suffering and death are ordered to truth. Death suffered to bear witness to the truth is martyrdom.

Today, as well, there exist truths and moral values for which one must be ready to give one's life. Of this witness, John Paul II teaches:

> [It] offers a contribution of extraordinary value … because it does not precipitate into the most dangerous crisis that can afflict mankind: the confusion of good and evil that renders impossible the construction and preservation of the moral order of the individual and the community. The martyrs, and more broadly all the saints in the Church, with their eloquent and fascinating example of a life totally transfigured by the splendor of moral truth, illuminate every age of history, reawakening moral sensibility. (Encyclical *Veritatis Splendor*, n. 93)

Martyrdom, as with all suffering, presupposes combat, a fight. We have already emphasized this. That Christian life is a struggle is one of the concepts that most frequently resounds in the New Testament where one reads, "He alone will be crowned who has fought according to what is right" (2 Tim 2:5). The gospel (from the Greek *euangélion*, or "good news"), in its original meaning, is the announcement of a military victory — in this case, the victory of Christ over evil and the powers of darkness.

The deeds of the martyrs of the first three centuries show us the intimate union that must exist between the Bridegroom and the Bride, between Christ and the Church, which is His Mystical Body. St. Paul says that a husband must love his wife as Christ loved the Church. The greatest expression of love is to offer one's life for his beloved. Jesus did so for the Church, and the first members of the Church, the apostles and their successors, did so for Christ. In this love, in this sacrifice, lies the Church's fecundity, which through the blood of the martyrs begot thousands of Christians and began its conquest of the world.

After three centuries of persecution, the decline of the Roman Empire had begun, as had the equally irresistible rise of the Church of Christ. In the person of His Vicar, the pope, Christ began to reign in the same city, in which the biggest empire in history had established itself. The feats of the martyrs are not a finished episode in time, confined merely to history. There is a place in the world where this lesson of martyrdom is alive and present: the Colosseum, the Flavian amphitheater, constructed by Vespasian, today a tourist attraction, but once a place of meditation where St. Leonard of Porto Maurizio had a large cross erected, and where St. Thérèse of Lisieux, while visiting Rome as a child, kneeled down and kissed the dirt, as if seeking in its furrows the smell of the blood poured out there by the martyrs.

Martyrdom is above all witness to the truth: it calls us to profess our faith publicly. It is an act of fidelity, fidelity to the Word of Christ to the point of death, which He transmitted to the apostles and from them to their successors. Fidelity, therefore, to the Church and to her Tradition: a tradition that is the truth of the gospel transmitted down to us by the written and spoken word, from generation to generation. We are the heirs of the Christians of the early centuries, and we must imitate their spirit. This is not easy, but we must ask for this. If they were faithful, it was thanks to the Holy Spirit who transformed them and sanctified them. We too can be transformed and sanctified, asking, as they did, for the intercession of the Virgin Mary, Mother of the Church, Queen of Apostles and Martyrs, the help of all those who over the course of history have fought the good fight.

CHAPTER II

# The Crisis of the Fourth Century

## 1. THE "CONSTANTINIAN SHIFT"

To live as good Christians, it is necessary to know the catechism that summarizes the doctrine of the gospel, the precepts of the Church, and the law we must respect to gain eternal life, because, as Jesus says, "He who has my commandments and keeps them, he it is who loves me" (John 14:2), and to observe them we must first know them.[23]

Today we are illiterate in religious matters, which is one of the reasons why the law of the Lord is not observed and Jesus is not loved. But if it is necessary to know the catechism, it is equally important to know the history of the Church, because the Church is a living organism, a Mystical Body that embraces all human history and has at its center the Incarnation of the Word, the event that took place two thousand years ago in Palestine, when God, the only true God, became man in the womb of the Virgin. This event radically changed history, which began to count its years from the birth of Christ.

We live in the era that since then has been called Christian, and we have the grace to be born as Christians: the two millennia behind us are our history and our roots—a history that we must know, because the history of the Church is the history of the Bride of Christ, which during its earthly sojourn is reliving the

---

[23] Radio Maria, conversation on October 19, 2011.

life of its Bridegroom and founder. We are part of the Mystical Body that is the Church, and to live in our time, we must know how the Christians who have preceded us, our brothers in the communion of saints, have lived the gospel, have faced challenges, have fought the good fight. We do well always to remember that the life of the Church has never been peaceful and calm: it has known trials, fights, persecutions in conformity with the words of the Gospel: "I send you out as sheep among wolves" (Matt. 10:16).

The first three centuries of the Church span from the Ascension of the Lord to the advent of the emperor Constantine in the year 312. This was the age of persecutions or, as one defined it, the age of the catacombs. This was one epoch in the history of the Church, its infancy, in which Christianity did not have free citizenship in the Roman Empire but was persecuted and repressed.

The emperors wanted to eradicate it and were convinced they could, because Christians refused to worship the Roman emperor as a divinity and repeated that they had to give to God what was God's and to Caesar what was Caesar's (Matt. 20:21; Mark 12:17; Luke 20:25). This maxim has always constituted one of the cornerstones of Christian thought.

From Nero to Diocletian, for three centuries, the persecutions raged, until the day when a young leader, Constantine (274–337), fighting Maxentius to conquer the throne of Rome, vanquished the army of his rival at Saxa Rubra, just north of Rome.

It was October 28, in the year 312. On the eve of this battle that would change the destiny not only of the empire but of the entire Church, Constantine had a vision and a dream. There appeared in the heavens a dazzling cross, and written on it was the phrase *in hoc signo vinces* (under this sign — the Cross — you shall be victorious). Then, as Eusebius and Lactantius tell us, the Lord appeared to Constantine in the night exhorting him to impress this cross on the standards of his legions. So it was under the sign of the cross that Constantine confronted Maxentius, and at the Milvian Bridge, at the very gates of Rome, he annihilated his enemy's army and took the imperial throne. This date marks an epochal turning point destined to go down in history by the name the "Constantinian shift."

The following year, 313, Constantine granted Christians full religious liberty with the Edict of Milan. They were no longer to be persecuted, but could walk with heads held high along the roads of the empire; construct their churches; celebrate their solemn rites; open schools, hospitals, and houses for orphans and the weak; and return to their places in the military, in the judiciary, and in the

Senate. They could Christianize society, instilling the life-giving breath of the gospel into the body of the empire that was sick unto death. It was the hour of triumph, celebrated by the first Christian historians like Eusebius of Caesarea.

Yet in these years of irresistible ascent, from the Edict of Constantine to that of another emperor, Theodosius (347–395), who in 380 made Christianity the sole religion of the Roman Empire, a new and terrible tempest struck the Church, a tempest so terrible that some would even long for the period of persecution again. It was worse this time, because the enemy was no longer external but within the Church itself. It was no longer physical violence, but the violence of heresy, the worst form of violence because it produces not the death of the body but that of the soul.

## 2. THE HERESY OF ARIUS

From its very birth, the life of the Church has been accompanied by errors and heresies. The father of heresy is considered to be Simon Magus, the Gnostic who wanted to buy the charisms of Peter and the apostles, and who crashed to the ground while trying to lift himself in flight with the help of the devil (Acts 8:9–10). But no other heresy was to have the diffusion and consequences of that which appeared at the beginning of the fourth century, and which seemed to shake the Church to its foundations. This was the Arian heresy, which took its name from its founder, the priest Arius (256–336), of Libyan origins, who arrived as a young man to the patriarchal city of Alexandria. Ordained deacon around 308 and priest two years later, Arius was, by 313, in charge of the church of Baucalis, one of the neighborhoods in Alexandria, where he began to preach a new doctrine.

Arius affirmed that God is one, eternal, and not begotten. Outside of Him, everything is a creature, including Christ, the Word of God. He affirmed that the Word, the second Person of the Most Holy Trinity, is not equal to the Father, but created by Him, as a middle point between God and man, and therefore of a different substance from the divine substance of the Father. Jesus Christ is not the Son of God by nature, but only by grace and adoption. The Holy Spirit, in turn, is the first creature of the Son and thus is inferior to Him.

Arianism was a heresy that struck the heart of the Trinitarian mystery, demolishing the very foundations of the faith and falsifying the most profound meaning of the gospel message. If in fact Jesus is not God, there is no longer an Incarnation or the redemption of humanity. Annulling the mystery of the Incarnation, the Arian heresy rendered Christianity more easily accessible to pagans who were astonished by the idea of a God become man, but, thinking of the divinized heroes of the ancient tradition, they could easily understand how a man, through his merits, could become God. On the other hand, in the Church, some theologians had held that the Father and Son were one and the same person. This was the heresy of Sabellius, which, though condemned, remained active as a tendency.

Finally, there was Arius's extraordinary ability to play on the meaning of certain words of Scripture, which aided the success of his heretical undertaking — for example, the statement "God created me" found in the book of Proverbs, which Arians considered prophetic of the Messiah, or again the passage in the Gospel according to St. John where Jesus says, "The Father is greater than me" (John 14:28).

For more than sixty years, a fierce battle raged among Christians in the East and West, in which the loftiest questions concerning the Divinity and men squared off in a mortal battle in defense of the truth. "If we struggle to comprehend this battle today," writes the historian Daniel Rops, "is it not because our age is weaker in faith and colder in temperament, and therefore no longer has recourse to such violence in resolving issues concerning the knowledge of God?"

When, around 320, the patriarch of Alexandria, St. Alexander, came to know the opinions of the priests under him, he invited Arius and his opponents to appear before a synod of hundreds of Egyptian and Libyan bishops that had been summoned to pronounce judgment.

At the synod in Alexandria, Arius presented his case with haughty surety. He knew he had the support of many who thought like he did. Among them was Eusebius, bishop of Nicomedia, a person of limitless ambition who, thanks to the geographical position of his city, was able to exert influence over the emperor. But if Arius had decided to put up a fight, there arose in his path the figure of a great Christian combatant: Athanasius, a little deacon just twenty years old, the secretary to Bishop Alexander. "His fragile appearance," writes the French historian, "concealed the indominable soul of one who would become the greatest adversary the heretic would encounter in his error."

The synod took place in a heated atmosphere. All but a few of the bishops present were on the side of Alexander — of orthodoxy, that is — and against the heretic Arius. There were dramatic moments. For example, when Arius was forced by his logic to affirm that Christ, insofar as he was a creature, could have sinned, the assembly let out a shout of horror. Arius was condemned, as well as some of the clergy who had sided with his theses. He received formal orders to submit or resign. For several weeks, he sought to preserve his role as priest, but he soon realized that to continue his fight he would have to leave Egypt. Thus, he abandoned his parish to seek support outside of his diocese. What had been up to that point just one of the many local agitations that the Church had already experienced was to become a vast movement that developed throughout the Christian East.

Under the pretext that Arius had been persecuted by his bishop, the ambitious Eusebius of Nicomedia welcomed him to his diocese. When Alexander discovered this, he sent a letter to his main colleagues explaining the issue and formally accusing the prelate of Nicomedia of intrigue. The Egyptian affair had transformed into a battle between two parties in the heart of the empire.

During the winter of 323–324, no one in the Christian East could ignore that a crisis was about to explode, one that could become a very serious matter. The bishops wrote each other letters, some favoring Arius, others against him. Alexander was reprimanded by Eusebius of Caesarea. The heretic himself, to confuse the matter, spread a "symbol" or creed in which, summarizing his theses, he skillfully wrapped them in many expressions with double meanings, misunderstandings, and ambiguities that could deceive many people of goodwill. This has always been the tactic of heresies: shun clear and precise expressions and mask error with a veil of ambiguity and confusion.

## 3. The Council of Nicaea

In the autumn of 324, the emperor Constantine definitively defeated his brother-in-law Licinius; the East was now under his control as much as the West. But when he entered the city of Nicomedia, he found the threat of a division in the heart of the Church. He was frightened by this and meditated on the matter for many sleepless nights. In the end, he decided to settle the problem once and for all. His ecclesial counselors, especially Osio of Cordova and the prelates of Antioch, persuaded him to call a plenary Assembly of Christianity to judge the matter, an assembly over which Constantine was to preside.

The Church had known this conciliar institution for quite some time. The first Council was held in Jerusalem in AD 49, when St. Paul and the apostles examined together the attitude to take regarding the Jewish problem. In the primitive Church, every time they had to decide serious points of discipline, they convened regional meetings, and in Africa and Italy these meetings took place regularly to maintain the bonds among Christian leaders. In the East, these meetings were more intermittent, but there had been many in Alexandria, Antioch, and even in Ancyra in Asia Minor. The idea was in the air of holding a council that would gather all Christianity and that could render concrete the unity of the Church in a general meeting. Constantine adopted the idea with elation. He sought religious peace in the empire. The universe, the *ecumene* as they say in Greek, had but one head: the emperor; the council that would gather the Church would be universal. Thus, it was decided to hold the first "Ecumenical Council."

During the winter of 324–325, the assembly was prepared. The setting that was immediately considered was Ancyra, but it was then judged to be too difficult to reach from the continent, and its position in the Anatolian highlands too cold for a springtime session. Thus, Nicaea was chosen, a city in Bithynia near Nicomedia and Byzantium, which was starting to be transformed into the imperial capital. Thus, the first Ecumenical Council of the Church was held in Nicaea in the year 325, convoked by the emperor Constantine.

The historian Eusebius writes that "the flower of God's ministers arrived from all of Europe, Libya and Asia," and that in just one house of prayer, as if it had been enlarged by Divine Power, he united Syrians, Cilicians, Phoenicians, Arabs, Palestinians, as well as those from Egypt, Thebaid, Libya, Mesopotamia, and even the bishop of Persia; there were also Macedonians, Thracians, Achaeans, Epirotians, and those who came from "the farthest of places, and from Spain, for example, an illustrious person." There was Osio of Cordova, Ceciliano of Carthage from Africa, and Marco, a Calabrian bishop, from Italy. Pope Sylvester II (314–335), who could not attend the council due to his old age, was represented by two Roman clerics, Vito and Vincenzo.

How many were these delegates from all Christendom? Eusebius of Caesarea said 250, adding that they were accompanied by many priests, deacons, and acolytes, all of whom he could not enumerate. St. Athanasius gives us another number: 318, which has become the traditional sum. It was, at any rate, a sizeable assembly in number and even more in the quality of its members. There were famous men: the healer Spiridione and James of Nisibis, both of whom it is said they had raised the dead; the Egyptian confessors of the faith, Potamone of Eraclea and Pafnuzio of Thebaid, who had both lost an eye during the persecution of Maximus; and Paul of Neo-Caesarea, whose hands had been burned by the red-hot irons with which Licinius had punished him.

The opening session took place on May 20, 325, in an atmosphere of enthusiasm. Little more than ten years had passed since the end of the age of persecutions, and now the persecuted were triumphant. Eusebius describes the imperial inauguration, the lunch banquet that Constantine offered the Fathers, and the pomp with which he presented himself to them on that historic day that marked the end of an era of persecutions. Ten years earlier (and just one year before for those in the territories recently under Licinius), life had been for the most part impossible and threats were constant; but now there was the splendor of the palaces, the majesty of the ceremonies, the guard of honor that presented their arms to the Christian dignitaries. The emperor had paid the expenses of the Council Fathers, placing at their disposal horses, carriages, and every type of material good they might need. It was clear that the emotions and the gratitude were immense.

The discussions began under the presidency of Constantine. As soon as the truly serious questions were confronted, they realized that there were two tendencies facing off that were irreconcilable.

We follow here the reconstruction of Daniel Rops. Arius was in the corridors, and be ably guided his group of supporters with his counsel. He was supported by some fifteen bishops in the assembly, among whom was Eusebius of Nicomedia, who was about to be reconciled with Constantine. There were many subtle maneuverings. Arius had his friends give an exhortation that he had prepared, in which he astutely equivocated on the contested points of his thesis, enveloping them in a willfully imprecise vocabulary. A group of bishops sought to fix everything by using in their definition of Christ only terms found in Sacred Scripture: could one not say, for example, that the Word is "of God," that he is "Son of God," that he is "the power and the image of the Father"? To which the Arians responded ironically that they gladly agree with these formulas insofar as they all could be understood to support their sense as well. Eusebius of Caesarea, for his part, attempted to save Arius, proposing a creed that left the door open to misunderstandings, but this was not successful.

Arius's supporters — some more explicit, others less so — used all the resources of dialectic, but the most profound Christian sentiment was against them. Beyond all their brilliance, one point was imposed by the very spirit of Christianity, which the deacon Athanasius presented as the cornerstone: the indisputable fact of redemption. Now the Redemption makes sense only if God Himself has become man, suffers, dies, and rises from the dead — if Christ is true God and true man at the same time. "The Word became flesh and lived among us"; the affirmation of St. John (1:4) supposes that the Logos is fully

God and not a divinized man following the pagan models. The son is not a creature. He has always existed and has always been at the Father's side, united to
Him, distinct but inseparable. He has always been infallible and perfect. The
Council, under the influence of Athanasius, adopted the term *homousios*, which
was translated into Latin as *consubstantialem*.

The adoption of this term to affirm the perfect equality of the Word and the
Father has remained fundamental for the Church all the way to our own time.
After having hesitated for several days regarding the necessity of promulgating a
new "symbol" that would clarify the old "symbol of the apostles" used in the
Early Church, they decided to redact this symbol of orthodox faith. A new "rule
of faith" was established, not substantially different from that which the early
Christians had followed, but more explicit, and composed in such a way that
error could no longer be introduced. This text is the Nicene Creed, which is
recited during Sunday Mass by the faithful, and we hear its exact and subtle affirmations: *gentium non factum, consubstantialem Patri* — begotten not made,
one in being with the Father.

The merit of the fourth-century theologians lies in having fought with intransigence to safeguard the divinity of Christ, the very essence of Christianity.
Every last part of the Nicene formula aimed at reducing the threat of heresy.
Arius was condemned. A crushing majority affirmed that the Son is truly God,
consubstantial with the Father. Only five bishops recanted before signing this
declaration, but given that the emperor had announced that he would use force
to make them accept it, three gave in and only two preferred to leave with Arius
in exile to the mountains of Illyria.

The Council of Nicaea closed after one month in a climate of triumph on
August 25, 325. The Arian question seemed answered forever. The end of the
Council coincided with the twentieth anniversary of the accession to the throne
of the emperor Constantine, and he offered all the prelates a sumptuous banquet
during which he gave a long discourse exalting the results, and inviting all of them
to maintain peace and to avoid all jealousy and discord, and to make his office
stand out as that "of a bishop on the outside," as he put it. Then the delegates departed, equipped with letters from the emperor for the faithful and bearing gifts.
"God has desired," said Constantine, "that the splendor of the truth triumph over
dissention, over schism, over the turbid and mortal poisons of discord."

The Council Fathers had just set off when three of them, including Eusebius of Nicomedia, retracted their signatures. The question was ready to

reemerge. A certain number of Eastern theologians, even those who were perfectly orthodox, were not far from thinking that the famous term "consubstantial" exaggerated the relations between Father and Son, and gave some advantages to the Modalists and Sabellians who wanted to see in the Son only a manifestation, a "mode" of the Father and not a distinct person.

The dogma of the Incarnation of the Word was attacked in every way. Besides the intransigent party of Athanasius and that of the Arians, a third party was emerging, that of the "Semi-Arians," divided into the sects of the Anomoeans, Homei, and Homoiusians, who recognized a certain analogy between the Father and the Son but rejected that He was "begotten, not made, of the same substance as the Father," as the Nicene Creed affirmed. While orthodoxy stated, "Christ is not a creature!," the nonorthodox added several treacherous words: "a creature like others." They thought that with this minor change, their doctrines could survive: the word *homoousias*, which means "of the same substance," they substituted with the term *homoiusios*, which means "of a similar substance." Between the two words there is only a minimal difference, but this apparently tiny difference was fundamental, and we must not ignore its importance. Between *homoousias* and *homoiusios*, there was an abyss: on one side the identity with God, on the other a mere resemblance, a simple nondissimilarity.

Defenders of the orthodox faith like Athanasius were accused of being obstinate over words, of being fanatics and intolerant. Against them, the party of innovators was to launch a boundless war that would last almost sixty years, and which St. Basil and the Christian historian Socrates compared to a furious "battle in the night."

The heretics, Arians and semi-Arians, understood that their success depended on two factors: the first was remaining within the Church; the second was obtaining the support of political power, and therefore of Constantine and his successors. This is what in fact took place, but it was a short-lived success.

If the Church was able to survive through such a trial, if in the end she came out not only intact but strengthened, as Daniel Rops concludes, she owes it to a meager legion of champions of the faith whom the Church had the good fortune of possessing. More than the miserable disputes through which heresy crumbled, what attracts our attention are these figures consecrated to God, passionately attached to the true Faith, solid as a rock in their positions, and whom nothing could defeat — neither intrigue, nor threats, nor exile, nor imprisonment. Two of them occupy the first places in this noble army: St. Athanasius and St. Hilary of Poitiers.

## 4. THE BATTLE OF ST. ATHANASIUS

St. Athanasius dominated the religious history of the Eastern empire in those turbid years. Daniel Rops writes:

> An extraordinarily penetrating intelligence accustomed to all the subtleties of the Eastern spirit, but capable of perceiving false appearances and avoiding traps, thanks to a positive common sense that can never be duped by anything; a marvelously tempered character, made of the same steel from which God had fashioned just centuries earlier his apostles and martyrs — at once agile and strong, direct in his intentions, expert in his maneuvers; furthermore, a profoundly religious soul, the type belonging to those great mystics for whom action is the effect and continuation of prayer, the type of mystic who in the worst struggles never forgets that they are God's. It was said he was at times intemperate, hateful in his fanaticism, ready to kindle violence and conflict wherever he went; but this is the calumny of his adversaries. No doubt, moderation cannot be imposed on a man of this world in a time when everything that nourished the Christian soul, that for the Church was a matter of life and death, was discussed. But if one often quotes the phrase of St. Epiphanius, "He persuaded, exhorted, but, if he found resistance, he used violence," we must also remember the words full of true Christian charity that St. Athanasius wrote about himself, "It belongs to religion not to coerce, but to convince."

Born in Alexandria around the year 300, Athanasius distinguished himself as a close collaborator to his bishop Alexander at the Council of Nicaea. In 328, when Alexander died, his disciple Athanasius rose to the episcopal throne. He remained bishop of Alexandria until his death forty-five years later.

Perhaps there has never been an episcopate as vexed in all Christian history. The difficulties began the day after his consecration. All the adversaries he had fought at Nicaea allied against the young bishop, from the radical Arians to the Semi-Arians, supporters of the two Eusebiuses. The number was great of those who could not tolerate Athanasius's public role, to which the episcopal see of Alexandria conferred power and prestige. This resentment led to a new Council held in Tyre in 335, at which the supporters of Eusebius determined to ambush

Athanasius. They accused him of having killed one of the schismatics, but the one presumed to be dead reappeared, confounding his accusers. They charged him with immodest acts and immorality, but the woman they had paid to give false witness could not even recognize him, and mistakenly identified another bishop who was indeed guilty of improper relations with her! Against Athanasius there existed, however, an organized lobby. He went to Constantinople to denounce the Arian intrigues, but Constantine took him for an agitator capable of disturbing unity. Athanasius was deposed and received orders to depart for Trier. This was his first of five exiles. Recalled from exile in 337, he was attacked again and forced to take refuge in Rome, while a heretic was placed in his episcopal see.

Athanasius was harshly persecuted by his own brethren and forced, from 336 to 366, to abandon his episcopal see five times, spending long years in exile and in determined struggles to defend the Faith, without concern for hardship or anxieties. "These are only passing clouds!" he would say, smiling.

In 341, while a Council of fifty bishops in Rome proclaimed Athanasius innocent, the great Council for the dedication of Antioch, in the presence of ninety bishops, ratified the acts of the Synods of Caesarea and Tyre, and placed an Arian in his episcopal see.

In 346, Athanasius finally returned to Alexandria for ten years, and was able to enjoy a margin of peace, bringing to completion a vast network of more than four hundred bishops faithful to the dogma of Nicaea, and writing his doctrinal works most worthy of consideration. In the meantime, however, two Semi-Arian bishops, Basil of Ancyra and Acacius of Caesarea, were able to gain the graces of the emperor. Constans, the sole master of the empire after the death of his brothers, under the influence of these advisers, multiplied in Italy and in Gaul the councils destined to destroy the doctrine of those orthodox bishops who were despised as "Nicene."

This was the low point of the Arian confusion. Pope Liberius (352–366), and after him Julius I, vacillated. The Council of Sirmium in 351 sought a compromise between Catholic orthodoxy and Arianism. At the Council of Arles in 353, the Fathers, including the papal legate, signed a new condemnation of Athanasius. The bishops were forced to choose between condemning Athanasius and exile. St. Paulinus (300–358), bishop of Trier, was nearly alone in fighting for the Nicene faith and was exiled to Phrygia, where he died from the maltreatment he suffered from the Arians. Two years later, at the Council of Milan (355), more than three hundred bishops in the West signed Athanasius's condemnation, and another orthodox father, St. Hilary of Poitiers, was banished to Phrygia for his intransigent fidelity to orthodoxy.

In 357, Pope Liberius, exhausted by the sufferings of exile and by the persistence of his friends, but also led by a "love of peace," signed the Semi-Arian formula of Sirmium and broke communion with St. Athanasius, declaring him to be separated from the Roman Church for his use of the term "consubstantial," as witnessed by four letters handed down by St. Hilary. Again, under Liberius's pontificate, the Councils of Rimini (359) and Seleucia (359), which constituted one large Council represented by the West and the East, abandoned Nicaea's term "consubstantial" and established an ambivalent via media between the Arians and St. Athanasius. It seemed that the spread of heresy had prevailed in the Church. "A dark night, sad and gloomy, covered the Church, because the lights of the world placed by God to illuminate the souls of the nations had been exiled," wrote St. Basil of Caesarea.

The twin Councils of Seleucia and Rimini, convoked by the emperor and considered ecumenical like that of Nicaea, are not today listed among the eight Ecumenical Councils of antiquity. They numbered up to 560 bishops, however — almost the entirety of bishops in Christendom — and were considered "ecumenical" by their contemporaries. It was then that St. Jerome coined the expression according to which "the world groaned and realized with amazement that it had become Arian."

St. Athanasius was forced into hiding, escaping to the desert where he arrived just in time to witness the passing of his old friend St. Anthony the abbot, the great hermit of Thebaid, Egypt. For six years, Athanasius was the "invisible patriarch" who continued to direct his Church from a distance, even though the emissaries of the emperor persecuted him unceasingly. He spiritually denounced Arianism and its by-products in his polemical writings, which circulated everywhere. With the death of Constans, he was finally able to return to Alexandria, and the Council he convoked there marked his triumph: all the confessors of the faith were present, proclaiming their unshakeable attachment to the dogma of Nicaea, to the Son consubstantial with the Father.

When he died in 373, St. Athanasius was the most famous among men, the highest authority of the Church. Just a few years after his death, the great bishop of Constantinople, Gregory of Nazianzus, celebrated him as "the column of the Church." In those same years, another emperor, the Arian Valens, not only fiercely persecuted the orthodox faith within the empire, but inoculated Arianism into the barbarian populations pressing on the borders. Under the illusion of binding them more strongly to Byzantium, he sent Arian missionaries to the Goths, who were then converted to heresy. However, Valens was defeated and killed precisely by the Visigoths at the Battle of Adrianople in 378, which marked the beginning of the progressive decline of the Roman Empire.

St. Athanasius, Father of the Church, left us an immense literary corpus despite his turbulent life — dogmatic works like *Against the Greeks* and *On the Incarnation of the Word*, as well as exegetical works like his *Exposition and Comment on the Psalms*, moral works like *On Virginity*, and historical works such as *The Life of St. Anthony*.

His defense of the orthodox faith was followed as an example in the East by the three Cappadocian Fathers: Basil of Caesarea, Gregory of Nazianzus, and Basil's brother, Gregory of Nyssa—and in the West by two other great saints: Eusebius of Vercelli and Hilary of Poitiers.

## 5. St. Hilary of Poitiers, the Athanasius of the West

St. Hilary of Poitiers (c. 310–367) has gone down in history as the "Athanasius of the West." This is a precise definition of his work, highlighting the fact that the foundation of his thought is the same as that of the great Alexandrian Doctor. Just like him, the saint of Gaul was moved by a passionate love for the incarnate Word, and he consecrated his life to the defense of faith in the divinity of Jesus Christ.

Hilary was born around 310 in Poitiers, to a wealthy pagan family that gave him a solid cultural formation. As an adolescent, he was struck by the prologue of the Gospel of John. As a young man familiar with spiritual matters, he meditated at length on the famous phrase *et Verbum caro factum est et habitavit in nobis*: the Word became flesh and dwelt among us (John 1:14). By means of this revelation, God was able to seduce his soul. Some years later, when he was already married and had a daughter, Hilary asked to be baptized. He later renounced marriage and asked to receive sacred orders. In 354, he became bishop of his native city.

This was the high point of the struggle against Arianism. It seemed as if Arianism was about to gain the victory. In 355, Hilary convened a synod in Paris that rejected Arianism. The champion of the Arian sect in Gaul, Saturninus of Arles, summoned a countersynod at Béziers in the South of France. Hilary rose with all his strength against the error, and this attracted the wrath of the pro-Arian emperor Constans, who had him sent to the opposite end of the empire. He was forced to settle in Phrygia in modern-day Turkey.

His sojourn there turned out to be advantageous. While he guided his diocese by correspondence, he studied Greek theology — of which the West had little understanding — and began to write his great dogmatic work against the Arians, *On the Trinity*. At this time, he sought to bring the Homousians, who were the most moderate among the Arian heretics, back to Catholicism. His prestige throughout the East was so great that the emperor thought it prudent to send him back to Gaul. This measure of clemency did not impede St. Hilary from launching an attack against the sovereign, a friend of heretics, with a pamphlet that was to circulate widely in a clandestine manner. Upon his return to Poitiers, he took up the fight once more. The Council of Paris in 361 was a prelude to the Council of Alexandria later convened by St. Athanasius. In Italy, all the Arians feared his arrival and banded together to keep him away. At the same time, he worked in Gaul to spread the monastic ideal; he multiplied his visits to the churches; and he wrote dogmatic tracts, commentaries on Scripture, and his *Essay on the Mysteries*, in which he studied the prophetic figures of the Old Testament. His work was truly prodigious and vast. When he died in 367, the whole of Gaul considered him a saint. In 1851, Blessed Pius IX proclaimed him a Doctor of the Church.

It was the Council of Constantinople, convened by the emperor Theodosius the Great in 381 under Pope St. Damasus (367–384), that marked the end of Arianism in the empire. At this Council, the Nicene Creed was reconfirmed almost to the letter, and it was determined that the Holy Spirit "proceeds from the Father, and together with the Father and the Son is worshiped and glorified." Thanks to Emperor Theodosius, Christianity was declared the state religion, and the work that had begun with the victory of Constantine at Saxa Rubra on October 28, 312, could finally be declared finished.

The sixty years that passed between the Council of Nicaea and that of Constantinople were years of confusion, bewilderment, and drama of conscience, during which Catholics asked themselves where the Church was in all of it. Cardinal Newman, in his book titled *The Arians of the Fourth Century*, writes that, in the age of the Arian crisis, "It was the Christian people who, under the protection of Providence, constituted the ecclesiastical strength of Athanasius, Hilary, Eusebius of Vercelli, and other great and solitary confessors who would have failed without their help."

St. Hilary writes that, during this period, the ears of the faithful who interpreted in an orthodox sense the ambiguous statements of Semi-Arian theologians were holier than the hearts of priests. "Hilary," writes Dom Guéranger, "had to fight pusillanimous churchmen who had become incapable of fathoming the supernatural essence of the Mystical Body of Christ, because naturalism had distorted their spirits."

The Church in the tempest, however, never lost its characteristics that always render it One, even when it seems divided and fragmented; Holy, even when the faults of her pastors besmirch her; Catholic, or universal, even when she seems to lose the certainty of her salvific uniqueness, and instead directs her efforts at just one part of believers in the world; Apostolic, even when among the successors of the apostles disputes and controversies arise. She enjoys the promise of indefectibility in her work of defending and preaching the Faith, of administering the sacraments, and of governing the faithful; in periods of crisis, great champions of faith like St. Athanasius and St. Hilary arise to remind them of this.

Today as well, the Church finds herself in a situation that is grave and arduous, and not only because of the persecution Christians are undergoing everywhere throughout the world, but also, and above all, because she appears harrowed and weakened, as in the period of the Arian crisis and in many other crises of the Church. It was Benedict XVI who reminded us of this, applying to our times the metaphor used by St. Basil to describe the years that followed the Council of Nicaea: a nocturnal battle in a raging sea.

Nothing worse could be imagined for the little boat of the Church than a situation like that evoked by the pope who, not by coincidence, announced that 2012 would be the Year of Faith.

For our part, we imitate St. Athanasius and all the saints, even those unknown, who raised the torch of faith in the fourth century, even at the price of being derided as intransigent fanatics. We ask them for their protection and for that of the Virgin Mary, *Auxilium Christianorum*, to face the trials that will come.

CHAPTER III

# Monks Conquer the World

## 1. MONASTICISM AS A CATEGORY OF THE CHRISTIAN SPIRIT

The first three centuries of the life of the Church were an era of suffering and persecution, during which Christians responded with generosity to the words of the Gospel: "If any man would come after me, let him deny himself and take up his cross daily and follow me" (Luke 9:23), and also, "You will be dragged before governors and kings for my sake, to bear testimony before them and the Gentiles" (Matt. 10:18).[24]

The early Christians did not hesitate to walk this path. They defended the truth to the point of shedding their blood, and martyrdom was the name the Church gave to this sacrifice. The age of the persecutions was also called the age of martyrs, because almost all the popes of the early centuries and many of the bishops and priests sealed their faith with martyrdom. The path of martyrdom was not, however, a circumscribed moment in the history of the Church, but a model to which innumerable Christians would be called throughout the centuries, to offer their lives in witness to Christ, the only Way, Truth, and Life (John 14:6).

We have seen, though, how in the fourth century an important shift occurred in the history of the Church known as the "Constantinian Shift": first,

---

[24] Radio Maria, conversation on November 16, 2011.

the Battle of Milvian Bridge, where Constantine's army, fighting under the standard of the Cross, defeated the pagan army of Maxentius; then, the Edict of Milan in 313, which conceded full religious liberty to Christians.

The Constantinian Shift, which marks the reconciliation of Christianity with the empire, has often been accused of betraying the gospel ideals, a Christian compromise with secular power. How many times have we heard it said that our faith needs to be purified of the accretions and residues of the Constantinian period so as to return to the origins of our faith, to the purity of primitive faith! That these accusations are false is demonstrated by the fact that, precisely in parallel with the so-called Constantinian Shift and in harmony with it, a new phenomenon developed in the fourth century characterized by the Christian rejection of the world and of every form of power. We are speaking of monasticism.

How can one reconcile, it might be asked, two apparently opposite perspectives: the social conquest of the world, namely its Christianization after Constantine, and the monastic flight from the world during that same period. To comprehend this, we must return to the words of the Gospel: "My kingdom is not of this world" (John 18:36). This does not mean that the Kingdom of Christ does not extend to the world or that in the world it is not realized, but rather that it has neither its origin nor its ultimate end in this world, because it is supernatural. Christians live in the world, however, and they must conquer it. The conquest of the world, its Christianization, can come about in various ways: monasticism is one of these, as is martyrdom, and as the Crusades were to be: these are ideal models destined to span the centuries — not in opposition to one another, but working in conjunction and arising from the same spirit of faith.

To understand monasticism in depth, we must understand well the nature of Christianity and the Church. Monasticism, in fact, is a form of complete dedication to God, through the faithful observance of the three evangelical counsels (Matt. 16:21): the renunciation of material goods (poverty), the renunciation of the pleasures of the flesh and the joys of family life (celibacy), and the renunciation, above all, of the independence of one's ego (obedience). Jesus sanctified marriage, but He also said, "Everyone who has left houses, or brothers, or sisters, or father, or mother, or children, or lands for my name's sake, will receive a hundredfold, and inherit eternal life" (Matt. 19:29).

Private property was legitimated by two commandments of the Decalogue, but Jesus says, "If you want to be perfect, go, sell what you possess and give to the poor, and you will have treasure in Heaven, and come follow me" (Matt. 19:21).

These renunciations are a free choice because they are *counsels*, not commandments, of the Lord. They are not orders, nor counsels addressed to all, but only to some. In a word, this is a vocation, an appeal that has resounded throughout history. The error, and even heresy, begins when one presumes to transform the evangelical counsels into obligatory commands for all. It was this — for example, the idea of a Church of "saints" or of the "pure" opposed to that of "sinners" — that inspired the first heresies of Marcion, Montanus, and Donatus, and that characterizes the secular religions of the twentieth century, such as communism, which would like to impose a community of goods by decree, denying the natural right to private property.

The institution of monasticism dates from the third and fourth centuries, but the search for forms of Christian perfection began in the Church in its very first years. Characteristically, those wanting to adopt the evangelical counsels would as a first choice embrace virginity, marking their separation from the world. Virginity, however, before being a physical state, is a moral choice. The first model we have of religious life is in fact St. Mary Magdalen, the sinful woman who, after the death of the Lord, left Palestine and with a few other companions (male and female) arrived miraculously in Provence to lead the life of a hermit for thirty years in silence and prayer. These were the years in which the apostles were spreading the gospel to every corner of the earth and sealing their testimony with martyrdom. St. Mary Magdalen accompanied their work of spreading the Gospel with her penance and her prayers.

## 2. Monasticism in the East

The first form of monasticism was called hermitical (from *eremo*, a deserted place) or solitary (the word "monk" stems from the word *monos*, or alone), signifying a type of life separated from men and entirely turned toward God. This came about in part because of the persecutions. From the biography of St. Paul of Thebes written by St. Jerome, we know that the future hermit took refuge in the mountains to escape persecution. St. Jerome was one of the first to use the term "anchorite" in the sense of "one who lives in desert places" (Epist. 22.36). God is not to be found in noise but in silence and meditation. In anchoritism, there are two degrees: some live entirely solitary lives; others, while living in separate cells, form a kind of colony around a church in which they gather for common prayer. Egypt was considered the home of early monasticism. Centers of Egyptian monasticism were the Natron Valley and the desert of Skete, south of Alexandria. To understand the mentality of the Egyptian monks, so different from our own, it is edifying to read the *Apo-phtegmata Patrum* (Sayings of the Fathers), a series of sayings attributed to the oral teaching of the Desert Fathers.

The Egyptian St. Anthony (251–356) is considered the founder of the an-choritic life. His biography was written in 357 by St. Athanasius, who knew him personally and was supported and counseled by him in his fight against Arian-ism. *The Life of St. Anthony* was translated into Latin and had a notable influence on the growth of monasticism in the West. Toward the end of the third century, he retired to the desert between the Nile and the Red Sea, living immersed in prayer and work. "He prayed continuously," his biography recalls, "and remem-bered everything — his memory took the place of books for him." He was not a priest or even a cleric, as were many hermits at that time, but around him there soon gathered many disciples attracted by this life of perfection, and thus the eremitical life spread first in Upper Egypt and then also in Lower Egypt.

The monastic form of life instituted by Anthony was that of the solitary who keeps separate from his peers and seeks to remain in face-to-face dialogue with God. Within the eremitical life, organization was lacking. If a monk stood out for his sanctity and wisdom, other monks allowed themselves to be guided by him, calling him their spiritual "father" (*abbas, apa, amba*: abbot). But a proper community did not exist. They soon realized that many candidates for perfection could not bear the dangers of absolute isolation, and that it was pos-sible, while still prescribing the desire for solitude, to have recourse to others in a reciprocal spirit of charity.

From the eremitical form, monasticism thus passed to the communitarian or cenobitic form. A first step toward this was made simultaneously in Palestine and in Egypt. The former Egyptian soldier of Constantine, St. Pachomius (287–347), began the eremitical life after his conversion, but later, toward 320, founded the first coenobium in Thebaid (Upper Egypt), gathering for the first time a group of monks who led a common life under the authority of an abbot, and wearing for the first time a monastic habit with a hood and a leather cinc-ture. The coenobium, an enclosure prohibited to the laity and above all to women, isolated the community from the world. A strict rule regimented daily life and time. Intellectual work went hand in hand with physical work, while frequent conferences taught the monks Sacred Scripture. Prayer was made both in common and privately. Nine communities, daughters of the first foundation of Pachomius, were established all over Egypt. His sister Mary founded two convents for women. At the end of the century, his congregation had no fewer than seven thousand monks.

In Palestine, where, according to Jerome, the first monk was Hilarion of Gaza, they began to call the monasteries by the name of *lauras*, which has been retained by the Greek Orthodox tradition. A laura (a Greek word meaning "village") was a true village of monks who constructed a group of cells, detached but near each other, surrounded by a hedge or a wall. That enclosure marked a boundary line: it was a cloister for those outside and a circle of unity for those within. St. Chariton, who lived as an ascetic in the vicinity of Jerusalem, is considered the founder of the lauras of Pharan, Donka (near Jericho), and Sonka (near Bethlehem). He and St. Hilarion spread their convents and hermitages throughout the lands familiar to us from Sacred Scripture.

Monasticism spread with prodigious rapidity. In Mesopotamia, Eugene, once a pearl fisherman and later a disciple of Pachomius, settled on the mountain of Nisibis. Other shepherd monks could be recalled, who prayed to God on the borderlands between Arabia and Syria, in the solitude of the steppe and in the midst of their roaming flocks. All of Asia Minor was soon penetrated by monasticism.

The true founder of Eastern monasticism was St. Basil the Great (329–379), who wrote a rule widely used throughout both the East and the West, and who became bishop of Caesarea and metropolitan of Cappadocia in 370. Basil belonged to a profoundly Christian family: the descendant of martyrs and son of upper-middle-class parents who had left everything to flee the threats of Diocletian. His sister founded convents, and two other brothers are canonized saints: Gregory of Nyssa and Peter of Sebaste. He was both a man of action and a great thinker, a worthy administrator, and a fervent believer. Around the years 357–358, Basil went on a long journey that took him to Egypt, Palestine, Syria, and Mesopotamia. Everywhere he went, he collected the experiences of the monks populating those deserts. After returning to Asia Minor, he became a monk as well, and settled, with several companions, in the region of Neo-Caesarea of Pontus, following the *Rule* of Pachomius with several adaptations.

In his writings on the ascetical life in community (known as *rules*), Pachomius summarized the ideal of cenobitic life in the following three points: first, love of God and one's neighbor as the perfect expression of the law of charity; second, the study of Sacred Scripture, understood as the highest manifestation of the will of God; third, the practice of the monastic life, considered as a perfect form of renunciation of the world.

St. Basil's reform tended to limit the number of monks in each monastery, allowing the superior to better direct them. For the spiritual flourishing of the community, it insisted on the development of the virtues of humility, patience, and charity. It was St. Basil who had the idea of annexing schools to the monasteries, an idea that would have decisive success for the future of Christian civilization. His rule has remained the basis of Eastern monasticism, as his liturgy has remained the basis of Orthodox liturgy.

In the East, other forms of monasticism spread as well, like the Stylites and the Enclosed. The Stylites took a vow to remain seated on a column that stood from three to eighteen meters high. Their founder was the Syrian St. Simon, called the Stylite (c. 390–459), because he spent thirty-seven years on a column near Antioch. After his death, one of the largest basilicas in Syria was built near the column.

The Enclosed, or recluses, earned their name from the fact that they would have themselves walled up in a cell for long periods of time, or for the rest of their lives, to dedicate themselves fully to contemplation, reading, and manual labor. The Council in Trullo established that no one could take up this form of life before having spent three years in a monastery, and that, once enclosed, he could no longer leave his cell. After a period of great success, this form of monasticism fell into disuse — although even today, on Mt. Athos, one can find recluses who spend their lives in absolute solitude, as prisoners of God. Today, this life choice might seem bizarre to us, but it is not *contra natura* — these monks took to its most extreme consequence the principle of renunciation of the world in order to gain eternal life. Of course, certain forms of modern life that openly violate all the laws, both natural and Christian, would have seemed absurd to these monks (as they often do to us).

During the fifth and sixth centuries, the number of monasteries continued to increase, as did their popularity. In 518, there were sixty-seven monasteries for men in Constantinople, and many for women as well. They occupied vast tracts of land, particularly along the Marmara Sea, where the famous monastery of Studios stood, renowned for its fidelity to the See of Rome during the Schism of Acacio (which became the See of the *Akoimetoi*, the "sleepless ones") founded in 405 by the monk Alexander. They led a common life, and, divided into various choirs, dedicated themselves unceasingly, even at night (hence the name), to the Divine Office.

The Council of Chalcedon gave juridical status to monasticism, placing monasteries under the jurisdiction of their respective diocesan bishops.

## 3. MONASTICISM IN THE WEST

It was thanks to Athanasius that monasticism spread from the East to the West. We have recalled the eventful life of St. Athanasius, bishop of Alexandria, exiled in the West by the Arian emperors and challenged by Semi-Arians because of his adherence to orthodoxy. He reached Trier, one of the capitals of the Western Empire, and in the mid-fourth century spent time in Rome as well. In this providential manner, he made known in the West the extraordinary life of St. Anthony and the Egyptian hermits, urging Western Christians to follow his example.

In Italy, the first centers of monasticism were in Rome and Milan, thanks to the two great Church Fathers St. Jerome and St. Ambrose. In Rome, a group of aristocratic women met under the guidance of St. Jerome, following his appeal for a new Christian nobility, to lead a more perfect life based on prayer and virginity. Among these women, we recall Marcella — who transformed her palace on the Aventine Hill into a sort of convent — as well as Fabiola, Proba, and Paola: all elevated to the altars. Dom Guéranger reminds us:

> The patrician class constitutes the better part of the monastic army in its formation in the West and communicates its character of ancient greatness; but among their ranks, sharing equal title with fathers and brothers, one finds virgins and widows, and sometimes even wives together with their husbands. It was Marcella who first obtained this direction from St. Jerome, and it would be Marcella who, once the master had passed away, would become a kind of oracle consulted by all, despite her humility, regarding the difficulties of Scripture. Following Marcella were Furia, Fabiola, Paola, names that recall their great ancestors: the Camilli, the Fabii, the Scipioni.

In Milan, St. Ambrose founded a monastery near the city walls. In Vercelli, St. Eusebius (d. 370) introduced the communal life for clerics; the same happened in Verona under the bishop Zeno (362–372), and in Nola where St. Paolino founded a monastery over the tomb of St. Felice in 395.

The fascination exercised by the fame of the hermits and monks in Egypt, Palestine, and Syria inspired many Christians in the West to set out for those lands. The Roman matron Melania, when left a widow, traveled to Palestine and in 378 founded a monastery on the Mount of Olives, followed some decades later by her granddaughter Melania the Younger, also a canonized saint. Jerome moved to Palestine in 386, followed by Paola and her daughter Eustochia. In Bethlehem, he founded two monasteries, one for men and one for women.

In Gaul, monasticism came to life with St. Martin (316–397), born in the land of Pannonia. After having served in the Roman army, he became a hermit near Poitiers, where St. Hilary was bishop, and of whom he became a disciple. Earlier we recalled the names of St. Athanasius, bishop of Alexandria, and Eusebius, bishop of Vercelli. Along with St. Hilary, they were not only staunch combatants against Arianism but also great promoters of monasticism. Their apostolic work against heresy was born of a profound spirit of prayer. While previously in the East, monks could not be priests, St. Martin established that they could also be ordained. At his bidding, the first monastery in Gaul was founded in Ligugé. Later, after becoming bishop, the saint wanted to preserve his monastic way of life, and so he built near Tours the abbey Marmoutier. Martin sought to reconcile his pastoral duties with the monastic life he promoted in Gaul, Spain, and Britain. He evangelized most of Gaul and was considered the protector of the Franks. When he died in 397, two thousand monks attended his funeral. The most venerated sanctuary in Gaul was constructed on his tomb.

In southern Gaul, St. Onorato (d. 492), later the bishop of Arles, founded a convent destined to have great influence on the island of Lerins, near the city of Cannes. St. Vincent of Lerins came from this monastery, as well as Salviano of Marsiglia and St. Cesario (470–542), later bishop of Arles, to whom we owe the first two monastic rules characteristic of Gaul: one for monks and the other for "Holy Virgins," adopted by St. Radegonda in Poitiers (560). At the end of the fifth century, there were 40 monasteries in Gaul, and a century later 240.

We must remember that the bridge between Eastern and Western monasticism was St. John Cassian (c. 360–435), a monk of the Dobruja (a region between the Danube and the Black Sea), founder of two monasteries in Marsillia for men and women, and the author (preceding St. Benedict) of a rule for Western monasticism. Among his works that have come down to us is the *Coenobitic Institutions* published in 417–418, which influenced the *Rule* of St. Benedict.

In Africa, the idea of monasticism was spread by St. Augustine, who learned about it in Milan and Rome, but who developed his own vision. He gathered around him members of the clergy to lead an ascetic life in community. The *Rule* of St. Augustine, written around 400, can be considered the most ancient monastic rule in Latin. Augustine provided for the founding of monasteries for virgins. In the one in Hippo, his sister was the superior. His Letter 211, directed to the nuns in Hippo, provided a foundation for many religious institutions to follow.

## 4. St. Benedict of Nursia

Monasticism came fully into its own in the history of the Church beginning in the fourth century when the era of martyrs gave way to that of monks. The new institution was welcomed by all Christians with the greatest of fervor. For three centuries, the model of perfection had been represented by martyrs whose relics were venerated and whose deeds were read. Now that the age of persecutions had come to an end, a new ideal of perfection arose, that of monks who also led extraordinary lives, and to whom, like the martyrs, were attributed great wonders. The Holy Spirit did not cease to aid the Church but continued to inspire new forms of holiness.

Certainly, there was no lack of resistance to the new form of life, condemned as too extreme and intransigent by pagans and by more moderate and mundane Christians. Even some bishops harbored diffidence for a way of life that seemed to them excessive or that appeared to constitute a critique of the bland Christianity of much of the clergy. In cities like Milan and Carthage, there were strong antimonastic reactions. Some bishops sought to discourage the new movement, which was growing in strength and numbers, but which seemed too independent from the authority of the bishops and too unsettling in the new fervor for life that it propagated.

However, the institution of monasticism marked an important stage in the development of Christianity. Daniel Rops recalls how we owe the habit of the "examination of conscience" to the writings of the Desert Fathers, and above all to St. Anthony, a practice greatly praised by St. Augustine. It was monks who inaugurated the practice of the spiritual direction of souls. Monasteries initiated the idea of the reversibility of merits, and the prayer of the cloistered was for the benefit of all humanity. St. Macarius the Egyptian cenobite exclaimed, "Happy the monk who considers with joy the progress and salvation of all his fellow men!" When martyrs were no longer there to redeem human misery, monks with their prayers took their place.

On the level of history, monasteries were to play a paramount role as well. They were the ones who, when the Barbarian Invasions were unleashed, aided many bishops destined to be the bastions of the Church and society. They were to be the ones who, in schools and in copyist workshops, would safeguard civilization amid the worst cataclysms. We owe to these men and women, providentially placed in this new institution, the survival of culture and the uninterrupted celebration of the Holy Sacrifice of the Mass and the Divine Office. The crowning of this epoch came by way of an extraordinary figure: St. Benedict, the father of the Christian civilization that arose from the ruins of Roman civilization.

St. Benedict was born in Nursia, Umbria, around 480 into a Roman patrician family. He ended his earthly existence in Montecasino on March 21, 543. His life was bound to three places: Nursia (today Norcia), his birthplace; Subiaco, where he had his most intense religious experience; and Montecasino, where he built a monastery destined to become part of European history.

In Subiaco, in the Valley of the Aniene, St. Benedict lived for three years as a hermit in a cave that is known today as the *Sacro Speco* (Holy Cave). Only after having quelled the desires of his flesh and vanquished spiritual temptations did he decide to leave this refuge and establish his first monasteries, providing them a new rule. The Abbey of Montecasino, the most famous monastery in Christendom, was founded in the year 529 on a mountain halfway between Rome and Naples, where pagan temples still stood. St. Benedict destroyed these temples and established there the first monastic community in the West. The foundation of this abbey represented the birth certificate of Christian Europe, which began to emerge after the fall of the Roman Empire.

In his homily *Exultent Hodie*, given on September 18, 1947, Pius XII described St. Benedict's mission: "He was a giant who opened new paths in a wayward century. Filled with the same spirit of all the just, as St. Gregory the Great said, he distinguished himself by his love of God and neighbor. He was serious and serene. He had a great influence on everyone. Tamer of his nature, decorated with angelic customs, celebrated for his gifts of prophecy and miracles, a new Moses, he established a law and conducted the people to sacrifice in the desert."

The law that Benedict established is the celebrated *Rule* of monks, which not only synthesizes his person and his work, but also constitutes one of the foundations of all Western spirituality. The great merit of the *Rule* lies above all in having harmonized and fused the preceding monastic rules, adapting them in an admirable fashion to the needs and habits of people in the West.

The *Rule* is made up of seventy-three chapters of varying length and has come down to us in three editions. The prologue and initial chapters (I–VIII) lay the foundations for the cenobitic life; the following chapters (IX–XVIII) provide norms for the liturgy and the common life; they define the spirit that must vivify the life of the monks as well as their private prayer; they establish the order of the abbey and regulate its functioning.

The *Rule*, "a little compendium of the gospel," as it has been defined, is a milestone of monasticism, a model for all the rules that determine later forms of religious life. Its fundamental characteristic is the common life of the monks as one large family.

The Benedictine monastery is a social organism sustained by the authority of the abbot, similar to a paterfamilias, who possesses broad powers to unite loving severity with discretion, and who understands the attitudes and weaknesses of the individual monks. Besides the three traditional vows of poverty, chastity, and obedience, the monks take a vow of stability: the fundamental vow of the Benedictine ideal is *stabilitas loci*, by which a monk binds himself when he enters to become part of a monastery.

Later in the Middle Ages, the so-called Mendicant Orders arose, characterized by an apparent instability due to their continual movement, walking the roads of Europe from one monastery to another. But this was a moment in history in which stability was the rule of society. Medieval society was an orderly society within which movement was possible as an expression of vitality, not of disorder. The time of Benedict was a time of great chaos. The *stabilitas loci* of the monks constituted an element of spiritual and moral stability, even before physical stability. The monasteries constituted, therefore, a stabilizing element in a society by that time deprived of order and without a center.

The principal task of the monk was the *opus Dei*, the divine service, to which all else was subordinated: reading, study, and manual work in the fields and in the monastery. The center of the monk's life was constituted by the liturgical office, celebrated night and day in common, according to the established hours. But the great novelty of St. Benedict with respect to Eastern monasticism is that of having associated prayer with intellectual and manual work. *Ora et labora* is the formula that summarizes the Benedictine ideal. From prayer (*ora*) arises and flows work (*labora*). This did not oppose prayer to work, but rather affirmed the primacy of prayer over works. This teaching applies above all in an age such as ours, characterized by feverous, incessant activity lacking the profound breath of prayer in work. The historian Giorgio Falco writes, "This, then, is the existence of the monk: praying, reading, working. Everything is disciplined: the calendar and the daily schedule, the liturgy, study, work, the amount they eat and drink, the service in the kitchen and laundry."

Modern man is immersed in the noise of exterior works and has forgotten the existence of that glance raised to God, the *opus Dei*, that gives the only possible meaning to his life. The monastic community was in fact conceived with two aspects in mind but fused into one, and having as their common principle love toward men and toward God. In the monastery, the vertical relationship toward God is fused with the horizontal one toward other men. "The law that governs this coexistence is that of love, all love, excluding self-love, namely the total renunciation of one's own desires, the abnegation of oneself in God and neighbor: in the brothers, in the novices, in the oblates, in the guest that knocks at the door, whoever he is, because in the guest one welcomes Christ." John Paul II stated, "Love invades and inspires everything, like in every true and healthy family: just think of that testament to charity, chapter 72 of the Rule" (*Discourse to the Faithful of Cassino*, September 20, 1980).

St. Benedict was proclaimed Patron of Europe by Paul VI on October 24, 1964. When St. Benedict died in 547, his work counted only three monasteries: Montecasino, Subiaco, and Terracina. A century later, there were more than a hundred Benedictine communities.

The proliferation of monasteries, according to Daniel Rops, is the most important event in the history of the Church in the Middle Ages: from the sixth century onward — and for many generations — kings, bishops, the great, and the rich competed to contribute to their foundation. Each community had on average two hundred men from all social strata. Even female abbeys multiplied to the point of having abbesses who had jurisdiction over double monasteries, one male and one female. The works they carried out in the territories around the abbeys were impressive: they tilled fields that had remained uncultivated after the fall of the empire and the Barbarian Invasions, they reclaimed marshlands, and they applied rational cultivation methods, created vast breeding farms of livestock. Villages, towns, and cities formed around monastic centers. Roads, bridges, and canals were appearing everywhere, while hospitals, almshouses, and abundant alms for the needy were used to alleviate the miseries of the time. The earnings of the monasteries were used not only for maintaining the community and embellishing the buildings, but also for works of charity, above all hospitals and hospices for pilgrims.

Their intellectual influence was no less profound. From their beginnings, monasteries had their schools and their scriptoriums, workshops for copying and transcribing codices, and in which the patient work of an amanuensis produced many books. The office of copyist required great commitment and sacrifice: *Si tres digiti scribunt, totum corpus laborat,* declared the scribe of Montecasino. The codices and texts, jealously guarded by the monks in their libraries, contributed to saving the cultural patrimony of the ancient world.

## 5. The Spread of the Benedictine *Rule*

The wide-scale spread of the *Rule* of St. Benedict in the Western Church was a slow process that contributed in a decisive manner to the evangelization of Europe. Outside of Italy, the first country where the *Rule* of St. Benedict was known and adopted was England, where St. Gregory the Great had sent Augustine of Canterbury on a mission.

When Augustine reached England, monasticism was already flourishing there. Over a century earlier, St. Patrick (385–461), of Scottish origin, had arrived in Ireland.

In England lived the Bretons, who were allied with the Romans long before the latter had retreated from their lands. They had fought the Picts alongside the Romans, the people who lived in the northern part of the island. A heretic came from these lands, Pelagius, who had come to Rome to propagate his errors. To fight Pelagianism, St. Germaine of Auxerrois (c. 378–448) organized a missionary expedition to the islands of Britannia in 432, taking as companion the young Patrick, sent as missionary by Pope Celestine I (422–432). Patrick worked in this land, obtaining extraordinary results and leaving it with a profoundly Catholic mark that was not to be lost through the centuries.

By 444, the monastery of Armagh in Ireland had become the metropolitan see and the most important center of ecclesial life in the country. One of the characteristics of Irish monasticism was its missionary zeal and its ability to expand. St. Colomban was to depart at the end of the sixth century from Bangor, near Belfast, the most famous of its monasteries. He then transferred around

591 to Gaul, where he founded the monastery of Luxeuil, and then to Vosgi. Colomban had an inflexible character and imposed deprivations and mortifications of every sort on himself. Forced into exile, he left for Italy with twelve companions, among whom was Gallo (550–645), who fell ill along the way and founded the monastery of San Gallo, today in Switzerland, while Colomban continued, fighting every sort of hardship, until arriving at Trebbia, near Piacenza, where he founded one last monastery, that of Bobbio, where he died in 615. The monasteries founded by Colomban and his disciples progressively adopted the *Rule* of St. Benedict. In the Carolingian Age, the *Rule* was adopted by all the monasteries of the empire (*Capitulare monasticum* of 817), with the help of St. Benedict of Aniane (c. 750–821).

The birth of monasticism was an extraordinary phase in the history of Christianity. This movement was not only an exceptional instrument for personal sanctification, by means of the radical application of the evangelical counsels, but it also elevated divine worship to incredible heights. It had a profound influence on social and political life, as nascent European civilization was being formed in the image of the monasteries and living in their spirit. For this reason, Pius XII called St. Benedict the "Father of Europe," stating that "while in the provinces the barbarian hordes were taking over, he who was called the last of the Romans reconciled *romanitas* (allow me to use this expression of Tertullian) with the gospel, and drew from this valid assistance in uniting the peoples of Europe under the banner of Christ and giving a fitting structure to Christian society. In fact, from the North Sea to the Mediterranean, from the Atlantic Ocean to the Baltic, legions of Benedictines spread, and with the cross, with books, with the plow, tamed those rude and uncivilized people" (Homily, *Exultent hodie*).

"The Benedictines are the fathers of European civilization," wrote Léo Moulin (1906–1996), recalling that even the rules of etiquette that we respect today at table (tablecloth, napkins, flowers, silence, cleanliness, sequence of foods, reciprocal courtesy, way of behaving) were invented by the monks who rendered food a matter of *pietas*: food received and consumed with gratitude and respect.

Etiquette, courtesy, and civil behavior are the fruit of Christian civilization, and the contemporary barbarization of customs is the fruit of the loss of the Christian spirit. This spirit, which has one of its highest expressions in the Benedictine spirit, is above all the spirit of prayer. This spirit of prayer, the Benedictine *opus Dei*, is above all the worship of God in the Holy Sacrifice of the Mass and in the Divine Office. Pope Benedict XVI, desiring to give renewed expression to this liturgical dimension, restored, with the Motu proprio *Summorum Pontificum* of July 14, 2007, full rights to the traditional Mass in the ancient Roman Rite, the same used by Benedict and his monks, and still celebrated today in many Benedictine abbeys in France and Italy, and which is progressively returning throughout the entire Church, benefiting souls to the greater glory of God.

CHAPTER IV

# Pagan Rome and Christian Rome

## 1. THE BARBARIANS AT THE END OF THE FOURTH CENTURY

Historical periods resemble each other — each is in some respects the prefigura-tion and image of a later one.[25] For this reason, we do well to linger on a particular historical period of the Church: the fourth century, which corresponds to the age in which the Roman Empire began its decline. Benedict XVI, in his *Discourse to the Roman Curia* given on December 20, 2005, compared our time to the period of the twilight of the Roman Empire, an institution that seemed immortal and yet, between the fourth and fifth centuries, fell into ruin.

It did not fall suddenly. A dark presentiment began to spread toward the end of the fourth century: the awareness that a world was collapsing, that something had ended and would not be able to rise again. This sentiment, observes Daniel Rops, was expressed in a general malaise—not only psychological, but political, economic, and social. One did not need to be a philosopher of history to notice it.

The memory of the order, peace, and universality of past times was only a sad regret. Even the simplest of citizens perceived that things were going badly, that they could not go on like this. The dissolution of a society brings with it various crises that overlap and intertwine with one other, rendering the situation irreme-diable — economic crisis, political crisis, and above all, a crisis of moral values.

---

[25] Radio Maria, conversation on December 21, 2011.

The economic crisis expressed itself in inflation, in the black market, in the devaluation of coinage, and by heavy taxation. Among the reasons for this economic crisis there was also, as in every age of decadence, a demographic decline. People stopped having children out of fear of the future and because they were immersed in a culture of hedonism and relativism. Corruption and dishonesty reigned. The imperial courts were places of all sorts of intrigue. "The halls of power," wrote Ammiano Marcellino, "are a seedbed of vices whose seeds are propagated everywhere."

At this time, according to Lactantius, the number of functionaries had begun to outpace that of taxpayers. One could neither work nor travel without the permission of an inspector. The agents of the state stole and plundered. It was not clear whether the court of Milan was in charge, or that of Trier, or Constantinople.

The Roman legion, which constituted the backbone of the empire, was no longer a reservoir of ancient virtues. There were no longer native Romans in the legion, because the enfeebled citizens no longer wanted to fight or to work. Conscripts cut off their thumbs to avoid having to pull the bowstring; barbarian immigrants filled the void left by Rome's citizens in the fields and in the army.

In this decadent society, barbarians arrived on the horizon as a new force. Rome harbored both fascination and fear toward this new power.

The word "barbarian" is of Greek origin and designates populations not subject to Roman domination, in particular the Germanic peoples who settled on the borders of the empire and then invaded it in the fifth century.

The borders of the Roman Empire extended over fifteen thousand kilometers, defended by a type of "iron curtain": the *limes* or *vallum*, a system of palisades, watchtowers, and trenches, which created an impressive example of military engineering. In the third century, the Roman *limes* stretched from the Atlantic and the North Sea all the way to the Caspian Sea, and included Europe from the Rhine and Danube, Britannia, Northern Africa, and Asia Minor, to Armenia and Mesopotamia.

On the borders of this immense empire were, to the East, Parthians and Arabs; on African soil, Ethiopians, Libyans, Berbers; to the North, the Germanic peoples who had not been conquered by the empire; while from Scandinavia, the Goths began to push toward the territory of the Vitula. Besides the Roman world throughout the Mediterranean and the barbarian world on its borders, there existed a third world in Asia which pushed on the barbarians from the East. These were savage hordes like the Huns who appeared on the Don and the Dnieper and were approaching the Danube.

The difference between the barbarians of northern Europe and those coming from Asia was that the former were willing to assimilate, integrating with the populations they conquered, while the latter carried out a policy of destruction and extermination, reducing the conquered populations to slavery.

The Barbarian Invasions did not overtake Rome suddenly. The first phase, between the second and third centuries, was characterized by peaceful and gradual infiltration into the territories of the empire by those attracted to Rome's high standard of living and its culture. A second phase of peaceful immigration followed, characterized by stable settlement within the Roman *limes*, not of individuals or fragmented groups, but of entire populations destined to become states within a state. These peoples did not arrive as regular armies, but as conglomerates of nomadic tribes with women and children, animals, and their belongings.

The empire was peacefully occupied until its borders were traversed by armed warriors intent on seizing the wealth and power of the lands of Europe. The migrations turned to invasions, then occupations, and finally the conquest of the Western Roman Empire, which, under the impact of the barbarians, crumbled and disappeared. The history of the relations between the barbarians and the Roman Empire had a watershed moment: August 9, 378, when on the plains of Adrianople in Thrace, the army of the Roman Empire of the East under the leadership of Valens (364–378) was defeated by the Visigoths. The Roman legion was annihilated, and Valens killed along with many high officials. The Roman army had never seen an undoing of such great proportions.

The religion of the barbarian people was Arianism. Valens, who was also an Arian, had sent a missionary, Ulfilas, to inoculate them with the Arian heresy. From that time, Arianism had become the national religion of almost all the barbarian peoples who had settled throughout the empire, and would remain so until the sixth and seventh centuries. Besides the Visigoths, the Vandals, the Ostrogoths, the Burgundians, the Suebi, the Alans, and the Lombards were all Arians. Some of these peoples, like the Vandals and the Ostrogoths, remained Arian until their extinction in the sixth century. Others completed their religious itinerary with a second conversion to Catholicism, as in the case of the Burgundians and the Visigoths in the sixth century.

And still other peoples, like the Lombards, remained Arian well after the seventh century. In this historical context, on the eve of the year 500, we can comprehend the importance of the conversion of the Franks with the baptism of their king, Clovis. The Franks were the only barbarian people that did not pass through Arianism on their way to orthodox Christianity. If Valens had not led them to Arianism, the Goths would have become Catholic and would have spread the true Christian civilization throughout the barbarian world.

In this situation of chaos and decomposition, while the barbarians pounded on the door, Christianity set down its definitive foundations.

The Roman state no longer had an authentic aristocracy aware of its tasks and duties. There were only sycophants, nobles in title and in pomp. The bishops were becoming the most authoritative men of their cities. In their dioceses they held vast power, almost absolute, which the gifts of the Holy Spirit rendered supernatural. The bishops were administrators, judges, directors of social programs — all that concerned the People of God passed through their hands. One can see, therefore, how all throughout the fourth century and concluding in the fifth, a real transfer of lay power into the hands of religious authorities was being prepared. "Christians," writes Daniel Rops, "feeling they were much better supported and organized by the bishops than by state functionaries, considered themselves increasingly to be sons of the Church rather than citizens of the empire."

The real aristocracy now belonged to the ranks of the Christians. It was both a political and ecclesiastical aristocracy. The typical case can be seen in St. Ambrose, one of the first Doctors of the Western Church, the one of whom the emperor Theodosius had to say, "Of all the bishops I have met, Ambrose alone truly deserved to be called bishop."

## 2. ST. AMBROSE AND THEODOSIUS

St. Ambrose (339–397) was born in Trier to an ancient senatorial family. He studied in Rome and soon reached the heights of his administrative career, becoming *consularis* (governor) of Northern Italy in Milan, which had been the capital of the Western Empire since 364. In 374, a fierce conflict broke out between Arians and Catholics due to the succession of the Arian bishop Assenzius. Ambrose, a young politician of only thirty-five, was chosen by both factions to become the bishop of Milan, despite the fact he was only a catechumen. After receiving baptism and Holy Orders, he transferred to his new role all his abilities, political and administrative, and proved to be an extraordinary pastor of souls.

There are events in the life of the Church that impress themselves upon us as symbols lasting through the centuries. The conflict between St. Ambrose and Emperor Theodosius over the massacre in Thessalonica was one such event.

In August 390, a revolt broke out in Thessalonica. The Gothic Butheric, commander of the Roman garrison, had arrested a homosexual who was also a very popular charioteer. The crowd rebelled and lynched the Goth. Theodosius was indignant and left the Goths free to avenge his death. They seized the opportunity at a circus event, massacring seven thousand people by sword. Theodosius, who had encouraged the massacre, was excommunicated by St. Ambrose. In a private letter, full of paternal affection, the bishop implored the emperor to admit his fault, assuring him that, if he were to ask forgiveness, he would be absolved and readmitted to communion.

For a month, Theodosius balked, supported by his court lackeys. But the scruples of his conscience won him over. On Christman Eve 390, the most powerful emperor on earth abandoned his sumptuous vestments and dressed in the miserable garb of a public penitent, expressed his repentance in the city square in Milan, and then entered the Basilica of St. Tecla where St. Ambrose readmitted him to the Church of Christ.

Professor Plinio Corrêa de Oliveira comments on the scene:

> This attitude of the spiritual power toward the temporal power recalls a principle that is quite dear to us. When one of the great ones among men (whatever his nature or title, and however exalted or glorified he might be in civil society) places himself in a position of defiance to the glory of God, it is the Church's mission to humiliate him.
>
> When human powers lose the right path, it is the mission of the Church to confront them and set them aright. It is the mission of the Church to emphasize that all things human, however elevated they may be, are nothing before God. In the face of eternity, human grandeur is reduced to nothing. At the end of the day, the only thing that remains forever as a value above all else is the Church, Holy, Catholic, Apostolic and Roman, namely the Church of God. Bossuet affirmed this with magnificent words: "The mission of the Church is the containment of the powers on Earth."

It was December 390. Ten years earlier, on December 28, 380, Theodosius had promulgated in that same city of Thessalonica an edict that stated, "All of our people must be united in the faith transmitted to the Romans by the apostle Peter, that which the Pontiff Damasus and the Bishop Peter of Alexandria profess; all must recognize, that is, the Holy Trinity of the Father, the Son and the Holy Spirit."

The spiritual unity that Constantine would not have dared to impose, and which Julian the Apostate had believed he could establish with neo-paganism, was established by Theodosius by means of the principle that the empire was one and so must the faith be one — the orthodox Catholic Faith.

Thanks to Theodosius, Arianism was definitively eradicated. In Constantinople, where it was still powerful, its last advocates were forced to cede their positions to Catholics. The emperor himself performed the Rite of Enthronement in the Church of the Holy Apostles of the new Catholic bishop of the capital, Gregory Nazianzus.

In January 381, an imperial edict proclaimed as law the faith of Nicaea, affirming "the indivisibility of the divine substance of the Trinity" and confiscating Arian goods, giving them to the "Nicaeans." Finally, in the spring of the same year, the Council of Constantinople, after many discussions, put an end to all the dogmatic questions that had arisen after Nicaea due to the spread of error, and hurled anathemas against all heretics — "eunomians or anomeians, Arians or eudossians, Semi-Arians or pneumatomachians, Sabellians and Apollinarists" — formulating a doctrine that was expressed in the famous Nicene Creed, the Creed of our Mass.

### 3. PAGANISM AND CHRISTIANITY

The barbarians were an enemy external to the Roman Empire. But there was an even more insidious enemy within the empire: the rebirth of paganism. The paganism of the fourth century was not the ancient religion of the Romans but a new religious philosophy, characterized by profound relativism. This religious and cultural relativism constituted a serious threat not only to Christianity but also to the empire itself.

The term paganism comes from *pagus*, village. The *paganalia* were the festivals of the *pagi*, the rural districts of ancient Rome (*paganicae feriae*); a paganus was a peasant farmer, an inhabitant of the *pagus*. The etymology helps us comprehend how the Roman Empire cohabitated with two forms of paganism: on the one hand, the often superstitious beliefs of the people of the countryside, a popular paganism that often boiled down to centuries-old animistic beliefs and a form of nature worship; on the other hand, for the more cultivated souls, the paganism of the fourth century was a civil religion, without dogmas or morality, a *religiosity* more than a religion, having no sacred texts or articles of faith but only a series of ritual gestures. This was a political religion that distinguished between the public sphere, in which one had to profess the polytheistic cult of the Roman gods, and the private sphere, in which each person was free to believe in what he wanted. It was, in the end, the cult of the *dea Roma*.

In the ancient world, besides Roman paganism there was also Greek, Egyptian, Nordic, Celtic, and Slavic paganism. Common to these forms of religiosity was polytheism, the veneration of a multiplicity of divinities in a proper pantheon. *Pantheon* (from the Greek *pan*, or all, and *théos*, or gods) indicates not so much a building as the sum of all the divinities of a religion.

The clash in the fourth century between Christianity and paganism was the clash between pagan relativism and those, such as Christians, who believed in one absolute Truth: Jesus Christ, the only Way, Truth, and Life (John 14:6). A decisive phase in the clash between Christianity and paganism was the controversy over the Altar of Victory between St. Ambrose and Symmachus, the two greatest representatives of the two cultures in conflict.

Quintus Aurelius Symmachus (345–405) was prefect of Rome in 384 and consul in 391. Ambrose, the former imperial functionary, was bishop of Milan from 347 to 397. Peers, and both from senatorial families, the two shared the same cultural formation, as well as family and social ties, but one represented dying paganism and the other the new Christian faith that was conquering society.

In the Western Empire, pagan opposition had its fulcrum in the senatorial aristocracy which continued to profess enthusiastically the veneration of Roman antiquity as well as the divinities and mystery cults of the East. The center of pagan resistance was always the Senate.

At the entrance to the Senate hall (*Curia Julia*) stood the Altar of Victory, installed by Augustus on the day of his return from Egypt (August 28, 29 BC). It was the public symbol of paganism. As the senators entered, they made an act of worship, burning a grain of incense.

The Western emperor Gratian (375–383) had ordered the removal of this altar. The Senate protested and sent the pagan Symmachus to Milan in 382 to obtain the revocation of the order, but Gratian, warned by Pope Damasus (366–384) via St. Ambrose, did not receive Symmachus.

Gratian was assassinated in 383, and Symmachus renewed his attempt with Valentinian II (383–392), who had succeeded his brother. Symmachus was

received, and he championed the cause of pagan Rome, but the emperor, persuaded by St. Ambrose, denied permission to bring the altar back (384). On this
occasion, Symmachus, who had become prefect of Rome in the meantime, wrote
a famous report on the Altar of Victory, to which St. Ambrose responded with two
letters (17 and 18) addressed to the emperor, in which he cautioned him, on pain
of excommunication, not to reinstate the pagan cult and privileges.

The apology addressed by Symmachus to Valentinian II in the late summer
of 384 was centered on religious relativism. His motto was, "Everyone has his
own customs, his own religion" (*Relatio* III.8). The true God is one, despite the
diversity of religions, yet "we cannot attain to such a great mystery by just one
path" (*Relatio* III.10). Symmachus was a relativist, convinced of the oneness of
a god who manifests himself in the plurality of religions. The good pagan he was,
he believed only in *dea Roma*, on whose lips he placed the words "Princes and
fathers of the patria, respect the old age I have attained through these sacred
rites. Leave me my traditional ceremonies, of which I have nothing to remon-
strate. Let me live as I wish, for I am free." But Ambrose replied, putting words
into the mouth of *Roma* as well, "I shall not blush at my age to convert along
with the entire world. It is true, indeed, that it is never too late to learn. Let old
age blush which knows not how to correct its ways" (*Epistola* 18.7).

Ambrose then reproached Symmachus for his incoherence: "Only now do
you speak of justice, pretending the equal right to speak? Where were these
discourses when Christians were not even allowed to breathe?" He claimed,
against every type of relativism, the absolute truth of the Christian religion. The
only true God is that of Christians (*Ipse enim solus verus est deus*), and there is no
hope of agreement between the two religions.

The clash between paganism and Christianity moved from the cultural
level to the military level and had its decisive moment in the Battle of the Frigidus, won by Theodosius in 394 against the last desperate attempt of paganism
to impose itself on the empire. This battle, as observes the historian Marta
Sordi, was considered by both Christians and pagans to be a true war of
religion.

On May 15, 392, the emperor Valentinian II died, killed by his general Arbogast, a pagan of Frankish origins. Three months later, Arbogast had the
rhetorician Flavius Eugenius (392–394) elevated to the imperial throne in the
West. Eugenius was an apostate Christian, like Julian, and had the support of the
Roman Senate. While Theodosius prohibited pagan worship in all of its forms,

Flavius Eugenius had the Altar of Victory placed once more in the Senate hall, and brought back processions in honor of pagan divinities to the streets of Rome. Theodosius did not recognize the nomination of Flavius Eugenius, and so moved with his troops toward Italy to face the usurper.

St. Augustine recalls the statue of Jupiter that pagans had brought over the Alpine passes on that occasion, while standards with the image of Hercules were carried by the army (*De Civitate Dei* V.26). The decisive battle took place near the River Frigidus (today the Vippaco), a tributary of the Isonzo, near Aquileia, on September 5 and 6, 394. It was characterized by extraordinary natural events: in the first phase of the battle, a solar eclipse gave the victory to Arbogast and Eugenius. In the second phase, at sunrise of the following day, after having prayed the entire night, and with the help of a strong wind that proved troublesome for the army of Arbogast, Theodosius routed his enemies.

Theodosius was only fifty years old, but after this victory over the usurpers in the autumn of 394, his health, which had never been strong, now deteriorated rapidly. He made arrangements for his succession: his firstborn son, Arcadius, would govern the East, while his second son, Honorius, the West. According to Theodosius's intentions, the empire would remain united, with two separate capitals, Constantinople and Milan. In reality, from the year 395, the two parts of the empire, East and West, were never again united.

Before dying, Theodosius received St. Ambrose in a lengthy colloquy and entrusted to him his two sons, so that he might be their counselor and keep watch over the empire. Theodosius died in Milan on January 17, 395, piously whispering the first word of the psalm for the dead: *Dilexi.*

As a testament, Theodosius left his two sons, the eighteen-year-old Arcadius (395–408) and the eleven-year-old Honorius (395–423), the exhortation to share all his devotion for the Church and his zeal for the Christian religion. "This religion and no other" were the words that Ambrose spoke to Theodosius: "Maintain peace and quiet in the state, banish war, give strength to the republic to subdue its enemies."

Several months later, as the empire was faltering and the barbarians were preparing their terrible invasion, gripped by sinister fears and with a heart full of sadness, St. Ambrose descended into the tomb on April 4, 397, on the vigil of the Day of Resurrection.

## 4. ST. AUGUSTINE

St. Ambrose was one of the first and greatest of the Fathers and Doctors of the Church. After his death, as darkness began to fall over the Roman Empire and the dawn of a new world awakened, two other great Fathers and Doctors kept watch over the Church: Augustine and Jerome.

Augustine was born on November 13, 354, in Thagaste (today, Souk-Ahras in Algeria), a large town in Numidia. Although born in Africa and probably of African ancestry, he was Roman in culture and language. His father was Patrick, and his mother, Monica, is also venerated as a saint by the Catholic Church.

A fervent Christian, Monica did what she could to cultivate religious senti-ment in her son, but as was the common practice (already being contested) in the fourth century, she did not have him baptized, in order to grant him the full benefit of a general purification at an older age. Augustine affiliated himself with the Manichean sect for nine years as a simple "auditor." In the meantime, he had become a professor in his native land and had begun to live with an unnamed woman to whom he often alludes in his *Confessions*. For a time, he was seduced by astrology but soon became disillusioned.

Toward the autumn of 383, when he was twenty-nine years old, he left for Rome. With the help of the pagan Symmachus, he obtained a teaching chair in Milan, and there came upon the books of the Neoplatonists, probably those of Plotinus and Porphyry. His mother followed him to Milan and became a disciple of St. Ambrose, weeping and praying for her son's conversion. When she asked St. Ambrose if her son would ever convert, the bishop responded with the famous words, "Woman, the son of so many tears shall never perish." He meant that she would see the rebirth of Augustine thanks to her intense and profound suffering.

One can imagine her joy when Augustine received baptism on April 24, 387, at the hands of St. Ambrose. Augustine and his mother then prepared to return to Africa. Before departing, they stopped in a lodge in Ostia, a port city of Rome. Standing at a window looking out over the sea, they began to converse about matters of God, a conversation that Augustine recalls with deep feeling in his *Confessions*.

Monica died in Ostia, and a few months later, Augustine returned from there to Carthage, retracing the route he had traveled as a young man with a heart overflowing with passions and uncertainties.

His elevation to the priesthood in 391 occurred in a most unforeseen man-ner. When the old bishop of Hippo, Valerio, expressed his desire to be assisted in his public speaking by a coadjutor priest, the people acclaimed Augustine. Then, in 395, Valerio conferred episcopal ordination on him, and shortly thereafter Augustine succeeded him as bishop of Hippo. He remained in this office until his death on August 28, 430, the third month of the siege of the city by Genseric, king of the Vandals.

After being nominated bishop of Hippo, Augustine wrote his masterpiece, the *City of God*. The theme of this extraordinary work is the perpetual and irreconcilable struggle carried out in history between two loves that originate two cities: "The love of self, taken to the point of despising God, which generated the earthly city; and the love of God, taken to the point of despising self, which generated the celestial city" (*De Civitate Dei* XIV.28).

The "City of God" he identifies with the Church — triumphant, pure, and militant — which unites the "sons of light," those faithful to God in Heaven and on earth. The Church Militant lives *in* the world but is not *of* the world. It is without sin, but not without sinners.

The "earthly city" he identifies with the *civitas diaboli*, the city of evil, understood above all as an infernal society of the damned, an earthly society that unites the "sons of darkness" as the adversaries of God. It lives in the world but is not identical to the human society living in history.

In the midst of these two cities, the celestial and the infernal, is the city of men, humanity living on earth, pilgrims in space and time, living out a period of trial. It is the object of contention between the other two enemy cities and constitutes the battleground between them. During its earthly existence, humanity is subject to the influence at times of the celestial city and at times of the infernal city. The destiny of the city of men is to be inclined toward either the celestial city or the infernal city, to be governed by one or the other. *Tertium non datur*: it is not possible for them to remain indifferent or neutral. "If society is not consecrated to God, it will be invaded by demons," says St. Augustine. The mission of the human city is precisely that of imitating the divine city and fighting the diabolical city.

There is a beautiful point to consider when meditating on St. Augustine. Plinio de Oliveira observed that Augustine wrote his great books as the Roman Empire in the West was falling, when everything led one to believe that the Catholic religion would probably be swept away during the Barbarian Invasions. In reality, Hippo and Carthage were so devastated that almost nothing remained standing in them, and the Catholic religion never again reestablished itself in these regions with its previous splendor. Yet while the future was uncertain, St. Augustine continued to write his books with great serenity. He died as the Vandals were entering his city.

The sack of Rome by Alaric in 410 was one of the most dramatic events of antiquity. Yet in the face of the devastation of what for them was the *dea Roma*, the great pagan rhetoricians, the disciples of Symmachus and Macrobius, were silent. It was St. Augustine who raised his voice before this terrible spectacle. *De Civitate Dei*, written by St. Augustine between 413 and 426, represents the model for the Christian conception of history.

The world as the saint had conceived it fell; the Middle Ages had arrived. It was the works of St. Augustine that inspired the medieval understanding of the state, the empire, and Christianity. Charlemagne (742–814) would listen to the *City of God* being read aloud while he ate lunch, and the empire he founded took inspiration from the ideas of St. Augustine.

## 5. St. Jerome

St. Jerome (347–420) is listed, together with St. Ambrose, St. Augustine, and St. Gregory, as one of the four great Doctors of the Western Church. Born in Zrenj, Dalmatia, in 347, he studied in Rome where he received baptism. He then traveled to the East, sojourning especially in Antioch. Returning to Rome in 382, he became secretary to Pope Damasus I and led various Roman nobles in the ascetic ideal, among whom were the matrons Marcella and Paola. He retired to the East, and in Bethlehem he undertook what would become his life's work, the translation of the Bible into Latin from Hebrew and Greek. His edition, the *Vulgate*, is still today the official biblical text of the Church.

St. Jerome gave witness in his letters to the terrible events at the start of the fifth century. It all began, one might say, on a winter's night in 406. On December 31 of that year, the thinly stationed Roman garrisons along the Rhine, near Mainz, sighted a shimmering mass of barbarians whom they had lost track of on the other side of the river. The Rhine was a thick sheet of ice that allowed the barbarians to cross over, invading the confines of the empire. The few who tried to resist them were massacred. These were Vandals, Alani, Suebi, entire tribes with women and children, wagons, cattle, and flocks that overwhelmed every resistance and spread throughout Gaul. Nothing could stop them. No city was spared, beginning with Trier, the ancient capital of the Western Empire. This was the beginning of the catastrophe. The two most fearsome barbarian populations were the Vandals and the Goths, the latter divided into two groups, the Ostrogoths and the Visigoths. Other peoples, including the terrible Huns, pushed at their heels.

A letter written by St. Jerome in Bethlehem in 409 offers us a stunning picture of the situation in which the empire found itself:

> If, up to now, some of us, though rare, are still in our own houses, it is not by our own merit, but we owe it to the mercy of God. Innumerable and ferocious populations have occupied the whole of Gaul. All lands between the Alps and the Pyrenees, between the Ocean and the Rhine, the Quads, the Vandals, the Sarmatians, the Alani, the Gepids, the Heruli, the Saxons, the Burgundians, the Alemanni, and o wretched state! The Pannonians, our enemies, have sacked everything. "Assur, indeed, has come with them." Mainz, that once illustrious city, was taken and razed to the ground. Thousands and thousands of people were butchered in its church. The overpowering cities of Rheims, Amiens, Arras, "the Morini, men of the farthest border" (Virgil, *Aeneid* VIII.l.727), Tournai, the Nemesi, Strasbourg, have all seen their inhabitants deported to Germany. The provinces of Aquitaine, Novempopulania, Lyon, and Narbonne have been completely razed to the ground, except for a few cities, which, nonetheless, due to the wars have been reduced to hunger and desertion. I cannot think about Toulouse without shedding tears. If it has not yet been demolished, it is the merit of its holy bishop Exuperius. Spain as well is about to receive the finishing blow; they live in constant terror thanks to the memory of the invasion of the Cimbri, and all the suffering others have endured once for all, they suffer continually due to the anticipated fear they hear about. I shall keep silent about all the rest so as not to give the impression that I despair of God's mercy. For some time now, the regions including those between Pontus Euxinus and the Julian Alps, which once belonged to us, are no longer ours; and since violating the borders of the Danube, they have been fighting across the territory of the Roman Empire for over thirty years. Through the shedding of our tears, we have lost them all growing old. (*Letters* 123.15–16)

The worst was yet to come. St. Jerome and his disciples were in Bethlehem when, in August 410, an immense army of Visigoths, Huns, Alani, and Scythians, led by Alaric, arrived at the gates of Rome without having encountered resistance. Alaric decided to assail Rome from the northeast side of the walls, so he placed his headquarters on the hill above the Salaria Bridge over the Aniene, today's Monte Antenne. "From the Temple of Jupiter Capitoline," writes Blessed Federico Ozanam:

One could see the smoke of the enemy encampment. In that predica-
ment, the Senate met and deliberated; as its first action, it had Serena,
the widow of Stilicone, nephew of Theodosius, put to death. The gods
demanded a victim, for it was said that the sacrilegious Christian had
entered the Temple of Cybele and removed the collar of the idol. Serena
was strangled following the ancient practice known as *more maiorum*.
But that last human sacrifice failed to save the nation.

On August 24, 410, the Salaria Gate was opened from within. The barbarian
wave invaded Rome, and the most celebrated city in the world was mercilessly
exposed to the fury of the barbarians who lit their fires on the slopes of the Capitoline Hill. Alaric ordered his men to respect the basilicas of the apostles but gave
license to sack the rest. Theft, arson, massacres all desolated the city that had
never, in eight hundred years, been invaded by an enemy.

News of the sack of Rome produced a sense of amazement and profound
consternation throughout the world. The sovereign city, the eternal city, had
been exposed to the outrage, mockery, and violence of the barbarians whom
Rome had crushed a thousand times.

St. Jerome's outbursts of grief are moving, as the successive and evermore
disheartening news of the fall of the eternal city reached him. "I was about to
translate Ezechiel when the news reached me in Palestine of the capture of
Rome by Alaric and of the barbarian devastation of the West. I was stunned and
could do nothing but weep." He exclaimed, "The most resplendent light has
been put out. The head of the world has been truncated, and in the ruin of one
city an entire empire has perished." He continued, "The city that had subjugated
all peoples has been conquered; the treasures of all the earth which it had gathered and accumulated is now spoil, reduced to a handful of ruins."

And still, as Rome's star was extinguishing, a new light was being lit: this
was Christian Rome, the Rome of the Apostles Peter and Paul, the Rome that,
unlike the pagan Rome, was to endure for millennia.

The light of this Rome that knows no twilight continues to illuminate the
world even when, as happens today, it seems immersed in darkness. The modern world has followed the self-destructive path of the Roman Empire; the
Church of Rome is destined to be established on the ruins of the modern world,
as happened already after the fifth century.

CHAPTER V

# Why the Roman Empire Fell

## 1. THE TWILIGHT OF THE ROMAN EMPIRE

The comparison made by Pope Benedict XVI between the crisis of our day and that which witnessed the twilight of the Roman Empire constitutes a point of meditation that deserves to be developed.[26]

The word "twilight" indicates a historical period, or a chronological itinerary, that represents the closing of an age. We know that the official date of the fall of the Roman Empire in the West is AD 476. In that year, the barbarian Odoacer, after having killed his rival Oreste, deposed the last emperor, the young Romulus Augustulus, and sent to Byzantium the imperial standards, satisfying himself with the title of king. The emperor in the East claimed from that moment the inheritance of Rome, at least until the year 800, when Charlemagne was crowned emperor and the ancient Roman Empire was reborn in the West as the Holy Roman Empire.

But the institutional crisis of the Roman Empire, which precipitated in 476 with the disappearance of the visible empire in the West, dates to at least a century earlier. We have already recalled the date of 378, when the legions of Rome were defeated by the Visigoths on the plains of Adrianople, and Valens II, the emperor in the East, fell on the battlefield. This was for Rome's army the worst

---

[26] Radio Maria, conversation on January 19, 2011.

defeat after the Battle of Canne. This event, the Battle of Adrianople in 378, marked the first great military victory for the barbarians over Rome, and opened the path to the great invasions that characterized the fifth century, the century of the definitive twilight of the Roman Empire in the West.

The external cause of this twilight and then collapse of the Roman Empire was the Barbarian Invasions. But the true, more profound causes of the decadence and end of Rome's empire are internal, and of a cultural and moral character. While the barbarian populations encroached on the borders of an immense empire that stretched from the Atlantic Ocean to the North Sea, down to North Africa, and all the way to the Caspian Sea and the frontiers of the Persians and Arabs, Roman society was immersed, thanks to paganism, in intellectual relativism and practical hedonism. For this reason, Benedict XVI affirmed in relation to the Roman Empire that the "degeneration of the load-bearing system of law and fundamental moral attitudes that gave them their strength, caused the rupture of the levees that, up to that time, had protected the peaceful coexistence among men. A world was waning." It was moral corruption that opened wide the doors to the Vandals, who in 406 had crossed the frozen Rhine, pouring into Gaul, and to the Visigoths who invaded the city of Rome in 410.

To understand the significance of those days, we must turn to the authors who lived in them, such as Orosius, Augustine, Jerome, and Salviano. St. Jerome, for example, wrote a famous letter from the solitude of Bethlehem, to where he had retreated, referring to what had been reported to him from Rome in the days following the arrival of Alaric's Visigoths:

> Terrible news is arriving from the West that Rome is besieged, that the safety of its citizens is being bought with the weight of gold, but after these extortions they continue the siege. They tell of those who have already had their goods taken and now wish to take their lives. My voice goes weak, tears inhibit me from dictating. The city that conquered the entire world has been conquered; no, it falls prey to hunger before being assailed by arms, such that they struggle to find someone to take prisoner. The desperate longing leads them to throwing themselves upon heinous food; the hungry tear each other to pieces, even a mother will not spare her child at the breast and devours the life she has just brought into the world.

These are dreadful scenes that show us the scope of the tragedy. When the refugees from Rome began to reach the East, they described the appalling scenes of the sack of the city. Jerome groaned with pain and wrote:

> Who would have believed that Rome, built on the victories it had achieved all over the world, would one day collapse? Or that all the coasts in the East, and in Egypt and Africa, would be populated with slaves from a city that once dominated the world? Or that the Holy City of Bethlehem would receive people, both men and women, who had earlier been nobles loaded with riches and gold, and now reduced to begging? ... The most resplendent lamp has been blown out. The head of the Roman Empire has been truncated, and in the ruins of one city the empire has expired.

These words give pause for reflection on how precarious and ephemeral every power, every wealth, every human honor is. It was meditating on the sack of Rome that inspired St. Augustine to compose his famous *City of God*, a classic of the Christian philosophy of history, which posits a struggle between two loves: the love of self to the point of hatred and indifference toward God, and the love of God to the point of hatred and indifference toward oneself. This vision of history has lost none of its validity in our times.

The Roman Empire collapsed because in it the moral and divine law had been transgressed. This is what history attests to, and what, throughout history, comes down to us as a warning. Today as well, foreigners are invading the West. For now, it is a peaceful, silent migration that could, however, transform into a bloody invasion. The barbarians were strangers to Roman civilization, but they assimilated to its culture and traditions. The new barbarians proclaim that they have no intention of integrating into our civilization, of which they adopt only the elements of decadence, refusing its culture and traditions.

Today, as always, the heart of man (and, as a consequence, the life of society) oscillates between two opposing enticements: the love for God, expressed in a respect for the order that He wished to give to the universe, to the point of renouncing our every instinct and desire to disrespect this order; or the love of self, giving free reign to our passions and our will to power, to the point of transgressing the law of God in our lives and in society at large. This is the dramatic possibility that history always places before us, and that not only the individual but also civilizations are called to choose between.

In the darkness of the fifth century, only the light of the saints shone bril-
liantly. They were the ones who comprehended what was happening and who
instilled supernatural trust when all seemed lost. "Christ is speaking to you:
Listen!" exclaimed Augustine. "He says, 'Why are you afraid? Did I not foretell
all that would happen? I foretold this so that your hope would turn, once the
verdict had been given, toward the true good, instead of darkening itself with the
world.'" All that happens in history, as in the life of each one of us, has a meaning
and a significance, known only to God.

Another prophetic voice, the priest Salviano of Marseille, wrote, "You la-
ment that God would allow all to fall into ruin? But no, God governs the world!
It is not true that he fails to care for the earth: it is the object of all his attention!"
If so many disasters occur, the cause must be found in us. "It is our sins which
give strength to the barbarians," exclaimed St. Jerome. "It is our vices which have
enfeebled the armies!"

The saints illuminated the darkest hours of history without seeing the consequences of their faith in the following centuries.

Twenty years after the sack of Rome by Alaric's Visigoths, the Vandals of
Genseric passed from Gaul into Spain, crossed the Strait of Gibraltar, and spread
throughout African lands, occupying the entire territory from Morocco to
Carthage.

The horrors committed by the Vandals in Africa were narrated by St. Augustine: children torn in half, virgins' breasts branded with incandescent irons,
the nobility impaled.

In the year 430, in the city of Hippo under siege by the Vandals, the bishop
who had guided the faithful of that city saw his end approaching, and with it,
that of all Christian Africa. Yet in the face of complete collapse, Augustine galvanized Christian souls, inspiring the defiant with a supernatural trust that
stretched far beyond the earthly destiny of those regions. His voice rose over the
centuries and repeated the divine words, "Heaven and earth shall pass away, but
the word of God shall not pass away" (Matt. 24:35). It was only when his voice
fell silent that the Vandals burst into the city.

In those same years, St. Nicasius was murdered in the Cathedral of Rheims;
St. Exuperius, bishop of Toulouse, resisted the Vandals until his deportation; St.
Lupo defended Troyes, his episcopal see; St. Eucherius of Lyon defended the
rights of the Church against the Burgundians; St. Anianus, bishop of Orléans, organized the defense of his city against the Huns and encouraged the population to

resist, allowing the Roman legion of Ezio time to reach Attila and defeat him; St. Paolinus became bishop of Nola right when Alaric was at the city gates, and offered himself as a slave to the invaders to free the only son of a widow; Quodvultdeus, St. Augustine's former deacon and later bishop of Carthage, organized the resistance against the occupying Vandals, only to be chased from his see by Genseric and put on a boat with neither sails nor oars, which miraculously went aground in Naples, where he died a confessor of the faith; St. Maximus, the first bishop of Turin, and St. Peter Chrysologus, bishop of Ravenna, were hammers to heretics and indefatigable defenders of threatened civilization.

Still today, we can find in Christian virtues the strength to fight the physical evil that threatens from outside and the moral evil that strikes us from within.

It is significant today that the accusations against our political class regarding the atmosphere of decline and moral decadence that typifies it are leveled precisely by those who have made moral relativism their program.

In Italy and throughout Europe, there exists a moral question, but the only ones entitled to intervene regarding this question are those who claim to hold perennial and nonnegotiable moral values. How can one who negates these values in principle reprimand those who transgress them? These are the contradictions of the present age, but contradiction is the notable characteristic of relativism.

## 2. A WORLD OF GRAY HAIR

From the fourth to the fifth century, barbarians invaded the territories of the empire, conquering them and devastating their cities. Arriving from the north and from the east, they reached its furthest extremes — the Atlantic and the Mediterranean — sacking Rome, *Caput Mundi*, the sacred and inviolate city that had laid down the law for the entire civilized world.

The enemy that Rome had to confront, and that would ultimately overwhelm it, was an external one; the deeper cause of the collapse, however, was not external in character, but internal. Neither was it political or militaristic in character, but rather of a cultural and moral nature. The Roman Empire collapsed because its foundation had been devoured and its strength was no more than an appearance. We shall try to develop this point to better comprehend the crisis we too are now facing.

The twilight of the Roman Empire, considered in the light of external causes — namely the Barbarian Invasion — is situated between two dates: 378, when the barbarians crushed the Roman legions at Adrianople, and 476, the official disappearance of the empire in the West. The cultural and moral crisis, however, dates not to the fourth or the fifth centuries but much earlier, and is attributable to the attitude of incomprehension and rejection that the Roman Empire held toward Christianity.

In the centuries following the birth of Christ, the Roman Empire professed an ecumenical religiosity that fused Greco-Roman polytheism with a syncretism of Eastern origin. The Pantheon was the cultic center of this religiosity par excellence, where all the forms of paganism, old and new, were gathered, with the one exception of Christianity.

In the empire, one professed a civil religion without dogmas and without a moral code, to which the state imposed a purely exterior adherence. Christians, who practiced a religion that was primarily interior, belonging to the heart and to the conscience but subjected to objective truth, refused formal adherence expressed by activities like the burning of incense in homage to idols.

The testimony of Christians was considered a dangerous form of intransigence and fanaticism by the authorities, although they professed the syncretistic equality of all religions. The verdict that condemned Christians took aim not at specific charges but at the *nomen ipsum*, the mere proclamation of Christianity.

The persecutions reached their height with Emperor Diocletian, who reigned until 305. It was one of the darkest moments in the history of the Church. Yet just a few years later, Constantine granted Christians full liberty, and they could finally profess their faith publicly and infuse their spirit into the laws promulgated in those years. It was the great Constantinian Shift, which celebrated its seventeen hundredth anniversary in 2012–2013. The rise of Christianity, from Constantine to Theodosius, was irresistible. But paganism did not surrender, and in the fourth century it unleashed a mortal battle against the Christian name.

The brief reign of the emperor Julian the Apostate from 361 to 363 involved the most acute expression of pagan hatred toward Christians, who were banned from holding magistrate and teaching positions, and were prohibited from receiving honors or high positions. After the death of Julian, the center of anti-Christian sentiment was the Roman Senate, the same Senate that had proclaimed in 37, just a few years after the death of Jesus Christ, its veto of Christianity.

The paganism of the second half of the fourth century was no longer a religion, but a relativistic philosophy that placed all religious worship on the same level, as opposed to Christianity, which affirmed the oneness of Christ as the only Way, Truth, and Life. The antipagan policies of Emperor Theodosius at the end of the fourth century did not eradicate this relativistic mentality, which hid behind the Roman Pantheon, opposing Christianity.

Paganism represented for Christians of the fourth century a worse enemy than the barbarians, because it was an internal enemy that impeded the Roman Empire from embracing Christianity completely. The gospel was not able to stop the moral disintegration, from the upper classes, who lived in luxury and idleness, to the commoners, inebriated with the bloody games of the circus. Divorce, prostitution (both male and female), homosexuality, and decreasing birth rates were widespread problems. The society of this period was decadent and corrupt — as St. Eucherius, the bishop of Lyon, defined it, "a world of gray hair."

## 3. SALVIAN OF MARSEILLE

We recalled St. Augustine's meditation on the fall of Rome, which the bishop of Hippo began composing in 410 following the sack of the Visigoths and finished right as the Vandals, having crossed Gibraltar, were quickly conquering Roman North Africa. Less well known, though equally evocative and profound, are the meditations of another Christian author of the fifth century: Salvian of Marseille and his *De Gubernatione Dei* (The governance of God). I have already had occasion to recall this passage, but it never loses its pertinence to our present times.

After having recalled how the members of the Senate in Trier, Germany, at the moment when the barbarians had penetrated the city walls, were intent on feasting and could not decide whether to interrupt the party, Salvian writes:

> While the arms of the barbarians were rattling around the walls of Cirta and Carthage, the people of Carthage were having a great time in the circuses and frolicking in the theaters! Outside the walls they were cutting people's throats, while within the people were fornicating. Outside, part of the population had become prisoners of their enemies, while on the other side, they were prisoners to their vices. It is difficult to say who had the worst of it: the former suffered a merely exterior, bodily captivity; the latter were slaves interiorly. Between these two mortal calamities, I think the lighter, for a Christian, was to suffer the enslavement of the body, rather than that of the soul; and the confirmation comes from what our Savior affirms in the Gospel: the death of the soul is much graver than that of the body.... Both outside and inside the walls, one heard the din of battle and

amusement; the shouts of those who were dying were confused with
the bedlam of those given over to their orgies, and one could hardly
distinguish the cries of the people who were dying in battle from the
uproar produced by the people in the circus. In the face of facts such
as these, what else could a rabble such as this do but demand their
own ruin while God did not yet wish to send them to damnation?

Carthage, the capital of Roman Africa, contended with Alexandria and Antioch
for primacy in dissoluteness, and enjoyed the reputation of being a "paradise"
for homosexuals. Salvian interprets the invasion of the barbarians as a chastisement for this moral transgression:

> "Could there have been, I ask you, a more unnatural vice than what I am
> saying, there in Carthage? ... In Carthage, that vice was no small thing
> but a plague, although the transvestites, in effect, were not so many. It
> happened that the effeminacy of some few would infect the majority.
> We know that for as few as assume shameful attitudes, there are many
> who are infected by the obscenities of that minority. Just one prostitute,
> for example, leads many men to fornicate; and the same happens with
> the abominable presence of a few homosexuals — they infect quite a
> few people. And I cannot say who is guiltier before God, since both the
> homosexuals and their victims are condemned, according to Sacred
> Scripture, to the same punishment: Effeminate men and homosexuals
> will not inherit the Kingdom of God.
>
> Now, what arouses more pain and consternation is that a crime such
> as that was seen abroad as belonging to the entire Roman population,
> and that the prestige of the name of Rome had been reduced to ashes
> thanks to a dishonorable stain of such monstrosity against nature.
> And this is the reason: When men dressed like women, and in their
> walk would swing their hips more than a woman does; when they
> would hang on their bodies certain pendants portraying heinous ob-
> scenities and cover their heads with feminine veils and hairpins; when
> all of this happened in a Roman city, the biggest and most famous of
> that province, was it not a disgrace for the entire Roman Empire? The
> fact that, in the very bosom of the state, one would permit such a de-
> testable scandal? In reality, an authority great and powerful enough to
> be able to prevent a great crime, insofar as it is not aware of it and al-
> lows it to be perpetrated, is behaving the same as if it had approved of
> its being committed. I renew my question, moved by pain, to those
> who are offended by me: Among which of the barbarian populations

have these events ever happened? Where have these actions ever been
allowed to be performed in the light of day?

Salvian wanted to demonstrate that the judgment of God is not only exercised
at the end of the world, but in every historical moment, and the barbarians who
invaded the West were an instrument of the judgment of God. Providence, which
draws good out of evil, makes use of such events to purify a corrupt and decadent
society, as Roman society was. Salvian's words deserve to be meditated upon. We
live in a period today in which the worst vices are fostered by mass media and
even inscribed in our laws as human rights. God is not disinterested in historical
vicissitudes, however. He draws good from every evil, but every evil must be
punished in time or in eternity, just as every good action will have its just reward
in time or in eternity.

## 4. St. Leo the Great

Pagan hedonism was one of the main causes of the collapse of the Roman
Empire, but it was not the worst enemy Christianity had to confront. The
barbarians were an enemy external to the empire; pagan hedonism was an
enemy within the empire, though external to Christianity. But there was an
even more insidious enemy within Christianity itself, and this was an enemy
worse even than the barbarians and paganism: the spirit of division and rebellion, of schisms and heresies, that came to compromise the unity of
Christendom.

The year 313 was the year of the Edict of Milan, by which Constantine
conceded full religious freedom to Christians. The Church exulted. A few years
later, in 325, the same Constantine summoned the first ecumenical council of
the Church in Nicaea, during which the Athanasian Creed was proclaimed
against the Arians. But Arianism had penetrated among the bishops, and only
ten years after Nicaea, two synods, at Caesarea and Tyre, condemned Athanasius for his fanaticism in ecclesiastical matters. Athanasius was deposed from his
episcopal see and sent into exile. From that point, one might say that his life
summarized the fate of the Catholic Faith. He was sent into exile five times, and
five times he returned to reaffirm the truth of the Faith.

It came to the point where a pope, Liberius, broke communion with Athanasius in 357, declaring him to be separated from the Roman Church. The
Councils of Rimini and Seleucia in 359 proposed an ambivalent *via media*

between the Arians and St. Athanasius. St. Jerome commented on this impasse, coining the expression "The world groaned and realized to its amazement that it had become Arian."

The mid-fourth century was one of the most confused periods in history. According to Blessed John Henry Cardinal Newman, the dogma of the divinity of Jesus Christ was preserved largely due to the people who remained faithful to their baptism, rather than the efforts of the *ecclesia docens*.

When Arianism had finally been weakened, there arose at the end of the fourth century new devastating heresies, such as the Donatist heresy and Pelagianism. Catholics were once more divided, and St. Augustine became, at the beginning of the fifth century, what Athanasius had been in the previous century: a champion of orthodox faith.

Christians, unable to form a cohesive society, were reduced to the condition of Babel and fell prey to the two great threats abroad: paganism within the empire and barbarians outside it. This situation of general confusion and disorientation constituted a profound cause of the twilight of the Roman Empire, a spiritual and moral twilight that also entailed political, economic, and social decline.

It was not difficult for the barbarians to prevail, and the fifth century was one of the darkest hours in the history of the West. Yet in this darkness, a star shone: while the Roman Empire was demolishing itself, a new empire, not political but spiritual, was being born in Rome — one that embraced the souls of the entire world, that challenged the ages, and that is still standing today, even in the hour of this new twilight, as new barbarians push against its doors and new pagans persecute the Christians within.

Dom Guéranger wrote:

> The empire fell bit by bit under the blows of the barbarians, but before inflicting humiliation and punishment upon them — the consequence of their crimes — Divine Justice would wait for Christianity, victorious under persecutions, to extend its branches high enough and far enough to quell the tempests of this new deluge; it was to cultivate again, and with complete success, the renewed earth and invigorated waters, purified and no longer devastated.

After the twilight of the Roman Empire, night fell on the West, but in the darkness a light shone announcing a new day of history. The authors of the fifth century discerned this light in the papacy, the first great European institution to rise from the ruins of Rome. Prosper of Aquitaine, a disciple of St. Augustine and author of a work titled *The Vocation of the Nations*, saw in Pope Leo I, the man who succeeded in saving Rome from the invasion of Attila, the catalyst of this rebirth. In August 452, a Roman delegation guided by Pope Leo confronted Attila, the chief of the Huns, along the River Mincio in northern Italy. We do not know what Leo said to him, but Attila, the Scourge of God, turned around and abandoned Italy, and so St. Leo the Great saved Rome, triumphantly proving wrong his pagan detractors who had attributed the loss of the empire to Christians.

In the fifth century, no individual had greater awareness of the twilight of the Roman Empire than Leo, but he also recognized the rise of a new Rome whose empire would be much more extensive and glorious than the ancient one. Christian Rome, founded by the Apostles Peter and Paul, had by then taken the place of the ancient pagan Rome founded by Romulus and Remus. No other empire was to attain the splendor of the Roman Empire. It seemed created to last millennia, and yet it too was subjected to the laws of time and history. Today, only ruins remain of pagan Rome. It is the law of everything that is human and earthly: the great successes and worldly triumphs are followed with ever greater rapidity by decadence, disintegration, and death. Pius XII reminds us of this in his discourse of January 30, 1944, in which he stated, "When, on the other hand, we find ourselves before the witness of our Christian past, however ancient it might be, we always feel something of the immortal: the faith they proclaimed lives on, multiplied indefinitely in those who profess it; the Church lives on, to which they belong, always the same throughout history."

St. Leo the Great (440–461) was the greatest architect of the romanization of Christianity, which took place in the fifth century, as the Roman Empire in the West was collapsing. "God made sure that the peoples would be gathered in one empire, of which Rome is the head, so that from it the light of the Truth, revealed for the salvation of all the nations, might more effectively be spread throughout all its members."

Leo was the great protagonist of his century, which saw the definitive fall of the Roman Empire in the West. No one had such full awareness of the inexorable decline of Rome as he did, but also of the rise of a new Rome, whose empire would be much more extensive and glorious than the ancient one.

CHAPTER VI

# The Conversion of the European Nations

## 1. THE CONVERSION OF CLOVIS

In the darkest periods of history, when all seems lost and nothing seems humanly possible, Divine Grace can produce miraculous and unexpected rebirth in order to bring about change.[27] It can happen today, as it happened in the fifth century after Christ, one of the darkest periods in the history of the Church. The Roman Empire was collapsing, but from its disintegration the Christian civilization of the Middle Ages was born. This new chapter of the history of Christianity and of European civilization was opened by the conversion of King Clovis and of his people, the Franks.

The country of the Franks was a primitive region covered in forests that extended into the heart of Europe along both banks of the Rhine. The Franks were a proud and courageous people of Germanic origin, like the Sicambrians, another barbarian tribe that was often confused with them. When the Franks crossed the Rhine at the beginning of the fourth century and settled in Roman Gaul, this nation had already encountered the gospel due to the work of ardent apostles like St. Irenaeus in Lyon, St. Diogenes and St. Germain in Paris, St. Saturninus in Toulouse, St. Martial in Limoges, St. Benigno in Dijon, and St. Nicasius in Rheims. In the first three centuries, the blood of martyrs had flowed

---

[27] Radio Maria, conversation on January 18, 2012.

in Gaul, as in all the other lands subjected to the empire. But with Constantine, Christianity emerged from the catacombs. Then, in the fifth century, Christian Gaul was conquered by the pagan Franks.

Born around 466, Clovis was a warrior of Germanic origins who came to power in 482 as king of the tribe of the Salian Franks. At this time, Roman Gaul was disintegrating into various kingdoms: to the southwest was the kingdom of the Visigoths, whose capital was Toulouse, and which extended south of the Loire down through Spain; between Lyon and Geneva was the kingdom of the Burgundians, divided again among three royal brothers; to the northeast, the kingdom of the Franks, now under King Clovis.

A distant similarity linked the Franks to the Kingdom of Christ. The birth of the Divine Redeemer had been preceded by extraordinary events: as a star was guiding the Wisemen from the East toward Bethlehem, the emperor Augustus, though unaware of the significance of his gesture, had ordered the closure of the temple of Janus as a sign of having attained peace in the world under his reign. To carry this out, however, it was necessary to cripple the tribes of the Sicambrians and the Franks, who had for years held the Roman legion in check in the German forests. When this finally occurred, and news of their submission arrived on Christmas Eve, it could officially be declared that peace reigned throughout the world. The Prince of Peace announced by the Prophets, the Savior, was born in Bethlehem in a temporarily pacified world; as Abbot Lemann tells us, the Franks and the Sicambrians were, so to speak, the messengers of the peace attained on earth in the days of Augustus.

Four centuries were to pass, however, before Divine Grace would touch the Frankish peoples. The instrument of grace was a young Burgund princess living near Lyon in Gaul, Clothilde. Burgundy was divided at the time into two kingdoms held by two brothers, Gundobad and Godegisel. Another brother, Chilperic, had died, or perhaps was murdered. His widow and two daughters, one of whom was Clothilde, were Catholics, although in Burgundy most of the population, as well as the two kings, were of the Arian faith. The Burgundians had become Christian, but then, around 440, they had converted to Arianism under the violent pressure of the Visigoths.

Clothilde, daughter of King Childeric, was born around 475, just a year before the Roman Empire in the West was to disappear (476). She was not yet twenty years old when an unexpected messenger came to her in the palace of her uncle, King Gundobad.

King Clovis had in fact called his most faithful servant, Aurelian, and had entrusted him a ring of betrothal to deliver to Clothilde with the request to marry him. The messenger dressed as a mendicant and, arriving in Lyon, sought to encounter Clothilde as she exited the church, where the young princess, as an angel of charity, showered alms every day on the poor of the city. When Clothilde appeared, Aurelian approached her and begged her to hear the important communication he had for her. He admitted to having been sent by the king of the Franks who wanted to marry her, and he gave her the ring.

Clothilde was disturbed, just as the Virgin Mary had been at the Annunciation, and answered with a murmur, "How can this be? It is not lawful for a Christian to marry a pagan prince." Aurelian assured her of Clovis's favorable disposition toward the Church and of his choice to marry a Catholic woman for his queen. Clothilde then responded, "If by means of this union I can bring your master to recognize the true God, then I accept." The young princess made the sign of the cross, accepted the ring of Clovis, and gave hers in exchange, telling the messenger, "Return immediately to your master and tell him to ask King Gundobad for my hand without delay, because any delay might be dangerous."

Clovis's ambassadors reached Gundobad with the official request, and Clothilde, upon interrogation, revealed she had already received Clovis's ring and had accepted his offer of marriage. Gundobad trembled but did not dare challenge the young king of the Franks with a refusal, for he was known for his boldness and valor. Thus, Aurelian led the princess to his master to become his wife, carrying her off on his cart pulled by oxen. Two days later, however, King Gundobad balked on his decision and dispatched his knights in pursuit of Clothilde. The young princess, warned just in time, abandoned the wagon for a charger and reached the camp of the Franks in time. Her nuptials with Clovis were celebrated in 493 at Soissons.

From that moment, Clothilde had but one desire: to convert the pagan king who had become her husband. In the king's heart, the desire to render his wife happy conflicted with his fear of irritating the pagan gods and of displeasing the warriors under him, who were imbued with pagan superstitions. Clothilde became a mother and convinced the king to have his young heir baptized, but when the child died immediately after baptism, Clovis burst into reproaches: "Had we consecrated him to the pagan gods he would still be alive!" The young mother responded with sweet firmness, "I adore my God in this trial, and I thank Him for having given me the honor of calling to Him my son, giving him a place among the angels."

A year later a second son was born, baptized with the name Chlodomer. The Lord allowed him to fall ill as well, arousing the irritation of Clovis. However, as Gregory of Tours tells us, "Clothilde prayed so ardently for the health of the child that God granted his recovery." The queen did not cease to pray for the conversion of her husband, and neither did this supplication go unheeded. All this occurred in the year 496. The Alemanni, one of the most ferocious Germanic tribes, had penetrated into Gaul. Clovis confronted them at Tolbiac, near Cologne. Both sides fought furiously, but the Franks, fewer in number, were about to succumb. Clovis had sought the help of his gods in vain. Turning heavenward, and with a thundering voice that momentarily dominated the din of battle, he exclaimed, "God of Clothilde, give me the victory and I will give myself to You!" The name of Clothilde hovered over the plain of Tolbiac, and the God of Hosts received the naïve if fervent prayer of this barbarian. The fate of the battle changed suddenly. Clovis's soldiers seemed to multiply, and as the Alemanni took to flight, Clovis became master of the battlefield. Now he had to maintain his promise. He did not await the encounter with his unknowing Clothilde, but on the return march, was instructed in the rudiments of the catechism by the holy hermit Vaast, the future bishop of Arras, who was riding next to him. As the queen rode out to greet them, the victorious warrior greeted her thus, "Clothilde, it was not I who vanquished the Germans, it was your God! And you, Clothilde, have vanquished Clovis!" Clothilde responded, "To God alone be the glory of these two triumphs."

St. Remigius (c. 440–533), the bishop of Rheims at that time, introduced Clovis to the mysteries of the Christian Faith, and the king of the Franks became in turn an apostle of the Faith to his companions in arms. He was profoundly moved whenever he heard the Passion of our Lord recounted, and clutching his sword hilt, exclaimed, "Ah, had I been there with my Franks!" Abbot Lemann writes, "From this outburst of knightly generosity, the soul of Christian France was born."

One day, standing before Clovis and Clothilde kneeling in prayer, the bishop Remigius invoked the protection of the Virgin Mary over the Christian king of the Franks, and suddenly the church was inundated by a heavenly light and a supernatural perfume, and they heard a voice say, "Peace be with you! Fear not, persevere in my love." Clovis and Clothilde prostrated themselves on the ground, while the holy bishop proclaimed, "Your posterity will govern this realm with nobility. It will glorify the Holy Church and inherit the kingdom of the Romans. It will not cease to prosper if only it walks the path of truth and virtue. Decadence can come only from evil customs."

St. Remigius wanted Clovis's conversion to be celebrated with all the pomp worthy of such an event. It was Christmas Day, 496. The Church of Rheims was illuminated by thousands of perfumed candles as the royal entourage arrived, preceded by the Cross and by the sacrament of Baptism, and then, as Gregory of Tours narrates in his *History of the Franks*, one heard the voice of St. Remigius resounding solemnly in the basilica, "Bow your head in silence, O Sicambrian; adore what you have burned, burn what you have adored."

As the other officers, divided into groups, received baptism following Clovis's example, the other soldiers beat their lances against their shields yelling, "Christmas! Christmas!" The bishop of Vienne, St. Avitus, addressed Clovis with these words, "Choosing for yourself, you choose for everyone. Your faith is our victory," and then said, "All those people who shall pass under your command, to the advantage of the authority that religion must exercise." When Clovis and his three thousand companions left the basilica regenerated and reinvigorated by baptism, leaving with them, wrote Blessed Ozanam, were fourteen centuries of the kingdom and the knights, the crusaders, Scholasticism, all the greatness of the centuries still to come.

But another miracle was to mark that date. In the primitive Church, the forehead of the baptized was anointed with holy oil immediately after the moment of baptism proper. That day, the clerics responsible for bringing the holy chrism to the baptismal font were not able to enter because of the crowd crushing around the church. That part of the ceremony was suspended. Then St. Remigius turned his eyes to the heavens and, crying hot tears, began praying in silence; and behold, a dove appeared, whiter than snow, carrying in its beak a little cruet full of holy chrism — an oil not extracted from earthly plants, but which came directly from the heavenly gardens. Anointing the king's forehead with this, St. Remigius stamped a supernatural seal on him. The same cruet would be used for the coronation of all French kings from Louis the Pius to Louis XVI. This vessel was shattered by the Jacobins during the French Revolution, but its fragments were recovered, and the chrism was once again used to crown Charles X in 1824.

Abbot Lemann observes that all European nations, in their response to the divine call, enacted and completed in a certain sense the mystery of the

Epiphany, when the Wisemen, according to the unanimous witness of the Church Fathers, were the firstfruits of the gentiles, *primitiae gentium*. Only for France was the mystery of Christmas added to that of the Epiphany, because it was on the day the Redeemer was born that the French received baptism, entering the Church as a nation.

As if to give supernatural confirmation of this vocation, on Christmas Day three centuries later, another king of the Franks, Charlemagne, would be crowned emperor in St. Peter's in Rome. As happened three centuries earlier, swords beat shields to the shout of "Christmas! Christmas!" According to Daniel Rops, this scene at the baptism of Clovis constitutes, along with the vision of Constantine and the crowning of Charlemagne, one of the three decisive events that determined the political fate of the Christian West. We must not forget this.

Six years later, Clovis marched against Alaric II, king of the Visigoths. At Vouillé in 507, Clovis defeated him, taking possession of the entire country, from the Loire to the Pyrenees. He stamped a religious character on the Franco-Visigoth War, the first waged by the Catholic Northern Gaul against the heretical South. When he had prepared everything for the undertaking, he said to his army captains, "It is deeply painful to me that these Arians possess a part of Gaul. Let us go with the assistance of God and, after having defeated them, let us subjugate their country to our lordship."

The domain of the Visigoths in France fell to pieces. By now, the Roman faith had triumphed in these lands. In this way, Clovis crushed the serious threat of a barbarian-Arian West. Before his ascension, the Gothic world ran from the Danube to the Rhine, to the Loire, and all the way to Gibraltar. In the heart of this Arian world, he constructed a center for the propagation of the Catholic Faith.

Clovis established his new capital in Paris, a little city at that time, known by the name of Lutetia: adorned with great satisfaction by the title of the Roman consul sent to them from Byzantium by the emperor Anastasius, recognized as the representative of *romanitas*. He convoked a national council of the Church at Orléans, with the participation of thirty-two bishops, imitating what Constantine had done at Nicaea.

It was said that in Clovis, three elements had been united for the first time: Germanism, Romanism, and Catholicism. In his person, "The barbarian was civilized, the German was Romanized, and the pagan became a Catholic."

On November 27, 511, Clovis died in Paris at the age of forty-five. He was the founder of the first royal dynasty of France, the Merovingians, and with him

France became "the firstborn daughter of the Church." French armies from Clovis to Charlemagne were to become the bearers of the Catholic Faith.

Next to his name we must not forget that of his wife St. Clothilde. A widow after twenty years of marriage, the queen of the Franks encountered many trials until finally retiring to Tours, near the tomb of St. Martin, to whom she was particularly devoted. She founded churches and monasteries in that region, practicing penance and works of charity. There she died on June 3, 545. Later, her body was transferred to Paris and interred next to that of Clovis and St. Genevieve (c. 422–502), patron of the capital. Her mortal remains were cremated in 1793 to avoid profanation at the hands of revolutionaries. They now repose in a basilica dedicated to her, where she is solemnly commemorated every June 3. The presence of the three lilies on the crest of the French monarchy is attributed to Clothilde as well. She had received a man carrying lilies sent by a mysterious hermit of the forest of Saint-Germain-en-Laye.

Clovis and Clothilde were great devotees of St. Martin (c. 315–397), a soldier from Roman Pannonia, Slovakia today, destined to become, as monk and bishop, a French patron saint and protector of the Merovingian dynasty and of the expansion of the kingdom of the Franks. He was one of the most important evangelizers of pagan Gaul. His disciple Sulpicius Severus wrote that "truly very few people before St. Martin's arrival had welcomed the name of Christ in those regions. His name was impressed on them by the miracles he performed, and, because of his example, there is no longer anywhere that is not rich with churches and monastic centers." "St. Martin's mission," writes Dom Guéranger, "was that of finalizing the fall of paganism, which, though it had already been chased out of the cities, still predominated in rural areas."

In 470, about a dozen years before Clovis had become king of the Franks, a great basilica was built in Tours over the tomb of the saint, already famous throughout Gaul for the wonders he performed for them. This church was destined to become a spiritual center of France, together with the church in Rheims and that of Saint-Denis, also tied to the Christianization of the country and of its monarchy.

The idea of Christian sovereignty, which emerged after Theodosius in the fifth century, survived in the Western imagination thanks to Clovis. His conversion and his reign predestined the Franks to reign over the future Christian empire. According to Fr. Grisar:

Whoever seeks in the course of the great upheavals of the fifth century a culminating point of history that would mark the beginning of the Middle Ages, finds in the exaltation of Clovis and in his baptism, in some sense at least, a better date than the year 476 ... because the rise of the Franks was more historically consequential than the fall of the empire.... While the Franks entered the Church without passing through Arianism, the remaining Germanic populations, except for those still living in the darkness of paganism, were Arians.

It was in the kingdom of the Franks that, at the end of the sixth century, the poet Venantius Fortunatus (530–607), having become in 567 a clerk to Queen Radegunde, composed a celebrated hymn: the *Vexilla regis prodeunt*. The occasion was to commemorate Emperor Justin II's (520–576) gift of a relic of the Holy Cross to the convent of Pictavium, sent in a precious reliquary at the behest of Radegunde. Here are the words of this beautiful hymn:[28]

> *Abroad the Regal Banners fly,*
> *Now shines the Cross's mystery:*
> *Upon it life did death endure,*
> *And yet by death did life procure.*
> *Who, wounded with a direful spear,*
> *Did, purposely to wash us clear*
> *From stain of sin, pour out a flood*
> *Of precious Water mixed with Blood.*
> *That which the Prophet-King of old*
> *Hath in mysterious verse foretold,*
> *Is now accomplished, whilst we see*
> *God ruling nations from a Tree.*
> *O lovely and refulgent Tree,*
> *Adorned with purpled majesty;*
> *Culled from a worthy stock, to bear*
> *Those Limbs which sanctified were.*
> *Blest Tree, whose happy branches bore*
> *The wealth that did the world restore;*
> *The beam that did that Body weigh*
> *Which raised up Hell's expected prey.*

[28] Translator's note: There are about forty English translations of this hymn. "According to John Julian's Dictionary of Hymnology, the following translation, dating from 1670, is by far the best rendering of the Vexilla Regis in common use." Vexilla Regis prodeunt: The Hymns of the Breviary and Missal, Catholic Cornucopia, cathcorn.org.

*Hail Cross, of hopes the most sublime!*
*Now in this mournful Passion time,*
*Improve religious souls in grace,*
*The sins of criminals efface.*
*Blest Trinity, salvation's spring,*
*May every soul Thy praises sing;*
*To those Thou grantest conquest by*
*The holy Cross, rewards apply.*

Thus, the *Vexilla Regis*, this hymn of Christian victory, comes to us from the distant sixth century.

## 2. Ireland, "the Island of Saints"

Besides the kingdom of the Franks, the light of the gospel illuminated another people: those who lived on the British Isles. This was a mysterious land, shrouded in fog and gusty wind, where despite the arrival of the Roman divinities, the local religions of the druids survived with vigor. These people worshiped water, the stars, and all the elements of nature. The gatherings of druids were held at night, illuminated by the light of the moon, which they considered to be a goddess.

The first of the lands of Britannia to welcome the gospel was Ireland, thanks to a young missionary named Patrick (385–461), who was destined to become the country's national hero. Born in Gaul (and a relative on his mother's side of St. Martin of Tours), Patrick was abducted by pirates at the age of sixteen and sold as a slave in Ireland, where he lived for six years as the keeper of his master's flock, suffering cold, hunger, and solitude. Once liberated, he returned to his homeland, though he retained for the rest of his life a memory of Ireland and a desire to return there for the sake of bringing the pagans the voice of the gospel. He would exclaim, "I hear calling me from Ireland the voice of children not yet born."

One night, Patrick had a vision in which a young Irish man of extraordinary beauty appeared to him. Holding in his hands a bundle of letters, he said to Patrick, "I am your angel, take these and read them," and he took a letter that began, "Voice of Ireland." Reading it, he heard the voices of many poor Irish who shouted to him, "We beg you, Patrick, come back to us and teach us the way of the Lord." He was moved to tears as the vision disappeared.

Obedient to the appeal of the angel and touched by the memory of his years as a slave, during which God had been his only faithful companion, Patrick shared with a monk, who had just returned from Britannia, his desire to leave for those islands and evangelize them. When, in 432, the bishop Palladino, who had been sent by Pope Celestine to the Scotti (as the Irish were called at that time) died, Patrick renewed his request. Pope Celestine consecrated him bishop, and Patrick departed for England, and then Ireland, where for thirty years, until his death in 461, he carried out prodigious missionary work.

Ireland at that time was called Hibernia, the "land of winter." Unlike the other British Isles, it had not known the yoke of Rome. The Roman legion had never trod its land. It was virgin soil. But it was also a land where magicians and wizards proliferated; warned by the devil, they announced that a young man with tonsured head would soon come to the island. Nothing was able to stop Patrick, however, who went on to conquer peacefully the heart of the Irish, thanks in part to a series of amazing wonders. The life of St. Patrick was characterized by prayer and penance. At the time of his death, the entire island had received a profoundly Catholic stamp, which it would never lose over the centuries. It boasted such a large number of Christian monasteries that it could legitimately be called the Island of Saints.

From 444, the monastery of Armagh in the northern part of Ireland became the metropolitan see and the most important point for the ecclesial life of the country. The ascetical ideal of the Irish monks was the *peregrinatio pro Christo* or *pro Dei amore*, the abandonment of one's own land to spread abroad, both on the islands and on the continent, the principles of the gospel.

"In those years," writes Daniel Rops, "the news was full of prodigious adventures about monks who, after taking vows, would never return to their native land, so as to roam everywhere preaching the gospel; or of whole crews setting off to sea without oars, the better to abandon themselves to the will of God; or of stone tubs that miraculously transform into navigable ships, leading the saints wherever Providence so wills."

The western coast of Great Britain and what we call the Land of the Scotti, or Scotland, saw the establishment of several monasteries erected for the sake of spreading the gospel: for example, Bangor in Chester, founded by St. Comgall, and Kentigern in Scotland, founded by St. Ninian. Farther away, always farther away, toward the most unknown countries, the most terrible, all for Jesus Christ! Not satisfied with having already created the abbeys of Darrow and Londonderry in Ireland, St. Columban, the ancient monk from Clonard, set off with twelve companions in 563 to convert the savage Pitti; they founded the monastery of Iona on a tiny island on the western tip of Scotland that would become a nursery for bishops — a true Scottish metropolis, where the gospel would set off toward Orkney, the Shetlands, the Faer Oer, the Last Thule of the ancients, and even to Iceland. To what dangers, to what often bizarre adventures did those audacious voyages subject the monks, we see in the entertaining legends of St. Brendan the Navigator, full of joyful or terrifying anecdotes: Mass celebrated on the back of a whale taken for an island, a vision of the gates of Hell where, amid glaciers, the fire of polar volcanoes erupts.... This is not only legend. When the Vikings discovered Iceland in the seventh century, they found that the Irish abbots had already established themselves and that every island in the North Sea had its colony of ascetics.

## 3. "Not Angles, but Angels"

Toward the end of the sixth century, a young monk was walking in the Roman Forum where the slave market was being conducted when he was struck by a group of young slaves with white skin, blond hair, and blue eyes — quite distinct from the majority of the other, darker-skinned slaves. "Where do they come from?" he asked. "From Britain." "Christians or pagans?" "Pagans." "What is their nationality?" "Angles," was the answer. "I would say *angels*, rather," exclaimed the young priest, adding, "Too bad the grace of God has not touched these beautiful heads." Some years later, the young monk was elevated to the papacy, and he would make history as Gregory the Great (c. 540–604).

What remained of the Roman Empire was prey to further devastation, but Gregory, born of a family of Roman nobility, wanted to entrust to the gospel of Christ the conquering mission that the Roman Empire had enjoyed. He was convinced that the work of evangelization was the primary mission of the Church, according to the mandate of its Founder: "Go into all the world and preach the gospel to all the peoples" (Mark 16:15). The faith was not promised to all *individuals*, but to all *peoples*. And the peoples, the nations, must be conquered by Christianity.

It was in the year 596 when Gregory, already pope for six years, decided to entrust to the monks of his Caelian Hill monastery, headed by the prior Augustine, the task of converting England. The Venerable Bede left us a detailed account of this undertaking, whose magnificent consequences Gregory could not have foreseen: it opened the path to evangelizing the peoples of Germany.

In Anglia, King Ethelbert of Kent (552–616) had married a Catholic princess, the Parisian Bertha, a descendant of Clovis, who became for her husband another Clothilde. The meeting between Augustine and the king was impressive: seated under a tree, surrounded by his warriors, Ethelbert watched an approaching procession of some forty monks chanting Gregorian hymns and bearing a large silver cross with the image of Christ painted on a canvas. "The history of the Church," wrote Bossuet about this scene, "has nothing more beautiful to offer."

The personality and persuasive force of St. Augustine, together with the influence of Queen Bertha, convinced the king of the Anglo-Saxons to allow Augustine the freedom to preach in his kingdom. Just a year later, on Pentecost of 597, Ethelbert converted to Catholicism. In the month of November of the same year, according to the instructions of the pope, Augustine was consecrated the first bishop of the English Church by the archbishop of Arles, the pontifical legate. The king ceded his royal palace in Canterbury to the new bishop, who made it the episcopal see and the center for the spread of Christianity throughout England. On Christmas Day, Augustine baptized, in one ceremony, ten thousand Angles.

The conversion of Ethelbert was momentous. After the baptism of Constantine and that of Clovis, no other event was more important in the history of Christianity. The Anglo-Saxon people came to know, thanks to these preachers of the gospel, not only the Catholic Faith, but also Roman law, which continued to maintain its universal importance even in places where the Roman state held no significance. The Benedictine monastery of Canterbury became the point of departure for a movement of religious and cultural unification that created in the West a new center of Christian civilization, defined by the English historian Christopher Dawson as "perhaps the most important event between the epoch of Justinian and that of Charlemagne." For this reason, Ethelbert can be considered the founder of the English nation, which before his conversion was a confused jumble of peoples without a shared religious identity.

In his moral writings on the book of Job, Pope Gregory the Great traced new horizons for the Church of Rome and compared her preachers to the clouds in the sky that irrigate and fertilize the parched furrows of the earth:

> The omnipotent Lord has covered with dazzling clouds the corners of the seas, such that, by amazing miracles worked by preachers, He might carry the Faith to the extreme limits of the world. Behold how it has now penetrated the heart of almost every people; behold how he has

united in one faith the far reaches of East and West; behold how the tongue of Brittanny, which knew only how to stutter its barbarian language, has begun to sing the divine praises of the Hebrew Halleluia.

## 4. St. Gregory the Great and "His Women"

If the conversion of the Franks and the Anglo-Saxons had come about in a painless manner, this was not the case for the Visigoths in Spain. Situated at one extremity of Europe, Spain was the last stronghold of Arianism, apparently impregnable, which was professed by the Visigoth kings. St. Leander (c. 549–601), bishop of Seville, was the great instrument of grace for Spain's liberation from this heresy.

In 567, King Liuvigild (525–586) ascended the throne in Toledo. He was a valorous German, though fanatically Arian. Liuvigild had married a descendant of St. Clothilde, the Frankish Ingund, an admirable woman of Catholic faith. Leander was tied to Ingund, and with her help was able to bring about the conversion of one of the king's sons, Hermenegild.

St. Hermenegild (564–585) was the first of the royal house of the Visigoths to abandon Arianism and embrace the Roman Faith. For this reason, he is called the Clovis of Spain. But unlike the Frankish king, his fate was sealed by martyrdom. The young prince was disinherited on account of his conversion, and when he sought to defend himself, gathering a militia, he was betrayed by his companions, defeated in battle, and decapitated at his father's order on Holy Saturday, in the year 585. His martyrdom was not without fruit, however. One year after the martyrdom of Hermenegild, in May 586, Liuvigild died in his palace in Toledo and was succeeded by his son Reccared, who overturned the policies of his father. The Catholic bishops were recalled from exile, and St. Leander, who had become the archbishop of Seville, was welcomed to court with full honors. Reccared became Catholic with the support of Leander and his brother Isidore (560–636), who was also destined to become bishop of Seville and a canonized saint. Thus, two Visigoth brothers — the martyr and the new king — brought about the conversion of their people due to the spiritual support of two other brothers, both saints and bishops in Seville successively, Leander and Isidore.

Isidore assisted his brother Leander at the Third Council of Toledo (May 8, 589), in which King Reccared solemnly abjured Arianism for himself and for his people, asking to be admitted to the orthodoxy of Catholic Faith. Thus began the Catholic history of Spain. When the Islamic tide swept across the Straits of Gibraltar, and Visigoth Spain collapsed, a group of Christian knights, inspired by the spirit of St. Leander and St. Isidore, formed the first nucleus of what would become the Christian *Reconquista*.

In the events we have narrated here, one fact draws our attention in particular: the decisive role played by women. "The believing woman," St. Paul had said, "sanctifies her unbelieving husband" (1 Cor. 7:14). This was never so true as in the time of the barbarians, when next to the Germanic warriors, often violent and brutal, we see the appearance of young princesses who converted their men with sweetness, as well as an inflexible strength in defending their faith.

St. Gregory the Great relied above all on three women: the Merovingian princess Bertha (560–616), queen of the Anglo-Saxons; the Visigoth princess Brunhilde (534–613), who became queen of the Franks; and in Italy, Princess Theodelinda of Bavaria (c. 570–628), the wife of Agilulf, king of the Lombards. Thanks to the influence of his fervently Catholic wife, Agilulf, though Arian, had his first-born baptized in the Catholic faith. This conversion, and that of many of the court nobles, was a fact of great importance, although it did not produce such lasting results as that of the conversion of Clovis. Theodelinda, together with Bertha and Brunhilde, formed a tryptic of feminine figures with whom Gregory had privileged relations, understanding the precious role of women in the new Christian world being born. St. Bertha, queen of Kent, and St. Theodelinda, queen of the Lombards, were both canonized by the Church.

It was thanks to Gregory the Great that the Catholic Faith truly began to flourish, and would become, for nearly a thousand years, the dominant religious force within Europe: Christendom. The hierarchy of the Church — its unity and its sense of discipline — along with its language, became the main civil institutions in Europe: the cement that held a disintegrating society together. Consider just the linguistic aspect: the English writer Hilaire Belloc reminds us that Europe possessed an infinity of dialectical variants. The form of Latin that the Church used was the same everywhere, and it unified the Church's rituals, which differed only slightly, if at all, from one province to another.

On the horizon of the chaotic sixth century, the Church was the only institution that remained standing, preserving the greatest treasures of civilization and, above all, imparting to Europe a new supernatural energy destined to renew it. Msgr. Umberto Benigni writes, "Gregory the Great was neither 'the first of the Pontiffs' nor the 'last of the Romans,' but was the first of the Pontiffs and the last of the Romans who, by sending missionaries to Brittania and corresponding with the monks on Mount Sinai, had the power and the occasion to show the entire civilized world the greatness of Papal Rome in the ancient civilized Rome, at the moment when the latter was vanishing forever."

## 5. St. Boniface and Germany

Through the evangelization of England, St. Gregory prepared the subsequent conversion of the Germanic nation.

If there is a European nation whose roots are eminently Christian, it is England, where, according to the historian Christopher Dawson, "It was the Church, and not the state, that opened the path toward national unity by means of its general organization, its annual synods, and its administrative tradition." But on the other hand, there has never been a period in which the influence of Anglo-Saxon culture on the continent has been as great as it was then. This was largely due to the influence of the Anglo-Saxon Boniface (673–754), the apostle to Germany, "a man who had a more profound influence over the history of Europe than any other Englishman who ever lived," as Dawson writes.

The one whom history venerates under the name of Boniface was called Winfred at his baptism; he was an Angle of Wessex, born in Kirton in Devonshire, who, like many other young men of his time, felt an attraction to the monastic life. During the winter of 718–719, St. Boniface was living in Rome near St. Peter's, and this sojourn would become important to his vocation.

The pope at that time was Gregory II (715–732), a lofty spirit, a man of great faith, fully aware of the mission of the Church. Significantly, at the moment of his election, he had chosen to reign under the name of the first Gregory. His encounter with Winfred was decisive. The glory that emanated from the English saint impressed the pontiff so thoroughly that he instantly placed all his trust in him, never to retract it until his death. The privilege of being the pontifical missionary to the Germans, which Winfred was requesting, was granted with enthusiasm: "You shall no longer be called Winfred, but Boniface, one who does good!"

"When he departed for the mysterious lands where pagan souls awaited him," writes Daniel Rops:

> Boniface was the representative of the pope — an itinerant bishop without a particular see, as Augustine had been in England, acting as a kind

of direct spokesman of St. Peter. For his entire life, the great missionary
would remain faithful to this oath of goodness granted him on the tomb
of the apostle. He would solicit the pope on every occasion for instructions and directives, receiving from him constant support, exchanging
correspondence with him that we can still read today, as beautiful as the
correspondence between the earlier Gregory and St. Augustine.

A remarkable pope, St. Gregory the Great, and a few religious and laypeo-
ple — among them several women — all animated by an ardent faith in God,
paved the way for the birth of Christian civilization amid the ruins of the Roman
Empire. Though the primary motive of these men was religious, their faith had
profound consequences in the political and social spheres as well. An indication
of what occurred can be found in the words Gregory addressed to Queen Brunhilde: "Carry out God's interests, and God will carry out yours" (*Epistles* 11.49).
There is in these words a philosophy of Providence that recalls the famous
Gospel passage "Seek first his kingdom and his righteousness, and all these
things shall be yours as well" (Matt. 6:33; Luke 12:31).

The promises of God are immutable: what was true in the fifth century is
true even in our own age, one that is in many ways more tenebrous than that
which saw the collapse of the Roman Empire. What seems to be waning today,
in fact, is not a pagan empire, but the very Christian civilization that emerged
and developed at that time. And yet, when men collaborate with Divine Grace,
God intervenes in history to maintain His promises.

CHAPTER VII

# The Youthfulness of Christian Europe

## 1. CHARLEMAGNE

The history of the Church is the history of the expansion of the Kingdom of God on earth, according to the mandate conferred by Jesus to the apostles.[29] "Go therefore and make disciples of all nations, baptizing them in the name of the Father and of the Son and of the Holy Spirit, teaching them to observe all that I have commanded you," says Matthew (28:19–20), and Mark adds, "The gospel must first be preached to all nations" (Mark 13:10).

The message of salvation is addressed not only to individuals but to the nations — and the history of the Church is the response of the peoples and nations to the appeal of the Redeemer. The nations are called to baptism just as individuals are, and they also are given a vocation that derives from it. The vocation of the peoples is that of conforming themselves to the design that Divine Providence has established for each of them. Providence has desired that a variety of nations join in unity toward their common end, which is for them, as for every man, the glory of God. The Catholic Church, custodian of the unity of Christian nations, is also the custodian of their diversity. It is called to respect, defend, and develop the vocation of every people by way of its individuality and originality.

---

[29]   Radio Maria, conversation on February 15, 2012.

Christendom, the fruit of the Passion of our Lord Jesus Christ, was intended, above all, to be a family of nations, diverse but united by the same law and by the same commandment of Divine Love.

The first people to respond to the Lord's call were the Franks, and for this reason France is called the firstborn daughter of the Church.

At the Mass celebrated in Le Bourget on June 1, 1980, John Paul II addressed this supplication to the French: "Today, in the capital of the history of your nation, I would like to repeat the words that constitute your title of honor: France, firstborn daughter of the Church, are you faithful to the promises of your baptism?"

Between the fifth and sixth centuries, France was an outpost for the missionary expansion of the Church, especially toward the British Isles. It was from the coast of Gaul that St. Patrick, and later St. Augustine of Canterbury, would set off. Those monks of the British Isles had been converted to the Church, and from St. Columban to St. Boniface, they in turn transmitted the flame of faith to Europe.

But the faith of St. Boniface was the fruit of three centuries of missionary heroism following the baptism of Clovis, and the English Boniface gave back to the Frankish people the flame he had received from it. It was Bishop Boniface who, in 751, bestowed the royal anointing on Pepin, king of the Franks, in the city of Soissons. After the baptism of Clovis, this event formalized the eternal alliance between the papacy and the kingdom of France.

Pepin the Short (714–768) was the son of Charles Martel, who had been victorious over the Arabs at Poitiers in 732 and the founder of the dynasty. The Battle of Poitiers has an analogous significance to the Battle of Lepanto: it erected an insuperable barrier to Muslim encroachment, saving Christianity from the domination of Islam.

Pepin's son, Charlemagne (742–814), had the merit and glory of inaugurating the Christian empire of the West, and he represented the prototype of the Christian hero and prince. He was above all a warrior who, in a series of arduous and always victorious military campaigns, extended the borders of Christianity from one side of Europe to the other. The River Ebro marked the border between the Christian empire and Muslim Spain, while the Danube marked the border between Christendom and the pagan populations of the East.

This empire included a great number of kingdoms, just as the Roman Empire had. After having defeated the Lombards in December 800, Charles arrived in Rome to venerate the tomb of St. Peter. On Christmas Day, Pope Leo III placed the imperial crown on Charles's head, proclaiming the famous phrase "Life and victory to Charles August, crowned great and peaceful emperor by the mercy of God!"

The Holy Roman Empire was not a pure and simple restoration of the Roman Empire that had preceded it. The empire was called "holy" for its religious character, and "Roman" because of its connection to the Roman pontiff and to Rome itself as the center of Christianity.

The emperor had a mission to defend the papacy, foster the missionary expansion of the Church, defend Catholic dogma against heresy, and establish peace and concord among Christian princes in accordance with the pope. Along with his military enterprises, he began an important work of political, cultural, and religious reconstruction. Charlemagne's greatest collaborator was Alcuin of York, an English monk and disciple to the Venerable Bede. Charlemagne had met him in Parma, Italy, and had explained to him his great plan for the rebirth of a Christian empire. Alcuin hesitated, torn between a desire to honor and serve the emperor and the temptation to retire to the peaceful cell of his monastery. Providence, however, had established the union between these great spirits, as often occurs in history.

Under the direction of Alcuin, a center of studies was created in the imperial palace in Aachen: the *Schola Palatina*, or Palace School. The court of Charlemagne became a great intellectual center thanks to the presence of the greatest talents of the age, whom he had gathered there. Alcuin produced a program of studies that was sent to all the episcopal and claustral schools of the realm, which would remain unchanged for the rest of the Middle Ages. The program included the seven liberal arts, distinguished by the *trivium* (grammar, rhetoric, and dialectic) and the *quadrivium* (arithmetic, geometry, astronomy, and music), and to which medicine and theology were later added. Charlemagne saw devotion to the Virgin Mary as the center of religious unity in his kingdom, and he had a magnificent church built in her honor in Aachen.

Charlemagne was an extraordinary personality with the loftiest of missions. The historian Giorgio Falco describes him in this way:

> The man demanded our sympathy by his very appearance: tall of stature with a robust body, a manly gait, and a winsome, luminous countenance with big, vivacious eyes. Scornful of foreign customs, he dressed according to the common Frankish style and always carried his sword; but on

solemn days, and in the presence of foreign ambassadors, he wore a crown adorned with jewels and precious fabrics. Much about him reflected his simple and robust ancestry. His favorite food was wild game, his favorite pastimes hunting and the baths. He had an open mind, and clear, easy, and abundant words, speaking in Latin, Frankish, and the Romance languages. His whole life he fostered an inextinguishable passion for knowledge, and had his sons and daughters instructed in the liberal arts. During his meals, he had a servant read the *De Civitate Dei* and the stories of the ancients, and he always kept a stylus and tablet under his pillow to practice writing during his frequent nocturnal vigils.

Emperor Charlemagne died in Aachen on the morning of January 28, 814, at seventy-two years of age and after a reign of nearly half a century. It was said that, shortly before his death, he was at table in a maritime city in Gaul when, on the sea's horizon, he saw ships arriving from the north. They were Viking pirates arriving with the intent to raid and plunder. Charlemagne gazed long at the scene, as if intuiting the future, and his barons saw him weeping. *Sunt lacrimae rerum* … there are tears that are born of certain things. Abbot Lemann observes that the tears gushing from the eyes of Charlemagne were a Christian testimony to the transience of his magnificent empire.

Charlemagne had dedicated his entire life to unifying and extending his kingdom, but it ultimately shattered after his death due to the fratricidal struggles launched by his heirs. The Treaty of Verdun of 843 sanctioned the fragmentation of Europe and the birth of the first nations, France and Germany. From that time on, Europe would no longer retain the political unity that had been established through the battles and sacrifices of Charlemagne.

Charlemagne's empire might appear to us as a failed project, a great but unfulfilled hope. A theology of history invites us, however, to move beyond our reflections. What characterizes the history of Europe and represents its vocation is, as we have recalled, the marriage of unity and diversity. Its diversity is that of its states, nations, languages, customs, and traditions, which in the Middle Ages achieved an equilibrium and a unified vision of the world, a vision born of the same faith, of a common law, and even of a common language — Latin. Alongside the papacy and the empire, the universities constituted the most important unifying elements of Europe as it was forming at the end of the first millennium. The University of Pavia, for example, was founded by Charlemagne around the year 770.

It became clear that the mission of Charlemagne was that of uniting Europe politically in order to unite it culturally. But once united culturally, its political unity nevertheless disintegrated, and out of its sundry parts were born the European nations of the ninth and tenth centuries, diverse yet united by their shared faith and values.

In the second half of the ninth century, the political unity created by Charlemagne disintegrated, and Europe plummeted one more into chaos. Christendom was devastated from the north by Scandinavian pirates and from the south by Saracen raiders. The former pushed into the very heart of France, while the latter conquered Sicily and dominated the Mediterranean.

After having sacked Bordeaux, Orléans, Rheims, and Paris, the Normans, guided by their chief Rollo (845–932), reached Chartres and put the city under siege. The townspeople raised high the relic of the Blessed Virgin Mary's tunic, sent by the emperor of the East, Nicephorus, to Charlemagne. The fate of the battle turned, and Rollo was for the first time forced to retreat. The monk Abbo, who was among the besieged, consecrated a poem to this event, sounding his praise for Mary the liberator: *Nec te Francus fugat, nec te Burgundus cedit, sed Regina Virgo* (O barbarian, it was not the Frank who put you to flight, nor the Burgundian who cut you to pieces, but the Virgin Mary, our Queen).

Rollo received in 911 both the sacrament of Baptism and the title of Duke of Normandy. Thanks to the assistance of Mary, the Normans entered the ranks of the family of Christian peoples, of whom they were to become indomitable defenders.

The inhabitants of Chartres, desiring to erect a monument in eternal gratitude to Mary, constructed in their city a cathedral of unprecedented beauty. The Normans, impressed by the majesty and splendor of this edifice, desired in turn to construct something similar in their capital in Rouen. We have a letter from 1145 in which Archbishop Hughes describes the construction of the cathedral dedicated to Our Lady, saying that no one was admitted to the worksite if he had not first confessed and done penance for his sins. Richard the Lionheart (1157–1199), King of England, asked that his heart be preserved in the cathedral of Rouen because "of the fervent devotion present in that place." And so it occurred, while the rest of his body was interred at his father's feet in the Abbey of Fontevrault in Anjou.

## 2. BRITAIN UNDER ALFRED THE GREAT

The destiny of England was mysterious. How did it happen that it was not conquered by Charlemagne and avoided falling under the dominion of the vast

Christian empire that spread from the Ebro to the Tiber, and from the Tiber to the Rhine and the Danube?

Abbot Lemann responds by saying that the British Isles remained free and independent in order to remain a kind of refuge in the midst of the tribulations that the European continent was to suffer in the turbulent period following the death of Charlemagne.

Its geographical location primed it for its role as a place of providential exile. The ninth and tenth centuries, which saw the decomposition of Charlemagne's empire, were shaken by wars, raids, revolts, and sufferings of every sort. Britain was a refuge, a lighthouse shining while the darkness of decay fell over Europe. The title of "Island of Saints" was attributed to Ireland, but also to England. In fact, on November 14, 1581, St. Edmund Campion (1540–1581) declared to the Anglican judges who were about to put him to death for his Catholic faith: "Condemning us, you condemn your ancestors: the priests, bishops, sovereigns, and all those who once represented the glory of England, the Island of Saints, and the most devout daughter of the Chair of St. Peter."

When the Normans invaded in 870, they advanced toward the monastery of Coldingham. The Abbess Aebbe, known as St. Aebbe the Younger, gathered her sisters and exhorted them to save their honor. After having raised her eyes to the Virgin Mary, she grabbed a blade and cut off her nose and upper lip. Her sisters imitated her, mutilating their faces one after another. When the Normans arrived the next day, they found the terrible scene. They set the monastery ablaze, and all the nuns died martyrs amid the flames, but having obtained the conversion of their executioners. St. Etheldreda (636–679) had been a novice in the monastery of Coldingham and sister to three other English saints: Ethel-burh, Seaxburh, and Vitburh — four sisters, all canonized by the Church, whose spiritual point of reference was the great bishop St. Wilfred (c. 633–709). Plinio Corrêa Oliveira considered St. Etheldreda to be "one of the seeds sown by God in the history of Europe to bring the Middle Ages into being."

Around the time of St. Aebbe's martyrdom, Providence raised up an English emulator of Charlemagne: the king of Wessex, Alfred the Great (849–899). He was the hero of the defense of the kingdom against the Normans, who had occupied the eastern and central regions of England and whom Alfred defeated on numerous occasions. Their king, Guthrum, chief of those who had massa-cred the nuns of Coldingham, converted and was baptized with the name

Aethelstan. The converted Norman warriors went on to Christianize England, just as other Normans had Christianized France.

Alfred's father had married Judith, the daughter of the Carolingian king, Charles the Bald. Alfred was thus a direct descendant of Charlemagne, and the Carolingian court atmosphere served as his model. He translated and disseminated throughout England the *Pastoral Rule* of St. Gregory the Great, the *Soliloquies* of St. Augustine, and the *Psalter* (of which he himself translated the first fifty psalms). During his reign, monasteries became centers of learning and instruction in the Sacred Scriptures and the liberal arts. Under King Alfred, the study of Latin and Christian culture reached their highest levels. Alfred the Great would later be venerated as a saint, and after him, St. Edward the Confessor (1043–1066), the last of the Anglo-Saxon kings. The most characteristic form of Marian devotion in England is attributed to King Edward: the consecration of his kingdom to the Virgin as "Mary's dowry." According to English marriage customs, the king offered England to the Virgin as her dowry, giving her all that he possessed; from that moment he no longer governed in his own name, but only as her vassal. In turn, the English people were proud to consider themselves Mary's "dowry."

## 3. The Feats of Covadonga

Another land, Spain, was situated, like Britain, on the western borders of Christendom. Beyond these lands were only seas and oceans.

When the apostles left Jerusalem, dividing up the regions to be evangelized, Spain was assigned to Zebedee's son, James, the brother of John, whom Jesus had privileged on Mt. Tabor to see Him in splendor, and in the Garden of Olives to witness His anguish.

James the Greater arrived in Saragossa in AD 39. He was praying one night on the banks of the Ebro, disappointed by the ineffectiveness of his preaching, when a dazzling light appeared to him on a pillar of jasper. It was a woman of incomparable beauty, surrounded by a procession of angels. He recognized her and prostrated himself before her.

Mary, according to a vision of the venerable Mary of Agreda in her *Mystical City of God*, spoke to him with ineffable sweetness the following words: "My son, minister of the Most High, be blessed by His right hand; may He sustain you and reveal to you the delight of His face." At this point, all the angels exclaimed, "Amen." Mary continued:

The exalted King has chosen this place that you might erect a temple to His glory here, where, under the title of my name, His name may be magnified, and where His treasures may be communicated in abundance; He will give free reign to His ancient mercies for the good of believers, and by means of my intercession they will obtain them, so long as they ask for them with authentic confidence and pious devotion. For His part, I promise them enormous favors and my protection, because this must be my residence and my inheritance. As a witness to this, this pillar with my image on its summit will remain here to endure with holy faith until the end of time. Begin the work without delay, and after having rendered this service, you shall depart for Jerusalem, because the Savior wants you to sacrifice your life where he offered His for the redemption of men.

In remembrance of the visit, the Virgin Mary left to James the pillar of jasper from which the name "Virgin of the Pillar" derives. Today, she is patron of Spain and her feast is celebrated on October 12. James built the chapel requested of him by the divine visitor, then left Spain to become Jerusalem's first bishop and the first martyr of the apostolic college. The chapel constructed by the apostle in Saragossa later took the name of Santa Maria del Pilar. From that moment, this image remained an unshakeable pilaster for the Catholic Faith in Spain.

The venerable Maria of Agreda also told how, when the Virgin was taken by angels from the banks of the Ebro back to Jerusalem, she asked the Lord that one of these angels should stay and keep watch over Spain, preserving its faith.

St. James was decapitated in Jerusalem in the year 41 by order of King Herod; according to tradition, his disciples, out of fear of the Jews, laid the saint's body on a ship and entrusted the task of his burial to Divine Providence. They too boarded the ship without a helmsman. The angel of the Lord led them safely ashore on the coast of Spain, where James's body was buried and miraculously rediscovered eight centuries later.

The history of Christian Spain is a history of martyrdom and of wars fought on behalf of the Faith. All of Spain remembers St. Leocadia, the virgin of Toledo and martyr under Diocletian. Turning her serene gaze toward her weeping companions, she said, "Forward, soldiers of Christ, rejoice with me in being judged worthy to suffer for the name of Jesus." The bishop Cixila (d. 783), in his biography of Ildefonsus, tells that on the feast day of St. Leocadia, when St. Ildefonsus (607–667), archbishop of Toledo, and the Visigoth king Recceswinth were gathered in the temple erected in her honor, the tombstone was raised, and Leocadia appeared and spoke with Ildefonsus in these words: "Ildefonsus, through you my Queen triumphs, who resides in the heights of Heaven." The archbishop, having recovered from the shock and wishing to attest to the miracle for posterity's sake, took the king's dagger and cut a piece of the veil that covered the head of the saint. He then took this relic, along with the sovereign's dagger, and placed them in the church in Toledo, where they are still venerated today.

Once the Roman persecutions had ended, Spain was invaded by the Vandals of Genseric. The Vandals passed on to North Africa and settled there, while other barbarians, namely the Visigoths, occupied the Iberian Peninsula. Like the Vandals, the Visigoths were Arians. Toulouse was the capital of their kingdom. They too were invaded by the Moors, who subjugated the peninsula in 711, raising the Islamic banner after fifteen months of fighting. This occupation lasted many centuries, but as Abbot Lemann observes, Providence, who seems to delight in paradoxes, assigned to Spain the vocation of becoming a bulwark against the Muslim onslaught.

At the hour when all seemed lost, a knight of royal blood, Pelagius (c. 690–730), incited resistance. He gathered his few men on a high mountain in the Asturias, where an image of the Virgin Mary was venerated in a cave. The destiny of Spain was there placed in his hands. This image has been known ever since as Santa Maria de Covadonga.

In 722, a handful of knights under the guidance of the same Pelagius defeated the Muslim army sent there to bring them to submission. Tradition has it that the Virgin appeared to Pelagius and his companions the night before the battle. The cry of Our Lady of Covadonga began the Reconquista, a military conquest against Islam that lasted for eight centuries.

After the very brief reign of Pelagius's son, Favila, his son-in-law, Alfonso I (739–757), took the crown and conquered part of Galicia, from Leon to Castille. Subsequently, Alfonso II (791–842) gave civil and ecclesiastical organization to the kingdom, establishing the capital at Oviedo, which became the main religious center of Catholic Spain.

During this period, the blood of martyrs was repeatedly shed in the Caliphate of Córdoba, in Andalusia, by the emir Abd ar-Rahman II (822–852), who resided there. Around 850, he imposed upon Christians a forced conversion to Islam. "What do you think of Jesus Christ and of Muhammad?" asked the Muslim judge to a priest named Perfectus. The Confessor of the Faith replied, "Jesus Christ is

God, blessed above all things. Muhammad, your presumed prophet, is one of the seducers of whom the Gospel speaks, who shall cause their followers to fall into the infernal abyss." He was immediately put to death, and the same fate was meted out to the merchant John, who died after receiving fifty blows of the whip.

This news provoked great commotion in the Christian community. Some monks came down from the mountains to proclaim their faith in the town squares of Córdoba. The most ardent was Isaac, from the monastery of Tabanos, who was put to death in 851. His body was hung in public to expose him to the scorn of the crowd. But far from frightening the other monks, this treatment aroused in them an even greater audacity. Every martyrdom, as the historian Ivan Gobry recalls, provokes the witness of other disciples of Christ who become martyrs in turn.

On September 16, there was a terrible execution of two monks who had come from the east: Rogelio and Servideo, one old and the other quite young. They entered the mosque during a ceremony and preached of Jesus Christ there. They had their hands and feet cut off first, and then their heads.

Under Abd ar-Rahman II, a council was convoked at which the archbishops and bishops of the South of Spain were gathered. The caliph tolerated Christians on the condition that they acknowledge Islamic authorities, and he wanted the bishops to condemn all Christians who, criticizing Muhammad's religion, were courting martyrdom. Martyrdom was not denounced as such, nor could it have been — it remains a highpoint of Catholic spirituality. But the bishops prohibited Christians from seeking it and condemned St. Eulogius, who exhorted public testimony against those bishops tempted to find a compromise. "St. Eulogius passed through the bitter trial of being condemned by a synod of bishops, but despite his sufferings," observed Plinio Corrêa de Oliveira, "considered it his duty to resist the unjust condemnation of wicked bishops, and thus his behavior gave us an example of authentic love for the Church. Obeying God rather than men, he effectively obeyed the Church, and the Church's authority would later recognize his rectitude."

Christians did not stop witnessing to their faith, however, and the caliph, possessed by fury, ordered the bodies of the martyrs to be exposed and burned publicly. He was then stricken with apoplexy and died without ever having spoken again. His successor, Moham, followed the same policy, and a new legion of witnesses to Christ enriched the canon of martyrs. We remember St. Fandila, St. Colomba, and St. Abbondius.

The year 859 saw the execution of St. Eulogius himself, the biographer and defender of the martyrs who preceded him. He had been elected bishop of Toledo but could not be consecrated before his death. He should be considered as the patron of all martyrs of Islam in the twenty-first century.

Meanwhile, in the north of Spain, under the reign of Alfonso the Chaste (791–842), the famous pilgrimage to Santiago de Compostella was set in motion by the rediscovery of the relics of St. James in 813. The place of discovery was given the name Compostella, the "field of the star." Bishop Teodomiro discovered in that place a tomb containing three bodies; one of the three tombs contained a severed head and the phrase: "Here lies Jacobus, son of Zebedeo and Salomé." Alfonso II ordered the construction of a temple on the site, and in 893, Benedictine monks established their residence there. The first pilgrimages to the tomb of the apostle began in Asturias and Galicia, and then from all of Europe.

In the twelfth century, a cry of fury rose in Islam when they learned that they were losing Spain, the land of their conquest. A holy war was proclaimed, and innumerable tribes populating North Africa crossed the Strait of Gibraltar to invade the Iberian Peninsula. Until that time, Christians in Spain had fought alone, relying only on the help of St. James, who had been sighted in the midst of bloody clashes with Muslims, killing many of them with his own hands. This gave rise to the sobriquet Santiago Matamoros: St. James, Killer of Muslims.

But this time, it was the Church that intervened. Pope Innocent III (1160–1216) made an appeal to all of Christendom. Sixty thousand knights from France, Italy, and Germany arrived at the foot of the Pyrenees, enrolling under the banners of the three Catholic kings of Navarre, Aragon and Castille, and Portugal. The Christian army descended on the Arabs from the Sierra Morena and dispersed them. This was the memorable Battle of Las Navas de Tolosa of July 16, 1212. Thanks to this victory, a process of unification between the Christian kingdoms began, which would lead to the formal union of Castille and Aragon by means of the marriage of Ferdinand II of Aragon and Isabella of Castille. The Virgin Mary, from the depths of that cave in Covadonga, had guided the heroic deeds of great men, such as the king of Castille, who, though by then a paralytic, had his men carry him into battle, where he confronted and defeated the terrible al-Manzar.

In this dreadful struggle, the height of Spanish valor was reached by "El Cid Campeador," Rodrigo Diaz de Vivar (c. 1048–1099). *Cid* means lord in Arabic, and *campeador* means peerless hero. The Moors bestowed this nickname upon

Rodrigo of Castille, who, after having defeated five of their kings, was recognized as their sovereign.

## 4. Christendom at the Dawn of the Year 1000

On Christmas Day in 496, Clovis was baptized, and on Christmas of the year 800, Charlemagne was crowned emperor.

But the history of Christianity knew yet another felicitous Christmas Day: that of 951, when King Otto of Saxony (912–973), the first to bear this name, married the princess Adelaide of Burgundy (931–999) in Pavia. Adelaide had been persecuted and imprisoned by Berengar II of Friuli, master of the Kingdom of Italy, because she had refused to marry his son. She was liberated by Otto I, whom she married and with whom she had three sons. Otto was destined to become emperor and Adelaide a saint. Glory was wed to supernatural virtue.

In 962, Pope John XIII invited the German king and his wife to Rome to kneel before the tomb of St. Peter, and there, amid the acclamations of the Roman people, placed the imperial crowns on their heads. This ceremony initiated the transference of the empire of the Franks to the Germans. It was the birth of what would be called the Holy Roman Empire of the German Nation.

Sanctity surrounded Otto's throne: St. Adelaide was his wife; St. Matilda (c. 890–968), his mother, retreated to the Abbey of Quedlinburg, which she had founded after becoming a widow; and St. Bruno I (925–955), archbishop of Cologne, was his brother. The latter acted as regent during Otto's second expedition in Italy. His successor to the imperial throne, Henry II (973–1024), was also declared a saint, as was his wife Cunegonde.

Adelaide educated her son Otto II (c. 955–983) both spiritually and politically; following his death, she aided her grandson Otto III (980–1002) as well. Adelaide ruled as regent until the young king came of age in 994. Otto III placed at the center of his governance the idea of *renovatio imperii*. The young emperor, son of Otto II and the empress Theophanu, united in himself the Germanic and Byzantine traditions, the legacies of Charlemagne and of Justinian. From 999, he and his court resided at a sumptuous residence on the Aventine Hill in Rome. Writing about himself, he referred to himself as "I, Otto — Roman, Saxon, and Italian — am servant of the Apostles and emperor by Divine Grace, the Augustus of the World." On Pentecost of the year 1000, in the ancient Palatine Chapel in Aachen, Otto III, having just been crowned in Rome, contemplated the mortal remains of Charlemagne, whose place of burial he had sought out.

On January 1, 1001, the son of Geza of Hungary, Duke Vajk, baptized with the name Stephen, became the first king of Hungary (r. 1001–1038). The crown was given to him at the hands of Pope Sylvester II, who granted him the title of *Rex Apostolicus* for having made of Hungary a Christian nation. Stephen consecrated his kingdom to the Blessed Virgin. After his death, he was elevated as patron of the nation and holy protector of Hungary. Both the Polish Duke Miezko and St. Stephen of Hungary made gifts of their nations to the pope. In a miniature from that period, one beholds four women in a state of obsequence before the pope: the women represent Rome, Gaul, Germany, and Sklavinia, the land of the Slavs, respectively.

The tenth century opened with the baptism of Rollo, Duke of Normandy, and saw the beginning of the Christianization of the Scandinavian peoples, beginning with Denmark, as well as that of the Slavs, Bohemians, Poles, and Hungarians. A new Christianity was being established at the dawn of the new millennium, when Otto III lay dying at just twenty-two, in Paterno, to the north of Rome, on January 23, 1002.

Another saint was about to succeed him on the throne in Germany: his cousin Henry III. He was to fight the hordes that were arriving from the East and continually attacking the empire. He gathered a vast army to respond to the aggression of these barbarians. He fought many wars and did so as a Catholic hero with the spirit of faith, trusting more in supernatural assistance than in natural powers. He asked God to win his battles for him. And God showed Henry how pleased He was with his prayers, intervening in miraculous ways on at least one occasion. When the two armies met, Henry's enemies fled, terrorized for no apparent reason. In reality, in order to terrorize the saint's enemies, God had shown them an angel leading a legion of martyrs. The Lord respects the prayers of combatants so much that, on this occasion, He granted them victory without even having to fight. With this victory, the pagan forces of the East had to retreat, and paganism lost its expansionist power.

But another danger was threatening Christendom: the presence of the followers of Arduin of Ivrea (955–1015) in Northern Italy. Arduin possessed a hegemonic desire that led him into conflict with the Church and with the empire. St. Henry, supported by many Italian bishops, entered Arduin's territory, defeated him, and proceeded on to Rome, where he gave homage to Pope Benedict VIII (d. 1024), who crowned him emperor of the Holy Roman Empire of the Germanic Nation. In a ceremony conducted in great splendor, he gifted

Henry a golden globe studded with pearls, representing the emperor's power over the entire world. But St. Henry refused to keep this treasure. Demonstrating his love for the Church, he offered the precious gift to the Abbot of Cluny, St. Odilo.

The role of St. Henry was also decisive in the conversion of King Stephen of Hungary, to whom he offered his sister, Blessed Gisela of Bavaria (980–1065), in marriage. She married Stephen and brought him to the religion of Christ. But the name of St. Henry is inseparable from that of his wife, another great saint — Cunigunde. Both made a vow of chastity, offering their marriage to the Lord. Today, they await the day of resurrection, united in the cathedral of Bamberg, which they had built.

After St. Boniface and Sts. Cyril and Methodius, St. Adalbert (956–997) was a great figure in the Christianization of the people of Eastern and Central Europe. Born in Bohemia, he abandoned his Slavic name Vojtech to take that of his protector, Archbishop Adalbert. He was a monk and a priest; in 983, he became bishop of Prague. He died a martyr at the hands of the pagans of Prussia near Danzig on April 23, 997. A similar fate awaited the monk St. Bruno of Querfurt in 1009, who, along with his eighteen companions, was martyred near the border between Lithuania and Russia. St. Adalbert was buried in Gniezno, and his veneration spread throughout Poland, Hungary, and especially in Bohemia, where he became a symbol of national identity.

The conversion to Christianity of the Russian people came about in 998, with the baptism of Prince Vladimir I (c. 956–1015). From the beginning of the eleventh century, the term "Rus'" (*Russkaya Zemlye*) signified the territories subject to the princes of Kiev, a Ukrainian city of great strategic importance due to its position at the intersection between the Baltic region, the Byzantine Empire, and the Abbasid Caliphate. In 988, the baptism of Vladimir brought the conversion of Russia to fulfillment. The *Chronicles of the Origins of Russia,* written in the twelfth century, narrate this conversion, which was followed by a widespread diffusion of Byzantine culture. A metropolitan see was erected in Kiev, which became the largest city in eastern Europe.

At the dawn of the year 1000, Christendom had spread to the East, as well as to the North, and Europe experienced a great demographic boom — and consequently, an economic one as well. But the greatest expansion was spiritual, what the chronicler Rudoph Glabro describes as a "white mantle of churches" that seemed to cover the landscape.

The year 1000 inaugurated a period of renewed youth in Europe. The historian Roberto Sabatino Lopez recalls a couplet written in the tenth century in a language that was no longer Latin, but not yet identifiable with any of the modern Romance languages: "*L'alba part umet mar atra sol / poy pasa bigil, mira clar tembras*" (The dawn brings the sun over the dark sea / then passes over the great hill, darkness is illuminated).

Plinio Corrêa de Oliveirawrites:

> [The Church] extended over all of Europe its hierarchical weave, and from the mists of Scotland to the slopes of Vesuvius, there blossomed dioceses, monasteries, and churches — whether cathedral, conventual, or parish — and around them the flocks of Christ.... By the power of these human energies revitalized by grace, kingdoms and noble lineages were born, as well as courtly customs and just laws, congregations and chivalry, Scholasticism and universities, the Gothic style and the songs of the troubadours.

These are our roots, but also our future, because nothing is impossible with the help of God, to those who love the Church and Christendom and who fight on her behalf.

CHAPTER VIII

# The Reform of the Church in the Year 1000

## 1. THE SCOURGES OF THE CHURCH IN THE ELEVENTH CENTURY

Light and shadow are interwoven throughout the history of the Church, although she is always divinely aided by the Holy Spirit, who transforms the shadows into light and leads ultimately to the good.[30]

The fact that supernatural guidance remains active throughout history, allowing the good to ultimately prevail over evil in the end, does not eliminate the tragic dimension of the life of individuals, of peoples, and of the Church itself, in whose existence good and evil, truth and error, are always opposed and in conflict.

This struggle is at times internal, because it can happen, as Paul VI said in a famous discourse, that the smoke of Satan enters the temple of God, that abomination enters the holy place.

This occurred at the end of the first millennium. The coronation of Charlemagne was an extraordinary event: it ushered in the birth of Christendom, by which, according to Leo XIII, "the philosophy of the Gospel governed states" (Encyclical *Immortale Dei* of November 1, 1885).

Yet once the empire of Charlemagne had come to an end (888), during that tumultuous epoch in which the first Christian nations were forming, a period

---

[30] Radio Maria, conversation on March 21, 2012.

began that Cardinal Baronius, in his *Annals*, defined as the "century of iron" — gloomy and dark because of its barbarity and rampant wickedness.

The great historian Cardinal Baronius warned his readers not to be scandalized if they were to see the abomination in the very sanctuary of the Church, but to consider the Divine Power that impeded the complete ruin of ecclesiastical society in that century.

This was a sad page in the history of the Church, which saw the succession, between 882 and 1046, of forty-five popes and anti-popes, fifteen of whom were deposed, and fourteen others who were assassinated, imprisoned, or exiled. One pope, Stephen VI (896–897), exhumed the cadaver of his predecessor Formosus (891–896), who had already been resting in the atrium of St. Peter's for nine months. Stephen presided over an actual trial against the deceased pontiff, held in the Lateran Basilica. The body of Formosus, still dressed in his vestments, was brought before a council of priests and bishops belonging to Stephen's faction. The cadaver was made to sit on a chair while a deacon responded to the accusations levied against his name. At the end of this macabre scene, Stephen condemned the memory of Formosus to perpetual infamy and declared all the acts of his pontificate null and void. After having him stripped of his vestments, he severed the three fingers used to impart the papal blessing, and had his desecrated corpse thrown in the Tiber. Later, the faction opposing Stephen had him imprisoned and then strangled to death. After this episode, the Roman clergy and populace remained divided into two parties, the Formosians and the Anti-Formosians, that disputed over the papacy for many long years.

Was the assistance of the Holy Spirit to the Church lacking during these years? Certainly not — in this dark period, during which unworthy representatives ascended to the papal throne, the Holy Spirit aided the Church just as He did when, as Cardinal Hergenröther writes, "throughout the entire first half of the tenth century, everything seemed shaken from its proper state; secular corruption seemed to inundate the Church and its strength seemed obliviated."

Two scourges devastated the Church from the tenth to the eleventh century: simony and the moral degeneration of the clergy.

The term and concept of simony derive its origin from the sacrilegious proposal made to the apostles by Simon Magus (Acts 8:12–24), a Samaritan known for his magical arts. He offered the apostles money to obtain from them the power to lay hands on Christians and communicate the gifts of the Holy Spirit. Simony, then, as St. Thomas Aquinas puts it, is "the premeditated and deliberate intention to buy or sell anything spiritual or that concerns the spiritual" (*Summa Theologica* II, II ae, Q 100).

The Church has always condemned the pretense of buying or selling something imbued with spiritual power. St. Gregory the Great testified in one of his correspondences to the existence of this abuse already in the sixth century, describing simony as a heresy (*simoniaca haeresis*). In the tenth and eleventh centuries, simony manifested in the form of selling ecclesiastical offices and was often tied to the problem of investiture (the allocation of ecclesiastical offices or benefices by secular authorities). This was a problem with the powers that belonged to secular authorities in matters concerning the Church, and, more generally, of a problem in relations between the Church and the state.

The other grave problem in that period was Nicolaism, a term that refers to the cohabitation of bishops and priests with women. The practice took its name from the Nicolaitans, mentioned in the letters to the churches of Ephesus and Pergamon (Rev. 2:6, 14–16) as "mendacious apostles" who presumed to have prophetic charisms but practiced immorality.

St. Irenaeus calls them disciples of Nicolas, one of the first seven deacons of the Church of Jerusalem (Acts 6:5–6), and considers them to be a branch of Gnosticism. In the eleventh and twelfth centuries, the term was used to stigmatize infractions against the rule of celibacy instituted for the clergy. This moral dissoluteness was not limited to the concubinage of the clergy, but unfortunately produced an even more abominable expression in the "cancer of the sodomitic infection"—the homosexuality among clergymen—which, as St. Peter Damian wrote in his *Liber Gomorrhanus*, raged "like a bloodied beast in the sheepfold of Christ."

Even in periods of doctrinal and moral crisis for the Church, however, the truth of Christ and His law remained immutable, and the Church continued to be holy in her dogma, in her sacraments, and in the souls that the Holy Spirit filled with His grace.

The Church is not occasionally, but constantly, under the influence of the Holy Spirit, who acts through ecclesiastical authority, as well as through the charisms distributed to all its members. And if it is true that the main beneficiaries of this assistance are the ministers of the teaching Church, the historian must never forget that the assistance of the Holy Spirit is expressed above all in sanctity, which, as Dom Guéranger explains, is distributed by the Holy Spirit throughout all the members of the Mystical Body.

## 2. ITALIAN REFORMERS

In the eleventh century, the Holy Spirit found in monasteries the spiritual resources needed to exit this profound crisis. In those centuries, there was in fact a prodigious rise and expansion of abbeys and convents spreading throughout Europe the law and spirit of the gospel. The roots of this flourishing are found in the works of St. Benedict of Nursia, whom we have already discussed.

The Benedictine family continued to grow throughout the ages, according to Dom Guéranger, and from the trunk of this massive tree were born four branches to which the Holy Spirit gave life and fecundity for many centuries: the Camaldolese, the work of Romuald; Cluny, the work of Oddo; John Gualbert's Vallombrosa; and Citeaux, the work of Robert of Molesme.

St. Romuald (c. 952–1027), son of Duke Sergio of Ravenna, entered the Benedictine monastery of Sant'Apollinare in Classe around 972, in the hopes of expiating a crime committed by his father, who had challenged his brother to a duel and killed him. Romuald, who was only seventeen, was a witness to this duel, and it left a terrible impression on him. This dramatic experience led him to the Lord, and in 1012, he founded the Camaldolese in Tuscany, whose constitution was redacted by Blessed Rudolfo around 1080, more than fifty years after the death of St. Romuald.

St. Romuald's disciple, St. John Gualbert (985–1073), founded the Order of the Vallombrosians in Tuscany in 1038; they were located not far from Camaldoli and shared its cenobitic character. Gualbert, like Romuald, was of noble birth, and he became a monk following some extraordinary events connected to the pardon he offered to the murderer of his brother. John Gualbert and his followers in Vallombrosa were major figures in the fight against simony, which resulted in the removal of Pietro Mezzabarba, the bishop of Florence, through the efforts of the Vallombrosian monk Pietro Igneus.

This reforming spirit was also manifested in St. Peter Damian (1007–1072), abbot of the monastery of Fonte Avellana, who was later nominated cardinal by Pope Stephen IX. Born in Ravenna and a follower of St. Romuald, Peter Damian retired to the hermitage at Fonte Avellana, transforming it into a center of austere and penitential spirituality, in contrast to the general relaxation of customs common to the clergy of his time. During the pontificate of Leo IX, he composed and sent to the pope his *Liber Gomorrhanus*, in which he laid bare the guilt of the clergy, beginning with the plague of homosexuality, and petitioned the pope to suppress this horrible wickedness. In the face of the Church's profound crisis, Peter Damian, in 1057, obeyed the wishes of the pope and left his monastery, accepting the nomination to become cardinal bishop of Ostia, near Rome, and committing himself to even greater responsibility in the difficult work of reforming the Church.

Speaking about St. Peter Damian in his general address of September 9, 2009, Benedict XVI said:

> [He] was a monk to his depths, taking on forms of austerity that today might seem to us excessive. In this way, however, he made of monastic life an eloquent witness to the primacy of God and a call to everyone to walk in the path of sanctity, free of every compromise with evil. He exhausted himself, with lucid integrity and great severity, for the reform of the Church of his time. He gave all his spiritual and physical energy to Christ and to the Church, remaining always, as he liked to call himself, Petrus, *ultimus monachorum servus* (Peter, the lowest servant of the monks).

The great twentieth-century author Plinio Corrêa de Oliveira recalls that St. Peter Damian disseminated a practice of penance called the "discipline," a sort of whip made of knotted cords. Perhaps we struggle to understand this practice today. "But spreading the practice," writes Professor Corrêa de Oliveira, "was one of the great services that St. Peter Damian rendered the Church, because in this way he promoted the spirit of penance."

The spirit of penance, according to Corrêa de Oliveira, "is much more than physical pain or the act of humility tied to the use of a specific instrument such as the discipline. The spirit of penance is the comprehension and adherence to the general principles on which the idea of penance is founded." What are these principles? Corrêa de Oliveira continues:

> Man is born with Original Sin, and must therefore combat the instincts and passions derived from it. Man is a sinner, and sin is an offense against the justice of the Divine Majesty, which requires reparation. This reparation must be a suffering proportional to the offense committed. Often this offense is an illicit pleasure we did not want to renounce. Just like the thief who has stolen money and is forced to return it, so the one who has enjoyed stolen pleasures to which he had no right before God must also carry out restitution, must restore equilibrium on the scales of Divine Justice. A person with the spirit of penance has understood the gravity of his sins. But even one who has no particular sin to

expiate can do penance. Penance is useful in this case to fight against the negative inclinations of the flesh and against the rebellious tendency of human pride.

Modern man abhors doing penance, and even more so, the spirit of penance. In most cases, films, novels, and social settings are thousands of miles away from the spirit of penance. The invitations to exacerbate pride and sensuality seem omnipresent, on the other hand. By spreading the use of the discipline, the hairshirt, and other instruments of penance, St. Peter Damian rendered us a service by helping us to conform to the spirit of penance and to remind us that we must fight against our bad inclinations.

## 3. THE SPIRIT OF CLUNY

The most profound of the monastic reforms was that of Cluny, destined to go down in history for its grandiose and lasting work of religious renewal in the Church.

    The Abbey of Cluny was founded on September 11, 910, in Burgundy, by William the Pious, Duke of Aquitaine; he conferred "on the holy apostles Peter and Paul what he possessed in Cluny," and determined that a monastery would be built, and that monks would gather there to follow the *Rule* of St. Benedict. The duke entrusted its fate to Berno (910–926), a man of great virtue who brought to the new monastery a group of monks who took their inspiration from the ancient Benedictine traditions. A series of holy abbots succeeded Berno at Cluny, and they spread their spirit throughout Christendom, transforming the men and the institutions of the Middle Ages.

    Blessed Berno's confrere, St. Odo, succeeded him as abbot from 926 to 942. Odo was continually traveling, seeking to spread and restore the Benedictine Rule. In Rome, in 931, Pope John XI took the monastery under his protection and gave to Odo full authority to oversee the reform of Cluny "in times when almost all monasteries are unfaithful to their rule." In just one monk, one found in full all the various virtues that were thinly spread throughout the other monasteries. According to Odo's biographer, "Jesus, in His goodness, drawing from the various monastic gardens, formed in one little place a paradise to irrigate from its wellspring the hearts of the faithful."

    St. Odo fostered a particular devotion to the Blessed Sacrament, and deplored the fact that this "sacrosanct mystery of the Body of the Lord, in which the entire salvation of the world consists," would be in his age, as unfortunately it is in ours, celebrated negligently by priests. Benedict XVI remembered St. Odo on September 2, 2009: "St. Odo was a true spiritual guide for both the monks and the faithful of his age. In the face of the 'vastness of vices' throughout society, the remedy he proposed with great determination was that of a radical change of life founded on humility, austerity, detachment from ephemeral matters, and attachment to eternal ones."

The foundational charter of Cluny gave the abbot the right to choose his own successor, and thus Odo designated Aymard (942–954), who was succeeded by Majolus (954–994). Born when Cluny was founded, and enjoying eighty-four years of life (910–994), Majolus held the role of abbot for 40 years during the second half of the tenth century, until 994. From 994 until 1109, over the course of 115 years, Cluny had only two abbots: St. Odilo, who sustained Cluny for 55 years (994–1049), and St. Hugh, who governed for 60 years (1049–1109). This continuity, along with the wisdom and sanctity of the two abbots, was, as the historian Ivan Gobry observed, the primary cause of the flourishing of this order.

St. Odilo, to whom we owe the celebration of All Souls' Day, was also the inspiration for the "movement of peace and the truce of God" that characterized Christian spirituality in the tenth and eleventh centuries. Hugo took the abbey to the height of its splendor, thanks to the relations he fostered with princes and sovereigns and the support he enjoyed from the popes who issued from the abbey under his governance: Blessed Urban II (1088–1099) and his successor Pasqual II (1099–1118). We also owe to Hugo the erection of a magnificent church, the largest in the world at that time.

In his address on November 11, 2009, Benedict XVI recalled that Cluny deliberately emphasized the central role that liturgy holds in Christian life:

> The monks of Cluny dedicated themselves with great love and care to the celebration of the liturgical hours, the singing of the Psalms, processions as devout as they were solemn, and above all, to the celebration of the Holy Mass; they promoted sacred music, desiring that architecture and art contributed to the beauty and solemnity of the rites; they enriched the liturgical calendar with special celebrations, such as the Commemoration of All the Faithful Departed at the beginning of November, which we have just celebrated; and they encouraged the veneration of the Virgin Mary. Great importance was reserved for the liturgy, because the monks of

Cluny were convinced that it was a participation in the heavenly liturgy. And the monks felt responsible for interceding at the altar of God for the living and the dead, given that many of the faithful asked them insistently to be remembered in their prayers.

Charlemagne once asked his wise minister and chaplain, Alcuin, "What is the liturgy?" The monk replied, "The liturgy is the joy of God!" The liturgy is the joy of God, explained Dom Gérard Calvet, because it is the public worship that His only Son, the Eternal Priest, renders Him; the priest who celebrates the Mass acts *in persona Christi*, making present on the altar, in an unbloody form, the sacrifice of the Cross. Moreover, the liturgy, affirms Dom Guéranger, is the "joy of the people," or rather the joy of men who have become sons of God, because men are made for God; they need redemption and sanctity to rediscover or maintain contact with the Holy God, and liturgy procures this for them. "In it, the Holy Spirit had the artistry to concentrate, eternalize, and manifest throughout the Body of Christ the inalterable fullness of the work of redemption, and all the supernatural wealth of the past, present, and future of the Church."

In the Abbey of Cluny, and in the monasteries that depended on it, the life of the monks was considered a continual preparation for the judgment of God. The monks, however, did not isolate themselves from the world for their own individual salvation but for that of all of society and for the glory of God. The monasteries of Cluny would become islands of prayer in the tumult of medieval society.

Cluny introduced other important innovations to Christendom:

✠ Every abbey was closely connected to its "mother house," whose abbot governed it. He was elected by the monks of Cluny but was head of the entire *family* that depended on Cluny. Cluny represented the first religious order in the history of the Church, understood as a group of religious houses having the same rule and dependent on the same superior.

✠ The monastery of Cluny, and the communities dependent on it, were recognized as being beyond the jurisdiction of local bishops and instead answered directly to the Roman pontiff. This produced a special bond with the See of Peter, and, thanks precisely to the protection and encouragement of the pontiff, the ideals of purity and fidelity that the Cluny reform sought to carry out were rapidly established.

⊹ Moreover, the abbots were elected without any interference by secular authorities, in contrast to what occurred in other settings. This gave power not only to the monastery of Cluny, but also to the papacy, to resist the lay powers that were strengthening in that period.

The monastic reform of Cluny spread rapidly throughout Italy, Spain, and England. At the beginning of the twelfth century, when Cluny reached its greatest power, the congregation numbered nearly twelve hundred monasteries, of which nine hundred were in France. Through monastic channels, important practices and devotions were developed and disseminated: the evening singing of the *Salve Regina*, devotion to the *Mater misericordiae*, the Office of the Virgin Mary, the Mass celebrated in her honor on Saturdays, servitude to the Virgin Mary, and even fervent devotion to the angels who, as it is said, mixed their voices with those of the monks in praise of God that rose unceasingly from these islands of sanctity.

## 4. St. Gregory VII

One of the greatest services the monks rendered to the Church was that of assuming the papacy. The Chair of St. Peter was occupied between 1057 and 1118 by five popes from Benedictine monasteries: Stephen IX (1057–1058), St. Gregory VII (1073–1085), Blessed Vittore III (1086–1087), Blessed Urban II (1088–1099), and Paschal II (1099–1118). Here we must pause to consider St. Gregory VII, Hildebrand of Soana (c. 1020–1085), who was the greatest reformer of his time and one of the greatest popes in history. He succeeded five popes who, with his assistance, had fought for what would later be called the Gregorian Reform. But none of them encountered the success or the difficulties that Gregory VII did.

Despite opposition from German and Lombard bishops, and despite his own reluctance, he was elected to the papacy on April 29, 1073, at fifty years of age. Upon election he stated, "I want you to know, dear brothers, what many of you already know: that we have been placed in this position and constrained, willingly or unwillingly, to announce the truth and justice to all people, above all to the Christian nations, because the Lord said *shout*, do not tire of shouting, raise your voice like a trumpet and announce to My people its crimes."

The new pope bravely faced the moral evil of his time. Just a few months after his election in 1074, Gregory summoned a council in Rome that approved two important decrees: one against priests who transgress the law of celibacy and the second against simony. He then sent out legates with letters to every corner of Christendom, insisting that bishops hold councils to promulgate observance of the decrees. In a second council in 1075, he condemned the lay investiture of bishops.

For Gregory, secular authorities were primarily responsible for the religious and moral decadence of the clergy, and a close relationship existed between simony and the policy of investiture. Public powers (the emperor, kings, dukes, and counts) nominated prelates, and at times ordained them, conferring upon them their crozier or ring, the sign of their religious office. Gregory's aim was to recover the dignity and independence of the episcopacy by opposing lay investiture by secular powers.

King Henry IV, as well as the clergy in Germany and Lombardy, rebelled against Gregory. The pope summoned Henry to Rome with the threat of excommunication if he refused to come. Henry then convoked a council at Worms and allied with the prefect of Rome, Cencius Frangipane, to depose Gregory. On Christmas Eve of 1075, Cencius entered the Basilica of St. Mary Major where the pope was celebrating Mass. With his men-at-arms, he pulled Gregory away from the altar, wounded his head, and took him prisoner. But only a few hours later, the people liberated the pontiff. Gregory held another council in 1076, at which he solemnly excommunicated Henry and declared his German and Italian subjects to be released of their bonds of fidelity. Writing to the German princes, he warned them not to take advantage of the king's excommunication but to seek his repentance.

The papal sentence was a terrible blow to Henry's power in Germany; many of the lords subject to him rebelled against him and summoned an assembly to nominate his successor. Recognizing the danger he was in, Henry set off for Italy to seek reconciliation with the pope. Gregory, in the meantime, had left Rome to travel to an assembly taking place in Augsburg, where he was guest in the Tuscan castle of Countess Matilda of Canossa, a close friend. It was January when Henry reached the castle. At first, Gregory refused to welcome Henry, who had arrived on foot wearing a cowl of coarse wool. The pope was indifferent to his unexpected penance, but the countess Matilda and Abbot Hugh of Cluny implored the pontiff not to dismiss the supplications of the repentant king. After three days of waiting, Henry was admitted to the papal presence, and Gregory absolved him of his excommunication on January 28, 1077.

Nearly seven centuries after Emperor Theodosius had kneeled in repentance before Bishop Ambrose of Milan, another emperor was kneeling before the religious authority of the Church. But Henry's repentance, unlike that of Theodosius, was not sincere. The sovereign did not remain true to his promise, taking up arms against Rudolf of Swabia, who had been elected emperor in his stead by the German princes.

Gregory VII reacted with determination, claiming papal authority. He synthesized his position in the *Dictatus Papae*, a collection of writings that explicate the relationships that must exist between the Holy Roman Empire and the papacy. The second proposition states that only the monarchy of the Roman pontiff "can in full justice be called universal." This universality refers to the spiritual sphere; the pope was not presuming that he should govern the empire directly. He was vindicating his right to exercise a decisive influence over society. Peter, according to Gregory, was proclaimed "sovereign over the kingdoms of the world," and to him God "subjugated all principalities and powers of the earth." Kings and emperors are not exempt from the divine and natural law to which all men are subject and of which the Church is custodian. This principle continues to be valid today, even in an age like ours, in which the ancient sovereigns have been replaced by modern parliaments with pretensions even more absolute and arbitrary than those back then.

A war was declared therefore between those faithful to the emperor and those faithful to the pope. Gregory found support in Matilda of Canossa (1046–1115), an extraordinary woman of Lombard ancestry. Matilda was married to Godfrey of Lorena, known as the Hunchback, who was assassinated in 1076. After the death of her mother, she had to govern her vast state alone. Not having heirs, she donated the territories to Gregory, a direct challenge to the emperor, given the rights that the sovereign claimed over them as feudal lord and also as her close relative.

Henry IV summoned a council in Brixen, at which he had the pope deposed, and decreed that Matilda be deposed and banished from the empire as well. The emperor traveled to Rome and besieged the pope at Castel Sant'Angelo. Gregory was deposed, and the anti-pope Clement was solemnly enthroned in his place. On Easter, Henry, along with his wife Bertha, received the imperial crown at the hands of the anti-pope. Robert of Guiscard then came to the aid of Gregory VII, but the sack of the city unleashed by the Normans provoked the reaction of the people, who, incited by the faction opposed to the pope, rose up in arms. Protected by Robert's men, Gregory was forced to flee and went into voluntary exile at Salerno. There, he renewed the excommunication of Henry and the anti-pope Clement, and he died shortly thereafter on May 24, 1085. It is said that his last words were *dilexi iustitiam, et odivi iniquitatem, propterea morior in exilio*, echoing the words of the psalmist: "I loved justice and hated iniquity, therefore I die in exile" (Ps. 44).

While Gregory VII was forced into exile, Countess Matilda of Canossa unexpectedly stormed the imperial army on July 2, 1084, at the battle of Sorbara, near Modena. She had succeeded in forming a coalition favorable to the papacy. She died in July 1115, after reigning for forty years. Her body was transferred to St. Peter's Basilica in the seventeenth century, where it still lies today.

It was thanks to a strong woman like Matilda of Canossa that Gregory VII, apparently vanquished, was able to triumph with the strength of his gospel message. This demonstrates the importance of the spiritual bonds that have so often brought saints together throughout history.

The message of St. Gregory VII is summarized in these words from his correspondence:

> God is our witness that, against depraved sovereigns and impious priests, no personal advantage motivated us, nor any worldly respect, but rather consideration for our office and for the authority of the apostolic see, which torments us every day. Better for us to face, if necessary, the fitting death of the flesh at the hand of tyrants than to consent with our silence, out of fear or convenience, to the ruin of the Law of Christ. We know, in fact, that our holy fathers said, "He who, in consideration of his office, does not oppose wicked men, has consented to them; and whoever does not eliminate the evils which must be suppressed, has committed them."

## 5. WHAT IS THE REFORM OF THE CHURCH?

The so-called investiture conflict lasted from the pontificate of Gregory VII to the Concordat of Worms in 1122. The term "investiture," which appeared only in the eleventh century, refers to the conferring of the symbols of the ring and crozier to the elected bishop. The problem of investiture is not a question of the selection of the bishop, but of the bestowal of power.

According to Catholic doctrine, the bishop is the successor to the apostles in the ordinary governance of individual churches (dioceses) under the authority of the Roman pontiff. It is historically verified that since the beginning of the second century, the "monarchical" episcopacy has been in place as a constitutional norm of the Church founded on the will of God (*iure divino*). St. Ignatius of Antioch (d. 107) attested that all the churches to which he wrote were endowed with just one bishop, recognized and venerated as their head.

The early Christian period had initiated a tradition by which the bishops would be nominated by the clergy, in harmony with the community of the faithful, and consecrated by the metropolitan of the province or by other bishops. During the Barbarian Invasions, the royal authorities actively intervened in episcopal elections. After Charlemagne, the *episcopatus* assumed a feudal character. Just as the king invested the civil office along with its constituent domains, so too was he given the power to invest the bishop with the rights attached to the episcopate, as well as with his religious functions. The fact that the king would confer the crozier as well as the ring, pronouncing the words *accipe ecclesiam*, means that the sovereign laid claim to the attribution of the *episcopatus* in its totality, without distinction between the spiritual and the temporal. In theory, the principle of canonical election remained intact, but it was emptied of content. The bestowal by royalty of the office of the bishopric — that is, of its annuities, its lands, and its honors — had been transformed into the bestowal of the episcopal see itself as an ecclesiastical office.

Against this intrusion of secular power, St. Gregory VII affirmed with clarity and force the rights of the Church. When, in 1119, the archbishop of Vienne, Guy of Burgundy, was elected pope, taking the name Callixtus II, he reinstated the teachings of Gregory VII. From the very start of his papacy, in a great synod held in Rheims in the presence of more than four hundred bishops, Callixtus II formally renewed the condemnation of investiture and the excommunication of Henry V. As the pope was pronouncing the words of excommunication, the bishops broke the candles they were holding to emphasize the solemnity of the anathema.

The new pope went to work in favor of peace in the Church, and after long negotiations, he signed, on September 23, 1122, the Concordat of Worms, which established that bishops would be elected by the clergy and the people, without imperial intervention, and that upon taking possession of their bishopric, they would receive temporal investiture from the monarch.

The emperor renounced the investiture of prelates with the ring and the crozier (symbols of spiritual authority) while maintaining the right to temporal investiture with the scepter. The agreement recognized the direct, universal supremacy of the Church on the spiritual plane and its indirect power in the temporal sphere. Callixtus II then summoned the fourth ecumenical council in the Lateran from March 18 to 27, 1123, which was also the first full assembly of bishops held in the West (all previous ecumenical councils had been held in the East). The agreement between Church and empire was solemnly ratified at the council, ecclesiastical discipline was restored with a series of canons against simony and in favor of priestly celibacy, and the holy war against the Saracens was promoted.

One must ask at this point what was, in essence, the reform of the Church from which all of this had arisen? *Reform* is the rectification of behaviors and the elimination of abuses that, over time, have proliferated; it is the return to a primitive spirit that has been lost, to the original laws that have been forgotten; it is the rediscovery of a lost identity. Whoever sets out to reform has gone in search of himself, wanting to substitute the old man with the new man, although it is the very same man.

Reform, when it is authentic, is inspired by the Holy Spirit and by the collaboration between Divine Grace and human will. Reform is opposed to revolution; it is continuity with the past, while revolution marks a rupture between past and present. Protestantism presented itself as a reform of the Church, but it was a revolution that began within the Church and concluded outside of it and against it. Reform is progress that does not deny the Tradition of the Church, but rather is nourished by it. Reform is, by definition, a return to the tradition of doctrine, in spirit and in customs. Everything that, in the name of a pseudo-reform, opposes tradition is really a revolution that, as such, must be fought.

St. Gregory VII in the eleventh century, St. Pius V in the sixteenth century, and St. Pius X in the twentieth century were all great reformer popes and great defenders of Sacred Tradition. It is moving to read the epistolary of two saints: Blessed Cardinal Schuster and St. Giovanni Calabria, who welcomed a profound reform of the Church in the 1950s in the years preceding the Second Vatican Council, which also proposed, without attaining its goal, a "reform" of the Church.

The pontificate of St. Gregory VII offers us a model of an authentic spiritual and moral reform of the Church, founded on the fullness of the authority of Peter's successors. From this Gregorian and Cluniac reforming spirit was born the cry "God wants it!" regarding the heroism of the Crusades.

Historians connect the First Crusade, announced by another pope from Cluny, Urban II, to the great reform movement of the Church in the eleventh century. Until the time of St. Catherine of Siena's own appeals for reform, the idea of the crusade would be inseparable from that of the renewal of society and the Church. The militant spirit of the crusaders and the penitential spirit of the reformers were born of the same love of the Cross that the hedonism of the day rejected, just as it does in our age, a thousand years later. Once more, only through the love of the Cross will we find the resources for a profound reform of the Church, which is also a crusade against its internal and external enemies.

# CHAPTER IX

# The Spirit of the Crusades

## 1. THE ORIGINS OF THE CRUSADES

The Crusades represent the culmination of the new civilization that arose at the dawn of the year 1000.[31]

By the term "crusade" is meant, in its strict sense, the military expeditions undertaken by the papacy with the aim of liberating the Holy Sepulcher between the eleventh and the thirteenth centuries. Historically speaking, they take place between the Council of Piacenza in 1095, at which Blessed Urban II launched the first appeal for the Crusades, and the fall of Acre, the last Christian bulwark in the Holy Land, in 1291.

In a broader sense, the Crusades can be understood as armed undertakings conducted in defense of the Faith and of Christendom. In this case, the Spanish Reconquista against the Moors, which was carried out over the course of eight hundred years—from the Battle of Covadonga in 722 to the fall of Granada in 1492—belongs to the Crusades. One might also include in later centuries the battles of Lepanto (1571), Vienna (1683), and Budapest (1686). The Crusades, in a narrow sense, were something different and more specific. At Covadonga and Lepanto, Christian knights fought to defend their faith but also their own land, threatened by Islam. The war in the Holy Land, however, was

---

[31] Radio Maria, conversation on April 18, 2012.

conducted for eminently spiritual motives. It was not a war of aggression undertaken to impose a faith, as Islam had done. The crusaders never carried out
forced conversions.

That which they promoted was only the liberation of the holy places that by
right belonged to Christians and had been wrongfully occupied by Muslims. It
is important to emphasize this: the main objective of the crusaders was never of
a political or economic order, but always eminently religious — the reconquest
of the Holy Land, or, later on, the preservation of the Christian Kingdom of Jerusalem created by the First Crusade. If the Spanish Reconquista and the Holy
Leagues promoted by St. Pius V and Blessed Innocent XI were noble enterprises, loftier still was the heroism of the Crusades, which still today appears as
one of the most luminous pages of Church history.

To understand the origins of the Crusades, one must first remember the
close ties that existed in the first millennium between Europe and the Holy
Land. In the land where Jesus was born, during the reign of Emperor Constantine, his mother, Helena, had discovered the wood of the true Cross and many
other important relics. From that time, Eastern and Western Christians never
stopped pouring into the Holy Land on pilgrimage to adore Christ in His sepulcher. From the furthest regions of Gaul and Germany, as well as from the Near
and Far East, thousands of Christians flocked to drink from the wellsprings of
their faith. The pilgrims took sea routes that departed from ports along the
Mediterranean, as well as land routes that were longer and less secure, crossing
the Byzantine Empire, Anatolia, and Syria. These pilgrimages, which required
crossing rivers and mountains in the worst of circumstances, were not inter-
rupted during the period of the Barbarian Invasions. The political and social
upheavals of those centuries made the Holy City of Jerusalem shine even
brighter, as the customs, rites, and memories of Christianity were preserved.

When the armies of Khosrow, king of Persia, invaded Syria, Palestine, and
Egypt, the Holy City fell to his power as well. The conquerors profaned the
churches and made off with the Cross of the Savior as booty. But the emperor
of the East, Heraclius (641–710), was able to defeat the Persians and liberate
Jerusalem. He brought back on his own shoulders, to the very summit of Calvary, the wood of the true Cross, which he considered the most glorious trophy
of his victories.

Worse disasters awaited Christians, however. At the beginning of the seventh
century, the religion of Muhammad appeared and promised its followers world

conquest. After seizing Persia and Syria, Muslims occupied Egypt, and from there reached all the way to the Atlantic shores. In 638, Jerusalem was taken by Caliph Omar (682–720), successor to the "Prophet." For Muslims, Jerusalem was a sacred city, because they believed that Muhammad had been led there by the Archangel Gabriel and then taken to the throne of Allah in paradise.

Throughout the lands subjected to Islam, Christians had the status of *dhimmi* and were deprived of their principal rights. They could continue to practice their worship in private, though without disseminating it and without criticizing Islam. They had to remain subject to their Islamic conquerors, to whom they had to pay a special tax just because they were Christians. They were even prohibited from riding horses and carrying arms. The sign of their *dhimmi* status was a leather belt which they could never remove. Pilgrims continued to come to the Holy Land, however, recalling that Jesus had been tortured and crucified in the places they were visiting.

At the beginning of the eleventh century, among the Turkmen who had converted to Islam in the Eurasian Steppe, there arose a new people united under a leader named Seljuk (d. 1010). His descendants, who called themselves Seljuks, occupied Persia and Iraq. In 1071, the Seljuk sultan of Baghdad defeated the Byzantine army at the Battle of Manzikert and captured the emperor of the East, Romanus IV (c. 1030–1072). As a consequence of this victory, Muslims occupied most of the Asiatic provinces of Byzantium. The situation of relative tolerance toward Christians that had developed over time now ended abruptly, and the Turks were now set on conquering Byzantium.

The Byzantine Empire was going through a phase of decadence. After the reign of Heraclius, eleven emperors were assassinated in their palace in Constantine, six retired to monasteries, and many were mutilated, blinded, or exiled. Corruption was destroying an empire that, over the centuries, had distanced itself increasingly from Rome, to the point of provoking a religious schism. Meanwhile, in the West, a new Holy Empire had arisen: that of Charlemagne and later of the Ottos in Germany.

At the beginning of the second millennium, Byzantium seemed to be in its death throes, while Europe was experiencing a tumultuous youth, one expression of which was the movement of spiritual reform launched by the Abbey of Cluny.

St. Gregory VII, who came from Cluny, had devised a plan to gather a great Christian army against the Turks. The liberation of the sacred sites represented, in his eyes, the culmination of the reform of the Church to which he had dedicated his entire pontificate.

In those same years, a pilgrim of unknown origins called Peter the Hermit had begun to travel throughout France, preaching with fiery words the necessity of aiding Christians in the East. He had been to Jerusalem and was moved by the sad state in which he had found the sacred sites. "Asia is under the power of the Muslims, all the East has fallen into servitude. No earthly power can assist us," the old patriarch of Jerusalem had told him through his tears. Peter replied by swearing that he would do all he could to convince the warriors in the West to intervene.

Peter the Hermit met Pope Urban II (1088–1099) in Rome, then crossed the Alps into France. He traveled on a mule, covered by a mantle of coarse material and clutching a crucifix. He preached with impetuous eloquence, from city to city, describing the sad conditions in the East and calling those in the West to liberate the Holy Land.

In those same days, the emperor in the East, Alexios I Komnenos (1081–1118), sent Urban II an ambassador to plead the cause of Constantinople, which was soon to fall to the terrible domination of the Turks.

Pope Urban II, like Gregory VII, had been formed spiritually by the ideals of Cluny and was very sensitive to this problem. In March 1095, he held a council in Piacenza, at which he announced his decision to convoke a synod that would sound an appeal to all of Christendom.

## 2. URBAN II AND THE COUNCIL OF CLERMONT

The council was held in the French town of Clermont, in November 1095. The city was packed with princes, ambassadors, and prelates who had hastened there from every part of Christendom. The assembly, under the direction of the pope, began with considerations of the reform of the clergy and ecclesiastical discipline, and then passed to matters regarding life within Christendom. A previous decree of the pope's had placed under the Church's protection orphans, workers, and all the weaker elements of the population. Then, during the tenth session on November 27, Urban II finally addressed the issue of holy war.

Peter the Hermit, sitting at his side, spoke first, describing the profanation and sacrilege he had witnessed. Urban II then spoke. He told of the outrages the Christian faith had suffered and concluded in a vibrant tone:

People of the Franks, people from beyond the mountains, people illustrious in many of your actions, chosen and loved by God, distinct from all other nations, both for the position of your country and for your observance of the Catholic Faith, and for the honor rendered to the Holy Church, to you our discourse and our exhortation is addressed.

We want you to know the grim reason that has brought us to your lands; what need of yours and of all the faithful has attracted us here. Sorrowful news has come to us from Jerusalem and Constantinople: the Muslims, a people so different from us, a people estranged from God, a race of inconstant heart, whose spirit was not faithful to the Lord, have invaded the lands of those Christians, have devastated them with iron, with theft, and with fire, and have taken as prisoners some of the inhabitants; others they have killed in miserable massacres, and they have either destroyed the churches of God from their foundations or have transformed them for their own religious worship.

After having described the massacres perpetrated by the Muslims, the pope continued:

To whom, therefore, does the burden of taking vengeance and reconquering these lands fall, if not to you to whom God has granted glory in combat, greatness in spirit, agility in limbs, and the power to humiliate those who resist you?

May your ancestors' feats, the rectitude and greatness of your king Charlemagne and of his son Louis, and of your other sovereigns who destroyed the pagan kingdoms and expanded the borders of the Church, goad your souls to action. Above all, may the Holy Sepulcher of the Lord our Savior, which lies in the hands of unclean people, and the sacred sites now shamefully and irreverently fouled by their filth, urge you to action. O strongest of warriors, sons of undefeated fathers, do not be degenerate, but remember the valor of your predecessors; and if the sweet affection of your children, parents, or consorts detains you, return to what the Lord says in His Gospel: "Whoever loves father or mother more than me, is not worthy of me. Whoever shall leave father, or mother, or wife, or children, or fields for love of my name shall receive a hundredfold in return and shall have eternal life." [...] May your internal feuds cease, your conflicts fall away, the wars abate, and all dissension and enmity come to an end. Take up the road to the Holy Sepulcher, tear that land from those wicked people and subjugate them:

that land was given to the sons of Israel, as the Scriptures say, where milk and honey flow.

O most beloved brothers, today you see manifested in us what the Lord says in the Gospel, "Where two or three are gathered in my name, there am I in their midst." If the Lord God had not inspired your thoughts, your voice would not be unanimous; even though it may have resounded with a different timbre, its origin was nevertheless the same — God has aroused it, God has inspired it in your hearts. May this be your voice and your war cry, since it comes from God. When you assault your bellicose enemies, may this be the unanimous cry of all the soldiers of God: *"Deus vult!* God wills it!"

The assembly of the faithful, swept by a supernatural enthusiasm, responded to the pope's words in a unanimous cry: *"Deus vult!* God wills it!"

Cardinal Gregory, who was to become Pope Innocent II, pronounced the formula of general absolution, and all those present kneeled, beat their breasts, and received forgiveness for their sins. They placed red crosses of cloth or silk on their garments. Ademar of Monteuil, bishop of Le Puy-en-Velay, who had been a knight prior to his ordination, was the first to take the cross from the hands of the pope. Bishops, barons, and knights imitated his example. From then on, those who committed themselves to the fight against the infidels were called "crusaders."

The Christians who responded to the appeal of Urban II considered themselves pilgrims in arms. The pope introduced the crusader's vow, which could only be unbound upon arrival in the Holy Land, and granted to participants, like those who fought the Moors in Spain, the remission of the temporal punishments imposed by the Church on sinners. This was the origin of the plenary indulgence.

Urban II also placed the families and belongings of the crusaders under the protection of the Church and of Sts. Peter and Paul. According to the decrees of the Council of Clermont, the crusaders were exempt from taxes and could not be punished for unpaid debts during their expedition. Joseph-François Michaud, a historian of the Crusades from whom we are drawing most of our information, writes, "It seemed that the French no longer had any other homeland than the Holy Land.... The fire that ignited in France spread to England, still agitated by the recent Norman conquest; to Germany, agitated by the excommunications of Gregory and Urban; to Italy, upset by political strife; and even to Spain, which was fighting the Saracens in its own lands."

The appeal of Urban II gave life to a great religious movement destined to survive for centuries. The crusader army was a tumultuous and colorful throng, made up of warriors of every background and circumstance. Michaud writes:

> Near the cities, under the fortresses, in the plains, in the mountains, tents and pavilions arose for the knights, along with altars for celebrating the Divine Office; everywhere preparations for war were in full swing. On one side, the clanging of arms and the sounding of trumpets could be heard, while on the other, psalms and hymns. From the Tiber to the Atlantic, from the Rhine to the Pyrenees, armies decorated with the cross could be seen, singing in anticipation of their conquests and swearing to exterminate the Saracens. Everywhere one could hear the war cry of the crusaders: *"Deus vult! God wills it!"*

At the Council of Clermont, Urban II had set as the crusaders' date of departure the feast of the Assumption of the following year, August 15, 1096. The princes and captains who guided the army would take various routes and then meet in Constantinople. But in the spring, a multitude of the faithful, lacking all organization besides the guidance of Peter the Hermit and Walter Sans Avoir, departed from the banks of the Meuse and the Mosel, heading toward the Bosphorus, anticipating the departure of the princes and their feudal armies.

En route, they crossed the lands of two peoples, the Hungarians and the Bulgarians, who had recently embraced Christianity but had preserved their warmongering tendencies. The disorganized throng of crusaders clashed violently with them, partly due to their own imprudence. They were dispersed or exterminated between the banks of the Danube and the plains of Bithynia. Peter the Hermit escaped death, while Walter Sans Avoir was slaughtered, along with his troops, in an ambush. The People's Crusade, as it was defined, ended in failure.

In the meantime, in August 1096, the second wave of crusaders began to leave Western Europe. This time it was a disciplined army, guided by the best knights of Christendom. From Central Europe came Robert, count of Flanders and head of the Frisians and Flemish, and Godfrey of Bouillon, Duke of Lower Lorraine, with the brothers Baldwin and Eustace and their cousin Baldwin from Bourg; the French had their champion in Count Hugh of Vermandois, the brother of King Phillip; the Norman princes were guided by

Robert, the firstborn of William the Conqueror, and by the Altavilla, descendants of Robert of Guiscard, who had conquered Apulia and Calabria and protected St. Gregory VII from Henry IV; among the Normans was Bohemond, Prince of Taranto, whom the authors of the time described as exceptionally large in stature and equally exceptional in his mastery of arms; he turned out to be the best strategist of the army, but also the most ambitious. With him was his nephew Tancred, the most religiously devout and chivalrous, along with Godfrey. Tancred's biographer says he was torn between the world's call and that of the gospel, but nothing could stop his warrior's enthusiasm when holy war was declared.

Stephen, count of Blois and Chartres, also took up the cross, considered among the wealthiest lords of his time. It was said that he owned as many castles as there are days in the year. The faithful asked the pope to ride at their head, but he chose as his apostolic legate the bishop Ademar, and nominated Raymond of Saint-Gilles, count of Toulouse, to lead his army; Raymond was a warrior of fifty-five who had had the honor of fighting in Spain next to Cid and of defeating the Moors on numerous occasions under Alfonso the Great. But the person of greatest prominence, known for his amazing physical strength, the purity of his manners, and his prudence as a commander, was Godfrey of Bouillon. One day in Syria, several Arab sheiks wanted to put him to the test, so they challenged him to decapitate an adult camel with one stroke of the sword — immediately the head of the animal rolled at their feet. Michaud writes, "He was always ready to dedicate himself to the cause of the unfortunate and innocent; he was considered a great model by princes and knights, a father to the soldiers, and a pillar of support for the people."

These were the knights whose deeds so many contemporary chroniclers narrated. Many of them were husbands and fathers, owners of estates and castles, yet they turned away from all they had with great generosity and with the knowledge that they were riding toward a doubtful fate, entrusting themselves only to the designs of Divine Providence. This should be sufficient to discredit those legends claiming that the Crusades were economic ventures promoted by avaricious conquerors.

## 3. TOWARD JERUSALEM

The Christian army crossed the Rhone at Lyon, passed over the Alps, marched through Lombardy and Friuli, and set off for Greek territory by way of the savage lands of Dalmatia. At last, they reached Constantinople. The Byzantine emperor had requested the aid of the Latins in defending the capital of the empire. However, he did not share the crusaders' aim to liberate the Holy Land and feared the presence of such a fearsome army in his capital. The dissension between the clergy in Rome and those in Constantinople contributed to the increasing antipathy aroused by differences in habits and customs. This discord provoked frequent clashes in which, as Michaud writes, "the Greeks displayed more treachery than valor and the Latins more valor than moderation."

The crusaders finally left Constantinople and headed toward the fortified city of Nicaea in Bithynia; famous for the two ecumenical councils held there, the city had since become the capital of the Turkish sultan. The Muslims viewed the city as a strategic position from which they could assault Constantinople and hopefully spill into Europe. The spectacle of the advancing crusaders was majestic and terrible to behold: tens of thousands of mounted knights and foot soldiers encamped near the city, which was protected by an incalculable number of towers and trenches. A chronicler of the time wrote:

> I do not believe anyone has ever seen or shall ever see again so many valiant knights. Fulcher of Chartres, among those present, counted nineteen nations represented in the Christian camp, so diverse in language and customs. Each of them had its own quarters, surrounded by walls and palisades. Lacking stone and wood for their entrenchments, they made use of the bones of the Christians who perished in the People's Crusade, massacred by the Turks and left unburied in the fields around Nicaea.

The crusaders made use of lances, swords, daggers, and maces, but also of the bow and crossbow, which were unknown in the East at that time. The princes and knights displayed on their banners images and symbols of various types, which they used to unite their own troops. These emblems, born on the battlefields of the Crusades, are the origin of the titles and crests of the nobility in the West. There is no greater title of glory for a noble than to claim descendancy from a crusader.

A year had passed since their departure, when, inside the walls of Nicaea on May 21, 1097, the crusaders won their first victory: the battle lasted the entire day and the victory cost the Christians two thousand men. The Saracens, however, scattered into the mountains, leaving four thousand dead in the plains.

From this moment, the siege of Nicaea grew more intense. The fortress began to crumble, but the intrigues of Emperor Alessio stole the victory from the crusaders. Alessio negotiated the surrender of the Turks; as the crusaders were preparing the final assault, the emblem of the Byzantine emperor was suddenly raised on the walls and towers of Nicaea. In treating the Turkish prisoners with excessive generosity, the emperor demonstrated to the Latins his lack of commitment to the war against his enemies.

The crusaders did not hide their frustration but continued their march through Asia Minor. In the mountains of Anatolia, the troops were often hindered by narrow passes, torrents, and precipices; in the plains, hunger, lack of water, and devouring heat created tremendous difficulties. The army was divided into two divisions: the first was guided by the princes Bohemond and Tancred of Altavilla, the second by Godfrey of Bouillon and Raymond of Toulouse. On the morning of July 1, 1097, the Turks descended in great numbers on Bohemond's army near Dorylaeum. Despite their valorous efforts, the Norman warriors were on the verge of defeat, when suddenly the army of Raymond and Godfrey appeared. Crushed by the furious charge of the Christian cavalry, the Turks were routed, and their camp fell into the hands of the crusaders, who found there immense treasures — especially camels, an animal then unknown in the West. After the battle, the Muslim prisoners recounted having seen angels fighting next to the crusaders. It was an epic victory that spread the fame of the "Franks," as the crusaders were then being called, all throughout the East and the West.

The population of Asia Minor was still almost entirely Christian and favored the advance of the Franks, welcoming them as liberators from the Muslim yoke. One of the crusader princes, Baldwin of Flanders, left the army and headed east to Armenia, where he arrived at the ancient Christian city of Edessa; the Byzantine prince Toros, who governed it as a vassal to the Turks, chose Baldwin as his heir. Shortly thereafter, an uprising overthrew Toros, and Baldwin found himself master of the city. No longer concerned about the liberation of Jerusalem, he gave himself solely to the governance of his new state. This was technically desertion, but, as Michaud observes, the principate of Edessa was useful as a bulwark against the Turks and Saracens; it was, until the Second Crusade, the first bastion of Christian power in the East.

After having passed over the Taurus and Amano Mountains, the crusader army sighted Antioch on October 21, 1097, the city where Jesus's disciples first assumed the name of Christians, and where St. Peter was named the first bishop of the nascent Church. The immense walls of Antioch, with their four hundred towers and bastions, were fearsome. It was the beginning of winter, and prudence would have counseled the army to attack the city only in the spring, when the weather would be more propitious and reinforcements would have arrived from Emperor Alessio, as well as from the West. But, as often happens in such moments, impatience took the upper hand, and the Christians attacked the city without the strength necessary to conquer it. Enthusiasm was quickly replaced by disappointment when the difficulties involved in taking the fortress became clear. Winter arrived and rains fell heavily day after day. The Christian camp in the valley was frequently submerged in water. Storms and flooding destroyed tents and pavilions. Cold and hunger began to claim a growing number of victims among the soldiers. Knights were forced to kill their horses for food.

Impregnable Antioch fell only thanks to a renegade Armenian by the name of Firuz, a tower guard who opened the city gates from within. The plot had been organized by Bohemond, dubbed the "Ulysses of the Latins" for this feat. Bohemond summoned a meeting of barons and announced that he had a way to bring down Antioch — with the condition, that is, that he be granted lordship over the city. The sudden attack was organized by Bohemond himself. On the night of June 3, 1098, his men scaled the walls and opened the gates for their companions, who poured into the city and managed to occupy it within just a few hours.

The city of Antioch fell into the hands of the crusaders in the first days of June, after eight months of siege. The following day, however, a formidable Turkish army, sent by the Seljuks of Persia and under the command of Kerbogha, emir of Mosul, appeared on the river Orontes. The warriors who had conquered the city immediately found themselves under siege, but by now they were exhausted by hunger and fatigue. Starvation in the city was tremendous. The situation seemed desperate; one of the leaders, Stephen of Blois, who was still outside of Antioch, was convinced that the cause had been lost when he saw the extent of the Turkish encampment surrounding the city. He set off for France. The Western world was indignant over his abandonment of the battlefield. Narrating Stephen of Blois's death in battle during the Second Crusade, William of Tyre said, "May God shine His mercy upon him, because only through death could he redeem the shame of his desertion."

A miraculous event occurred for a Christian from Provence, Peter Bartholomew, who declared that St. Andrew had appeared to him and revealed to him the place where the Holy Lance was to be found — the lance with which Longinus had pierced the side of Christ. Bartholomew rediscovered the lance tip under the flagstones of the Cathedral of St. Peter, and this discovery galvanized the crusaders, who saw in it the proclamation of imminent victory. Emir Kerbogha, sure of his military superiority, was amazed when he saw the city gates of Antioch open and a massive throng of crusaders rushing through them. In the front ranks was Hugh the Great, though weakened by a long illness, bearing the standard of the Church. All the princes, knights, and barons, except Raymond of Toulouse, who had been wounded, led their men forward. Preceding them was Bishop Ademar wearing armor and the papal habit. "Exhausted by hunger and fatigue, the crusaders," as Michaud writes, "were sustained only by the hope of winning or dying."

The fields around Antioch were inundated with Muslim warriors, whose leader, Kerbogha, seemed invincible. The clash was epic, but the Muslims were overwhelmed by the persistence of the crusaders. Kerbogha, who had announced the defeat of the Christians to the Caliph of Baghdad and the Sultan of Persia, fled wildly toward the Euphrates.

Robert the Monk recalls how, in the thick of the melee, an angelic militia was seen descending from Heaven, guided by the martyrs St. George, Demetrius, and Theodore. According to the accounts of some historians, the infidels left one hundred thousand men dead on the field, while the crusaders left only four thousand, who were counted among the martyrs.

The summer was blazing hot, and the crusaders decided to remain in Antioch until the end of autumn, but in the coming months, many of them fell victim to a terrible epidemic. Ademar of Puy succumbed as well, without having seen the Holy Land, like Moses.

The number of those who had departed for the Crusade was over two hundred thousand, the majority of whom died in combat, or of hunger and illness. The army that succeeded in conquering the sacred sites numbered fewer than fifty thousand combatants. But even this did not keep them from pursuing their aim.

## 4. THE LIBERATION OF THE HOLY CITY

In January 1099, the crusaders continued their march toward Jerusalem. The path was long, marked with skirmishes and battles that lasted until spring. The harvest blanketed the fields, and the Christian soldiers could see, rising in the distance, the mountains of Lebanon. Between the mountains and the sea, the fields were covered with tall olive trees. Keeping near the coast, the crusaders arrived at the walls of the ancient city of Ptolemais, which they called St. John of Acre; next, they occupied Lydda, ancient Diospolis, known as the place of St. George's martyrdom. In Beirut, Tyre, and St. John of Acre, the terrorized local emirs offered the soldiers necessary provisions, while other Muslims rushed to Jerusalem to defend it with all their strength. At Emmaus, Godfrey of Bouillon sent his cousin Baldwin of Bourg, along with Tancred of Altavilla and one hundred knights, toward Bethlehem, where the Savior was born. The Christians of the city, who formed a large majority, came out in procession with their crosses and hymns to welcome their liberators, after four centuries of oppression. Carried away by the festive atmosphere, Tancred and his companions stopped in the Church of the Nativity and, as one chronicler tells, "saw the manger where the sweet baby Jesus rested, He who made Heaven and Earth." On June 6, 1099, Tancred's banner was planted on top of the Basilica of the Virgin Mary.

On this same night, a sudden eclipse shrouded the earth in darkness. No one slept, and the crusaders, now just a few miles from Jerusalem, set out in haste at dawn. When the sun appeared on the horizon, the entire army advanced with unfurled banners, and the domes of the Holy City were revealed to their sight. The front rows burst out with the cry "Jerusalem! Jerusalem!" The name flew from mouth to mouth, and the cry was repeated by forty thousand armed pilgrims, echoing across Zion and the Mount of Olives. The knights dismounted in order to advance on foot; all repeated their oaths to liberate the Holy City from the sacrilegious domination of the Muslims. Arriving at the walls, the crusaders readied themselves for battle. Robert of Normandy took the northern side of the city at the Damascus Gate; Robert of Flanders positioned his men in front of the present-day Notre Dame de France; Godfrey of Bouillon and Tancred took the western side, near the Jaffa Gate and the citadel; and finally, Raymond of Toulouse took the south at Mount Zion.

It was mid-June, and the heat was unbearable. They lacked water. On June 13, the crusaders attempted a first attack but were easily repelled, as they lacked the ladders and siege engines necessary to take the city. As if by miracle, a little fleet from Genoa arrived in Jaffa carrying provisions and construction materials. The crusaders went immediately to work building catapults, enormous ladders, and wheeled towers to position beneath the walls. It was a lengthy and arduous task, especially because of the heat.

On July 8, the Muslims were surprised to see the crusader army, barefoot and unarmed, walking around the Holy City intoning prayers. Finally, on the dawn of July 14, 1099, the trumpets sounded in the Christian camp; the crusaders ran to their arms and the siege engines began moving at once. From the bastions, the Muslims fired a torrent of arrows and poured boiling oil on the crusaders who tried to scramble up the walls. The violent clash lasted twelve hours, until darkness divided the combatants. Suddenly, the crusaders saw St. George appear on the Mount of Olives, shaking his shield and signaling them to enter the city. At this point, nothing could stop the determination of the Christian combatants.

It was midnight of July 15 when Godfrey's tower, advancing through a tempest of arrows and fire, succeeded in establishing a gangway at the wall. Godfrey of Bouillon was the first to burst into the Holy City, followed by his soldiers, who spread throughout the streets of Jerusalem annihilating all resistance. Raymond of Aguilers, an eyewitness, claims that the seas of blood rose up to their knees. Among the crusaders, word spread that Bishop Ademar, and many other companions who had died during the siege, had appeared in the first ranks of the army and had planted the banner of the cross on the towers of Jerusalem. The Muslims were by now trying to escape in every direction, as Jerusalem resounded with the shouts of the crusaders, "*Deus vult!* God wills it!"

A chronicler tells us that, on the evening of that same day, the crusaders "washed their hands and feet, changed their bloodied clothes for clean ones, and went to the Sacred Site barefoot." Gathered on Calvary, in the silence of the night, the Christian army demonstrated such piety that it seemed the men must have come from a hermitage rather than a horrendous massacre.

The last battle of the First Crusade was that of Ashkelon, on August 12, 1099. Once again, a chronicler tells us, "The battle was fierce, but the Divine Power accompanied us in such a great and powerful way that we made short work of them. The enemies of God were blind and speechless; although their eyes were open, it was as if they could not see the knights of Christ and did not dare oppose them because they were terrorized by the Divine Power."

The Holy City now needed to be governed. The crusaders chose Godfrey of Bouillon, whom the chroniclers described as a lion on the battlefield and a cenobitic monk in daily life. Standing over the place where our Lord had worn a crown of thorns, he asked to be called "defender and first advocate of the Holy Sepulcher." It was only after his death that his brother Baldwin I (1108–1118), succeeding him on Christmas Day of the year 1100, took the title of Christian King of Jerusalem.

The crusaders marched thousands of miles amid difficulties of every sort, defeated the Turkish and Egyptian armies, and reconquered the Holy City of Jerusalem for the first time in 450 years. It was a historic defeat for Islam. For the West, it provided a model that would last for centuries.

## 5. The Crusades as a Category of the Spirit

There were seven, or perhaps eight, Crusades, depending on the criteria one uses to define them. They saw moments of extraordinary natural and supernatural heroism, illustrated by names such as Baldwin IV (1161–1185), the Leper King, who fought on his stretcher, and St. Louis IX (1214–1270), the perfect model of a Christian knight.

The most illustrious crusaders were those belonging to the military orders like the Knights Hospitaller (later called the Knights of Malta), the Teutonic Knights, and especially the Templars, for whom St. Bernard of Clairvaux wrote a *Rule* approved by the Church. Those Catholics who criticize the Crusades must remember that the Crusades were always promoted, organized, and directed by the Church, which considered the crusader army to be its own. Unable to personally participate, the pontiffs were represented by pontifical legates, who carried out the important role of counselor and representative of the supreme authority of the army.

There exists a close connection between the crusades and martyrdom. But the heroism of the Crusades was, in a certain way, even greater than that of martyrdom, because martyrdom is a trial that overtakes the martyr only suddenly. The dramatic alternative to fidelity to Christ is the cowardice of apostasy, which leads directly to the gates of Hell. Even one who does not have a heroic vocation is obliged to give witness, even to the point of shedding his own blood.

Crusades, as opposed to martyrdom, demand a *choice*, a heroic vocation dedicated to fighting for the Church and for Christian civilization. This entails being prepared to die not only on the battlefield but in all the harsh trials of daily life. In the expedition to liberate the Holy Sepulcher, the number of those who died from exhaustion, hunger, and sickness was greater than that of deaths in combat. This is to say nothing of the terrible spiritual and moral trials caused by parting from their loved ones, by their uncertain future, and by the betrayal they sometimes suffered at the hands of their Christian brethren.

The philosophy of the Crusades is antithetical to a certain ecumenical spirit widespread among Christians. Today, one believes that good and evil have the same rights, and that religious freedom can be understood as the right of all religions to be considered true. The Crusades presuppose, on the other hand, a Christian theology that tells us that evil and error have no right to reign, and that there is no truth outside of Jesus Christ and his Gospel, the only Way, Truth, and Life (John 14:6).

Those convinced of this must desire with all their strength that evil be uprooted from society and that only good shall triumph. This must be desired with an intensity greater than that of those who believe, in the name of relativism, that the Christian roots of society must be ripped up, if necessary, by force.

For this reason, St. Bernard wrote with theological surety in his *De Laude Novae Militiae*:

> The knights of Christ can fight the Lord's battle with peace of conscience, without the least fear of committing a sin when they kill the enemy and without the least fear of dying. In this case, death inflicted or suffered for Christ's sake has nothing criminal about it, and often involves the merit of glory. As with the former, one gives glory to Christ, so with the latter, one attains Christ himself. Christ willingly accepts the death of the enemy as punishment, and even more willingly gives himself as consolation to the soldier. The knight of Christ kills with a peaceful conscience and dies with even greater assurance. In dying, he favors himself; in killing, he favors Christ. And it is right that the soldier carries the sword. He is the minister of God for the punishment of the wicked and for the exaltation of the good. When he kills the wicked, it is not a homicide but, so to speak, a "malicide"; it is necessary to see in him both a conqueror in the service of Christ and a defender of the Christian people. If he dies, one must not think he is dead, but that he has attained eternal glory.

Of course, one must distinguish between the error and the errant. If our Lord poured out His blood for every creature, He did so in order that His kingdom might triumph over society. That this might come about, one must see God not only as merciful, but also as *just*. The Crusades were an expression of His justice, along with those who have dedicated their lives to fighting evil and error, responding to those words of the Gospel that console us but also urge us on to fight: "Seek first the Kingdom of God and his righteousness, and all these things shall be yours as well" (Matt. 6:33).

# FROM THE MIDDLE AGES TO THE FRENCH REVOLUTION

# Foreword

IN FEBRUARY 2010, I began my monthly collaboration with Radio Maria, where I hosted a program called *Christian Roots*. This collaboration lasted until February 2014.

Most of my talks on Radio Maria concerned Church history in particular. I am convinced that history enables us to comprehend the present age in depth, because everything is new in history, and yet all events repeat themselves. The history of the Church is, in every period, one of persecutions and rebirth, of apostasy and conversion, of defeat and triumph. In Catholic formation, the study of these events ought to accompany that of philosophy and theology, because it is in history that metaphysical and moral principles are made concrete, and it is in history that each one of us lives and makes his choices. For a Catholic, however, history is not only a secular "teacher of life"; it is above all a key for discovering the laws that govern the temporal and eternal destiny of men. As Dom Prosper Guéranger reminds us in his magnificent essay *The Christian Meaning of History*, "Man has been called by God to a supernatural destiny; this is his end; the history of humanity must bear witness to this."

I had Dom Guéranger's lesson in mind when, in 2012, I collected a part of my conversations with Radio Maria for the editor at Sugarco, covering the first millennium of the Church, under the title *The Church in the Storms*. I now present the second part of those conversations, following in chronological order from the Middle Ages all the way to the French Revolution and the birth of the Catholic Counter-Revolution. In the future, I hope to be able to add a third volume that follows the events of the Church down to our own tumultuous days.

The title of this volume remains the same as Volume I because the history of the Church is like that of a little boat buffeted by the waves in a tempest. Not everyone has heard of the dream of Don Bosco, in which the saint witnesses a raging naval battle during a tempest. In the midst of the vast sea, two tall columns arose next to each other. On top of one was a statue of the Immaculate Conception, *Auxilium Christianorum*; on the other was an enormous Eucharistic Host, on which was written *Salus credentium*. All the efforts of the admirals were aimed at leading the ship between the two columns. When the helmsman, who Don Bosco recognized as the figure of the pope, fell gravely injured, immediately those around him ran to his aid and helped him to his feet. The helmsman was struck a second time, fell once more, and died. A cry of victory and rejoicing arose among the enemies. But as soon as the pilot died, another took his place. As the adversaries began to lose heart, the new leader, overcoming every obstacle, led the boat to the two columns and anchored it securely to them. Then a great upheaval occurred. All the ships began to flee that, to that point, had fought the admiral's ship, that of the pope, and scattered and shattered, crashing into one another. Some sank, and others that had fought valorously came and anchored at the columns as well. Complete calm then reigned over the sea.

"The enemy ships," explained Don Bosco, "are persecutions. They prepare terrible distress for the Church. That which has been up to now is nothing compared to what will happen. Her enemies are portrayed in the ships trying to sink the flagship. Only two means remain for saving it amid such dangers and disarrays: devotion to Mary Immaculate, frequent Confession, and Holy Communion. We must employ every means and do our very best to practice them and have others practice them everywhere and by all."

Don Bosco's vision is the supernatural confirmation of the image that St. Basil used to characterize the age of the Council of Nicaea, and that Benedict XVI applied to our own troubled times: a naval battle raging on a storm-tossed sea.

It is undeniable that, throughout history, the mystical ship of the Church has always faced storms and tempests, overcoming them all. St. Augustine's *City of God* describes, as the theme of universal history, the struggle between two cities, the *Civitas Dei* and the *Civitas diaboli*.

The City of God is identified with the Church, understood as the heavenly Church (triumphant and purging), as well as the earthly Church, militant on earth. She lives in the world, without being of the world. She is without sin, but not without sinners.

The earthly city is identified with the *civitas diaboli*, the city of evil, understood as an infernal society of the damned and, in a secondary manner, as an earthly society that unites the children of darkness, adversaries of God. It lives in the world but is not identifiable with human society that lives in history.

Between these two cities, the celestial and the infernal, is the city of men, humanity living on the earth, pilgrims in space and time, living out its period of trial. It is the object of contention between the two enemy cities and constitutes the battleground between them. Throughout its earthly existence, humanity suffers the influence at times of the heavenly city, at times of the infernal city. The destiny of the city of men is to tend either toward the celestial city or toward the infernal one, to be governed by one or the other. The City of God is always victorious through the Cross, while the city of Satan is always defeated, despite its renewed daily attempts.

From the fourteenth century on, this clash was expressed as an implacable struggle between the Church and a revolution that attacked it, trying to destroy its cultural and social fruits in Christian civilization. The starting point of this volume is the Middle Ages, therefore, an epoch that produced a culture, as well as a political and social order, in conformity with the basic and perennial principles of natural and divine law. This was the age in which, as Pope Leo XIII wrote in *Immortale Dei*, "the philosophy of the gospel governed states," and "the force and sovereign influence of the Christian spirit had penetrated the laws, the institutions, and the customs of the nations, in all the orders and bureaucracy of the state." The same Leo XIII, in *Annum Ingressi*, summarized the history of the struggles and triumphs of the Church as a war, whose genesis, forms, and woeful consequences he examined.

The pontiff identified the phases of the anti-Christian revolution in the rebellion of the "so-called Reformation of the sixteenth century" and in the "proud and derisive philosophy of the seventeenth century." He stated, "The tragic and deleterious systems of rationalism and pantheism emerged from these sources, which established under new appearances the ancient errors already victoriously refuted by the Fathers and apologists of Christian times."

The process described by Leo XIII is also the narrative thread of these pages. The dream of modern civilization opposed to medieval civilization has never been attained. The history of modernity is the history of a profound crisis caused by humanism, the Protestant Reformation, and the French Revolution, all of which are aspects assumed by the anarchical and egalitarian spirit throughout the centuries. The return to Christendom, which is realized by and identified in the Catholic Church, is the only solution to the evils afflicting society, which are destined to intensify.

The "battle in the night" between the Church and its enemies has tragically grown worse, and the lightning bolt that struck St. Peter's the evening of February 11, 2013, the day on which Benedict XVI announced his abdication, seems the symbol of the storm in which the Barque of Peter finds itself. However, the path of the Church throughout the centuries, as Pius XII wrote in his *Discourse to Catholic Action* on September 12, 1948, is both a triumphal march and a *Via Crucis*. The Catholic Counter-Revolution of the nineteenth century, to which I turn in the concluding pages of this volume, constitutes the premise of that religious, cultural, and moral restoration of the civilization that I am sure Divine Providence has reserved for our near future.

*Roberto de Mattei*

CHAPTER I

# The Light of the Middle Ages

## 1. WHEN THE PHILOSOPHY OF THE GOSPEL GOVERNED STATES

The Church is both a divine and a human reality, spanning two thousand years of history. These two thousand years separate us from the Incarnation, Passion, and death of Jesus Christ, God and man, crucified under Pontius Pilate, as we recite every Sunday in the Creed, emphasizing the historical and material dimension of that event. The Jesus Christ of history is the same as the Jesus Christ of Faith.

In two thousand years, the Church has preserved the integrity of her doctrine, the continuity of her apostolic hierarchy, and the supernatural fecundity of her history. "Heresies, scandals, defections, conquests, and revolutions have not shaken her," writes Dom Guéranger. "Ejected from one country, she penetrated another; always visible, always catholic, always conquering, and always under trial."

The Church was born from the blood of Christ shed on the Cross and received its baptism by the Holy Spirit, who transformed the apostles on the day of Pentecost. They had the mission of carrying the gospel to all nations, of Christianizing the world, ordering it to Christ, the only King and Lord of human society.

At times we hear it said that the Church is behind the times: several years or even a century behind the transformations occurring in the world. It is an unfortunate phrase, profoundly erroneous, because the one who pronounces it assumes as his supreme criterion of judgment what happens in history and, in the name of history, judges the Church. That is not the case. The Church is the standard of measurement for human events, and any society or historical period must be judged in the light of what the Church thinks.

A Christian judges history by the Church's standard of judgment and not the Church by the standard of history. For this reason, we affirm that recent years and recent centuries have seen humanity's regress, not its progress. Humanity is regressing, has de-civilized in recent centuries, especially in the past two hundred years, because it has wandered from its center, which is the Church, which is Jesus Christ, the apex of history and of the universe.

The world has not moved forward, but rather moved backward, and has wrecked itself from a religious and moral point of view. The mission of the Church is not that of chasing the world in this wreckage, but of proclaiming the immutable truth of Jesus Christ, the only Way, Truth, and Life.

Never before in history has human society been so far from Christ — not even in the early centuries, those of paganism and persecutions. The pagans persecuted the Church, but did not recognize Christ. They were barbarians, not savages like the Europeans who, after having known the truth and the beauty of the Catholic Faith, have turned their backs on it, falling into apostasy, the silent but real apostasy of Europe, discussed by John Paul II (Exhortation *Ecclesia in Europa*, June 28, 2003) and Benedict XVI (Discourse to the Bishops of the United States, April 16, 2008).

But if today we live in a dark hour, perhaps the darkest ever experienced by the Church, has there ever been a historical period of true luminous faith for the Church and for all society?

The answer was given by Pope Leo XIII in *Immortale Dei*, in these words:

> It was the time when the philosophy of the gospel governed states, when the force and sovereign influence of the Christian spirit had penetrated the laws, the institutions, the customs of the nations, in all the orders and bureaucracy of the state, when the religion of Jesus Christ was placed firmly in that honorable degree that was its due, flourishing in the shade of the favor of princes and of the just protection of magistrates; when the priesthood and the empire proceeded in concord, agreed upon daringly in the friendly reciprocity of services. Ordered in this manner, society benefitted from fruits more precious than one can imagine, the memory of which shall last thanks to

innumerable historical monuments that no craft of its enemies shall be able to falsify or obscure.

## 2. The Origins and Nature of the Middle Ages

The name of this period when "the philosophy of the gospel governed states" is the Middle Ages. The origin of this term and of "medieval" as a concept is tied to a reductive historiographical vision that seeks to characterize this historical period as a long "night," a parenthesis between the "light" of the classical world and the "rebirth" of the modern age. This was the conception of the Renaissance humanists, of the Enlightenment philosophers, and of Marxists in the twentieth century.

The black legend about the Middle Ages proposed by Marxist and Enlightenment historiography has fallen definitively, however, and no serious historian today would accept considering the Middle Ages as a parenthesis of obscure barbarism. The term "Middle Ages" has shed every negative caricature to indicate simply the historical period that more precisely ought to be denoted as "Christian civilization" or "Christendom": a historical epoch, namely, in which all society, in its institutions, laws, and customs, conformed to the Magisterium of the Church—in which Christianity exercised its civilizing mission, forming all social life. Medieval Christianity was therefore the human society that carried out in history the Catholic ideal with greatest perfection.

All medieval society conformed harmoniously to the natural order ordained by God Himself in creating the universe, and to the supernatural order established in its redemption and inspired by the Church. For this reason, Pius XII affirmed that "it is just to recognize in the Middle Ages and in its mentality a note of authentic catholicity: the undeniable certainty that religion and life formed an indissoluble unity." The pope, bishop of Rome, was recognized as the immediate representative or Vicar of Jesus Christ on earth. As the French historian Régine Pernoud writes, "In practice, Christianity can be defined as the 'universality' of Christian princes and peoples who obey a single doctrine, are animated by one Faith and recognize therefore one spiritual Magisterium."

The roots of the Middle Ages go back to the fourth century, when the Church was granted its freedom by Constantine. But when we speak of medieval civilization, we mean a historical period that can be delimited by two symbolic events: the crowning of Charlemagne, on Christmas night of the year

800, and the Slap of Anagni suffered by Boniface VIII on September 7, 1303. The Slap of Anagni overturned the founding act of Christendom, accomplished when, in St. Peter's, Charlemagne rendered homage to Pope Leo III and received from him the imperial crown. The violation of the Pontifex Maximus at the hands of Phillip the Fair's emissaries at Anagni contains, on the other hand, the entire itinerary of secularization that would absorb the spiritual and moral spheres into the political over the coming centuries.

For this reason, although the Middle Ages was formed long before 800, it is from Charlemagne onward, as John Paul II affirms, that "an extraordinary age [begins]," an age that, "despite human limitations and the shortcomings present in every time, was characterized by an impressive cultural, economic, and social flourishing."

Medieval civilization was compact, organic, and unitary. Its philosophy of life could be summarized in the words of the angel in Bethlehem: "Glory to God in the highest and peace on earth to people of good will" (Luke 2:14). Both private and public life had their supreme point of reference in God's glory. The most heinous crime was sacrilege. Public legislation, customs, and habits were oriented toward God. The Middle Ages can be defined as a theocentric society because everything referred to God, the Alpha and Omega, the beginning and end of every created thing.

For this reason, the clergy was considered the first social class, and the pope the loftiest figure in all humanity. Medieval society was hierarchical, but anyone, noble or plebian, could become a priest, bishop, or pope; in other words, the pinnacle of the social ladder was available to all.

This medieval theocentrism has been opposed by an anthropocentric vision of the universe founded on the dignity and rights of man, but never have these rights been so openly violated as in the modern era. The more one hears talk of promoting human dignity, the more we see that same dignity trampled. Today's man has become merchandise, a number, a fragment in a liquid society that respects nothing and consumes everything.

No other period has had such a high conception of personal dignity as the Middle Ages. Feudalism was a complex system of hierarchical and personal bonds. Hierarchy means ordering goods according to their value. As the historian Christopher Dawson writes, "In every aspect of medieval civilization, we find the conception of a hierarchy of goods and values, and of a corresponding hierarchy of orders or 'states' and vocations that binds together the entire matrix of human relations in such a manner as to form an orderly spiritual structure extending from earth to Heaven."

Hierarchy presupposes a personal relationship among men. The human person is always at the center, precisely because he is situated in a chain of orderly relationships linking Heaven and earth. The feudal pact established, on an interpersonal level, the reciprocal rights and obligations of the higher and the lower. No other period has so valued the personal relationship, the agreements between men, that are expressed in the oath. To violate one's given word was considered a serious stain. Faith and honor were, and remained for many centuries, the basis of social relations. "What the Middle Ages felt and expressed," observes the philosopher Bertrand de Jouvenel, "is that every man had a superior. This superior was his lord, his superior, his sovereign, who in his turn had a lord, a superior, a sovereign."

Ancient Greco-Roman society, even in its highest forms, was not able to recognize the dignity of the human person. The category of person was forged in the first centuries of Christianity, when the Church was fighting against Christological and Trinitarian heresies that denied the oneness of the person of Jesus Christ or the one divine nature in three persons, Father, Son, and Holy Spirit. Jesus Christ is one *person* in two natures, his human and divine natures.

What is a person? Christianity explored this concept theologically and applied its reflections to human society. Before Christianity, nine-tenths of mankind were slaves. Slaves had no rights, not even to their own lives. In the Athens of Pericles, as in the Rome of Augustus, it was taken for granted that men were slaves to other men. Thanks to the preaching of the gospel, Europe discovered and promoted the natural equality of men, attaining the eventual abolition of slavery. Only with the establishment of medieval Christianity did there exist for the first time in history a society without slavery. All are one in Christ: for Christians there are no longer Greeks or barbarians, free men or slaves (Gal. 3:28). The medieval feudal serf, although obliged to work his master's land, was not without rights, especially his right to life. These same rights are trampled underfoot by modern society.

## 3. THE AGE OF CATHEDRALS

Medieval man had a profoundly Catholic spirit, which he expressed in his approach to the reality around him. He looked around and observed that reality was not found in what one sees and touches, in the sensible world of appearances, but within and beyond things; what the senses behold is purely a reality of phenomena. All created reality is a symbol, a sign, imperfect and limited, of a more profound and truer reality.

In the First Letter to the Corinthians (13:12), St. Paul says that we now see God's perfection reflected in creatures, but in an unclear manner, as "through a glass darkly." In other words, creatures are like a mirror in which the perfection of God is imperfectly reflected. Every creature, reflecting imperfectly some of the infinite perfections of God, is a symbol and sign of that higher, more profound truth. The French writer Ernest Hello said that the glory of the Middle Ages was that it never considered creation as a thing as such, isolated from its Creator. In this sense, there was never a historical period that attained such great scientific cognition, if, by science, we understand the capacity to penetrate, as far as is possible for man, some of the secrets of the universe: "True science breaches and goes beyond all systems. It knows things as they are, not as the human spirit is pleased to consider them. It knows them as God has made them and not as man dreams they are. The system finds in nature the image or the imprint of its Creator. Science finds in nature the image or the imprint of God."

This metaphysical spirit is reconciled with the great practical sense of the Middle Ages, with its love of concreteness and horror for abstraction. The historian Régine Pernoud recalls that jurists spoke in this period of the "crime of novelty," meaning everything that produces a violent brutal rupture with the natural course of things or with their traditional state. From this concreteness was born the love of created reality, because nature does not deceive. What deceives are dreams, abstractions, utopias. They delude man and lead him to sadness. Medieval man, on the other hand, was not dour or sad, but joyful, with a keen sense of humor. He does not know depression, but the joy of living. It is the joy of existing, a glee that pervades his philosophy, architecture, and every aspect of his social life. Medieval man did not know depression because he was psychologically and spiritually stable. He lived on certainties, with a template of absolute values with which he could interpret all of reality. These values were shared.

The worldview of Dante and St. Thomas that was transformed into stone in the cathedrals was also the vision of the humblest of medieval serfs. Medieval man had a critical sense infinitely superior to contemporary man because his secure criteria of judgment allowed him to discern truth from error, justice from injustice, the saint from the imposter. Medieval man was not credulous like modern man, but intellectually pure, innocent in the logic he applied to the reality around him. Today's man has an enormously superior quantity of information compared to medieval man but remains crushed under the weight of his confused ideas, incapable of giving them order.

Psychological and intellectual stability also conveys stability to the family and the home. Every existence is centered on the family, the home, on the stability of the place where one lives. The family was the key to the Middle Ages. The entire society was constructed around the model of the family, and the history of nations was identified with the great dynasties and family lines around which the nations gathered. And yet these men of the Middle Ages, so tied to their roots, were in perpetual movement. The Middle Ages witnessed immense mass migrations, the most intense circulation the history of the world has ever known. This was the movement of students and professors from one university to another, from Bologna to Oxford, from Paris to Cologne. It was above all the movement of the great pilgrimages. "If one attempts to summarize the concerns of the age, one realizes that they can be found in two words, two opposite poles, though not contradictory: home and pilgrimage," writes Régine Pernoud.

The medieval period was an age of social stability, and therefore of peace, of that true peace for men of goodwill that is the tranquility of order. Consider the institution, established by ecclesiastical authorities, of the peace of God, which obliged lords to refrain from war during the most important periods of the liturgical year; the Lateran Council of 1179 prescribed this from sunset on Wednesday to sunrise on Monday of every week in the periods running from Advent to the Octave of the Epiphany and from Lent through the Octave of Easter.

The Middle Ages was an era of beauty. Beauty is perhaps "the most attractive and fascinating itinerary for attaining the encounter and the love of God." Benedict XVI affirmed this in a homily dedicated to the idea that Romanesque and Gothic art, symbolized by the cathedrals, allowed entire Christian generations to be educated in the Faith throughout the Middle Ages. "It happened that the world, ... shaking off its old rags, desired to reclothe itself everywhere in the white garments of new churches." The world described by these words of the French monk Radulfus Glaber (*Historiarum* 3.4), one of the most important medieval chroniclers, was that which from the eleventh to the thirteenth century saw an incredible number of churches towering over the European landscape, either new or restructured, which the pope defined as "the true glory of medieval Christianity." In the words of Pope Benedict:

172

THE CHURCH IN THE STORMS

Everything was oriented and offered to God in the place where the liturgy was celebrated. We can better comprehend the sense that was
attributed to a Gothic cathedral considering the text of an inscription
cut into the central portal of Saint-Denis, in Paris: "Passer-by, if you
wish to praise the beauty of these doors, do not allow yourself to be
blinded by the gold, or their magnificence, but rather by the strenuous
labor. A famous work shines here but may Heaven desire that this famous work that shines make the spirits shine that with the luminous
truths one might walk toward the true light, where Christ is the true
door." The strength of the Romanesque style and the splendor of the
Gothic cathedrals remind us that the *via pulchritudinis*, the path of
beauty, is a privileged and fascinating route for approaching the mystery
of God. (Audience on November 18, 2009)

Medieval cathedrals tell us that God is light, in the true sense of the word. The art
historian Hans Sedlmayr explained that one cannot study a Gothic cathedral without
analyzing in depth the function that is celebrated therein. "All works of art are in a
specific relationship to light, intentionally or not, not only by means of the structure
of their body or their surfaces, but also due to their color, which is born of a co-
mingling of light and shade, different from one moment to the next. Pure light
'informs' matter. The more it penetrates it, the more matter becomes luminous and
expandable, and the more bodies become thin, light, pure, simple, luminous; however, the more matter refuses light, the more light's capacity for dilation and
movement diminishes; bodies then become more opaque, dense, dark, heavy, defined
and compact." God is light in the true sense of the word. "*Deus lux dicitur proprie
et non traslative*," in the words of the medieval philosopher Robert Grosseteste.

The divine light of the Middle Ages was the light of a civilization that allowed itself to be illuminated by God and radiated that light. In fact, it is the
Enlightenment (the civilization of light) that is in fact characterized by the loss
of light, by the darkening of reason, but also by the darkness in the arts, which
are the reflection of the soul. Sedlmayr observes that from the end of the eighteenth century, light lost the transparence that made reference to a light that is
mysterious and spiritual, both in painting and in architecture. In the 1800s, light
was swallowed so to speak by color, which it was previously independent of and
superior to. Then color was lost, and art precipitated into the abyss of nothing-
ness, into the dark whirlpool that reflects the nihilism in which we live today.
Tenebrous modernity contrasts with medieval luminosity.

## 4. AREAS OF DARKNESS IN THE MIDDLE AGES

The Church reached the height of its prestige and influence in the Middle Ages, which can be defined as the Christian era par excellence.

The light of the Middle Ages certainly had its dark areas as well, which we would be naïve to conceal. The investiture conflict, which for over a century pitted the popes against the emperors, is one of these shadows. The harmony between the Church and the empire, the proclaimed goal of all, was realized only partially, and at a great price. There were not only kings and emperors who failed in their duties, but also priests, bishops, and even popes.

The popes and the bishops, however, received the criticism and listened to the candid remonstrances directed at them. A great historian of the Church, Joseph Cardinal Hergenröther, recalls, for example, that Pope Paschal II (r. 1099–1118) humbly accepted being rebuked for having allowed King Henry V to force him into signing the Treaty of Ponte Mammolo in 1111, which contradicted the firm position of St. Gregory VII in the investiture conflict. The dogmatic principle *Ubi Petris ibi Ecclesia* did not prohibit the possibility of criticism of the pontiffs for love of the Church of Christ, of which they were not always worthy vicars.

According to Cardinal Hergenröther, medieval society reached its apex under the pontificate of Innocent III (r. 1198–1216), born Lothar of Segni, a pontiff who reestablished the authority of the Church, revived religious sentiment in Christendom, aided the Crusades, and struck hard against new heresies through the Inquisition. The high point of Innocent's pontificate was the convocation of the Fourth Lateran Council, which opened in November 1215 in the presence of twelve hundred bishops, abbots, religious superiors, and representatives of all the Christian nations. Seventy canons were issued on faith, customs, and discipline. One of these canons was the principle according to which there is no salvation outside the Catholic Church.

Despite his greatness, however, Innocent III was not without faults on the personal level. A Flemish nun, St. Lutgard of Tongres, reported that immediately after his death, the pontiff appeared to her devoured by flames. He was in Purgatory, condemned to be there until the Day of Judgment, punished by God for several sins he had committed in life. St. Robert Bellarmine commented on this, saying, "If a pope as worthy of praise as he was, who seemed in the eyes of all to be holy, finds himself subjected to the most horrible torments until the end of the world, what then is reserved for other ecclesiastics, religious, and the faithful?"

The powers of Hell sought to overthrow medieval civilization, provoking two great heretical movements: the Cathars and the Waldensians.

The first great medieval heresy to spread widely was that of the Waldensians, begun by the rich merchant of Lyon, Peter Waldo (1140–1205), who began preaching poverty and penance, based on the Holy Scriptures. The underlying theme of his preaching was the return to a primitive, evangelical Church.

Waldo attended in person the Third Lateran Council of 1179 and was authorized by Pope Alexander III (r. 1159–1181) to preach penance, as long as he avoided placing in doubt the theological and moral foundations of the Catholic Faith. If he and his disciples had observed the rule imposed on them, as St. Francis would later do, schism and heresy could have been avoided. But Waldo did not obey and was repeatedly condemned by the pontiffs. The Waldensians then organized themselves as a sect separate from the Church, adopting a doctrine of a spiritual Church opposed to an institutional Church, quite similar to the concept of the Donatists in the fourth century. Going further still, they attributed to themselves, thanks to the presumed holiness derived from their poverty, the right to confer the sacraments of Baptism, Confirmation, and Eucharist, without having received Holy Orders. Waldo presumed to exercise all the powers of the priesthood, and even that of the episcopate, without ever having been ordained priest or consecrated bishop.

To escape the condemnation of ecclesiastical and civil authorities, the Waldensians settled in the Alpine valleys of Piedmont. Their preferred center was the city of Pinerolo and the area of Torre Pellice. Much later, around 1533, they adopted the doctrinal principles of Protestantism: justification by faith alone, reduction of the sacraments to two, the Calvinist interpretation of the Eucharist, and the doctrine of predestination. The Waldensian movement ended up being nothing more than an appendage of Calvinism.

Much more widespread and deeper was the heresy of the Cathars, who saw themselves as an alternative religion to Christianity.

In his *Social History of the Church*, Msgr. Umberto Benigni observed that the Middle Ages inherited from the ancient heretical groups an unhealthy humus in an area that was not only extensive but also quite important, because it constitutes the junction between south and north in Western Europe, the lands that in a nearly horizontal line, from the northeast Iberian peninsula through Southern

Gaul and subalpine Italy, reach the Gulf of Trieste on the Adriatic. This was the zone where the heresy of the Cathars (the "pure ones") was born, which assumed the name Albigenses in France, from the city Albi, in Provence, where they had one of their main centers.

The Cathar movement offered a complete cosmology that clearly opposed Christian cosmology; for this reason, some have placed in doubt their status as heretics in the proper sense, because their conception of the world was born and formed outside of the Christian tradition.

The Cathars considered the world to be a contemptible reality that proceeds from the devil, from which we must be liberated. The reason for this is that the world was created by an evil god, that of the Old Testament, who according to them was Satan himself. The goal of life is therefore found in the liberation of material bonds, in order to return to the heavenly abode. Marriage was condemned because it perpetuates physical life, which is evil. Even the state and family were condemned as earthly and visible societies. They also condemned oaths and military service. The Cathars considered voluntary suicide to be the ideal of holiness. What they called *endura*, or the practice of allowing oneself to die of hunger or to meet some other violent end, was the ideal of perfection. Euthanasia had an analogous value to suicide.

Furthermore, the Cathars practiced the *consolamentum*, a type of baptismal sacrament that consisted of the imposition of hands. There was neither veneration of images nor of the saints, but several forms of liturgy including a sort of "sacred meal."

The Cathars considered the Church to be filled with temporal goods and sinful, and so contrasted it with their own church, poor and "evangelical," which rejected every form of possession. Nevertheless, they too were organized following the model of the Church, and had a hierarchy with their own bishops. Their wide diffusion throughout Southern France, particularly in the region of Albi, led them to make alliances with several feudal lords who were preparing to fight the French kingdom. The county of Toulouse, under Raymond V (r. 1148–1194) and Raymond VI (r. 1194–1122), was especially infested.

Pope Innocent III, concerned by the progress of this heresy, sent his representatives to direct the evangelization of the contaminated countries, prescribing the use of peaceful means. On January 15, 1208, however, the papal legate Peter of Castelnau was assassinated by the Cathars. Innocent III then invited Christian nobles to unite in a crusade against the heretics. This crusade was directed by Count Simon de Montfort (1150–1218), already a valorous crusader in the Holy Land, who defeated the Cathars in the decisive Battle of Muret on September 12, 1213, but later died in combat in 1218. The name Simon de Montfort is often forgotten today, but we can consider him a great martyr of the Catholic Faith.

## 5. HOLINESS IN THE MIDDLE AGES: FROM CLUNY TO ST. BERNARD

Every age has had its saints, but one can rightly say that the medieval period was an age of sanctity. We are not speaking only of the saints officially elevated to the honor of the altar, because the Middle Ages was as sober in proposing models of holiness to the faithful as the contemporary age is generous and overabundant. We are speaking of the common holiness of daily life, which is so exceptional today, and for this reason needs to be emphasized. Sanctity is complete conformity with the will of God. In modern society, which rejects God in principle and in fact, living an ordinary Christian life requires a heroic effort, perhaps even a miracle. In the Middle Ages, when everything spoke of God to man, man spoke daily with God.

A review of all medieval saints would be impossible. We shall recall some of the more significant names in the various historical periods.

The tenth century, when many popes were going through a moral crisis, was the century in which the virtues of the monks excelled the most. It was these men who made their monasteries into centers of Church reform. The holy abbots of Cluny come to mind, who followed one another in holiness from 909 to 1057, from Berno to Odo, from Majolo to Odilo, from Hugh to Peter the Venerable, disseminating throughout Christendom a new spirit that transformed the men and institutions of the Middle Ages.

The eleventh century can be epitomized in St. Gregory VII (r. 1073–1085), who raised high the banner of the *Dictatus Papae*, the document proclaiming the superiority of the pope over the emperor in the religious and moral fields, claiming for the papacy the most elevated and eminent power on earth. This doctrine was represented in the art of the epoch as well. The pope was always represented on a higher step, while the emperor was on his left, on a lower step, and even lower than the emperor were the kings and sovereigns of the temporal sphere, and then, little by little, all the members of the Catholic hierarchy that governed the spiritual sphere.

Gregory VII gave his name to the most profound reform of the medieval Church, a true reform that restored the integrity of doctrine and the purity of customs, not pseudoreforms like many that are announced in our days, covering with the slogan of reform the desire to humiliate the papacy and mutate the fundamental principles of the gospel message. Gregory VII wanted to complete his spiritual reform by proclaiming a great crusade, but the honor of being the first to proclaim war on the Muslim infidels fell to one of his disciples, Blessed Urban II. The Crusades represented the high point of the Middle Ages.

The following century, the twelfth, can be summarized in the figure of St. Bernard of Clairvaux (1090–1153), of whom Ernest Hello wrote that "he carried in himself the entire twelfth century, and not without pain.... It is impossible to write the history of his life without writing a history of the entire world during his lifetime." One would need to investigate the theological and philosophical discussions, the political and military events, and enter into the silence of the cloister and the tumult of affairs to find the luminous and peaceful presence of St. Bernard, ardent preacher of the Crusades, who wrote the military *Rule* of the Templar Knights, an acute theologian who defeated Abelard, the wise counselor of popes and sovereigns, as well as mystics like St. Hildegard of Bingen (1098–1179). When one of his disciples, Bernard Pignatelli, was elected pope under the name of Eugene III (r. 1145–1153), Bernard wrote a text to his spiritual son, the *De Consideratione*, explaining to him how to be a good pope; as Benedict XVI said, "It remains recommended reading for popes of all times" (General Audience on October 21, 2009).

St. Bernard was deeply devoted to the Virgin Mary, of whom he said, "De Maria numquam satis." Tradition has attributed to him the title of Mellifluous Doctor, meaning that his praise of Jesus and Mary "flowed like honey," touching the heart of souls. For good reason, a century and a half after his death, Dante Alighieri, in the last canto of his *Divine Comedy*, placed on the lips of the Mellifluous Doctor the sublime prayer to Mary: "Virgin Mother, daughter of your Son, / humbler and higher than creatures, / fixed term of eternal council ..." (*Paradise* 33.1ff.).

St. Bernard has given us the *Salve Regina*, the *Memorare*, and the following beautiful prayer:

> In danger, in anxiety, in uncertainty, think of Mary, invoke Mary. May she never depart from your lips, from your heart; and that you may be able to

obtain the assistance of her prayer, never forget the example of her life. If you follow her, you cannot go astray; if you pray to her, you will never despair; if you think of her, you cannot go wrong. If she sustains you, you shall not fall; if she protects you, you have nothing to fear; if she leads you, you shall not tire; if she is well disposed toward you, you will reach your goal. (*Hom. II super "Missus est,"* 17: PL 183.70–71)

## 6. St. Dominic and St. Francis

If St. Bernard occupied with his magnificent presence the entire twelfth century, in the thirteenth there arose, almost contemporaneously, two great luminaries of the Church: St. Francis of Assisi (1182–1226) and St. Dominic de Guzman (1170–1221). St. Francis was the response of Divine Providence to the heretical challenge of the Waldensians, while St. Dominic was the response to the Cathars.

Dominic was born in Caleruega, Spain, around 1170. He belonged to a noble family of old Castille and was educated in a famous school in Palencia. Ordained a priest, he was elected canon of the cathedral chapter in his diocese, Osma. The bishop of Osma, Diego, soon noticed Dominic's spiritual qualities and solicited his collaboration. When Bishop Diego and Dominic sought the pope's counsel, the pope asked the latter to dedicate himself to preaching against the Albigensian heretics who were devastating France. This apostolate demanded profound study and piety. St. Dominic founded the Order of Preachers to become specialists in the fight against heresy. He wanted his brothers to dedicate themselves without reserve, uniting their knowledge of Sacred Scripture to that of theology and philosophy.

The Virgin Mary rewarded Dominic, entrusting to him the Holy Rosary as a privileged weapon in the fight against the enemies of the Faith, a vocal and mental prayer consisting of 15 Our Fathers and 150 Hail Marys. The new way of praying became so popular and was so enthusiastically received that prodigious spiritual fruits were immediately seen. This can be explained only by the promise the Virgin made to him when she said, *"Eam precandi formula omnes doce."* The victories won against the Albigenses were due to this devotion as well. Simon de Montfort fought with arms, while Dominic de Guzman fought spiritually with prayer and preaching. The assistance of the Virgin Mary was so great that the crusaders of de Montfort defeated the heretic army that was much more numerous than the Christian army. This fact amazed people throughout the world, who recognized that the victory was due to the power of the Most Holy Rosary.

Next to St. Dominic stands the figure of St. Francis. He was born in Assisi in 1182. An illness sparked the beginning of his life of perfection, and he resolved to give away all he possessed. The gospel was his sustenance, his consolation, the remedy to all his sufferings, to all trials, and one day he was to say to his brothers, "I am saturated by the gospel, I am full of the gospel." The gospel became his life; when he wanted to give a rule of life to his friars, he wrote in the first pages, "The rule and the life of the Friars Minor is this: Observe the holy gospel of Our Lord Jesus Christ." Following the example of Jesus, he embraced poverty, and, in front of the bishop of Assisi, he removed his clothes, saying, "Now I can truly say, 'Our Father, who art in Heaven.'" Thus began his life of joyful, voluntary, and beloved poverty, not the poverty of affliction and resentment that we too often see in the world.

Francis prayed often and for long periods before the crucifix in the old Church of San Damiano. One day, Christ on the cross came to life three times and said to Francis, "Go, Francis, and repair my house that is in ruins." Deeply moved, Francis replied, "I shall go joyfully, O Lord, and do whatever you tell me!" The house that was about to collapse was not only the old solitary chapel of San Damiano. As Benedict XVI recalls:

> St. Francis was called to repair this little church, but the ruinous condition of this edifice was a symbol of the dramatic and disturbing situation of the Church itself at that time, with its superficial faith that neither formed nor transformed life, with its clergy lacking in zeal, with the cooling of its love; an interior destruction of the Church that also caused a decomposition of its unity, with the birth of heretical movements. Nevertheless, in the center of this church in ruins is the Crucifix and it speaks: he calls for renewal, he calls Francis to do manual labor to repair concretely the little chapel of San Damiano, symbol of the deeper call to renew the very Church of Christ, with the radicalness of his faith and with his enthusiasm for the love of Christ. (Audience of January 27, 2010)

This experience, probably in 1205, leads one to think of another similar occurrence in 1207: the dream of Pope Innocent III. In his dream he saw the Basilica of St. John Lateran, the mother church of all churches, collapsing, and a friar propping up the church on his shoulders to keep it from caving in. Benedict XVI observed:

On one side, it was not the pope who was trying to keep the church from collapsing, but a little, insignificant religious, whom the pope recognized as St. Francis who had come to visit him. Innocent III was a powerful pope, with deep theological formation, as well as great political power. Nevertheless, it was not he who was renovating the Church, but a little, insignificant religious: St. Francis, called by God. On the other hand, however, it is important to note that St. Francis did not renew the Church without or against the pope, but only in communion with him. The two realities go together: the successor of Peter, the bishops, the Church founded on the succession of the apostles, and the charism that the Holy Spirit created in that moment to renew the Church.

The pope approved the Order of Friars Minor, and with its fervor, its love for poverty, and its apostolic zeal, it not only repaired the ruins of the Church of Christ, but would go on to construct a new Christianity in the lands of the infidels with the blood of its martyrs. Francis, the first among the founders of modern orders, sent his sons into the regions of the infidels and when, after several months, he learned that five of them had received the palm of martyrdom in Morocco, he exclaimed with joy, "Finally, I have some bishops!" His bishops, as Dom Guéranger emphasizes, were martyrs. After having founded his work, he dreamed only of offering Jesus his own blood as a testimony, and crossed the sea three times to preach Christ in the presence of the infidel sultan. But God bestowed another martyrdom on him, which took place in 1224: while in prayer, a seraph appeared to him and impressed upon his body the wounds of the Crucified One as a sign of the love the saint nourished for the Lord.

Two years later, Francis, already very ill, had the brothers carry him to St. Mary of the Angels, where he died after having exhorted his friars to love poverty and to defend the Faith of the Roman Church. After having sought Jesus, after having lived on Him, after having loved Him, Francis uttered this song as he was dying: "*Voce mea ad Dominum clamavi, ad Dominum deprecates sum … Me exspectant iusti*" (I call to the Lord with all my voice and ask my Lord … The just await me … they shall give witness to the recompense that God shall give me) (Ps. 140).

St. Francis was not a priest, because he judged himself unworthy to ascend the altar, but reminded priests of the greatness of their call, kneeling before them and kissing their hands. He wrote to cardinals, bishops, and princes: "I beg you, my lords, kissing your hands, take care that the Body of Jesus is treated worthily and is duly respected by all." At the Church of San Damiano, he founded an order of virgins under the direction of his spiritual daughter St. Clare (1193–1253), as well as the Third Order, to give to people living in the world an efficacious means of sanctification in the practice of religious virtues.

Pope Gregory IX entered St. Francis and St. Dominic in the canon of saints. Dante, in his *Divine Comedy*, places in the mouth of St. Bonaventure, a disciple of St. Francis, an admirable panegyric to St. Dominic and his disciple St. Thomas Aquinas, as well as an equally splendid exaltation of St. Francis (*Paradiso* XI.43–117; XII.22–105).

## 7. ST. LOUIS, KING OF FRANCE

Next to these great founders of religious orders, we find saints who were kings, queens, and princes, such as St. Ferdinand of Castille (1201–1252) and St. Elisabeth of Portugal (1271–1336); St. Margaret (1045–1093), Hungarian by birth, then Queen of Scotland, of which she is the patron, and also mother of two saints, Matilda (d. 1118) and Edmund (d. 1100). In Hungary, after St. Stephen (969–1038), there is St. Elisabeth of Hungary (1207–1231) and her aunt St. Hedwig (1174–1243), duchess of Poland; and then there is Blessed Umberto III, Amadeo III, Luisa of Savoia, and many others not officially recognized by the Church, but who lived and died in holiness.

Among all these figures, the name of St. Louis IX (1214–1270) shines brightest. The son of Louis VIII of Lyon and Bianca of Castille, he succeeded his father in 1226 under the regency of his mother, only to assume full powers in 1242, after his marriage to Margaret of Provence. He was a model sovereign, pious and just, a perfect knight and crusader.

This model figure was opposed in the thirteenth century by that of another sovereign, Emperor Frederick II (1194–1250), the creator of an absolute state that was bureaucratic and centralized, whose foundations he did not build on God, as the medieval sovereigns had done, but on his self-aggrandizement and will to power.

Always faithful to the Church, Louis IX set off in 1248 for the crusade called by Innocent IV and remained in the Holy Land to fight until 1254. Frederick II, who had on numerous occasions asked Louis to seek the pope's mediation in his conflict with him, sought to undermine the success of the crusade, warning the Muslims of an expedition organized by Louis. St. Louis wanted to convert the Muslims, as St. Francis had done in 1220. Frederick II, on the other hand, never desired anyone's conversion to Christianity, but rather expressed respect and admiration toward Islam. St. Louis constructed the Sainte-Chapelle in Paris to hold the Crown of Thorns which he had acquired from the Byzantine emperor for an enormous sum. Frederick was an unbeliever and disseminated the tale of the "three impostors" (Christ, Moses, and Muhammad). St. Louis lived chastely, while Frederick was a dissolute man. The Church excommunicated Frederick II several times, and canonized St. Louis IX.

Frederick II was found dead on December 13, 1250, at fifty-six years of age, excommunicated by the Church and unrepentant. An English Franciscan, Thomas of Eccleston, tells of a confrere who saw, at the time the emperor died, five thousand knights riding into the sea, making the water boil, as if their armor were made of molten metal. When the friar asked who they were, one of the knights replied that it was Frederick II and his knights who had entered the fires of Mt. Etna.

While Frederick II laid dying, Louis IX was fighting in the Holy Land; he ended his days twenty years later, in Tunisia, on August 25, 1270. The Church canonized him in 1297. Modernity ignores St. Louis and exalts Frederick II, seeing in him its precursor.

We, on the other hand, remember St. Louis in the words of his testament, in which he addressed his son with these words:

> Beautiful son, the thing I wish to teach you is that you must set your heart to loving God; because without this no one can be saved. Keep guard not to do anything that might offend God, namely mortal sin; to the contrary, you should prefer to tolerate any torment so as not to commit mortal sin.... Preserve good customs in your kingdom and make bad ones cease.... Do not be greedy toward your people and do not burden them with taxes and tribute, unless you are in great need.... Love what is fruitful and good; hate all that is evil, wherever it is.... In administering justice and righting wrongs for your subjects, be loyal and inflexible, without looking to the right or the left, but always uphold justice; sustain the claims of the poor until the truth comes to light.... Beautiful and dear son, I give you all the blessings that a good father can give a son. May the Blessed Trinity and all the saints protect and defend you from all evils; and may God give you the grace to do his will always, that he be honored through you, and that you and I may, after this life, be together with him and praise him without end. Amen.

Thus did Christians of the Middle Ages live and die; thus did princes, kings, and emperors exercise their power. Certainly not all were like this, but the most noble and the holiest, in an age that tended toward nobility and sanctity, were. One who lives in an ignoble age like ours must hope that the world and the Church will rediscover that spirit and establish on the ruins of the modern world a civilization even more resplendent and luminous than medieval civilization.

CHAPTER II

# The Crisis of Medieval Christianity

### 1. The Fourteenth Century and the End of the Middle Ages

History has known periods of progress and development as well as periods of decadence and crisis. Medieval civilization was one of great material and moral progress; the fourteenth century was one of profound crisis and decadence, and was to mark the end of the Middle Ages, just as the fifth century of the Christian era saw the collapse of the Roman Empire.

When one speaks of the fourteenth century, many think of the Middle Ages. For example, it is often thought that the novel *The Name of the Rose* by Umberto Eco faithfully captures the pinnacle of the Middle Ages. Rather, the historical background of intellectual and moral decadence in which the plot is set actually portrays the moment of crisis of the Middle Ages. The fourteenth century is in fact the century that witnessed the great religious, political, and social upheaval that set the stage for the modern age, an era running from the Renaissance down to our own days, and whose guiding principle is precisely the loss of the medieval world's spirit and vision.

A great historian and philosopher of history, Plinio Corrêa de Oliveira wrote in his masterful work *Revolution and Counter-Revolution*:

> In the fourteenth century, one begins to observe in Christian Europe a
> transformation of mentality which over the course of the fifteenth

century became increasingly clear. The desire for earthly pleasures was gradually transformed into a lust for them. Diversions became increasingly frequent and sumptuous. Men took better care of themselves. In their clothing, their fashions, their language, their literature, and their art, the growing longing for a life full of delights of fantasy and of the senses was producing gradual manifestations of sensuality and frivolity. A slow deterioration of the seriousness and austerity of older times could be noted. Everything tended toward the merry, the delicate, the frivolous. Hearts were being detached little by little from a love of sacrifice, from true devotion to the Cross, and from aspirations to holiness and to eternal life. The knighthood, in other periods one of the highest expressions of Christian austerity, became amorous and sentimental. Love literature invaded every country, as did the excesses of luxury and its consequent avidity for turning a profit.

This moral climate, penetrating the intellectual spheres, produced clear manifestations of pride, such as the enthusiasm for pompous, vacuous disputes, for sophistical, inconsistent argumentation, for fatuous exhibition of erudition, and the adulation of old philosophical tendencies over which Scholasticism had triumphed and which, with the relaxation of the old zeal for the integrity of the Faith, were now coming to life under new forms. The absolutism of legal scholars who paraded their self-important knowledge of Roman law found in ambitious princes a favorable echo. And keeping step with this was the gradual extinguishing in great and small alike of the wherewithal of past times for containing royal power within legitimate limits.

The Middle Ages was undermined by two heretical movements: the Waldensians and the Cathars, countered by the great figures of St. Francis and St. Dominic. St. Thomas Aquinas (1225–1274), with his *Summa Theologica,* had raised formidable bastions against the theological and philosophical errors that were then corroding the foundation of the medieval world. The attack against the Church and Christendom developed on a deeper level, weakening the supernatural and militant spirit that had characterized the medieval Christian. The weakening of the crusader spirit was the alarming signal of an epochal change.

St. Louis of France, the last great crusader king, died in 1270, in North Africa. From then on, the Christian armies would lose their passion and their trust in the help of God that had worked extraordinary victories for them. The relaxation of customs, greed, and discord had penetrated even the military orders, like the Templars, which constituted the model of Christian combat. On May

28, 1291, the Muslims succeeded in conquering St. John of Acre, the last Christian fortress in the Holy Land. It was a crucial event because it closed the epic period of the Crusades. But another symbolic event was around the corner.

## 2. THE SLAP OF ANAGNI

On December 24, 1294, Cardinal Benedetto Caetani was elected to the papal throne, taking the name Boniface VIII. He reigned as pope until 1303. He was born in Anagni around 1230 to a noble family. Tall and domineering in stature, he was a man of lively intelligence who had distinguished himself as an eminent jurist and diplomat, being made cardinal in 1281 by Pope Martin IV. He obtained the pontifical tiara following the renunciation of Celestine V, the monk-pope, whom Pope Boniface did not hesitate to comfort and support in his tormented choice to abdicate.

The situation in Europe at the time of Boniface's election was confused and turbulent. In France, Phillip the Fair reigned (1285–1314), finding himself in great financial difficulty on the heels of a foolish spending policy that exceeded the revenue of the Crown. The sovereign sought to lay his hands on the possessions of the clergy, but was met by the opposition of Boniface VIII, who in *Clerici laicos* threatened to excommunicate him. Open war began between the pope and the king of France, who was supported by the jurists who taught in the universities in Toulouse, Montpellier, and Orléans, and who opposed Roman law to the canon law of the pontifical court.

On the basis of Roman law, they theorized the absolute sovereignty of the prince (*princeps legibus solutus*) and the extension of the *ius regium* to the point of reforming the national Church. They were the first to attack the juridical foundations of Christian and medieval civilization, with abstract logic resembling that of the Enlightenment philosophers of the eighteenth century. Phillip the Fair's jurists set the foundations for Gallicanism, a system of theological and juridical theories that affirmed the autonomy of the Catholic Church in France. This was a sort of "national path" or "French path" toward Catholicism that saw its moment of maximum development in the following centuries.

The pope condemned the presumption of Phillip the Fair in *Ausculta Fili* on December 5, 1301, and then summoned a synod of French bishops, at which he read *Unam Sanctam*, published on November 18, 1302, which treated the relations between temporal power and spiritual power. In this important document, Boniface VIII reaffirmed the positions stated in St. Gregory VII's *Dictatus Papae*.

The pontiff asserted that the Church is one, holy, catholic, and apostolic, and that outside of it there is no salvation. This Church wields two swords: a spiritual one, used directly by the priesthood, and a temporal one, used by princes according to the indications of the Church. The dogmatic conclusion of *Unam Sanctam* is the following: "We declare, we say, we pronounce, and we define that every human creature is, for the necessity of salvation, subject to the Roman pontiff." This means that every man, including Christian princes and kings, if he wants to save his soul, must conform his conduct, both public and private, to the laws of the Church and to the spiritual and moral authority of the Pontifex Maximus. The pope, according to Boniface, is by divine authority above all kings and kingdoms, not because he exercises absolute temporal authority over them, but in the sense of being invested with the relative superiority that is appropriate to spiritual things over the material ones, to the supernatural and divine order with respect to the merely natural and human order.

After the publication of *Unam Sanctam*, by which Boniface VIII reaffirmed the rights of the Church, William of Nogaret, one of Phillip the Fair's jurists, denounced Boniface as a usurper, a heretic, and a Simonist in an indictment read to the royal council on March 12, 1303. Phillip gathered the Estates General of the kingdom and had the pope deposed. On September 7, 1303, a brigade of French soldiers led by Nogaret and by the Roman Sciarra Colonna broke into the Apostolic Palace in Anagni. The pope, clothed in the papal cape, with the golden crown on his head and the keys of Peter in his hands, sat in silent recollection on the throne as his assailants struck his cheek with an iron glove. The French emissaries imprisoned the Head of the Church for three days. Liberated by the people of Anagni, Boniface VIII returned to Rome where, under the weight of the offense suffered, he died on October 11, 1303.

This was a most serious and profoundly symbolic episode that overturned the foundational act of Christendom: that Christmas night in the year 800 when, in St. Peter's Basilica, Charlemagne rendered homage to Leo III and received from him the imperial crown. If by the term "Middle Ages" we delineate the period of Christianization of society inaugurated by the coronation of Charlemagne, the date that likewise symbolically closes this period is 1303, the year of the aggression at Anagni. The outrage committed by the envoys of the king of France against Boniface VIII constitutes in fact a new conception of society emancipated from the spiritual and moral authority of the Church.

The gesture of Sciarra Colonna reveals a whole itinerary of secularization that over the course of centuries would lead to Renaissance humanism, the Enlightenment, and the totalitarianism of the twentieth century. This itinerary denies the distinction between two powers, characteristic of the Western and Christian tradition, absorbing the spiritual sphere through the sacralization of the figure of the sovereign, emancipated from the Church, and then of the people, the class, the party.

After the attack at Anagni and the death of Boniface VIII, there began one of the most dramatic periods in the Church's history, which saw the transfer of the papacy to Avignon and the Great Schism of the West. The end of the medieval period was manifested in the fourteenth century, which opened as dark and dramatic as the previous century had been luminous.

## 3. THE AVIGNON CAPTIVITY

Succeeding Boniface VIII, who died in Rome on October 11, 1303, was Blessed Benedict XI (r. 1303–1304), Niccolò Boccalini, the general of the Dominicans and bishop of Ostia. He struck the perpetrators of the sacrilege at Anagni with excommunication, but absolved Phillip the Fair from all the censures he might have faced following the affair. The king of France knew how to profit from the situation. Pressured by him, the archbishop of Bordeaux, Bertrand de Got, was elected pope with the name Clement V (r. 1305–1314), who in the conflict between Boniface VIII and Phillip the Fair had assumed a neutral position. Giovanni Villani, in his *Istorie Fiorentine* (III.80), reports that in May 1305, just a few months before his election, Bertrand had a meeting with Phillip the Fair in a forest near the Abbey of Saint-Jean d'Angely, where the king supposedly promised the archbishop of Bordeaux the pontifical tiara on condition of reconciling him unconditionally with the Church and condemning the memory of Boniface VIII. In fact, even without this simoniac pact, Clement's election was a success for the policies of Phillip the Fair. The coronation ceremony was held in Lyon on November 14, 1305, in the presence of the king of France.

With Clement V began that period of the papacy called the Avignon Captivity, which lasted seventy years, 1308 to 1378, comparable to the seventy years of exile experienced by the Jewish people during what was called the Babylonian Captivity (587–517 BC). After his coronation, celebrated in Lyon, Clement promised to return to Italy but was never to fulfill this intention. From 1309 on, he resided in Avignon, a little city on the Rhone River, which had belonged to the count of Provence, Charles of Anjou, since 1290. The new pope satisfied Phillip the Fair in all that was asked of him, cancelling all the acts of Boniface against him. The king, desirous of taking possession of the wealth of the Templars, accused the order of terrible crimes: idolatry, blasphemous rites, and immoral practices. On October 13, 1307, Phillip had all the Templars living in France imprisoned and their possessions confiscated. The pope protested against the sovereign's actions, which violated ecclesiastical law, but then, awed by the confessions extorted under torture and fearful of the sovereign's threats, he ordered an ecclesiastical tribunal to conduct a general investigation. At the general council held in Vienne between October 1311 and May 1312, the majority of Council Fathers, although composed mostly of French clergy tied to Phillip the Fair, were not able to demonstrate the guilt of the order suppressed by Pope Clement V with an administrative decree (not by force of a juridical verdict) *Vox in excelso*. In 1314, the Grand Master James de Molay, although insisting until the end on the order's innocence, was burned at the stake like many of his confreres. This was the tragic end of an order that had won glory on the battlefields of the Crusades.

After Clement V, John XXII (r. 1316–1334) rose to the papal throne, definitively establishing the Apostolic See in Avignon; he was followed by Benedict XII (r. 1334–1342), who built the enormous papal palace in Avignon; Clement VI (r. 1342–1352), under whose pontificate Cola di Rienzo attempted to establish a republic in Rome; Innocent VI (r. 1352–1362); Blessed Urban V (r. 1362–1370), the most pious of these popes; and Gregory XI (r. 1370–1378), who in 1377, distressed by the prophetic warnings of St. Catherine of Siena and St. Brigid of Sweden, made his return to Rome.

These seven popes, five of whom were never to see Rome, were nevertheless bishops of Rome, because an indissoluble bond exists between Rome and the papacy. St. Peter was bishop of Rome, and Jesus Christ said to Peter and to his successors, "You are Peter, and on this rock I shall build my Church, and the gates of Hell shall not prevail against it."

It has often happened throughout history that popes were forced to flee Rome, either in exile or imprisoned. But in the case of Avignon, it was a culpable exile, willed by the popes themselves. One pope, Urban V, a Benedictine, proposed to return the papacy to Rome and returned to the Eternal City amid great acclamation. But he was then deceived into returning to France to resolve a controversy between two sovereigns. The Lord made known to him through St.

Bridget that death was awaiting him if he returned to France, and that he would never see Rome again. The prediction came true. After just a few months from his return to Avignon, he died. Pius IX beatified Urban V for his life of penance, but St. Bridget had a dream in which she saw him passing through Purgatory.

The Avignon exile, considered in its entirety, did great harm to the papacy. The voice of the pope heard from Avignon did not have the same accent as it did when heard from Rome. The absence of the pope from Rome shook the trust and moral authority that the papacy enjoyed in the age of Innocent III and Boniface VIII, and provoked the difficult historical crisis that had as its direct consequence the Great Schism of the West (1378–1417).

## 4. WILLIAM OF OCKHAM AND MARSILIUS OF PADUA

Under the pontificate of John XXII, open conflict arose between the pope residing in Avignon and Duke Ludwig of Bavaria, elected emperor under the name of Ludwig IV (r. 1314–1347). The pope did not recognize the emperor's election without his own papal approval. The emperor accused John XXII of heresy, while the pope excommunicated Ludwig and liberated his subjects from the bond of obedience (1324). The German sovereign travelled to Italy and, on January 27, 1328, had himself crowned emperor in the name of the Roman people by a layman, Sciarra Colonna (1270–1329), the author of the attack in Anagni against Pope Boniface VIII. He then had John XXII removed from the papal throne and declared a heretic. As anti-pope he procured the election of an Italian Franciscan of the spiritualist current, Pietro da Corvara, who took the name Niccolò V (r. 1328–1330), but who later retracted his errors and died in Avignon in 1333.

As Phillip the Fair had been supported by the French jurists in his clash with the pope, so Ludwig of Bavaria was encouraged by two ideologues: William of Ockham (1285–1347) and Marsilius of Padua (1279–1343).

The figure of the modern intellectual was born in this period: one who proposes to change the world through an ideological construction. Such was William of Ockham, a Franciscan who turned his back on the true spirit of St. Francis and on the one who had been his master, Blessed Duns Scotus (1266–1308). Ockham was the main representative of a philosophical current that marked the end of medieval Scholasticism: nominalism.

The term "nominalism" indicates a theory that denies the existence of universal concepts, or at least denies their correspondence to concrete realities. Already in the twelfth century, the philosopher Abelard (1079–1142), resolutely opposed by St. Bernard, had stated that universals are only "the meaning of denominations" (*nominum significatio*): universals exist only in the intellect, although they signify real beings. Ockham develops this thesis, maintaining that the universal exists only in the soul of the knowing subject without a correspondence to anything that is real in the objects. The universal present in the soul is a simple *signum*, a conventional symbol; that sign is only an abstraction and a production of the mind, without meaning on the ontological level of reality.

For nominalists, there exist only individual things, not general ones. If we speak, for example, of love, of freedom, of justice, we are speaking of concepts that exist in the intelligence of a subject, but not in the reality of things. Visible reality is thus separated from the invisible. But also, as concerns social life, concepts like family, authority, and the state all lose their meaning. There exists the individual man, the individual woman, individual children, but not the family as a universal and invisible reality. Society is reduced to being an agglomeration of concrete individuals. The common good is the sum of the particular goods. From nominalism, two philosophical systems were to arise: rationalism, according to which nothing really exists outside the human mind, and empiricism, according to which nothing exists outside what we can come to know through our senses. Common to both systems is subjectivism, a consequence of the negation of the objective reality of universals.

In 1324, Ockham was excommunicated and sided with the duke of Bavaria. Ockham denied the dependence of the emperor on the pope, to whom, in his opinion, no temporal power should be attributed, neither over kingdoms nor over any type of possession, because Christ, of whom St. Peter is vicar, professed and requested of his successors absolute poverty. The supremacy of the pontiff is of a purely spiritual nature, therefore the pope is not infallible and can err in matters of Faith. It is licit to make appeal against him to a general council.

No less revolutionary was Marsilius of Padua. He had studied in Paris where he fell under the influence of legal scholars like William of Nogaret and various Averroist philosophers, like the disciple of Siger of Brabant, John of Jandun. Marsilius allowed for no other authority than Sacred Scripture, interpreted not by the pope, but by a general council representing the *universitas fidelium*, the entirety of the faithful, composed of clergy and laity. Like Ockham, he also presumed that political power was completely independent of ecclesiastical authority. He held moreover that sovereignty resided in the people. Marsilius enshrined his theories in the *Defensor Pacis*, in which he announced the revolutionary ideas that prefigure the theories of Rousseau.

After having been condemned by Pope Gregory XXII in 1326, Marsilius offered his services to Ludwig of Bavaria, like William of Ockham. The sovereign welcomed him as a counselor and had himself crowned emperor on the basis of his doctrine. Despite the condemnation by John XXII, the errors of Marsilius and William of Ockham enjoyed wide dissemination, undermining the foundations of the great Scholastic edifice that had reached its peak with Aquinas.

If the thirteenth century, the high point of the Middle Ages, had been a period of peace, the fourteenth century was one of "permanent war" in Europe. War broke out on the Iberian Peninsula and in southern Italy between the Angevins and Aragon over the dominion of Sicily and the Kingdom of Naples. In the Baltic there was the struggle between Lithuanians and the Teutonic Knights. Above all, the century exploded in the clash between France and England, which took the name of the Hundred Years' War (1339–1453). The medieval period had never known a conflict of such duration and proportions. But a new danger knocked at the door.

The fall of Adrianople in 1362 marked the emergence of the Ottoman Turks into Europe. A new Islamic wave was crashing against the Byzantine Empire, and in the following century would destroy it.

## 5. A Fame, Peste, et Bello Libera Nos, Domine

Those with a supernatural Christian spirit know that Heaven and earth are bound by an invisible, though real and profound, relationship. Nature is subjected to man, and man must recognize that he is subject to God. If man rebels against God or alienates himself from Him, nature too will become estranged and rebel against man. So it has happened in every period of spiritual and moral crisis. So is it happening today.

This conviction of the Church is expressed in the ceremony of supplication, or prayers in which men invoke protection for the earth and liberation from the great scourges that have always threatened humanity: war, famine, and pestilence. Their aim was that of "liberation from the scourges of God's justice and drawing down the blessings of his mercy on the fruits of the earth." "*A Fame, Peste, et Bello Libera Nos, Domine*," writes the historian Roberto Sabatino Lopez in *The Birth of Europe*, was the liturgical invocation in the ceremony of supplication that "recovered over the course of the fourteenth century all of its dramatic relevance." As Lopez observes:

> Between the tenth and twelfth centuries, none of the great scourges that reap misery for humanity seems to have afflicted it to any great extent; neither pestilence, of which no one spoke in this period, nor war, which took a much smaller number of victims. Moreover, the agricultural horizons were enlarged by a slow warming of the climate. We have proof of the retreat of glaciers in the mountains and of icebergs in the northern seas, in the extension of viticulture to regions like England where it is no longer practicable today, in the abundance of water in the regions of the Sahara recovered from the desert.

Quite different was the scene in the fourteenth century, which saw natural catastrophes and serious religious and political upheavals coincide.

The climate in the Middle Ages had been mild, like its customs. The fourteenth century, on the other hand, was to face a sudden harshening of climatic conditions. Historians have detected in this period the advance of alpine and polar glaciers. When the southern limit of glaciers is lowered and precipitation increases, the springtime thaws cause the water that could not be held in forests to descend ruinously into the valleys, causing flooding and mudslides, eroding arable land. This leads to a diminished harvest and to malnutrition and death among the inhabitants of a region.

The rains and floods of the spring of 1315 brought a general famine that struck all of Europe, but especially the northern regions, causing the deaths of millions of people, one-fifth of Europe's population in all. Lopez observes that over the course of the fourteenth century, Greenland, which had previously been occupied by Scandinavians, was abandoned due to the excessive cold and malnutrition. They could no longer find food to eat. King Edward II of England (1284–1327), who governed the most prosperous nation in Europe of that period, stopped in St. Alban on August 10, 1315, and could not find bread for himself and his retinue. Hunger spread everywhere. The elderly voluntarily refused their food in the hope of allowing the youth to survive, and the chroniclers of the age wrote of many cases of cannibalism.

One of the main consequences of famines was what another historian, Alberto Tenenti (1924–2002), defined as "agricultural de-structuring." In this period, there were "incredible movements of agricultural depopulation" characterized by flight from the land and the abandonment of villages; forests were invading fields and vineyards. Agriculture represented at that time the main source of income for the population. As a consequence of the abandonment of their fields, a sharp reduction in the productivity of the soil resulted, and an impoverishment of the livestock holdings followed. This led to other consequences for working the land: a contraction in the number of plows was proportional to the decrease of oxen.

If bad weather provoked famine, this in turn weakened the health of the population, opening the path to disease. The historians Ruggero Romano and Alberto Tenenti have shown how, in the fourteenth century, the recurring cycle of famine and epidemics was intensified. The last great pestilence had broken out from 747 to 750. Nearly six hundred years later it reappeared, striking four times over the course of a decade and annihilating at least a third of Europe's population, more than that in urban areas. The first epidemic was the terrible lung infection of 1348–1350; the second that overtook it lasted from 1360 to 1363; the third from 1371 to 1374; and the fourth from 1381 to 1384. The plague came from the Far East, on board merchant ships departing from Caffa in the fall of 1347, reaching Constantinople, the first city to be infected, and then arrived in Messina. Over the course of the next three years, it infected all of Europe, all the way to Scandinavia and Poland. This was the plague described by Giovanni Boccaccio in his *Decameron*. Italy lost half its population. More than numbers, it was individual destinies that gave a concrete idea of the plague's devastation.

Agnolo di Tura, a Sienese chronicler, lamented not being able to find anyone to bury the dead, and of having to bury his five children with his own hands. Giovanni Villani (1276–1348), a Florentine chronicler, was killed by the plague so suddenly that his account breaks off in mid-sentence. Florence at the time of Dante had more than one hundred thousand inhabitants; after the first great wave of the plague, it had fifty thousand. In France as well, the plague, together with the sad economic situation and war, saw innumerable victims, among them a third of the cardinals gathered in Avignon.

The medieval period had been characterized by strong demographic growth. Describing the city of Milan, which at the end of the thirteenth century was perhaps the most populous city in Europe, the medieval poet Bonvesin de la Riva writes that "the population is growing every day, and the city is expanding into new buildings." The population of Europe, which around the year 1000 had exceeded forty million and by 1300 had reached seventy million, after a century of wars, epidemics, and famines sunk back to forty million, a decrease of more than a third.

The famines, pestilences, and wars of the fourteenth century were interpreted by the Christian people as signs of God's chastisement, recalling the words of the Gospel, *"et erunt pestilentiae et fames et terraemotus per loca"* (and there shall be plagues and famines and earthquakes in various places) (Matt. 24:7). This was not the end of the world, but the end of an age. As always throughout history, natural disasters have accompanied the infidelity and apostasy of the nations. It happened at the end of the Christian Middle Ages and seems to be happening today: sin has always brought upon the nations the chastisements of God.

## 6. ST. CATHERINE AND ST. BRIDGET

The thirteenth century was a century in which sanctity flourished and thrived in Europe. The fourteenth century was more like a desert in this aspect. Dom Guéranger writes that, in the fourteenth century, Christianity seemed to lose heart, due in particular to naturalism and sensualism. "It seems that God in this century was stingier with the saints. Besides the illustrious St. Catherine of Siena, we find no other saint in this period whose work had such a vast echo. The historian cannot fail to notice this characteristic trait of a decadence that had only just begun, but instead must study in depth the sublime figure of Catherine of Siena, who epitomized all the supernatural vitality of her time."

The popes have spoken much of her. Canonized in 1461, St. Catherine of Siena was declared patron of Italy by Pius XII. In 1970, Paul VI proclaimed her Doctor of the Church, and John Paul II later declared her co-patroness of Europe. Born in Siena in 1347 in a very large family, Catherine died in Rome in 1380 at just thirty-three years old. At the age of sixteen, moved by a vision of St. Dominic, she entered the Dominican Third Order, in the female branch of the Mantellates. She never became a nun, much as St. Francis had refused the priesthood. Staying within her family home, she confirmed her vow of virginity made privately when still an adolescent, dedicating herself to prayer, penance, works of charity, and above all the aid of the sick. She was twenty-eight when on April 1, 1375, while preaching the necessity of the war for the liberation of the Holy Land, Catherine received the stigmata of Christ. Her confessor, Blessed Raymond of Capua (1330–1399), wrote that the stigmata were "in the form of pure light radiating from her hands, her feet, and her side."

As the fame of her sanctity spread, every social class sought her counsel: nobles and politicians, artists and common people, the consecrated, and ecclesiastics, including Pope Gregory XI, who at that time was living in Avignon and whom Catherine energetically exhorted to return to Rome. Catherine was convinced that the popes must return to Rome from Avignon, that they should reform the customs of the Church and call a new crusade against the infidels, to rediscover around the banner of the Holy Cross the unity and concord of the Christian people.

Catherine insistently admonished the pastors of the Church not to allow their negligence to lead the flock to perdition. She wrote to the cardinal bishop of Ostia, "Alas, keep silent no more! Shout with a hundred thousand tongues. I foresee that through keeping silence the world has rotted, the Bride of Christ has blanched, her color stolen, because her blood has been sucked out of her, namely the Blood of Christ."

Moved only by her profound love for the Church, the saint from Siena always invited sacred ministers, beginning with the pope—whom she called, "Sweet Christ on earth," to be faithful to their mission. Before dying, she said, "Leaving the body, in truth I have consumed and given my life in the Church and for the Holy Church, a matter for which I am singularly grateful."

Next to St. Catherine of Siena, we must recall another extraordinary woman of this age, Bridget of Sweden. Born to a pious noble family at the castle of Finster in 1303, she was married at fourteen and had eight children who distinguished themselves like their mother for their holy lives. When she was left a widow, Bridget distributed her goods to the poor and, though never requesting religious consecration, settled in the Cistercian monastery of Alvastra. There her divine revelations began, which accompanied her for the rest of her life. Bridget herself dictated these revelations to her confessor-secretaries, who translated them from Swedish into Latin and collected them in an edition of eight volumes titled *Revelations*. As Pope Benedict XVI writes:

> Reading these *Revelations*, in fact, we are challenged by many important themes. For example, the description frequently returns, with very realistic detail, of the Passion of Christ, to which Bridget always nurtured a privileged devotion, contemplating in it the infinite love of God for men. On the Lord's mouth that speaks to her, she audaciously places these words: "Oh my friends, I love my sheep so tenderly that, if it were

possible, I would like to die many more times for each of them, that
same death that I suffered for the redemption of all."

The revelations of St. Bridget were directed, in the form of severe reprimands,
to all believers of her time, and above all to religious and political authorities,
that they might live their Christian life coherently. In 1349, Bridget left Sweden forever and travelled in pilgrimage to Rome. Not only did she intend to
participate in the Jubilee of 1350, she also sought to obtain from the pope
approval of the rule of a religious order she hoped to found, called the Holy
Savior, composed of monks and nuns under the authority of an abbess. This
is an element that should not surprise us: in the Middle Ages there existed
monastic foundations with both male and female branches, practicing the
same monastic rule.

In Rome, Bridget dedicated herself to a life of intense apostolate and prayer,
in the company of her daughter Catherine. From Rome, she visited various Italian sanctuaries on pilgrimage, in particular Assisi, the home of St. Francis, to
whom Bridget fostered particular devotion. Finally, in 1371, her great desire was
crowned: a journey to the Holy Land, where she travelled in the company of her
spiritual children, a group Bridget called "the Friends of God."

During those years, the pontiffs were sojourning in Avignon, far from
Rome. Like Catherine of Siena, Bridget appealed to them urgently, that they
would return to the Apostolic See in the Eternal City. Also like Catherine, she
proclaimed the necessity of a new crusade.

She died in 1373, before Pope Gregory XI returned definitively to Rome,
and was solemnly canonized in 1391 by Pope Boniface IX. She left us the fifteen
famous *Orations* to which great promises are tied. We hope that in reciting with
all one's heart the following prayers, our souls might receive the same benefits
that St. Bridget mentioned when she wrote:

> My most beloved brother, I was immersed in the greatest bitterness of
> life, pain, sickness, and poverty, and abandonment afflicted me. Every
> evening, I read these orations with love and my life was miraculously
> transformed and the Lord, faithful to His promises, filled me with joy,
> well-being, riches and consolations. What Jesus did for me, a miserable
> sinner, He will do for you too, my beloved brother.

## 7. CARTHUSIANS: NEVER REFORMED, NEVER DEFORMED

The fourteenth century was a century of confusion, of suffering, and of fear, in which the end of the world seemed near, announced by saints like the great Dominican preacher Vincenzo Ferreri (1350–1419). But Providence had different plans. Spiritual decadence did not spare the great monastic orders, with one exception: that of the Carthusians. Throughout the centuries, over 151 Carthusian monasteries have been founded in Europe.

St. Bruno, born in Cologne in 1030 and raised in France, founded the order of the Carthusians in 1084, taking its name from the valley of the Grande Chartreuse in the French Alps, the place where he and six companions sought solitude to dedicate themselves to the contemplative life. He was guided by a vision he had in a dream: seven stars that led seven pilgrims toward a mountain called "Carthusia," *Chartreuse* in French. From the very beginning, the Carthusian life was characterized by a combination of hermitic and cenobitic life. The Carthusian lives alone, but also in community — alone because each monk has his own cell where he is supplied with all he needs to live in poverty; in community because he participates in the liturgical life with others.

Chartreuse is formed by a cloister, in the middle of which is a garden and a cemetery. Around these are the cells of the monks. Different from many other religious orders, the Carthusians can proudly say they have never abandoned the original spirit of prayer and penance. It is said of this nine-hundred-year-old order that it has never been reformed because it has never been deformed: "*Carthusia, numquam reformata quia numquam deformata!*"

Even today, the Carthusian spirit lives on. Among the many Carthusian monasteries in Italy, we remember the one in Farneta near Lucca (Tuscany) and the one in Serra San Bruno in Calabria, where St. Bruno, the founder of the order, died in 1101. In the twentieth century, a great spiritual author also lived there, Francesco di Sales Pollien (1853–1936), author of books such as *Lived Christianity*, *The Interior Life Simplified*, and *The Plant of God*. From the Carthusian hermitage of St. Bruno in our own century, the spirit of St. Bruno reaches us to help root the life of those who struggle in the world in a spirit of recollection and prayer.

*Lived Christianity*, the masterpiece of Dom Pollien, ends with the exhortation of St. Paul to the Ephesians:

> Finally, be strong in the Lord and in the strength of his might. Put on
> the whole armor of God, that you may be able to stand against the wiles

of the devil. For we are not contending against flesh and blood, but against the principalities, against the powers, against the world rulers of this present darkness, against the spiritual hosts of wickedness in the heavenly places. Therefore, take the whole armor of God, that you may be able to withstand in the evil day, and having done all, to stand. Stand therefore, having girded your loins with truth, and having put on the breastplate of righteousness, and having shod your feet with the equipment of the gospel of peace; above all taking the shield of Faith, with which you can quench all the flaming darts of the evil one. And take the helmet of salvation, and the sword of the Spirit, which is the Word of God. This is the armor of the soldier of God. It is well tempered and gives certainty of splendid victories. (6:10–18)

# CHAPTER III

# The Age of the Great Schism

## 1. THE CONCLAVE OF 1378

The fourteenth century was one of the most dramatic in the history of the Church. It was the century of the Slap of Anagni suffered by Boniface VIII in 1303 and of the transfer of the papacy to Avignon from 1308 to 1377. But it was also the century of the Great Schism of the West, the worst crisis in the Church since Arianism.

It all began on March 27, 1378, when, fourteen months after his return to Rome from Avignon, Pope Gregory XI died. For the first time in seventy-five years, a conclave was to be held in Rome.

The term "conclave" comes from the Latin *cum clave* and indicates a closed setting in which the Sacred College of Cardinals gathers to elect a new pope. For it to be valid, the election must be carried out according to the procedure established by the Church, but a validly elected pope has the power to change the concrete manner of election. This explains why, throughout the centuries, the participants of the conclave have been the Roman clergy, the people of Rome, secular princes (both licitly and illicitly), and finally cardinals, who are nominally the representatives of the clergy of Rome and of the dioceses around the city, but represent in fact the universal Church.

The first conclave as we understand it today was held in Viterbo from November 1268 to September 1271. The city authorities, after many months of vain hopes, locked the electors in the bishop's palace, walled up all the entrances, placed the cardinals on a diet of bread and water, and even went so far as to remove the roof of the building. These severe measures obtained the desired effect, and the pope who was finally elected, Gregory X (r. 1271–1276), promulgated the constitution *Ubi Maius Periculum*, which constitutes the birthdate of modern conclaves. This constitution established that the cardinals had to gather in the building where the pope died, in a perfectly sealed place, subjecting themselves to a regime of life the more austere the longer the election was protracted. From the beginning, an oath was demanded of the participants to respect the secrecy of what was happening within the conclave.

One hundred years had passed since the conclave of Gregory X, when another pope of the same name died, Gregory XI (r. 1370–1378). At the conclave of 1378, held in the Vatican in the Chapel of St. Niccolò, substituted today by the Sistine Chapel, sixteen cardinals participated of the twenty-three cardinals living at that time. Of these, most were French and were called "limousines," meaning those from the South of France. This was a logical consequence of the long Avignon Captivity, in which the popes had been French and had nominated French cardinals.

As the cardinals were entering the conclave, the people were in an uproar, shouting, "We want a Roman, or at least an Italian!" On April 8, the College of Cardinals chose as Gregory XI's successor the archbishop of Bari, Bartolomeo Prignano, a learned canonist with an austere lifestyle, who was not a cardinal and therefore was not present at the conclave. On that same day, the people burst into the conclave to demand the election of a Roman pope, but the cardinals did not dare announce the election of Prignano and had them believe that the newly elected pope was the elderly cardinal Francesco Tibaldeschi, a native of Rome. The following day, however, Bartolomeo Prignano was enthroned, taking the name Urban VI (r. 1378–1389), and on April 18 he was crowned in St. Peter's. All Christendom considered his election legitimate, because the threats on the cardinals took place in the Vatican after the election had occurred.

The French cardinals thought that "the newly elected pope would be malleable and docile, but they were wrong. Immediately after his election, Urban VI announced a program of radical reform, beginning at the highest ecclesiastical levels. *"Ego intendo mundare Ecclesiam et ego mundabo."* Urban's desire for reform was more than justified, but according to St. Catherine of Siena (who supported him), he lacked moderation and prudence in carrying out its execution, embittering the cardinals who had elected him.

In the month of July, twelve French cardinals, along with Cardinal Pedro de Luna from Aragon, met in the city of Anagni where, on August 2, they posted a declaration in which they called the Roman See vacant, saying that the election of Urban VI was invalid because it had been extorted by the Roman populace through rebellion and tumult. Urban VI was proclaimed an "antichrist, apostate, devil, and tyrant." The queen of Naples, Giovanna I, and the king of France, Charles V, assured their protection, and on September 20, the rebel cardinals elected in the Fondi cathedral Cardinal Roberto of Geneva as the new pope, taking the name Clement VII (r. 1378–1394). After a vain attempt to occupy Rome, Clement took up residence once again in Avignon. Thus began the Great Schism of the West.

## 2. Material Schism and Formal Schism

The word "schism" indicates a division, a fracture in the ecclesial body, and is not synonymous with heresy, which instead signifies doctrinal error. Christendom had experienced the Eastern Schism in 1054, which separated the Eastern Orthodox Church from the Roman Catholic Church. This division still endures today. The Western Schism was a division that shook Western Christianity for nearly forty years, from 1378 to 1417. While the Eastern Schism was a schism in the true sense of the word, because the Orthodox refused and still refuse to recognize the primacy of the bishop of Rome as pontiff of the universal Church, the Western Schism was a material schism, de facto, but not a formal schism, of intent, because neither side intended to deny the primacy of the papacy. There were no doctrinal errors on either side. Urban VI and Clement VII, and their successors after them, were convinced of the legitimacy of their canonical election. It was a matter of understanding who was the legitimate successor and Vicar of Christ. Today the Church says that the legitimate popes were Urban VI and his successors, but the question then was precisely one of knowing where the true Church was.

From 1378, Christianity was divided into two "obediences": recognizing Clement VII were France, Spain, Scotland, Castille, Portugal, Savoy, Aragon, and Navarre. Faithful to Urban VI were Northern and Central Italy, the Holy Roman Empire, England, Ireland, Bohemia, Poland, and Hungary.

For forty years, European Catholics lived a daily drama. Not only were there two popes and two Colleges of Cardinals, but often in the same dioceses there were two bishops, two abbots, two parish priests. "One king arises against another," wrote Ludolph von Sagan, "one province against another; the clergy, the learned, families have all been divided." And because the two popes excommunicated each other, all the faithful in Christendom found themselves excommunicated by one pope or the other.

St. Catherine of Siena, who had worked so hard for the return of Gregory X to Rome, was convinced of the legitimacy of Urban's election and his right to govern the Church. According to the historian Ludwig von Pastor, it is thanks in part to her influence that Urban VI was able to establish himself in Italy. She was in those years for the papacy what Joan of Arc would be for the French monarchy. The virgin of Siena wanted to carry on her shoulders the weight of a Church divided into two adversarial camps. Her health was worsening, but from January 1380 through all of Lent, she walked to St. Peter's every morning, until she was confined to her bed, awaiting death in the profound sadness of seeing the Church in a worse situation than that which she had sought to remedy by bringing the pope back to Rome from Avignon. She affirmed that there was no worse period than that in which she was forced to live. Catherine died at thirty-three on April 29, 1380, taking to her tomb the martyrdom of the Church she carried in her heart.

Next to Catherine of Siena and Catherine of Sweden, who supported Urban VI, there were other saints who were obedient to Avignon, such as St. Vincenzo Ferreri, Blessed Peter of Luxemburg, and St. Colette of Corbie. The situation was so confused that there was no clear way out.

## 3. SCHISM AND CONCILIAR THEORIES

At the beginning of June 1394, the University of Paris presented King Charles VI with a long defense that proposed three ways for extinguishing the schism: the first, the *via cessionis*, required both popes to renounce the throne spontaneously; the second, the *via compromissi*, entailed arbitration by an impartial college that would decide the legitimacy of the claimants; the third, the *via concilii*, counseled that the matter be entrusted to the decision of an Ecumenical Council. The route suggested by the Sorbonne as the simplest and safest route was that of the free resignation of one of the two popes. On September 16, one of the two died suddenly, Clement VII, the pope of Avignon. It seemed the time had come to resolve the matter. It would have sufficed that the cardinals not proceed with the election of another pontiff and that the pope of Rome resign. Instead, the cardinals in Avignon elected a new pope, Pedro de Luna, an austere and obstinate man who forcefully claimed his rights and who reigned with the name Benedict XIII (r. 1394–1422). Following Boniface IX, the Roman popes were Innocent VII (1404–1406) and Gregory XII (1406–1415).

The debate continued among theologians. The point of departure was a passage of the *Decretum* of the jurist Gratian (c. 1075–1145), the most authoritative collection of ecclesiastical laws of the age, which said, "The pope has the right to judge all, but can be judged by no one, unless it has been discovered that he has deviated from the Faith" (*A nemine est judicandus, nisi deprehenditur a fide devius*) (*Dist.* 400, c. 6). The rule according to which no one can judge the pope (*Prima sedes non judicabitur*) admitted, and still admits, one exception: the sin of heresy. This was a maxim on which all could agree, and which could be applied not only to a heretical pope but also to a schismatic pope. It created a whole series of problems, however: What does *a fide devius* actually mean? Must the heresy be notorious and manifest, or private and hidden? And who can judge the pope, if no one in the Church is superior to him? These were the problems on the table. The case of a heretical pope is still allowed today by traditional theology because this hypothesis in no way limits the supreme power of the pontiff. It is not a matter of deposing a heretical pope, but of verifying that a pope has lapsed in his function due to heresy.

Quite different, however, is the doctrine of conciliarism that was affirmed in this period. It stated that a heretical or schismatic pope could be deposed by a council, because the assembly of bishops is superior to the pope. The main proponents of this doctrine were the chancellor of the University of Paris, Peter d'Ailly (1350–1420), later a cardinal in Avignon, and the theologian Jean Gerson (1363–1429), another chancellor and professor in Paris. In 1410, the work *De Modis Uniendi ac Reformandi Ecclesiam in Concilio Generali* appeared, which summarized the conciliarist theses circulating at that time. The Church, it said, rests upon popular sovereignty; the representative of the Christian people is the council, which is superior to the pope, and the council can depose him and proceed to a new election; the convocation of a council lies solely with the emperor, with the approval of secular princes, against the will of the cardinals.

## 4. THE COUNCILS OF PISA AND CONSTANCE

These ideas, together with the unresolved schism, led some cardinals on both sides to seek a solution in a general council that opened in Pisa on March 25, 1409, with the aim of inviting both rival pontiffs to abdicate, or if they refused, to depose them. And so it happened.

In the eighth and ninth sessions (May 10 and May 17), the Council of Pisa declared itself ecumenical and representative of the universal Church, and attributed to itself the competence, as a supreme tribunal, over the two popes; during the fifteenth session on June 5, the sentence was read that deposed both rival pontiffs as "schismatic and heretical" and declared the Roman See vacant.

During the nineteenth session, on June 26, the College of Cardinals, dominated by the strong personality of Baldassare Cossa, elected a third pope, Pietro Filargo, of the Friars Minor, a native of Candia and archbishop of Milan, who took the name Alexander V (r. 1409–1410). The following year, he was succeeded by Baldassare Cossa himself, who took the name John XXIII (r. 1410–1415). But neither Gregory XII nor Benedict XIII recognized the validity of the council, nor did they accept its decisions. The Council of Pisa was neither ecumenical nor legitimate, because it was an acephalus assembly, without a pope summoning it or presiding over it. "During the first nineteen sessions," observes Cardinal Hergenröther, "the council had no pope, and without a pope there cannot be an Ecumenical Council."

At this point, John XXIII, with the support of the German emperor Sigmund (r. 1410–1437), took the initiative of calling another council, which opened in the imperial city of Constance on November 5, 1414. Constance was a city of little more than five thousand inhabitants. During the council, it swelled to a hundred thousand. Participating at the council were 29 cardinals, 3 patriarchs, 185 archbishops and bishops, and 18,000 ecclesiastics. It was, therefore, a much more important and solemn event than that in Pisa.

John XXIII had the goal of being recognized as the sole pope, of confirming the Council of Pisa on which his legitimacy was based, and of leading the Council of Constance to these conclusions. To obtain these goals he had created many Italian cardinals to support him. Emperor Sigmund had taken seriously, however, his role as defender of the Church, and at the council the idea began to gain traction of the necessity of a *via cessionis*, the renunciation of all three popes.

The most important prelates, like Cardinal Peter d'Ailly and Francesco Zabarella (1360–1417), and the chancellor of the University of Paris, Jean Gerson, were convinced that the unity of the Church could be reestablished only if all three popes were obliged to renounce their own election. To overcome the Italian majority, the French and the English were able to define the vote as expressed not by *capita singulorum*, by head count that is, but by *nationes*, by national groups.

The right to vote was given to France, Germany, England, Italy, and later to Spain, the five principal European nations. This was a profoundly revolutionary idea. In the first place, the nations—political entities, that is—entered significantly in the life of the Church, subverting the dependent relationship that they had always had with the Church up to this point. Second, and above all, the principle that saw in the pope the supreme arbiter, moderator, and judge of the council was unseated, placing authority instead with the Council Fathers.

For this reason, the historian Giorgio Falco wrote that, at Constance, the adult Europe of nation-states rebelled against its Mother, the Roman Church, preparing a case against the papacy itself and the entire Catholic system of the Middle Ages. Another historian, Alois Dempf (1891–1982), defined the parliamentarism of Constance "the only voice declaring itself sovereign in the Church."

On March 20, 1414, there occurred a twist in the plot: John XXIII, disguised as a halberdier, fled Constance fearing the Council would depose him. His flight produced universal consternation, but Peter d'Ailly, who exercised great authority, and the French theologians pushed for the continuation of the council. On March 23, Gerson gave a discourse in which he established twelve propositions relative to the universal council that he stated to be superior to the pope and independent of him for its convocation.

A few days later, the council recognized itself as legitimately assembled and decided to continue its sessions: in the fifth session of April 6, it approved through the voting of the nations the celebrated decree *Haec Sancta*, in which it solemnly affirmed that the Council, assisted by the Holy Spirit, represented the entire Church Militant, and received its power directly from Christ: therefore every Christian, including the pope, was obliged to obey it in matters of Faith, Church unity, and reform in its head and members.

The decree *Haec Sancta* was integrated, on the disciplinary level, by that of the thirty-ninth session, *Frequens*, of October 9, 1417. It stated that Ecumenical Councils must be made a stable ecclesiastical institution and consequently, to use the words of Hubert Jedin, "a type of court of appeals to control the papacy." If this decree had been applied, it would have carried out the revolutionary injunctions of *Haec Sancta*.

Pope Gregory XII rectified the irregularity of the Council of Constance, and thus it is considered an Ecumenical Council of the Church today, such that both pontiffs, Martin V and Eugene IV, ratified its acts. Historians and theologians explain, however, that *Haec Sancta* was not a dogmatic definition because it lacks the typical expressions of this genre of definition, expressed in formulas such as *anathema sit* and by verbs such as *order, define, establish, decree,* and *declare.* The actual importance of the decree was in its disciplinary and pastoral character. Cardinal Alfred Baudrillart explains in the *Dictionaire de Théologie Catholique* that the Council of Constance did not intend to promulgate a dogmatic definition when it published *Haec Sancta,* and for this reason the Church could later repudiate it.

In the meantime, John XXIII had fled to Burgundy and was captured and brought back forcefully to Constance, where on May 29 he was deposed for simony, scandal, and schism, and excluded from future election along with the other two popes. Gregory XII consented at that point to abdicate on the condition that his bull summoning the council would be read in public. The Council recognized him as a cardinal and nominated him bishop of Porto and permanent legate of Ancona, but Gregory died in Recanati before the new pope was elected, on October 18, 1417. Benedict XIII remained inflexible, although he was abandoned even by the nations of his own obedience and deposed as a perjurer, schismatic, and heretic on July 26, 1417.

The new pope, Odo Colonna, was elected on November 11, 1417, a Roman who took the name Martin V (r. 1417–1431), after the saint whose feast day it was when he was elected. The Council of Constance was dismissed on March 21, 1418, with the generic approval of the new pope. The disorder that troubled the Papal States forced Martin V to remain in Florence for nearly two years until his solemn entrance in Rome on September 28, 1420, which he found in a desolate state.

## 5. THE CONDEMNATION OF CONCILIARISM

In deference to the decree *Frequens,* Martin V summoned another council, which opened in Pavia on April 23, 1423. Two years later, following an epidemic, the council transferred to Siena, where it continued until February 25, 1424, with scarce results. Martin V decided on the city of Basel as the setting for the next council, but then died on February 23, 1431, before the council could gather. The assembly opened under his successor Eugene IV (r. 1431–1447), upon whom the Council Fathers attempted to impose the conciliar doctrine of Constance.

Eugene IV retracted the work of the council, transferring it to Ferrara and then to Florence. Most of the Council Fathers, however, opposed the transfer and remained in Basel. The Council of Basel deposed the pope as a heretic and elected Duke Amedeo VIII of Savoy with the name Felix V (r. 1439–1449), the last anti-pope in history. Eugene IV, from Florence where he had moved the council, hurled excommunication at the antipope and those gathered in Basel. The council convoked in Ferrara is considered the legitimate continuation of the Council of Basel and is listed with it as the seventeenth Ecumenical Council of the Church.

The Council of Florence was very important for two reasons. First, an authoritative delegation of the Eastern Church participated in it, led by the Patriarch of Constantinople Joseph II and Emperor John VIII Palaiologos, the two highest authorities in the East. The theological discussions were long, but in the end, they reached an agreement that brought the schism to an end. On July 16, 1439, the decree *Laetentur Coeli et Exultet Terra* solemnly sanctioned the reunification of the Eastern Church with Rome.

Second, conciliarism was definitively condemned and the doctrine of the supreme authority of the pope over the Church was confirmed. On September 4, 1439, Eugene IV, "*sacro approbante concilio*," condemned Basel's interpretation of the Council of Constance and solemnly defined "that the Holy Apostolic See and the Roman pontiff have primacy over the whole universe; that the same Roman pontiff is the successor of Blessed Peter, Prince of the Apostles, the authentic Vicar of Christ, head of the entire Church, Father and Doctor of all Christians; that our Lord Jesus Christ transmitted to him in the person of Blessed Peter full power to feed, support and govern the universal Church, as is attested also in the acts of the Ecumenical Councils and sacred canons."

Conciliarism was later condemned by the Fifth Lateran Council; by the Council of Trent, with the *Professio Fidei Tridentina*; and by the First Vatican Council in *Pastor Aeternus*, which solemnly reaffirmed the primacy of government of the Roman pontiff.

## 6. St. Vincent Ferrer and St. Bernardine of Siena

Even in the most tempestuous periods of history, God never abandons His Church, but raises up prophets, mystics, combatants who open the way for great rebirths. While Christianity was torn by the Great Western Schism in the fourteenth and fifteenth centuries, a saint who saw himself as the angel of judgment, Vincent

Ferrer, travelled throughout Europe proclaiming the imminent coming of the Last Judgment.

Vincent was born in Valencia, Spain, in 1350. At eighteen, he entered the Order of Preachers and was consecrated priest in the year in which the Great Schism of the West broke out. He sided with the pope in Avignon, Benedict XIII, and became his chaplain, but later left the pontifical court and spent the next twenty years of his life as a preacher in Provence, Liguria, Savoy, Switzerland, Northern Italy, and then in Flanders, France, and Spain, obtaining by his zeal the conversion of innumerable public sinners and even of Muslims and Jews. He was a saint of extraordinary austerity, received everywhere as a prophet, an apostle, and a wonderworker. Overcome by his exertions and old age, he died in 1419 in Vannes, Brittany, where his remains are interred. He was canonized in 1455 by Pope Callistus III at Santa Maria Sopra Minerva in Rome.

One wonders how people would react today before a St. Vincent Ferrer reminding them that everything is ephemeral on earth and that the judgment of God looms over men, nations, and history. Dom Guéranger recalls the people of that time:

> [They] beat their breasts, crying for mercy, and converting to the Lord. Today, the thought of Jesus Christ presiding in judgment in the clouds of Heaven no longer stirs Christians in the same way. They believe in the final judgment because it is an article of faith; but they do not tremble in expectancy of that day. They continue sinning for many, many years; then one day, by a particular grace of Divine goodness, they convert; but most of these neophytes continue to live a tepid life, thinking as little as possible about Hell and blame, and even less about the judgment with which God will bring this world to an end.... But this was not the case during the Christian era, when souls converted in sincerity. Love ruled over the fear in their souls, but fear of God's judgment was always alive in their minds, and in this they remained always anchored in the good they attained. But today, few Christians think about their situation on the day when the heavens will be rent with the sign of the Son of Man, Jesus, no longer as Redeemer but as Judge, who will come to separate the goats from the sheep.

And yet periods of crisis and difficulty, like all disasters, are permitted by Providence to reawaken the faith of men, raise their eyes to Heaven, and remind them of their immortal destiny and that supreme justice awaits every man.

Among those who heard St. Vincent Ferrer's preaching in Alexandria in 1408 was a twenty-eight-year-old Franciscan, Bernardino of Siena. He was deeply moved by the fiery words of the Spanish Dominican and decided to set off on an apostolate of preaching throughout Italy. His mission ended in the city of Aquila where he died on May 20, 1444.

Bernardino preached above all against the worldly mentality of nascent humanism, and inculcated devotion to the Holy Name of Jesus. When he entered a city, he raised a banner on which was displayed the monogram of the Name of Jesus (IHS) surrounded by twelve rays of sunlight and crowned by a cross. He would set the banner next to the pulpit, and often carried and distributed small tablets with the same symbol. In private homes, public buildings, and churches in the cities he visited, he would write in large letters the monogram of Christ. Then, in the spring of 1437, while preaching during Lent in Viterbo, Pope Martin V called him to Rome on grounds that the devotion to the Holy Name that he was preaching had been accused of heresy.

The saint travelled immediately to Rome, where he was met with disdain and treated as a heretic. Dominican and Augustinian theologians diligently examined his writings by order of the pope, and it was established that a pontifical commission should publicly try the offender. Many Franciscans, among them another future saint, John of Capistrano, hastened to the Curia to defend their confrere. Some fifty doctors gathered in St. Peter's for the solemn judiciary audience, while Bernardino appeared with John of Capistrano and Matteo da Girgenti. Pope Martin V attended the memorable discussion in person, surrounded by cardinals, theologians, and religious. Bernardino defended himself from the accusations with calm humility, and John of Capistrano spoke in his defense with passionate oratory. The pope declared Bernardino innocent, removing all censure from him, and conferred to him the authority to proclaim the Word of God everywhere and to expose to public veneration "the sweet Name of Jesus." From that time this devotion spread widely.

## 7. St. Joan of Arc

Four years later, on May 30, 1431, St. Joan of Arc died, burned at the stake at only nineteen years of age, while gazing on the Crucifix and pronouncing over and over out loud the Name of Jesus. As Benedict XVI said at the audience on January 26, 2011:

Dear brothers and sisters, the Name of Jesus, invoked by our saint in the last moments of her earthly life, was the continual breath of her soul, like the beating of her heart, the center of her entire life.... Jesus was always given first place in her life, according to her beautiful expression, "Our Lord is served first." This French saint, cited numerous times in the *Catechism of the Catholic Church*, is particularly close to Catherine of Siena, patroness of Italy and of Europe. They are, in fact, two young women of their people, lay and consecrated in virginity; two committed mystics not in the cloister, but in the midst of the most dramatic realities of the Church and the world of their times. They are perhaps the most characteristic figures of the "strong women" who, at the end of the Middle Ages, fearlessly brought the great light of the gospel into the complex vicissitudes of history. We can place them next to the holy women who remained on Calvary, near Jesus crucified and Mary His Mother, when the apostles had fled and Peter had denied Him three times. The Church in that period was living through the profound crisis of the Great Western Schism which lasted nearly forty years. When Catherine of Siena died in 1380, there was a pope and an anti-pope; when Joan was born in 1412, there was a pope and two anti-popes. Along with this laceration within the Church, there were continual fratricidal wars among the Christian nations of Europe, the most dramatic of which was the interminable Hundred Years' War between France and England.

The English occupied at that time part of France, where King Charles VI found himself in the impossible situation of intervening in the struggles that lacerated the country. But God has always had a predilection for France, "the firstborn daughter of the Church," thanks to the baptism of Clovis at the end of the fifth century, and Joan of Arc was chosen by Him to display His love for the kingdom of France.

Joan was born in Domrémy, a little village on the border between France and Loraine, in January 1412. Her parents were well-off peasants, known by all as excellent Christians. At thirteen, she began to hear "celestial voices" and said that she saw St. Michael, St. Catherine of Alexandria, and St. Margaret of Antioch exhorting her to rise and fight for the salvation of France. At first, Joan resisted, but the voices continued for five years with the same insistence, revealing her mission. When she no longer had any doubt that God was calling her to fight for France, she succeeded in gaining an audience in Chinon with the Dauphin of France, the future King Charles VII, to propose to him her plan for liberating the city of Orléans, attacking the Burgundians, the allies of the English. Before meeting her, the sovereign had decided to put her to the test by dressing as a common man, mixed in with the nobles present in the vast hall of the castle.

Joan had never seen him before, but she went straight to him and said, "I come on a divine mission to aid the kingdom and your majesty; the King of Heaven orders, through me, that you be consecrated and crowned in Rheims, and that your majesty assumes his role, as the kings of France have always been, as representative of the King of Heaven." Charles had her examined by several theologians of the university, whom she convinced of the reality of her visions and of the rectitude of her intentions. In April 1429, the king gave her permission to ride, clothed in white armor, with his banner and sword, at the head of the army marching to the aid of Orléans. Joan was given no official command, though she exercised an irresistible fascination over the soldiers, because she fought with them and wounded, killed, and was injured like them.

On May 8, Orléans was liberated, and by June 12 Jargeau was taken. On June 18, Joan led the troops to victory at Patay, where two thousand enemy soldiers were killed, and many English nobles, among them the famous Talbot, were taken prisoner, while the French lost only three soldiers. An arrow struck Joan in her shoulder under the fortress of Tournelles, but did not prevent her from taking this victory. The fame of the young virgin warrior spread throughout France and Europe, and all now called her the "Maid of Orléans."

Her mission culminated in the coronation of King Charles VII in Rheims, on June 17, 1429. Joan stood with her banner at the foot of the altar throughout the ceremony, one of the most extraordinary in history. Her prodigious actions aroused envy and resentment, however, even among the politicians and ecclesiastics surrounding the sovereign. Joan was contrasted in her military plans. On September 8, she valorously fought under the walls of Paris and was again wounded. A year later, in September 1430, she ran to the aid of some companions who had been taken by the enemy in Compiègne, but this time she was taken prisoner. Shut in a horrible prison, she attempted to escape twice. Finally, she was handed over to the English on October 24, for ten thousand gold scudi, as booty of war. Neither the court nor the king of France hastened to save her.

On December 23, she was led to the city of Rouen, where a long and dramatic trial was carried out from February to May 1431. This was an unjust trial, presided over by two ecclesiastical judges and led by a large group of theologians from the famous university of Paris, who accused her of being a heretic, excommunicated her, and condemned her to burn at the stake. Joan proclaimed to the very end her love for the Church and for the king of France. Against the imposition of the tribunal, she insisted on wearing the clothes of a soldier to show her fidelity to the mission she had received. This was one of the most severe charges the judges brought against her. We have two historical sources of exceptional value regarding the trial: the Trial of Condemnation (*PCon*), which contains the transcript of the long interrogation of Joan and reports the saint's own words; and the Trial of Nullity of the Condemnation, or "rehabilitation" (*PNul*), which contains depositions of nearly 120 eyewitnesses from her entire life.

Joan's appeal, on May 24, for the pope's judgment of her case was rejected. On the morning of May 30, she received Holy Communion in prison for the last time and was immediately conducted to her execution in the old market square. Amid the flames, she reaffirmed the truth of her divine mission, shouting, "The voices did not lie to me."

Nearly twenty-five years later, the Trial of Nullity opened under the authority of Pope Callistus III, ending in the solemn verdict that declared her condemnation null (July 7, 1456). The pontiffs Leo XIII in 1894, Pius X in 1909, and Benedict XV in 1930 proclaimed Joan of Arc venerable, blessed, and saint, respectively.

Joan of Arc epitomizes and transmits to our age the enduring spirit of the Middle Ages. Providence chose a humble shepherd girl to offer an example of martial virtue taken to its fullest expression. The chaste and combative spirit of Joan of Arc, her warrior virginity, is diametrically opposed to our world that lives immersed in impurity and cowardice. We must fight like her, with complete purity of doctrine and character in the defense of our Faith.

CHAPTER IV

# The Popes between Humanism and Crusade

## 1. THE JUBILEE OF 1450

The Jubilee of 1450 seemed to mark a new era for the Church after the dramatic events of the Avignon Captivity and the two religious schisms that had lacerated the West: the Great Schism (1378–1417) and the Little Schism (1433–1447). With the rise of Nicholas V (r. 1447–1455) to the papal throne, peace was slowly returning to the Church. Even the dissidents who had rebelled at Basel in the name of conciliarist ideas accepted his authority. Their anti-pope, Felix V, submitted, returning to his identity as Amedeo VIII of Savoy.

The proclamation by Nicholas V of a Great Jubilee was welcomed enthusiastically by Christendom. On Christmas of 1449, the pope personally opened the Holy Door at St. John Lateran Basilica and pilgrims began to flow in from everywhere. The Holy Year of 1450 renewed the pomp and splendor of the first Great Jubilee, invoked by Boniface VIII in 1300. Ludwig von Pastor writes, "Pilgrims from every nation in Europe rushed to Rome of all ages and conditions: Italians and Transalpines, men and women, young and old, healthy and sick, rich and poor. With their long pilgrim's walking stick, wide-brimmed hat adorned with a seashell hung at their backs, they marched along the great routes singing and reciting prayers."

Once they arrived in Rome, the pilgrims crossed the Tiber at Castel Sant'Angelo to reach St. Peter's and venerate the tomb of the Prince of the

Apostles, the veil of Veronica, and the great relics of Christendom that the pope
had exposed for the public. The flow of pilgrims was so great that an eyewitness
compared them to the swarming of ants. Thanks to this unexpected flood of
crowds, the apostolic coffers were able to settle their debts, allowing the pope to
carry out his grandiose projects, beginning with the urban renewal of the Eternal City.

Rome had returned to its place as the center of the world, the capital of
Christianity, and Nicholas V planned to transform it so as to increase the authority of the Church and the dignity of the papacy. One of the most glorious
days of the Holy Year was the canonization of the holy preacher Bernardino of
Siena, who had died in 1444, just six years earlier, and who was already venerated everywhere. The ceremony was held on the solemn day of Pentecost, May
24, 1450. From the large Franciscan convent of the Ara Coeli came a procession
of three thousand Friars Minor, among whom were several illustrious preachers
destined to be canonized as well, such as John of Capistrano, Giacomo della
Marca, and others. Among the multitudes of pilgrims was the great saint of the
stigmata, Rita of Cascia. This enthusiasm, this multitude of pilgrims from every
corner of Europe, this solemnity of religious gives us a framework for understanding an epoch of intense Christian Faith. Yet, next to its light, many shadows
were darkening this framework.

## 2. BETWEEN HUMANISM AND CRUSADE

A serious threat came from the East. On November 10, 1444, a coalition of crusader
armies led by the king of Hungary and the king of Poland Ladislaw III (r. 1424–1444)
was shattered against the troops of Sultan Murad II, with three times their number,
at Varna in Bulgaria. Among the fallen Christians was King Ladislaw and the papal
legate Giuliano Cesarini (1398–1444), while the commander of the army, Giovanni
Hunyadi (1407–1456), who had liberated Serbia from the invaders, barely escaped
capture after fighting valiantly. This was a decisive victory for the Ottoman Empire,
allowing it to consolidate its hegemony in the Balkans.

But the most serious threat was within Christendom. A new way of thinking
and feeling had progressively taken hold in all Italy and from there was infecting
Europe. The Christian vision of life placed God at the center of the created universe. The medieval period was, in this sense, a theocentric civilization, in which
every reality was ordered to God. The new conception of the world, on the
other hand, placed man at the center of the universe and substituted earthly

happiness, founded on love of self, for supernatural happiness, founded on love of God. This philosophy of life, *humanism*, did not deny Christian truths in principle, but proposed a human ideal that de facto denied the redeeming value of the sacrifice of the Cross.

In the medieval period, the spirit of sacrifice knew its highest expression in the Crusades, a movement of souls in which the whole of Christendom embraced the Cross, choosing it as a public insignia, and fought and died in its name. Substituting the austere and combative spirit of the Crusades with a hedonistic state of soul, humanism sought to reconcile the law of the gospel with the principles of the world. The spirit of the Crusades and the worldly spirit were incompatible. Pleasure is the illusory happiness of one's body, enjoyed in the present moment. Sacrifice is the renunciation of immediate goods to attain higher goods through effort and abnegation of oneself. Pleasure is the expression of the pagan spirit; sacrifice, of the Christian spirit. These two tendencies clashed in the fourteenth century and placed even the popes before a dramatic crossroads, between the worldly spirit of humanism and the austere, combative spirit of the Crusades.

The first leader of humanism in Rome was Lorenzo Valla (1405–1457), the author of a dialogue *On the Pleasures or on the True Good* in which he celebrated a pagan-style hymn to pleasure. This work was conceived in dialogue form among three people who represent three different doctrines: Leonardo Bruni explicates the pagan doctrine of the Stoics; Antonio Beccadelli, called the Panormita, the likewise pagan doctrine of the Epicureans; and Niccolò Niccoli, that of Christian humanism. In reality, Valla was closest to Panormita, who derides in the dialogue the monastic virtues and affirms that prostitutes are more useful to humanity than nuns.

Lorenzo Valla was also the author of a celebrated defamatory work on the Donation of Constantine that the historian Ferdinand Gregorovius called "the most audacious attack against the temporal power of the pontiff that a reformer had ever dared to make." If the Donation of Constantine was false, said Valla, the pope must strip himself of every temporal power and the Romans must rebel against his dominion and restore the ancient Roman Republic. Despite these seditious ideas, Valla was secretary to popes and a canon of the Lateran Basilica, where his tomb can still be found. This makes clear the extent to which humanism had penetrated even ecclesiastical spheres, along with moral corruption.

The new humanistic direction had been affirmed in the Roman Curia from the beginning of the 1400s, under the pontificate of Innocent VII (r. 1404–1406), who had called many humanists to his service—"even some," writes Ludwig von Pastor, "whose admittance projected a sinister light on the conditions of that time." The German historian gives the example of the humanist Poggio Bracciolini (1380–1459), who occupied the lucrative office of apostolic writer under eight popes, working in the Curia for half a century.

According to Pastor, two currents existed in humanism: one Christian and one pagan. It was the latter one that, in fact, prevailed. The Church did not condemn it because, though formally it was a heterodox doctrine, it was difficult to condemn a disposition of one's soul. "In addition," observes the German historian, "the followers of the pagan Renaissance studied how to avoid even the shadow of allowing their science to touch theology in any way, and knew well how to make everything appear as an innocent passion, that could not be seriously persecuted without making the persecutor look ridiculous."

The first humanist pope was Nicholas V, the pope of the Jubilee of 1450, whose pontificate marked a shift in the history of the popes. With Nicholas V, according to Gregorovius, "Humanism sat on the Throne of Peter." His election was unexpected, because in the Sacred College there were cardinals like the Spanish Juan Carvajal (1399–1469), universally esteemed, as Pastor recalls, "for his extraordinary greatness and the profundity of his character." Nicholas V, however, although he had never written anything of importance, passed as a very learned man, and the reputation soon spread around the world that Rome had a pontiff unequalled in intelligence, culture, and liberality. Pastor calls him "the most liberal of his liberal age." Nicholas V was the first pope of the Renaissance, the first true benefactor of the humanists who had a dominant position in the Curia. Lorenzo Valla was named apostolic writer. The Pontifical Court welcomed not only Poggio Bracciolini, but also Francesco Filelfo, Giannozzo Manetti, Leon Battista Alberti, and the negotiator of codes, Vespasiano da Bisticci. The latter told his friends that when he was still in Florence, he would have invested in two things, if he could have afforded it: "that were in books and walls." This was the program of Nicholas V, who spent the great sums received from the Jubilee of 1450 on enriching the Vatican Library's collections of books and codices, and carrying out grandiose architectural projects.

The pontificate of Nicholas V seemed to open a new golden age for the Church, but was afflicted by two events that, as Msgr. Cristiani recalls, placed the pontiff before a dramatic reality. The first was the plot of Stefano Porcari (1453), a humanist who wanted to overthrow the papacy and restore the Roman

Republic. Porcari sought to put into practice the ideas of Lorenzo Valla and complete the program of Cola di Rienzo (1313–1354), the tribune who had presumed to emancipate the city of Rome from the pope in the fourteenth century. The plot was discovered, however, the humanists who supported him drew back, and Porcari was hanged in Castel Sant'Angelo along with his fellow plotters.

In that same year, the pope received a message that nearly crushed him: on May 29, 1453, the young sultan Mehmed II (1432–1481) had conquered Constantinople and had entered the Hagia Sophia over the cadavers of five thousand Christians. After eleven centuries, the Byzantine Empire disappeared from history, and in its place arose the terrible empire of the Turks. Nicholas V, stricken by grave physical and moral suffering, died on March 25, 1455, and was buried in St. Peter's.

### 3. The Project of a Crusade: Callistus III, Pius II, Paul II

In the conclave that followed, the Spaniard Alfonso Borgia (r. 1455–1458) was elected, taking the name Callistus III. St. Vincent Ferrer had predicted his election long before. Callistus was a great jurist and was the least humanistic of the popes of this period. Immediately after his election, he made a solemn vow to the Holy Trinity to spend all the money of the Church, and if necessary his own life, on a crusade against Islam. To realize this plan, he published a bull on May 15, 1455, calling for a crusade and entrusting the Franciscans to preach it. The Franciscan John of Capistrano carried out an extraordinary role in this undertaking, dedicating his life to exhorting the faithful to rise up against Islam, which was advancing along the Danube to conquer Central Europe.

In June 1456, a Muslim army of a hundred thousand men led by Sultan Mehmed II besieged the city of Belgrade, considered the last outpost of the Christian world. Three men, whom the pope called "the three Johns," hastened to the aid of the besieged city: John of Capistrano; John Hunyadi, leader of the Christian armada; and Cardinal Juan Carvajal, the papal legate. The pope had invited all Christians to pray, instituting in particular the evening *Angelus* as a prayer against the Turks. John of Capistrano, seventy years old by now, did not abandon the field of battle for eleven days and nights, inciting the soldiers to have faith in Jesus Christ in every moment of the conflict. The prayers and the valor of Christians were crowned by a sensational victory on July 21, 1456. Mehmed II had been wounded and was forced to sound the retreat. To celebrate the victory of Belgrade, Callistus III instituted the feast of the Transfiguration celebrated on August 6, which recalls when Jesus manifested to his disciples his divine splendor on Mt. Tabor. The pope wanted to symbolize the immense joy that transformed Europe in that moment. This great victory demonstrated to the West that, when united, the Christian forces could have chased the Turks back into Asia. In that same year, both Capistrano and Hunyadi died, the two main protagonists of the victory, and two years later, on August 6, 1458, the day of the feast of the Transfiguration that he had instituted, Pope Callistus died as well. In June of that same year, Muslims invaded Attica, the city of Athens fell, and the banner of the crescent moon was raised over the Acropolis.

Eighteen cardinals participated at the conclave, which opened on August 16, 1458. The election of Cardinal Enea Silvio Piccolomini, who took the name Pius II (r. 1458–1464), raised concern. Pope Piccolomini was a humanist who had a boisterous youth. He was distinguished more as a writer, poet, orator, and diplomat than for his religious life, and had adhered to the conciliarist party of the anti-pope Felix V. With age, however, his ideas had matured and he decided to reform his ways, renouncing the works of his youth. He was bishop of Trieste, then of Siena, created cardinal by Callistus III, and finally, at only fifty-three, was elected to the papal throne. At the moment of his election he said, "Forget about Enea, receive Pius." In confirmation of the change in his life, he reaffirmed papal primacy in the bull *Execrabilis* in 1460, announcing the excommunication of anyone who might appeal to a council against the pope. In the same year he also announced a crusade. The six years of his pontificate were characterized, as Pastor writes, "by a sublime idea to which all other interests had to be subordinated: the liberation of Europe from the shame of Ottoman dominance through a general crusade of Christian princes and nations."

Under Pius II's pontificate, in May 1462, a new source of wealth for the patrimony of St. Peter was discovered: alum mines in Tolfa just north of Rome, which allowed for the prolongation of the war against the Turks. This mineral, necessary at the time as a pigment, previously had to be imported from the East. Pius II decided to allocate the profits to the war against the Turks. On October 22, 1463, the pontiff proclaimed a new crusade and announced that he would assume the command himself, hoping that his example would draw other Christian sovereigns. Europe was immersed in hedonism, and the spiritual fire that had animated the Crusades had been extinguished.

Among the states on good terms with the Holy See was the duchy of Burgundy. On February 17, 1454, Phillip the Good, duke of Burgundy, issued the

Vow of the Pheasant, so called because the duke and his court had solemnly promised to participate in the crusade during a banquet, over a pheasant brought to his table, "living and adorned with an ornate golden necklace." But the duke betrayed his word and went so far as to steal the money collected for the crusade. The news that Phillip of Burgundy had broken his vow seemed nearly unbelievable to the pope, and given that it arrived on Good Friday, he declared that it was worthy of the sufferings of the day of the Passion. The pope counted on the help of the Republic of Venice and, though seriously ill, set off for Ancona to sail with the little crusader army he had summoned. When the Venetian fleet finally reached the port of Ancona considerably late, Pius II could barely reach the window to admire the ships. The following day he died. It was August 14, 1464. That same day, George Castriota, called Skanderbeg, obtained an incredible victory against the Ottomans in Ohrid, Albania.

## 4. George Skanderbeg and Pomponius Laetus

With the death of the pope, the crusader army disbanded, but George Skanderbeg continued his victorious campaign against the Turks of Mehmed II. Skanderbeg was born in Albania in 1405, the son of Prince John Castriota. He was captured by Muslims as a child and taken to the court of the sultan, where he grew up and distinguished himself for his extraordinary military qualities. But one day, with a group of Albanian patriots who were fighting alongside him, he abandoned the Ottoman army, returned to his homeland, and conquered the fortress of his native city, Kruje, proclaiming himself the vindicator of his family and his nation with the words "It was not I who brought you freedom, but I found it here in your midst."

Thus began his extraordinary military career. From 1443 to 1468—at one point, for nearly twenty consecutive years—Skanderbeg fought untiringly against the Turks, always at the order of the popes. His majestic posture was united with his immense energy and exceptional physical force. In battle, he was seen to have split in two trunks the enemy force, armed from head to foot. Although he spent his entire life in battle and had killed hundreds of enemies with his own hands, Skanderbeg was never wounded, save for once when he was hit in the shoulder. A supernatural power protected him, and for this reason, after his death, when the Turks conquered the city of Alessio where he was buried in the Cathedral of St. Nicholas, they opened his tomb and divided his bones among themselves, bound them in gold and silver, and carried them around their necks as amulets.

In 1466, the Albanian hero arrived in Rome to ask for assistance. The Venetian Pietro Barbo had just been elected pope with the name Paul II (r. 1464–1471). The pontiff was struck by his imposing stature, welcomed him with great honors, and accompanied him into the assembly of cardinals. There Skanderbeg spoke of the Turkish successes, of the danger they represented for Italy and of the necessity of supporting Albania, the last Christian bulwark in the Balkans.

Nicholas V had conferred on him the title "Champion of Christendom," reconfirmed by Callistus III, Pius II, and Paul II. When Skanderbeg died two years later, on January 17, 1468, almost all Albania fell into the hands of the Turks. It is said that at his death, the sultan exclaimed, "A lion of such mettle will never again arise on the earth! Finally, Europe and Asia are mine. Woe to Christianity, she has lost her sword and her shield!"

While Skanderbeg sought heroically to defend Christendom, the humanists attempted to overthrow the papacy. The main disciple of Lorenzo Valla was Julius Pomponius Laetus (1428–1498), who succeeded him as professor at the Sapienza University in Rome, where he held the chair of rhetoric. Pomponius Laetus exalted the last pagan emperor Julian the Apostate, wore buskins and a toga in the manner of the ancients, and wandered about the ruins of ancient Rome as if raptured in ecstasy, seeking inspiration. He despised Christian religion and professed paganism, venerating "the genie of the city of Rome." His house on the Quirinale was packed with fragments of antiquity—books, inscriptions, and coins. He founded a literary society that took the name Academy Romana, with the aim of exhuming ancient Latin language and culture.

The initiates in this society, which Gregorovius defines as "a classic Masonic lodge," considered themselves a fraternity: they renounced their own names (they "un-baptized" themselves) and assumed ancient ones: we do not even know the true name of Pomponius, for example, who considered himself the Pontifex Maximus, though it is known that he was the illegitimate child of Giovanni Sanseverino, prince of Salerno. They dated their writings from the foundation of Rome (*ab urbe condita*), rejecting the use of the Christian calendar. Their way of living was Epicurean and materialistic, and they were famous for the impure vices they practiced, such as homosexuality, in the manner of the ancient pagans.

After the plot of Stefano Porcari, the followers of Pomponius Laetus prepared their own act of rebellion—the assassination of Pope Paul II and the proclamation of a republic—but the conspiracy was discovered and the Academy Romana was suppressed. The strength of the humanist party did not diminish, however, as it acted on public opinion at the time, defaming Paul II, one of the few popes of the fifteenth century who tried to preserve the Christian spirit of Rome.

## 5. THE POPES OF THE RENAISSANCE: FROM SIXTUS IV TO INNOCENT VIII

St. Catherine of Siena outlined for the popes a way of governing that has remained applicable ever since: that of the reform of the Pontifical Curia and the renunciation of all ambition to power and human grandeur, of following Jesus Christ on the Via Crucis. This way inevitably leads to crusading against one's enemies, whether internal or external to Christendom. The humanists, on the other hand, who celebrated through the arts and letters the cult of man, proposed to the Church an embrace of the world and the melding of the religion of Christ with the religion of man. This, unfortunately, was the tendency that prevailed. When Paul II died on July 26, 1471, Pope Sixtus IV was elected (r. 1471–1484). Born Francesco della Rovere, he was a Franciscan from Liguria. From this pope until Leo X, the party of the humanists dominated the papacy. But in this period, according to historians, the worldly element prevailed in the College of Cardinals, in the Curia, in the upper clergy, and consequently throughout all Christian life. The pontiffs became temporal sovereigns, protectors of the sciences and the arts, competent in politics and warfare, but not primarily men of God. The Church became worldly, and this secularization paved the path for the Protestant Reformation.

Among his first actions, Sixtus IV allowed the reopening of the Academy Romana, suppressed by Paul II, appointing to his service several of its exponents, formerly condemned by the preceding pontiff, such as Bartolomeo Sacchi, known as the Platina—an intimate friend of Pomponius Laetus, who was nominated prefect of the Vatican Library and charged with writing a history of the popes. "Nothing better demonstrates the victory of humanism over monasticism," writes Gregorovius, "than the fact that Sixtus IV, although a Franciscan friar, gave the task of compiling the history of the papacy to an academic who had been tried for having renounced Christianity." Pomponius was able to resume his lessons at the university as well. The meetings of the Academy Romana were held in his home, at the Gardens of Constantine on the Quirinale in Rome.

Under the pontificate of Sixtus IV, the Turks took control of the wealthy Genovese colony of Caffa on the Black Sea on June 6, 1475, while their attacks in Moldavia and Wallachia increased. The borders of the Venetian states were subjected to continual incursions. In fall 1477, the Turks crossed the Isonzo and the Tagliamento Rivers in northern Italy. Venice resigned itself to signing a peace treaty with harsh conditions. The Turks dominated the Mediterranean, where only the island of Rhodes resisted, heroically defended by the Knights Hospitaller, today recognized as the Knights of Malta. In 1480, the Turks landed in Apulia, and on August 11, the city of Otranto fell into their hands. Of the twenty-two thousand inhabitants, twelve thousand were killed and the others taken as slaves. On August 14, Ahmed Pascià ordered a search among the survivors for all men over fifteen. They found about eight hundred. They were offered the choice of apostasy or decapitation. According to tradition, an old woolworker replied in the name of all, "To this point we have fought for our country, to save our goods and our lives. Now we must fight for Jesus Christ and to save our souls." In groups of fifty, the prisoners were taken to the hill called Minerva outside the city (today called the Hill of Martyrs) and were decapitated. Their bodies were left unburied for a year, until August 15, 1481, when the city was conquered by Christians, when their remains could be worthily honored. Antonio Primaldo and the other martyrs of Otranto were canonized on May 12, 2013.

Sixtus IV, whose name is tied to the Sistine Chapel, died on August 12, 1484. Ludwig von Pastor writes:

> In Pope Sixtus IV, next to many excellent and praiseworthy qualities, we see weaknesses and defects of no lesser import; much light, but also dense shadows.... Egidio of Viterbo might have exaggerated when later he dated this period as the age of corruption, but no one doubts that Francesco della Rovere, formed in a cloister and unexpert in the ways of the world, conducted the Barque of Peter into dangerous waters abounding in rocks.

After a very tumultuous conclave, a native of Genoa, Giambattista Cibo, ascended the papal throne in very difficult conditions, under the name Innocent VIII (r. 1484–1492). His entire reign was distraught by the war waged against the Holy See by the king of Naples, Ferdinand I. In the year of his death, July 5, 1492, Innocent VIII had a dream in which he contemplated a divine revelation: a hand wielding an unsheathed sword appeared to him, and on it was written, "*Gladius domini super terram cito velociter*" (Soon the Lord's sword shall strike the earth). In that same year, on January 2, the Moors were definitively run out of Spain with the fall of Granada, and on October 12, Christopher Columbus discovered America.

## 6. FROM ALEXANDER VI TO LEO X

The Church was approaching one of the darkest moments in her history. "The salt of the earth in many cases had become insipid, but where the purity of customs vanishes, there too will faith struggle to remain intact," writes Pastor, adding that in this period, "The immorality of the clergy was so widespread and egregious that voices circulated calling for priests to get married." In the conclave of 1492, Cardinal Rodrigo Borgia was validly elected, "but through simoniac intrigues," taking the name Alexander VI (r. 1492–1503). Cardinal Hergenröther wrote that in his life, Borgia had not thought of anything but "satisfying his passions, enriching and exalting his family," and "in his time as pontiff continued this type of life for a long time, such that his pontificate served to discredit the Holy See, which he was profaning in the eyes of the whole world."

Rodrigo Borgia—who, before pursuing the ecclesiastical life, had made a career as a soldier—was renowned for his immorality. With one of his lovers, Vannozza de' Cattanei, he had fathered Giovanni, Cesare, Lucrezia, and Jofré, and his papacy was dedicated to nepotism and the accumulation of wealth. Lucrezia, his favorite daughter, was at the center of innumerable rumors and calumnies. The firstborn, Giovanni, duke of Gandia, was assassinated and thrown into the Tiber. No one could say who had murdered him. Suspicion fell upon Lucrezia's husband, Giovanni Sforza, as well as on her brother Cesare Borgia. The latter was made archbishop of Valenza by the pope and then cardinal, the true black soul of the pontificate. Niccolò Machiavelli took him as a model in writing *The Prince*, outlining the figure of an ambitious man without scruples, who does not balk at any means for attaining his objectives, embodying the maxim "The ends justify the means."

During the pontificate of Alexander VI, the execution of Girolamo Savonarola was carried out in Florence. After repeated warnings, he was excommunicated for not having ceased his preaching and for having opposed the unification of his monastery with those of the Roman province. Savonarola was completely correct in combating the humanism of his age, but he imprudently made an appeal to the council against a "simoniac, heretic, incredulous" pope. For this reason, his case is still debated today.

The pontificate of Alexander VI has long been a battle cry for enemies of the Church, presented as an indelible stain, like the Inquisition or the Crusades. But while the Inquisition and the Crusades were luminous pages that Catholic historians ought to proudly claim as their own, there is no reason to hesitate in admitting the faults of Alexander VI.

The First Vatican Council proclaimed as a dogma of the Faith the supremacy of the Roman pontiff over the universal Church and his infallibility when solemnly defining a dogma on faith or morals. But when in the conciliary hall the anti-infallibility fathers put forward cases of the moral unworthiness and even deviance from the Faith of some of the popes, the relator of the dogma, Msgr. Vincenzo Gasser (1809–1879), bishop of Brixen, clarified that one could cite the case of a morally unworthy pope, or of one who erred in his governance, or even of one who deviated from orthodox faith, without ever impairing that pope's supreme power of governing and the possibility of infallibly defining a dogma, under specific conditions. This does not mean that the Church, as such, can err. The Church is always holy and immaculate, in its life and in its doctrine, considered as a whole, although not in each of its individual members, even the pope.

Alexander VI was immoral in his behavior before and after his election as Pontifex Maximus. The same election was due to plots and intrigues, and to think that it was the work of the Holy Spirit would be an offense to the third Person of the Holy Trinity. Catholic doctrine is different from Lutheran or Calvinist doctrine, according to which man is not free, but rather determined by grace. It is a doctrine of the Faith that meritorious actions are the consequence of the action of grace and of free human will that corresponds to it. Grace is a supernatural influence that we receive in greater or lesser measure according to the divine plan, but it is always sufficient for our salvation. There are moments in our lives, and especially in the life of the Church, in which grace is superabundant. This is the case with the election of a pontiff. The cardinals united in a conclave are assisted by the Holy Spirit, who does not however infallibly determine their choice, but demands that their will correspond to His influence.

No theologian, nor any Catholic, could hold that the choice of Alexander VI bears the stamp of the Holy Spirit's illumination of the twenty-three cardinals who elected him. If this failed to happen in that election, one can presume it also did not happen in many other elections and conclaves that resulted in weak, unworthy popes, inadequate for their high mission. The Church is great precisely because it survives the pettiness of men. An immoral, inadequate pope may be elected. It might happen that the cardinals in the conclave refuse the influence of the Holy Spirit and that the Holy Spirit that aids the pope in the fulfillment of his mission is refused. This does not mean that the Holy Spirit has been defeated by men or by the devil. God, and He alone, is capable of drawing good from the evil committed by men, and therefore Providence guides every event in history. But the fact that God draws good from the evil that men commit—as happened in the first sin of Adam, which was the cause of the Incarnation of the Word—does not mean that men can commit evil without guilt. And every fault must be recompensed, in Heaven and on earth. And so it was for the pontificate of Alexander VI.

After the twenty-six-day pontificate of Pius III, Cardinal Giuliano della Rovere, nephew of Sixtus VI, ascended to the papal throne with the name of Julius II (r. 1503–1513) and was one of the greatest personalities of the age. Not only a capable politician, Julius II was a warrior pope who commanded his troops in person. But he is remembered in particular for his patronage of the humanists. He entrusted Bramante with the reconstruction of the new St. Peter's, whose first stone was laid in 1506. Michelangelo followed his orders for the frescoes in the Sistine Chapel and sculpted for his tomb the famous statue of Moses. Raphael executed for Julius II the paintings in the Stanza della Segnatura and those of the Stanza of Heliodorus in the Vatican. Under his pontificate, the demolition of the venerable Constantinian Basilica of St. Peter was carried out to make room for the new one. The stupendous ancient columns of the Constantinian church were destroyed, and the tombs of the ancient popes broken to pieces. The ancient basilica was the world's sanctuary, rich in treasures and memories, guilty of having been erected in a "barbarous" century. From this wreckage was born, however, the masterpiece that is the current Basilica of St. Peter, center of Christianity and of the Universal Church.

Julius II summoned the Fifth Lateran Council on May 10, 1512, the eighteenth Ecumenical Council in the history of the Church. It was called to discuss the reform of Church life, at that time characterized by the nomination of ignoble prelates, the accumulation of benefices, the inobservance of the obligation of residence for bishops, and the infraction of clerical obligations. The opening discourse was pronounced by Cardinal Egidio of Viterbo, who spoke of the necessity of reform in the Church. He offered the memorable axiom, still debated today, "Men must be changed by sacred realities, not sacred realities by men."

Julius II died on February 21, 1513, and the council was continued by his successor, Leo X (r. 1513–1521), the thirty-year-old Giovanni de' Medici, a cardinal, although not yet an ordained priest at the moment of his papal election. He was the son of Lorenzo the Magnificent (1449–1492), raised in the luxury and pomp of the

Medici house, having as teachers Poliziano and Marsilio Ficino, a humanist who sought to unite in his person the cult of Plato and the cult of Christ. Leo was therefore a perfect son of humanism. He gathered around him the most celebrated artists and men of letters, such as Michelangelo, Raphael, and Ariosto, and sent out learned explorers in search of precious antiquities, buying ancient manuscripts from abroad. Under his pontificate, the Fifth Lateran Council concluded in March 1517, just months before Martin Luther nailed his Ninety-Five Theses to the cathedral door in Wittenberg. The Fifth Lateran Council was not able to promote the necessary reforms of the Church and can be considered a council of missed opportunities, as emerges sadly from the words of the final decree announcing its closure: "Numerous times the cardinals and prelates of this commission have told us [Pope Leo X] that they no longer have any questions to discuss or examine, and that for months no one has brought anything new to them."

At the first news of the Protestant revolt, Leo X defined it arrogantly as "a squabble among monks." Rarely in Church history has such incomprehension of approaching storms been displayed. Ludwig von Pastor concludes the volume of his history of the popes—dedicated to Leo X—stating that his pontificate was "fatal to the Roman See":

> Light of sentiments and jocund, he continued to dedicate himself thoughtlessly to pleasures quite worldly even after the great tempest had broken out, which was to tear from the Roman See a third of Europe. In all things a genuine son of the Age of the Renaissance, surrounded by his artists, poets, musicians, comedians, clowns, and courtesans, Leo X abandoned himself with frightful calm to the vortex of life in the world, without the least regard as to whether his pleasures behooved a spiritual lord or not.

The force of these words cannot be overestimated. Corruption was certainly more grievous under Alexander VI: though he had not committed doctrinal errors, his pontificate "was a disgrace for the Church, whose prestige suffered the most profound wounds." According to Pastor, nevertheless, the worldliness of Leo X was "more dangerous for the Church," because it was "much more difficult to combat."

## 7. ST. FRANCIS OF PAOLA

Throughout her history, the Church has faced the tempests without being overcome by them. So too, in the fifteenth and sixteenth centuries, when pagan humanism was the dominant mentality even among the popes, the Church countered through its heroes: saints such as Bernardino of Siena, John of Capistrano, Giacomo of the Marca, Antonio of Florence, and Lorenzo Giustiniani, to name but a few. The characteristic of the saints of this period is their immersion in the supernatural. An exemplary case is St. Francis of Rome (1384–1440), foundress of the Oblates of Tor de' Specchi, famous for her dialogues with angels and her visions of Heaven and Hell; also exemplary is St. Catherine of Bologna (1413–1463), abbess of the Poor Clares in Bologna, who became famous for her prophecies, miracles, and struggle against the devil. In particular, we remember St. Francis of Paola (1416–1507), born in Calabria to a poor family. He dedicated himself to the eremitical life of mortification and gathered around himself a group of disciples he called "minims."

St. Francis of Paola was the saint of charity and penance. Bossuet said that he purified his charity with his penance and sanctified his penance with his charity. In an age immersed in sensuality, Francis preserved his baptismal innocence and imposed on the order he founded, the Minim Friars, the most severe Lenten abstinence, to be observed by solemn vow, always and everywhere, throughout their entire lives. What characterized the mission of Francis was the task God gave him of opposing the moral depravation of humanism by his austere and penitential life, affirming against the paganism of his time the primacy of the Cross and the supernatural. His life was a series of uninterrupted miracles. He reminds us that God is master of nature and its laws and that he alone can, through miracles, surpass its laws, which remain insurmountable for men.

Francis had power over created things: over storms that calmed at his word, over the waters that solidified under his feet as when he crossed the Strait of Messina on his mantle laid over the waves, over the rocks that moved or halted at his command. Resuscitating the dead is perhaps the greatest miraculous manifestation. St. Francis of Paola resuscitated at least nine dead people. His fame was so universal that it reached the king of France, Louis XI (r. 1461–1483), the most powerful sovereign in Europe, who was so amazed by the news of his virtues that he had Francis visit him, that he might meet an authentic saint before he died. Francis of Paola stayed in France as a living reproach to the worldly and a model for reformers afflicted by the evils of the Church. He died at ninety-one in Plessis-les-Tours on April 2, 1507. St. Robert Bellarmine wrote that, on the eve of the Protestant heresy, the Lord wished in a certain way to contrast the rigid mortifications of St. Francis of Paola with the rebellious sensualism of Luther, demonstrating what the path of authentic Christian reform should be.

The reform of the Church is always necessary, just like personal reform for each one of us, and the saints continue to be our models. The Church navigates even today through dangerous waters, and there is no other route to follow than the rejection of the sirens of the world, taking up the path of abnegation, sacrifice, and struggle, which is the only path that puts the soul at ease and opens the gates of Heaven.

CHAPTER V

# Protestant Revolution and Catholic Reform

## 1. THE ORIGINS OF THE PROTESTANT REVOLUTION

There are dates in history that have symbolic value because they mark a rupture between two periods and represent, so to speak, a revolution. Such were the dates of 1917, marking the outbreak of the Bolshevik Revolution in Russia, and 1789, the beginning of the French Revolution. Equally important as a date is 1517, the year in which Martin Luther published his religious manifesto against the Church of Rome. What followed was called the Protestant Reformation. It was not a true reform, however, but a revolution born within the Catholic Church, promoted by priests and religious who had lost the Catholic Faith and sought to substitute it with a new one.

We choose to term it the Protestant *Revolution* and not the *Reformation* because reform and revolution have a foundational difference. Reform restores, whereas revolution destroys. And the essence of the Protestant Revolution, as for every revolution, was not what it wanted to construct, but what it wanted to destroy: its objective was the annihilation of the Roman Church and, above all, the papacy that epitomized it. The decadence of the papacy between the end of the fifteenth and the beginning of the sixteenth centuries facilitated this endeavor. Behind the appearance of a great force, the framework that the Church and European society offered at the start of the sixteenth century was desolate.

The new humanistic mentality had created a mortal embrace between the Church of Rome and the world. The popes lived as splendid Italian princes: they were great humanists like Nicholas V, refined diplomats like Alexander VI, and warriors like Julius II, but their temporal interests prevailed over their concern for the supernatural; the episcopate was corrupt, religious life decadent.

Many consider the Protestant Reformation to have been a reaction to the abuses of the Church, to restore the revelation of Jesus Christ to its primitive purity.

The spark of the Protestant Revolution was in fact the "scandal" of indulgences, against which Martin Luther (1483–1546) was reacting. This was not a cause but rather an occasion. Indulgences, according to Catholic doctrine, effect the total or partial remission of the temporal punishment due for sins committed. Tied to indulgences are religious practices and at times almsgiving, but to obtain them one must be in the grace of God, confess one's sins, and receive Communion. They can be neither sold nor bought. Humanists, through the weapons of philology, derided indulgences as well as the veneration of saints and relics, monastic life, devotions, and all ancient traditions in general. They advocated an "interior" or "evangelical" Christianity, stripped of optional and exterior elements and reduced to the essential.

This was the cultural terrain in which Protestantism took root, which picked up the themes of evangelical humanism. The latter represented a transition from pagan humanism to Protestantism. Its champion was Erasmus of Rotterdam (1466–1536), who wielded at the beginning of the sixteenth century a cultural influence similar to that of Voltaire two centuries later. Erasmus was a Dutch monk who passed his time travelling, rarely celebrated Mass, and when he was in his monastery, dedicated hours to reading the Latin classics. His proclamation of the supreme freedom of the Christian, his invitation to direct access to the Scriptures without mediation, opened the path to Luther. On the other hand, the Protestant historian Roland Bainton wrote that the Lutheran call to the simplicity of the New Testament, the annoyance of Scholastic subtleties, the condemnation of indulgences, and the rejection of veneration of relics and of the saints all aligned perfectly with the humanist program.

## 2. MARTIN LUTHER'S REBELLION

Martin Luther was born in Eisleben, Thuringia, on November 10, 1483, into a family of peasant farmers. He studied at the University of Erfurt, in an environment saturated by humanism. His life changed on July 2, 1505, when he was caught in a terrible storm on the road from Erfurt to Mansfed, with lightning striking all about him. Terrorized, he made a vow to St. Anne that he would become a monk if he survived the storm. Two weeks later, on July 17, he entered the monastery of the Augustinian Hermits in Erfurt. His father and friends, who knew his impetuous and violent temperament, disapproved of his choice. His was a hasty, immature vocation, the consequences of which would weigh on him for the rest of his life. Two years later, Martin Luther was ordained a priest, and on May 2, 1507, he celebrated his first Mass. His superiors sent him to study in Erfurt and Wittenberg, where he became a professor of theology. The ferment of his passions rendered the observance of his monastic rule unbearable, which tormented Luther and placed before him the distressing question of his salvation. In 1510, he was sent to Rome, where he sojourned a month, due to mission for his order. He was shocked by the worldliness and corruption of Renaissance Rome.

The occasion for Luther's rebellion was the preaching of the Jubilee indulgence for the construction of the new St. Peter's Basilica in Rome. On October 31, 1517, Luther nailed his Ninety-Five Theses against indulgences to the door of the castle church of Wittenberg. This gesture aroused an enormous uproar, especially because Luther had been encouraged by the humanist party and the German princes who wanted to emancipate themselves from both the Church of Rome and the Holy Roman Empire. Luther's ideological shift occurred in 1518, it seems, following the so-called Experience of the Tower. While he was in the convent latrine, situated in a tower, he had the sudden idea that personal salvation derives only from faith, not works. From that point on, the idea that progressively took shape was this: human nature is radically corrupted by Original Sin, the center and source of every evil in man; sin is invincible, and not even Baptism can cancel it; as a consequence, there are no good or bad human actions, and every action by man is necessarily evil. Man cannot help but sin.

The invincibility of sin renders the divine law impracticable. Man is not therefore justified by observance of the law, by means of his good works, but only by faith in God, regardless of works. God has given man an impossible law, so that from the knowledge of its impracticability and from the awareness of the nullity of works, faith might be born in man. The phrase *pecca fortiter, crede fortius* aptly summarizes Luther's thought.

Absolute passivity is the only possibility for communicating with God, on whom everything depends. If everything depends on God, without the cooperation of man, it is God who infallibly decides who to save and who to condemn. Among the mass of the damned, God, out of pure goodness, chooses His elect. There is no freedom either in the elect or in the damned. God concedes faith to His elect. This is the theory of predestination that Calvin would later take to its extreme consequence.

When these ideas began to spread, Pope Leo X, after having underestimated the revolt, sent several theologians to combat Luther. On June 15, 1520, Leo issued a bull condemning forty-one propositions extracted from Luther's writings. But Luther, before he even knew about this document, had written to a friend on July 15, 1520, "The die is cast. I scorn forever the fury and the favor of Rome." On August 1, he published his manifesto, *To the Christian Nobility of Germany*, in which he proclaimed the equality of all Christians thanks to their universal priesthood, and recourse only to the Bible as a source of truth. In October of the same year, he published another booklet, *On the Babylonian Captivity of the Church*, in which he reduced the sacraments to two: Baptism and Communion, making their efficacy depend, however, only on justifying faith.

On January 3, 1521, Leo X decreed Luther's excommunication with the bull *Decet Romanum Pontificem*. Luther was summoned to the Diet opened by Emperor Charles V at Worms on January 28 of the same year. "The pope," said Luther on April 18, 1521, "is not the arbiter in matters regarding the Word of God and the Faith. The Christian must examine and judge for himself." Bainton comments, "Here we have the core and the consistency of Protestant individualism." The object of Luther's attacks was not the deformations of medieval Catholicism; rather he considered Catholicism itself a deformation.

On May 26, 1521, the Edict of Worms banished Luther from the Holy Roman Empire. As Luther was leaving Worms, the elector Fredrick II of Saxony had him abducted by a group of knights to save him, and kept him hidden in his castle at Wartburg near Eisenach, where he stayed for ten months (June 1521–March 1522). There he dedicated himself to various writings and to the translation of the Bible into German, which he finished many years later. During the period in which Luther, excommunicated by the pope and banished from the Holy Roman Empire, remained hidden in the Wartburg castle under the protection of the prince elector of Saxony, a radical wing began to form among his followers that sought to push the nascent movement into extreme positions. One of these followers, Andreas Karlstadt (1486–1541), celebrated in civilian clothing the first "evangelical Mass" of the Reformation on Christmas Day 1521 in Wittenberg. He omitted the elevation of the Host and all references to sacrifice, and allowed the participants to take Communion themselves under both species.

The city of Wittenberg was in turmoil: priests were marrying, monks were leaving their monasteries, the Mass had changed, and altars, images, and crucifixes were being destroyed. Furthermore, Luther's preaching lit the flame of religious and social revolt, the Peasants' War of 1524 to 1525. Luther intervened to bring the movement under control. Addressing the German princes, he incited them to repress the revolt in these words: "Dear Lords, free us, help us … run them through with the sword, slit as many of their throats as you can…. The ass wants cudgeling and the people want governance by force."

While in open war with the peasants, Luther united himself in sacrilegious marriage to Catherine von Bora, a nun who had left the convent two years earlier. He had six children with her. The last of his descendants bearing his name died in 1759, but there were 1,035 "Lutherids" still living in 1936 scattered around the world (among them the socialist agitator Liebknecht and the industrialist Zeiss).

In 1526, the Diet of Speyer conceded to the princes and to the free cities the right to embrace Protestantism. Exercising this faculty, various German states passed over to the new religion, among them East Prussia, which was a fiefdom of an ancient and valorous knight order, the Teutonic Knights, which had distinguished itself on the battlefields of the Crusades in the Holy Land and in the conversion of the Baltic nations. The Teutonic Order depended directly on the pope, but its grand master Albert of Brandenburg broke off relations with Rome, embraced Protestantism, and seized possession of its immense ecclesiastical patrimony. This was the origin of what would become the Prussian state.

The Diet of Speyer, convened again in 1529, prohibited the introduction of any further changes in Germany. The first dissemination of Protestantism came about through the printing press and by local preachers who were often apostate friars preaching from city to city. Protestants grew in number above all thanks to the support of the German princes who formed a League that transformed Lutheranism into a political and military force that could challenge the emperor of the Holy Roman Empire, Charles V.

Charles V (1500–1558), the grandson of Maximillian Hapsburg, Maria of Burgundy, Ferdinand of Aragon, and Isabel of Castille, was at that moment the inheritor of an immense territory that spanned from the far reaches of Eastern Europe across the ocean to the new colonial possessions in the Americas. His

dream of reconstructing the universal Empire of Charlemagne was shattered by
Martin Luther, who lacerated the religious unity of Christendom, opening the
path to the birth of new nation-states. Luther's work was continued in Switzerland by the apostate parish priest Ulrich Zwingli (1484–1531) and above all by
John Calvin.

## 3. JOHN CALVIN

John Calvin was not Swiss, as many believe, but French. He was born in 1509 in
Noyon, Picardy. His father, Gérard, a businessman, clashed with the bishop whom
he served as secretary, and died excommunicated. His older brother was a priest,
but also died excommunicated in 1537. Guided by his father into an ecclesiastical
career as well, Calvin entered the Montaigu College in Paris in 1523 (where he
studied for several weeks with Ignatius of Loyola), but had to abandon his studies
for a crime, sodomy it seems, for which he was sentenced the death penalty, but
which was later commuted with the mark of infamy on one shoulder. We shall
ignore the reasons for his abandonment of the Faith. We only know that his
cultural formation, like that of Luther, was humanistic, and that in Basel he published his *Institutes of the Christian Religion*, which is the "summa" of his thought.
While Luther wrote many booklets and pamphlets, but no systematic work, the
little book of Calvin, at first published in six chapters, was slowly enlarged until
the final edition had four books and eighty chapters.

Calvin eventually settled in Geneva, where he had sojourned twice, first
from 1536 to 1538, and then from 1541 to 1564, the date of his death. In this
second phase of his life in Geneva, Calvin exercised a terrible dictatorship and
displayed the most severe intolerance, having those who did not think like him
expelled from Geneva and even executing those whom he declared heretics, like
Michael Servetus, who was burned at the stake in 1535 under the accusation of
having denied the Holy Trinity.

Calvin's doctrine began where Luther's ended. Luther started with the total
corruption of human nature and arrived at salvation through faith alone. Calvin
pushed Luther's theses to their extreme, theorizing absolute predestination that
makes God into an unbearable tyrant. It may be summed up as follows:

1) Man, radically corrupted by Original Sin,
   is condemned to damnation.

2) God, by a gratuitous and mysterious decision, decrees *ab aeterno* to remove the elect from condemnation. Salvation is like the clemency that follows a merited death sentence.

3) Predestination, which is the decree by which God establishes the eternal, irrevocable destiny of every man, is not the consequence but the cause of our faith. We are saved, or damned, not as a consequence of our merits, but because God has predestined us. Nothing can change this destiny, for it is not subject to appeal.

As with Luther, Calvin also reduces the sacraments to two, Baptism and the Eucharist, but went further than Luther, reducing the latter to a mere commemoration, a simple symbol. Luther was a violent, passionate personality, whereas Calvin was a cold and proud man. Calvin died in 1564. Luther had preceded him to the tomb in 1546.

## 4. Henry VIII and the Anglican Schism

Protestantism spread to England, although while Luther began with a heresy and ended in schism, in England the reverse occurred: the rupture with the Church began with schism and ended in heresy.

Henry VIII ascended the throne in 1509. He was a young, brilliant prince, a lover of luxury and pleasures, ambitious and jealous of his authority. In all things he was obliged by his lord chancellor, Cardinal Thomas Wolsey (1471–1530), an equally ambitious and compliant minister. When Luther began to attack the doctrine of the Church, Henry VIII refuted him in writing, defending the sacraments, such that Leo X conferred upon Henry the title Defender of the Faith (1521). But several years later, the sad issue of his marriage exploded, which was at the origin of the schism in England. Henry VIII was charmed by a lady of the court, the Irish Anne Boleyn, and wanted to divorce his wife Catherine of Aragon, with whom he had already had a daughter, Mary Tudor. This matter of the king's passion was described by the historian Ludwig von Pastor as "almost demoniacal." Pope Clement VII, to whom the king appealed for his divorce, opposed him inflexibly. Clement VII was not an intransigent pope, but he could not concede this on the principle of the indissolubility of Christian marriage. Cardinal Wolsey, charged with not being able to convince the pope, was accused of treason and condemned to death. Power then passed into the hands of Thomas Cromwell, who resorted to extreme measures to satisfy the king.

The legitimate wife of the king, Catherine, was chased from court, and Anne Boleyn took her place, being married in secret to the king in 1533. The primate of Canterbury, Thomas Cranmer (1489–1556), close to Anne Boleyn, hastened to annul the king's first marriage and to confirm the second. On June 1, 1533, Anne Boleyn was crowned queen consort of England. The pope could not keep silent in the face of this scandal and confirmed that only the first marriage was valid before God. The king then had approved and promulgated the Act of Supremacy by which, in 1534, the Anglican schism was consummated. By this act, Henry VIII declared himself the head of the Church in his kingdom and demanded the clergy and functionaries to take an oath by which they recognized the supremacy of the king over Rome. By means of the Act of Succession, he established Elizabeth as heir to the throne, the illegitimate daughter he had with Anne Boleyn.

Sadly the episcopate and the clergy, both religious and diocesan, submitted en masse to the desires of the sovereign. Only a few courageous men heroically resisted unto martyrdom. Among these was Thomas More (1478–1535), former chancellor of the kingdom, who did not hesitate to submit his resignation rather than follow the ill-advised path the king had embarked upon. For his refusal to swear the oath required by the Act of Succession, he was arrested, locked in the Tower of London, stripped of all his possessions, and condemned to execution on July 6, 1535.

These were the years in which Machiavelli theorized the primacy of politics over morality. Thomas More represented the opposite: politics that bends to the demands of morality, to the point of the supreme holocaust of martyrdom, the supreme primacy of truth or, as John Paul II said, of conscience which, when founded on the truth, securely directs man's actions toward the good. "Precisely for his witness, rendered to the shedding of his blood, to the primacy of truth over power, St. Thomas More is venerated as an everlasting example of moral integrity." This Christian conception that affirms the primacy of moral values to the point of sacrificing the supreme good of life is antithetical to the Machiavellian concept that elevates one's will to power to supreme rule, to which all other moral values must be sacrificed. Fifteen days before More, the bishop of Rochester, St. John Fisher (1469–1535), counselor and confessor to Catherine of Aragon, had faced his own death with the same courage. From the heights of the scaffold, Fisher made his profession of Catholic Faith, kneeling down and reciting the *Te Deum* and Psalm 70, which begins, *"Domine in te speravi, non confundar in aeternum"* (Lord, I have hoped in you, may I not be rebuked forever). In 1935, four hundred years after their deaths, Pius XI canonized these two great heroes.

The Anglican schism now mutated into a vast regime of confiscation of ecclesiastical property. Monasteries were invaded, sacked, and sold, and the booty enriched the Crown on one side but also the landed gentry on the other, a new social class that became ardent supporters of the Reformation. Henry VIII died in 1547, after having executed two queens (his wives), two cardinals and archbishops, eighteen bishops, thirteen abbots, and five hundred priors and monks. After him reigned the young Edward VI (1537–1553), son of Henry VIII's third wife, Jane Seymour. Edward was only ten when he ascended the throne, and the kingdom slipped toward pure Calvinism under the leadership of the archbishop of Canterbury, Thomas Cranmer, who brought from the continent some of the worst Protestant preachers, like the apostate friar Bernardino Ochino, former general of the Capuchin Order. In 1549, the Anglican *Book of Common Prayer* was published, accompanied by forty-two articles of the new religion.

Edward VI died in 1553 and was succeeded by a Catholic queen, Mary Tudor (1516–1558), the only legitimate child of King Henry VIII, born into the Catholic Faith, which she never abandoned. Her brief reign gave a short five years of breathing room to Catholics. "Catholic Mary," as she was called, liberated Catholics who had been unjustly imprisoned, and had heretical Lutherans and Calvinists sent to jail, contributing to the dark legends that were created about her. But she died prematurely, and under Elizabeth I, who reigned for more than forty years from 1558 until her death in 1603, the definitive separation of England from the Catholic Faith was completed.

Anglicanism represents the part of Protestantism that is closest to the Catholic Church, although the episcopal consecrations that have been performed from the schism down to our day are considered invalid by the Catholic Church. The archbishop of Canterbury was given primacy over England, but he is not an authentic bishop, bound to the apostles in legitimate succession.

Luther and Calvin, however, were dragged to the left by a swarm of sects, of which the Anabaptists were the model. They were given this name because they denied the validity of Baptism administered to children and so had them rebaptized as adults. Within their ranks there developed a rationalist current called Socinianism, named for its founders Lelio and Fausto Sozzino of Siena, who, in

the name of the principle of Sola Scriptura, unmediated by any religious authority, dissolved all dogmas, beginning with that of the Trinity.

Based on the same principle, Anabaptists and Socinians concluded that all
the faithful were free not only to scrutinize every belief but to practice the morality that agreed most with them. The Anabaptists went so far as to reject
private property and to call for the mandatory pooling of goods. Professor
Plinio Corrêa de Oliveira observed of the disorderly tendencies of man:

> [They] have already in potency, in the first instance of their great explo-
> sions, all the virulence that will later be revealed in their worst excesses.
> In the first denials of Protestantism, for example, were implicit the anar-
> chical longings of Communism. If, from the point of view of explicit
> formulation, Luther was no other than Luther, all the tendencies, all the
> states of mind, all the excesses of the Lutheran explosion already bore
> within them, in an authentic and full manner, even though still implicit,
> the spirit of Voltaire and Robespierre, of Marx and Lenin.

## 5. The True Catholic Reform

The great theme of Church reform runs throughout the sixteenth century, as it
had in many preceding periods. The 1500s opened with the Fifth Lateran Council,
summoned precisely to promote this necessary reform of customs and discipline
in the Church. But the words that echoed in the assembly had no practical consequences. And yet, in these tempestuous years, even before Luther appeared on
the horizon, groups of ardent piety arose in the Church called Companies of
Divine Love. The movement was born in Genoa around Catherine Adorno de'
Fieschi (1447–1510), known at the time as St. Catherine of Genoa, and had as
their founder a layman, Ettore Vernazza. Belonging to this company was Gaetano
of Thiene (1480–1547) and Gian Pietro Carafa (1476–1559), who founded the
Order of the Theatines, whose name comes from the fact that Carafa (later to
become Pope Paul IV) was then bishop of Chieti (Theatum).

To combat cupidity, the Theatines embraced apostolic poverty and abandoned themselves entirely to Divine Providence. In them, a new form of
religious life was inaugurated, that of clerics regular, who practiced the evangelical counsels, professed public vows, and led a common life according to a rule.

Leo X's successor, Adrian VI (r. 1522–1523), born Hadrian Florent of
Utrecht, was a reformer pope opposed by the Italian humanists for his moral

rigor. Two issues were close to his heart: the union of Christian princes in fighting the Turks, and the reform of the Roman Curia, but the brevity of his pontificate impeded him from carrying out his projects, in particular "the giant war against the swarms of abuse that were perverting the Roman Curia as well as the entire Church." Even if he had a longer reign, the evil rooted in the Church was too deep, observes Pastor, "for one pontiff alone to be able to produce the great change that was needed. All the evil that had been committed over many generations could be ameliorated only by long, uninterrupted labor."

Adrian VI understood the gravity of the evil and responsibility of men in the Church, as emerges clearly in an instruction which, in his name, the nuncio Francesco Chieregati read to the Diet of Nuremberg on January 3, 1523. The German historian considers this a document of extraordinary importance, not only to learn about the reform ideas of the pope, but because it is an unprecedented document in Church history.

After having refuted the Lutheran heresy, in the last and most noteworthy part of the instruction, Adrian VI treats the defection of the supreme ecclesiastical authority in the face of the innovators. The pope gives the following explicit instruction to the nuncio:

> You will say that we openly confess that God allows these persecutions of the Church to occur due to the sin of men and in particular of priests and prelates; it is certain that the hand of God has not weakened to such a degree that He cannot save us, but it is sin that detaches us from Him to such a degree that He does not hear our pleas. Sacred Scripture clearly teaches that the sins of the people have their origin in the sins of the clergy and thus, as Chrysostom notes, our Redeemer, when He wants to purge the infirm city of Jerusalem, went first to the temple to punish all the sins of the priests, like a good doctor who cures the illness from the root.
>
> We know well that many detestable matters have manifested themselves in this Holy See for some years now: abuses in ecclesiastical affairs, impingement of precepts; in fact, everything has turned for the worse. It is no wonder that the sickness has spread from the head throughout the members, from the popes to the prelates. All of us, prelates and ecclesiastics, have deviated from the way of the just and for quite some time no one has done the good. All of us must therefore give honor to God and humiliate ourselves before Him: each one of us must meditate why he has fallen and straighten his ways lest he be judged by God on

the day of His wrath. Thus, in our name you shall promise that we shall work assiduously that the Roman Court first of all be improved, from which all these evils have begun; so, as from here the sickness has spread, from here shall begin its cure, to accomplish this we consider ourselves all the more obliged because everyone desires this reform.

We have never coveted the papal dignity and we would gladly have closed our eyes in the solitude of the private life; gladly would we have renounced the tiara, and only the fear of God, the legitimacy of the election, and the danger of a schism have induced us to assume the office of supreme shepherd, which we do not wish to exercise out of ambition, nor to enrich our relatives, but to give back to the Church, the Bride of God, her first beauty, to help the oppressed, to raise up learned and virtuous men, in general, to do all that is required of a good shepherd and a true successor of St. Peter. Let no one be amazed, however, if we are not able to eliminate with a single stroke all the abuses, for the illness has deep roots and has branched out widely. One step shall be taken at a time, and initially the most serious and most dangerous maladies shall be remedied with appropriate medicines so that, with a hasty reform of everything, matters will not be muddled even more. For good reason does Aristotle say that sudden change is dangerous to a republic.

After Adrian VI, Giulio de' Medici ascended to the throne with the name Clement VII (r. 1523–1534). Under his weak papacy, the terrible Sack of Rome of May 1527 occurred, carried out by the Lutheran Landsknecht. The Catholic emperor, Charles V, was irritated by the pope's political and military alliance with the king of France, Francis I, and thus allowed the German mercenaries (the Landsknecht) at his service, Lutherans all, to enter Rome, and gave them license to sack it. It is difficult to describe the extent of the devastation and sacrilege carried out in their ferocious hatred against the center of Catholicism. "Hell is nothing compared to the appearance Rome now wears," one reads in a secret report of May 10, 1527, cited by Pastor.

The unlimited license to rob and kill lasted eight days. They raged with particular cruelty against ecclesiastics: nuns were raped, priests and monks were sold as slaves and killed, and churches, buildings, and homes were destroyed. It was only after the terrible sack that life in Rome changed profoundly. The climate of religious moral relativism dissolved, and the general misery gave the sacred city an austere and penitential aspect. Pope Clement VII commissioned Michelangelo to paint the Last Judgment in the Sistine Chapel, as if to immortalize the psychological drama the city of Rome and the Church had suffered in those years. The people of Rome saw in this the chastisement of God. The Landsknecht were an instrument of divine wrath against the pagan Rome of the Renaissance, as the barbarians of Alaric had been against pagan Rome in the late Roman Empire. In the fifth century, pagan Rome was punished because it resisted the rise of Christianity; in the sixteenth century, papal Rome was castigated because it embraced paganism. These two sacks of the city were moments of destruction analogous to natural disasters, like earthquakes or epidemics. They destroyed the urban spaces, upset daily life, and crushed optimism, recalling men to meditate on the meaning they give to their lives. From a supernatural perspective, they can be understood as an expression of God's justice, but also of his immense mercy. Throughout history, the city of Rome and the Church came out of these experiences purified and more faithful to their mission. What history teaches us is no different from the lessons of theology, and is perennially valid.

## 6. THE COUNCIL OF TRENT

In just a few years, great reformers began to appear. The sixteenth century was a time of terrible trials. Dom Guéranger writes:

> St. Gaetano dominated the first half of the century nearly alone; but as soon as 1550 came around, a marvelous flourishing blossomed on the boughs of the ancient tree of the Church; and while Protestantism's conquests finally came to a halt, it pleased God to show that the Roman Church had lost nothing because it had preserved the gift of sanctity.

The figure of Ignatius of Loyola (1491–1556) stands out as one of the giants of the sixteenth century. At the service of the viceroy of Navarre, he was injured in the siege of the castle of Pamplona and, during his convalescence, became convinced that the only true Lord to whom he ought to dedicate his life was Jesus Christ. In the grotto of Manresa, he conceived of the *Spiritual Exercises,* an inspired book that, according to St. Francis de Sales, has produced more saints than the letters of the alphabet it contains.

On September 27, 1540, Pope Paul III approved the Society of Jesus, founded by Ignatius. To the three traditional vows of poverty, chastity, and obedience, the Jesuits added the promise of going wherever the pope sent them. While Ignatius founded the Society of Jesus that worked against Protestantism for the reconquest of Europe, Rome was dominated by the figure of St. Phillip Neri (1515–1595), a very different saint from St. Ignatius, but one closely tied to him. He often visited the catacombs, praying before the tomb of one of the martyrs, and regularly made the pilgrimage of the seven churches. Slowly, there formed around him a little group of the faithful, gathered in the Church of St. Jerome of Charity, a group that took the name of the Oratory.

In Spain, St. John of God (1495–1550) founded a congregation called Fatebenefratelli due to their habit of begging for alms for the sick, during which St. John would cry out in the streets, *"Fate bene fratelli, per voi e per l'amor di Dio!"* (Do good brothers, for yourselves and for the love of God!). In the year of St. John's death, St. Camillo de Lellis (1550–1614) was born in Abruzzo. Though at first a soldier, a swashbuckler, and a gambler, he converted in 1575 and founded a religious institute, the Camillians, who take an additional vow of aiding the sick even in times of plague. His religious wear on their chest the red cross that would later become the symbol of all health workers. He too was a disciple of St. Phillip Neri.

In those same years, St. Antonio Maria Zaccaria (1502–1539) founded the Barnabites, true disciples of St. Paul, to whom we owe the practice of adoration of the Most Holy Sacrament. St. Girolamo Emiliani (1486–1537) founded the Somaschi Fathers for the exercise of charity toward orphans and deviant women. The tenor of the new religious orders was very similar: a life of rigorous mortification, the rejection of all forms of worldliness, abandonment to Providence, and zeal for souls. This legion of saints flowered before, during, and after the Council of Trent, which was the Catholic response to the Lutheran Revolution.

The Council of Trent, the nineteenth Ecumenical Council of the Church, was at the center of this great work of reform. The assembly lasted eighteen years, from December 13, 1545, to December 16, 1563, dedicated "to the praise and glory of God, the growth of faith and Christian religion, the uprooting of heresy, the peace and unity of the Church, the reform of the clergy and of the Christian people, and the confusion of the enemies of the name of Christian." Three popes guided the council through their legates and, though not personally present, approved its decrees: Paul III (from 1545 to 1549), Julius III (r. 1555–1559), and Pius IV (r. 1559–1585). The last announced the full and unconditional approval of the canons of Trent.

Thanks to the Council of Trent, the Church enjoyed a period of doctrinal restoration and profound renewal of customs from the second half of the 1500s to the first half of the 1600s. The Council discussed whether the doctrinal or pastoral aspect should prevail: if it was the moment for theological definition and condemnation of errors or that of reform of discipline and ecclesiastical customs. They decided that the two aspects were inseparable, but in a period of doctrinal confusion such as the one of that time, the Church needed above all to define the truth and condemn errors. Of enormous importance were the doctrinal decisions of the Council regarding Sacred Scripture and Tradition; Original Sin and justification; the sacraments; and the sacrifice of the Mass. No less significant were the disciplinary decrees that contributed to the development of an authentic Catholic Reformation that alone could beat back the Protestant Revolution. The Church's Faith was reaffirmed with clarity, without leaving room for equivocation and without the need for interpretation.

## 7. St. Pius V: A Model Pope

Two other great saints should be remembered: St. Charles Borromeo and St. Pius V. St. Charles Borromeo, the son of Count Gilberto Borromeo and Margherita de' Medici, sister of Pius IV, lived from 1538 to 1584. As archbishop of Milan, he rigorously applied the spirit and letter of the decrees of the Council of Trent. The diocese of Milan was immense, extending beyond Lombardy into parts of Veneto, Switzerland, and Liguria. Charles Borromeo not only lived there for eighteen years but visited all the parishes in this territory, even the most remote and forsaken, giving the example of a life of zeal, penance, and prayer. The plague of 1576 offered him the opportunity to display the full depth of his charity. On that occasion he led a procession walking barefoot, carrying a relic of the Holy Nail of Christ, to obtain the remission of the outbreak. He was canonized in 1610. He is considered the patron saint of seminarians and spiritual directors. If St. Charles Borromeo represents still today a model bishop, St. Pius V (born Michele Ghislieri) represents a model pope for his firmness and the sanctity of his governance.

Ghislieri was born in 1504, in the diocese of Tortona. At fourteen, he entered the Order of Preachers and was sent to the University of Bologna to study theology, which he later taught for sixteen years. He was nominated general inquisitor and commissioner of the Holy Office in 1551, a task that brought him much persecution, but allowed him also to lead many heretics back to Catholic truth. His virtues were appreciated by Paul IV, who chose him for the episcopal see of Nepi and Sutri near Rome, then for the cardinalate. These honors did not alter his austere way of life. On January 7, 1566, he was elected pope, taking the name Pius V.

His entire life was a struggle. Dom Guéranger says of him:

> In the agitated times in which Pius V was called to guide the Church, error had invaded a large part of Christianity and threatened the rest of it. Astute and accommodating in places where it could not spread its audacity, error coveted Italy; its sacrilegious ambition was to over-throw the Apostolic See, and drag the entire Christian world without exception into the darkness of heresy. Pius defended the threatened peninsula with his inviolable dedication. Even before being elevated to the honors of the papacy, he had often exposed his life to save cities from its seduction. A faithful imitator of Peter Martyr, he never re-treated in the face of danger, and the emissaries of heresy fled whenever he approached. Ascending the Throne of Peter, he knew how to fill innovators with a salutary fear. He uplifted the courage of Italian sovereigns and, with moderate severity, succeeded in throwing back beyond the Alps the scourge that would have dragged Europe into the destruction of Christianity, if the states of Southern Italy had not created an invincible barrier. Heresy was halted.... The work of St. Pius V to regenerate Christian customs, to establish the discipline of the Council of Trent, to publish the Breviary and the Missal sub-jected to reform, rendered his pontificate of just six years one of the most fruitful in the history of the Church.

On his deathbed, taking a last glimpse at the Church on earth that he was abandoning for the one in Heaven, and desiring to implore for the last time the divine goodness in favor of the flock he was leaving exposed to so many dangers, he recited with his nearly inaudible voice the verse of an Easter hymn: "Creator of men, deign on this day filled with the joys of Easter to preserve your people from the assaults of death." Having uttered these words, he fell asleep in peace. His body was buried in the Basilica of St. Mary Major. The name of Pius V is indissolubly linked to the liturgical restoration that takes his name and with the extraordinary victory at Lepanto against the Turks—and his memory is dear to many for these reasons.

The history of the sixteenth century teaches us that the true reformers are the saints, who do not attribute to the Church the faults of men, but take those faults upon themselves, like our Lord. They did not presume to change the constitution of the Church, but strained to change themselves and, through their example, to change others. The Church is always holy, but men of the Church are often not. The reformer is the one who works for the Church to be holy in her members like she is in her Founder, in her soul and in her essence, from her head (the pope and bishops) to her feet (the faithful).

False reformers, on the other hand, are those who want to change the Church, those who maintain that the cause of evil is not to be found in the men of the Church but in the Church herself, and so wish to change its way of governance, the sacraments, and her teaching, adapting them to their own opinions or those of the world. They say they are doing this to return to the gospel message, and thus they reject the Tradition of the Church and invoke the Sacred Scripture, or better their own reason, their own sentiment, to interpret the passages of Scripture without a *regula fidei* as their guide.

The Church throughout history has known the pseudoreform of heretics and the true reform of the saints. Pseudo-reformers included the Cathars and the Waldensians in the thirteenth century, the Protestants in the sixteenth century, and the modernists in the twentieth. All around us we hear the false appeals for a structural reform of the Church. Our response can only be the example of the saints, who united the moral integrity of their lives to the complete fidelity to the Tradition of the Church, which is nothing more than the message of Jesus Christ, always alive, always pertinent, laden with all the memories of the past and with all the hopes for the future.

CHAPTER VI

# The Missionary Church in the Sixteenth and Seventeenth Centuries

## 1. THE UNIVERSALITY OF THE CHURCH

In the years in which the Protestant Revolution was lacerating Christianity and wresting the Catholic Faith from entire populations, Divine Providence opened immense new spaces for the Church's apostolate. In the fifteenth and sixteenth centuries, thanks above all to Spanish and Portuguese navigators, the frontiers of Christian civilization were enlarged, and a period of missionary heroism began.

The Church is by her nature missionary because she disseminates a saving truth. The teaching of Jesus Christ is not an intellectual doctrine reserved to just a few initiates, but a truth that preserves souls from Hell and opens to them the gates of eternal happiness in Paradise. For this purpose, Jesus entrusted his disciples with the mission of going into the whole world and preaching the message of salvation to every creature (see Mark 16:16). "Go therefore and make disciples of all nations, baptizing them in the name of the Father and of the Son and of the Holy Spirit, teaching them to observe all that I have commanded you" (Matt. 28:19). "You shall receive power when the Holy Spirit has come upon you; and you shall be my witnesses in Jerusalem and in all Judea and Samaria and to the end of the earth" (Acts 1:8).

*To the end of the earth*: the Christian message has a universal reach. The Church is called *catholic* precisely because it is universal. The adjective *catholic* comes from the Greek word χαθολιχός (which derives from the adverb χαθόλου, meaning in general, total), which means "universal." The missionary spirit flows therefore from the catholicity of the Church. The Old Testament had already announced the Kingdom of God as a universal kingdom that must reunite all the nations of the earth. In the vocation of Abraham, father of the Israelite nation from which the Messiah would come forth, God pronounced the promise of the future redemption and of His kingdom: "In you shall be blessed all generations of the earth" (Gen. 12:3).

Jacob, the son of Isaac, also received a similar promise from God: "Your descendants shall be like the dust of the earth, and you shall spread abroad to the west and to the east and to the north and to the south; and by you and your descendants shall all the families of the earth bless themselves" (Gen. 28:14). These words of God's promise refer not only to the potency of the Jewish people but also to the universal diffusion of Christianity.

In the visions of the prophets, the contours of this universal kingdom of God in the New Covenant become increasingly clear. Isaiah saw the future Church of Christ as such: "It shall come to pass in the latter days that the mountain of the house of the Lord shall be established as the highest of the mountains, and shall be raised above the hills, and all the nations shall flow to it" (Isa. 2:2).

The obvious meaning of this universality is geographic, in the sense that the message of Christ is destined for all peoples of the earth. There is also a temporal universality, however, which is the extension of this message throughout time. While all things pass and nothing survives the time it is allotted, the Church is perennial, she resists all ages, vivified by her Tradition. She will never be substituted by a better salvific institution. The place of the Church of Christ will never be taken by a Church of the Holy Spirit. Such a thesis, sustained by Joachim of Fiore and many other heretics, contradicts Sacred Scripture and the Magisterium.

This universality of the Church in space and time can be termed "external" catholicity, signifying that the Church is not bound to one nation or to one political system, nor to a particular culture: it is above everything because it lives in everything. It is not restricted in a particular way, but transcends all geographical, cultural, and political barriers.

But there also exists an "internal" catholicity of the Church, which refers to the truth revealed in its fullness, in the integrity and totality of the gospel message, sent to all peoples throughout history.

When preaching the universality of the Church, one should not think so much of the numerical extension throughout the world, in the sense that the Church of Christ should have more followers than any other religious confession. If one were to see in large numbers an essential trait of the Church, this would have as a consequence that the Church of Christ is distinguished only in a numerical and quantitative manner, while instead it is recognized qualitatively for its origins from above, from God who reveals, contrary to all other religious formations that draw their origin from below, from men. The Catholic Church is not only something *more* than every other religious formation, but is something *different*, like Christ her founder is different from all other founders of religions.

The Catholic Church is universal not so much because it de facto reaches all men and all nations, but because in principle it is capable of reaching them thanks to the oneness of its doctrine, its sacraments, and its apostolic succession from Christ, which enables it to offer every man what he needs to fulfill his nature. Whoever enters the Church of Christ has no need, in order to be a Christian, to sacrifice his own natural qualities. He does not need to cease being that particular person, that concrete individual, or being a member of a certain ethnic group. To the contrary, his nature is transformed by this, elevated and purified to reach its true form.

The capacity of the Church to bring all men and peoples to salvation is one of its *intrinsic properties*. The Church, being ordered to all men and nations and having the ability to adapt to all individual and collective particularities, was already catholic when it was still confined to the tight space of the Cenacle in Jerusalem and could count only about 120 members. For the same reason, it was catholic when St. Jerome was forced to sigh, saying that the whole world had become Arian. It will remain catholic when, at the time of the antichrist, the prophecies of the Revelation of St. John shall be fulfilled, and the people of God shall be reduced to a little troop of persevering faithful.

But if the Church's mission cannot be reduced to the numerical extension of its members, neither is it indifferent to this aspect. In fact, the Church, ordered to the salvation of all men and nations, would be unfaithful to her nature if she did not aspire to fulfill what she is capable of carrying out. The more numerous are the men whom she reaches and fills with the good of salvation given to her by Christ, the more intensely does she fulfill the mission she has been called to fulfill. In this sense, it is important that the Church spreads throughout the world and has many followers, more than all other religions. And this is the specific task of the missions.

## 2. THE MISSIONARY VOCATION OF THE CHURCH

The missions are the highest manifestation of the catholicity of the Church. It is important to highlight one aspect in particular that is often misunderstood. The mission is not a generic work of the apostolate carried out to save the individual soul of the nonbeliever, but has a specific and institutional aim: to extend the kingdom of God to all peoples by means of the *plantatio Ecclesiae*. The formation of the eternal Church that will be the definitive, perfect, glorious plant is the aim of all that is done in time and space. This work is, therefore, both sacramental and institutional, not so much of conversion of souls as of the sanctification of peoples and places.

Indeed, the Redeemer and St. Paul, speaking of the evangelizing mission, insist that Christians must instruct, baptize, and Christianize not only all individuals but also and especially "all nations," all peoples. St. Augustine comments thus:

> The existence of the Church is therefore necessary where the nations still do not enjoy it; this is not, however, with the aim of having every individual who exists in that land obtain the possession of the Faith, since the promise of salvation was extended to all the peoples but not to all individuals; to possess the Faith is not a matter for everyone.

The Faith was not promised to all individuals, but only to all the "nations"; the mission, according to St. Thomas Aquinas, aims precisely at bringing the Faith to those nations that have not yet known, or no longer know, the gospel, incorporating them into the visible Church.

As the expression itself indicates, the *plantatio Ecclesiae* requires that the Faith not only be grafted like a shoot but also nourished and protected, just like the seed and the plant in the famous Gospel parable, so that it can take root, grow, and flourish; the gospel requires deep roots and social promotion — in other words, the conversion not only of individuals but also of environments, of ethnic groups and peoples, of institutions; it demands the construction and diffusion of

Christian civilization, essentially through the mediation of a system of adequate institutions. To extend the Kingdom of God, the Church must take root in civil life, and surround and support it with all the human means available; this requires a Christianity parallel to evangelization, namely a Christian society.

The Church has the duty to "establish all things in Christ," in conformity with the command of St. Paul. The missions must work therefore "not so much merely to preach and obtain individual conversions, as above all to tend to the Christian permeation of ethnic groups, to render possible and to facilitate the construction of true Christianity first, and then of truly complete Churches."

Pius XII said:

> The missionary is an apostle of Jesus Christ. He does not have the office of transplanting specifically European civilization in mission lands, but to render those peoples who boast of millenary cultures ready and suitable to receive and assimilate the elements of Christian life and customs which easily and naturally agree with every healthy civilization and confer to it the full capacity and power to ensure and guarantee human dignity and happiness. Indigenous Catholics must be true members of the family of God and citizens of His Kingdom (cf. Eph 2:19), without ceasing to be citizens of their earthly homeland. The great objective of the missions is to establish the Church in new lands and to put down solid roots there to be able one day to live and develop without the support of the work of the missions. The work of the missions is not an end in itself: it tends with fervor to that lofty objective, but she withdraws when it has been reached.

This missionary vocation of the Church was reproposed by John Paul II, who stated:

> The mission *ad gentes* has this objective: to found Christian communities and develop churches unto their complete maturity.... It is above all necessary to seek to establish everywhere Christian communities that are a sign of the divine presence in the world and which grow and become churches.... This phase of ecclesial history, called the *plantatio Ecclesiae*, has not ended; to the contrary, in many societies, it has yet to begin.

The conception of the mission as *plantatio Ecclesiae* manifests the public and institutional aspect of the Church as the Mystical Body and *societas perfecta*, which "governs peoples and nations in the name of and by the authority of Him who

is the Way, the Truth, and the Life, guiding both to the conquest of true civilization, to the attainment of the ultimate and highest end."

This public and civilizing mission of the Church is denied by secularism,
which seeks to limit the jurisdiction of the Church to the field of the individual
conscience.

## 3. St. Francis Xavier

The Church, insofar as it is catholic, bearer of a universal salvific message addressed to all men and all peoples, has always been missionary, and always will
be until the end of time. Her missions *ad gentes* accompany her history. Before
using the word "mission," the Church made use of other expressions to indicate
the same reality: "*Dilatatio fidei*," "*Propagatio fidei*," "*Evangelii Praedicatio*," "*Min-
isterium Verbi*," "*Praedicatio apostolica*." The term "mission," which today tends to
be substituted by "evangelization," entered into Catholic language above all thanks
to Ignatius of Loyola, who proposed to the Society of Jesus he founded the "*voto
de las missiones*," the availability of its members to accept any destination and task
or mission in any place or territory.

And of the thousands of missionaries, in all religious orders, one in particular perfectly incarnated the missionary spirit: St. Francis Xavier of the
Society of Jesus.

Francis was born into a noble family on April 7, 1506, in the castle of Xavier
in Navarre. He studied at the University of Paris, where Ignatius of Loyola was
his roommate. Ignatius succeeded in transforming the young Francis from a
model student dedicated to his university career to a champion of the gospel.

"For what does it profit a man, to gain the whole world and forfeit his life?"
(Mark 8:36), Ignatius repeated to Francis, until finally it touched his heart.
Francis Xavier was won over by Ignatius of Loyola and decided to follow him.
On June 24, 1537, Francis was ordained a priest in Venice. In the spring of 1539,
he took part in the foundation of the Society of Jesus and, a year later, when the
pope and King John III of Portugal asked Ignatius for missionaries to go to the
Portuguese colonies in India, Francis was chosen in place of a companion who
fell ill and was left paralyzed. At the last moment, Francis Xavier, who had at first
not been considered, had to prepare for the journey. It was March 14, 1540. He
travelled to Lisbon, was nominated apostolic nuncio to India, and left for Goa.
He dreamed, "I bore an Indian on my shoulders and he was so heavy that his
weight nearly crushed me."

After a horrible journey under limp sails that dragged out for thirteen months, during which he lavished spiritual assistance on the three hundred passengers, they finally arrived in Goa, on the western coast of India, where he began his apostolate (1542). He gathered the indigenous youth along the roads by ringing a bell and taught them the catechism through songs, to help them assimilate it better. After five months, the governor of the Indies sent him to the south, where the Portuguese had constructed their fortresses and launched their commercial enterprises, and were baptizing the indigenous people and prisoners of war without sufficient preparation.

With the help of interpreters, Francis immediately translated into their languages the main prayers and truths of the Faith. Then, for two years, he walked from village to village, at times using simple means of transport, exposed to thousands of dangers, establishing churches and schools, teaching, curing, adjudicating their disputes, and being greeted everywhere as a saint and a healer. "So great is the multitude of converts," he wrote, "that my arms are often sore from baptizing so many and my voice gives out for having repeated the Creed and the Commandments in their language." In one month, he was able to baptize ten thousand fishermen of the coast of Macua, in Travancore. While he was busy administering the sacrament, he received news that six hundred Christians in Manaar had preferred to be killed rather than return to paganism. "I am so tired of living," he wrote, "that the best thing for me would be to die for our Holy Faith."

In the following years (1545–1547), he opened new fields for the apostolate. Arriving in Malacca in December 1547, Providence had him meet a fugitive Japanese named Anjiro, wanting to become a Christian to liberate himself from the remorse brought about by a crime he had committed in his homeland. The saint was so fascinated by his tales about Japan and its inhabitants that an ardent desire to go there to evangelize was born in him. He set off in the company of Anjiro, who served as his interpreter, and anchored on the island of Kyushu on August 15, 1548. Prince Shimazu Takahisa (1514–1571) welcomed him, and while he studied the language, Anjiro converted more than a hundred relatives and friends to Catholicism. Francis wrote:

> I shall flee to Japan: I have already lost too much time, and I wish to lose no more.... My heart is pierced by a great power of attraction. No fear of dangers shall withhold me, so ardently do I desire and hope to spread

our holy religion in that country.... One thing encourages us, God
knows, to go to Japan: that those who are his image can learn to know
their Creator and glorify him.... I want to push the frontier of the Holy
Church still further.... Thus, I have the certainty that our undertaking
shall succeed.

An extant image shows the saint in the year 1551 travelling to Myako, then the
capital of Japan, on foot through the snow, through forests, without eating regular
meals. The last fifteen miles he raced with the *kulis* of a caravan to get there before
them. He was delighted finally to be able to preach the joyful news of God. In
the winter of 1551, he was recalled to India on urgent matters. By that time there
were already about two thousand Christians in Japan. His efforts had turned his
hair gray.

After Japan, he set off on another project: China, the land of the Great Wall.
But despite the order of the king, his Portuguese compatriots had abandoned
him. The *Santa Croce*, the ship that was to take him to China, was confiscated by
the governor of Malacca, who publicly denounced the saint as a forger of papal
and imperial seals. Without succumbing to discouragement at this setback,
Francis continued his journey by makeshift means and, on April 17, 1552,
landed on the island of Shang Chuan with his Chinese servant convert, Antonio
di Santa Fe.

Shang Chuan was a deserted and uninhabited island, a refuge of pirates and
contraband smugglers. Sailors had constructed huts of palm fronds for their
brief sojourns there. Francis sent his last European companion back to Malacca
because he was afraid of being taken prisoner by the Chinese. In October 1552,
a smuggler told Francis he would take him secretly to Canton for two hundred
ducats. The date and the price were fixed. In November, the cold and storms
came. Francis climbed a rock to look for his ferryman, but he did not come.
Francis was tired and ill. From the last ship that had dropped anchor he had received in alms a piece of clothing and some almonds. "Until today I have desired
to live in order to serve God and increase the glory of his name; today my nos-
talgia gives way to something stronger: to rise to Heaven and contemplate the
Lord." During the journey, the drinking water ran out. Francis touched the sea
water and turned it fresh.

During the bitter winter, the saint contracted pneumonia and, lacking all
medical care, died in a hut on December 3, 1552, after having prayed repeatedly,

"Jesus, Son of David, have mercy on me! Oh Virgin, Mother of God, remember me!" Only the cross remained for him: he rested his gaze on it as he surrendered his spirit to God. His body was buried in the northern part of the island in a trunk filled with lime. Two years later it was transported whole and intact, first to Malacca and then to Goa, where it is venerated in the Church of Good Jesus. Pope Paul V (r. 1605–1621) beatified him in 1619, and Gregory XV (r. 1621–1623) canonized him in 1622. It has been estimated that the holy missionary baptized roughly forty thousand pagans.

## 4. Send Me Wherever You Wish, Even to India

From Goa in India, Francis's arm was brought in triumph in a reliquary throughout the regions of his mission, all the way to Rome, where it was presented to the Holy Father. Today, this relic is preserved in the Church of the Gesù in Rome, enshrined in an altar across the nave from the body of St. Ignatius. The general of the Jesuits preserves in Rome some fifteen thousand letters of young Jesuits of St. Francis Xavier's time, begging to take Christ to the ends of the world. The fire of the Holy Spirit had spread among his confreres and his faithful.

In a famous letter from January 15, 1544, St. Francis Xavier wrote:

> Ever since I arrived here, I have not stopped for a moment; I go assiduously to the villages administering baptism to the children that have not yet received it. Thus, I have saved a great number of children who could not tell their left hand from their right hand. The children prevent me from saying the Divine Office or from eating or resting until I have taught them some prayer; now I have begun to understand how it is that the Kingdom of Heaven belongs to them.... Many in these areas have not become Christians simply because there is no one to baptize them. Quite often it comes to mind to go through the universities of Europe, especially in Paris, and shout here and there like a madman and disturb those who have more knowledge than charity with these words: "Oh, what great number of souls, all your fault, excluded from Heaven and chased into Hell!" Oh! If they would give as much thought to this as they do to their books, they might render an account to God for the knowledge and talents they have received! Verily, many of them, disturbed by this thought, dedicating themselves to meditating on divine matters, would dispose themselves to listening to what the Lord says to their hearts, and would set aside human ambitions and affairs, and would place themselves totally at the will of God. They would certainly

shout from the depths of their hearts: "Lord, here I am, what do you want me to do? Send me where you will, even to India."

This letter by St. Francis Xavier is a missionary manifesto, but also, we might say, a Christian manifesto. "Lord, here I am, what do you want me to do? Send me where you will, even to India." How many times throughout history has a similar appeal resounded in the heart of Christians in Europe, who face suffering and dangers, to answer this call of God to save souls, to enlarge the Kingdom of Christ? The Jesuit missionaries who were martyred in Japan on a hillside in Nagasaki between 1617 and 1632 were responding to this call. The Church has recognized the martyrdom of 205 of them, proclaiming them blessed.

But how many sons of the Church, how many theologians, how many politicians and Catholic intellectuals today seek tranquility, physical and economic well-being, and success, and to obtain these results are compromised by the world? The missions remind us that the Christian is not made for pleasure, for wealth, for honors, but for sanctity and for heroism, and in this narrow though secure way, can obtain happiness in time and eternity. Today our Indies are the cities in which we live, our families, our workplaces, our schools, our universities, our mass media, from which Catholics are often excluded, and which should be reconquered with a missionary spirit.

## 5. OUTSIDE THE CHURCH THERE IS NO SALVATION

Why has the missionary spirit been lost in our time? One of the reasons can be traced to a certain religious relativism that has spread among Catholics in recent decades, especially in the aftermath of Vatican II.

The missionary activity of the Church is founded on the principle that was proclaimed a dogma of the Faith by the Fourth Lateran Council and by the Council of Florence: "The universal Church of the faithful is one and outside of it absolutely no man can be saved." The Church has as its goal the salvation of souls, precisely because it knows that outside of it there can be no salvation. Jesus Christ shed His blood for the salvation of all men and He wants all men to be saved. To realize His salvific plan, He founded the Church, endowing it with the necessary means for reaching this end: faith, the sacraments, and legitimate authority. Salvation outside of the Church is possible only in extraordinary cases, but these are exceptions, not the rule. The exception is a secret that only God knows. It is for us to know the rule, which is that the sole means of salvation is through the Church, because she alone is, by divine will and institution, the depository of the means of salvation, and the only way of access to God and to Christ.

For this reason, as Blessed Pius IX affirmed in *Singulari Quidem:*

> One is the true Church, holy, catholic, apostolic and Roman; one the Cathedra founded on Peter by the word of the Lord (cf. Matt. 16:18); outside of it there is neither true faith not eternal salvation, because one cannot have God as his Father if he does not have the Church as his Mother, and wrongly does one deceive himself thinking he is part of the Church, when he is separated from the Cathedra of Peter, on which the Church is founded.

This is a dogma of faith: it does not exclude from salvation those who are outside the Church due to invincible error, but they are ordered to it at least by implicit desire, which includes supernatural faith and charity. They are deprived, however, of the assurance of salvation, and the ordinary means to attain it. In the same years of the heroic missionary efforts, in the esoteric secret gatherings of humanists and of some Protestant sects, new theologies of salvation were being elaborated. But if it is possible to be saved outside the Catholic Church, the missions make no sense. For this reason, the misunderstood ecumenism rampant today is diametrically opposed to the missionary spirit.

One cannot cite a lack of love for one's neighbor and of a spirit of mercy as the cause of this. Pius XI proclaimed St. Thérèse of Lisieux the patroness of missions, together with St. Francis Xavier. Pius XII wrote to the superior of Lisieux that it was a great marvel for all Christians that a little Carmelite nun, who died at twenty-four, could be placed at the head of the missionary army. But the saint demonstrated how, "in order to be a missionary, one must have a missionary soul."

One must simply recall the words from the *Story of a Soul* to say all that one can on the apostolic spirit of St. Thérèse: "I would like to be a missionary, but not only for a few years, but rather to have been one from the foundation of the world and remain in that vocation until the end of time." Such missionary zeal that embraces the entire world and all times led her to choose (something that might surprise a superficial spirit) the Carmelite Order, where silence, hiddenness, and the perfect sacrifice of herself gave to her elevated vocation the most complete power and efficacy. And if her illness had not kept her in France, she would have sailed for Vietnam to become a member of the Carmel in Hanoi and thus render manifest her ardent desire to reconcile in concrete form mission and contemplation. Her entire life in the heart of her order can be seen as a life at the service of the missions. In Heaven as well, she promised to offer her prayers to this end, according to what she assured her spiritual brother, the missionary in China Fr. Roulland, on the eve of her death. St. Thérèse was the same saint who had longed to die on the battlefield, as a crusader or a papal guard.

If there is a saint characterized by sweetness, in whom we find not the least element of harshness, arrogance, or fanaticism, it is St. Francis de Sales (1567–1622). His sweetness according to some biographers was his dominant and characteristic virtue. St. Jane Frances de Chantal (1572–1641), his spiritual daughter and cofounder with him of the Nuns of the Visitation, although she held in high regard the sweetness of Francis de Sales, admired an even more dominant virtue in him: his zeal for the salvation of souls. The first time St. Francis de Sales celebrated as bishop in his cathedral, he could not withhold his tears. His brother, Louis de Sales, asked him the reason for his tears. He responded, "Because I see my Church in Geneva in the shackles of heresy and sin and instead of having an angel to break these bonds, she only has me, your brother, a poor sinner." The saint of sweetness understood with perfect clarity the concept of the exclusivity of truth, of the Catholic principle *Extra ecclesiam nulla salus*, the notion of heresy and of sin. It was from his intransigent love of Catholic truth that his charity, sweetness, and zeal were born.

It is to this zeal that the Church owes the return to her bosom of over seventy thousand heretics. St. Francis de Sales had no ideological tolerance toward them, and he offered them no compromise. With extreme charity, tolerance, and moderation, he was able to bring these souls from error to truth in many cases—a sweet but intransigent saint, firm in the truth. The more he was tolerant, the more he was virtuous, and the more virtuous, the more he was permeated by the truth of the Faith.

## 6. MISSIONARY SPIRIT AND CRUSADER SPIRIT

St. Francis de Sales would have reconquered the city of Geneva, occupied by Calvinists, by force of arms, and was saturated by the same missionary spirit that animated the great saints of the Counter-Reformation. The contemporary crisis sinks its roots into the modern spirit of doubt, of searching, of cultural and moral relativism that established itself in Europe with the Enlightenment, and which presents itself as antithetical not only to the spirit of the Crusades but also to the missionary spirit. The missionary spirit and the crusader spirit are expressions of the same Catholic *sensus fidei* that runs throughout the centuries, and which Christians must rediscover.

We shall do so by reading the words of Pius XII, which he addressed to the Pontifical Mission Societies on June 24, 1944:

> Could there be a more explicit manifestation of the profound awareness of her mission to all regions and to all peoples that the Bride of Christ has, than her missionary activity of the last few centuries? Certainly, the idea of catholicity has always been alive in the Church, which, faithful to the mandate of her divine Founder, "Go out into the whole world, preaching the gospel to every creature" (Mark 16:15), has set her hand to missionary work always and everywhere, opening doors that had been closed to the gospel. Thus, after becoming the teacher of truth to the peoples of the ancient Roman Empire, she won the Germanic and Anglo-Saxon peoples to the Faith and charity of Christ; even before the sixteenth century, she founded the first churches in China, in the Far East, as in Greenland and the Canary Islands, in the New World.
>
> But the work of evangelization naturally could not reach its full development until the opening of the Age of Discovery, around 1500, which gave rise to that missionary movement, in the proper and most specific sense, that later in the Old World and New World continued expanding until it became a powerful popular movement, insofar as it attracts all classes of Christian society, particularly the most humble, and all the sons of the Church inspired to contribute in quite varied ways to the propagation of the Faith. This movement recalls to our mind the memory of the enthusiasm for the Crusades, which from the end of the eleventh century and for nearly all of the thirteenth century held Western Christianity in anxious anticipation.
>
> And yet it seems that future history shall place the missionary work of the modern era on an even higher level than the great deeds of the medieval Crusades. The crusaders tended to attain their goals mostly with the arms of war and of politics. Missionary work labors with the sword of the spirit (cf. Eph 6:17), of truth, love, abnegation, and sacrifice. The crusaders proposed the liberation of the Holy Land, and particularly of the Holy Sepulcher of Christ, from the hands of infidels: doubtless a noble and lofty goal! Beyond that, they had to serve and defend the Faith and Christendom against Islam. Missionary work does not stop at securing and protecting its positions. Its aim is to make the entire world into the Holy Land. It aims at taking

the kingdom of the risen Redeemer, to whom every power in Heaven and on earth has been given (cf. Mt 28:18), His empire in hearts, throughout the earth to the very last hut and least man who lives on our planet.

## 7. THE CANADIAN MARTYRS

Leaving Asia, we go now to Canada, where the first Jesuit missions among the Native Americans landed in Quebec in 1625, led by Fr. Charles Lallemant (1587–1674). Two years later, at the behest of Cardinal Richelieu, a company of one hundred associates was founded for the purpose of funding the missionary activity. Unfortunately, in the summer of 1628, England easily took possession of Canada, which lacked any form of defense. The missionaries were sent home.

A new mission arrived in Canada in 1632, led by Fr. Paul Le Jeune (1591–1664). In accord with their parents, he sought to catechize the indigenous youth as boarders in the missions.

Fr. John de Brébeuf (1593–1649), who had carried out his apostolate among the Hurons during his first sojourn, returned among them in 1633 with two other priests. From hut to hut, they began to teach the catechism to young people and adults. But several shamans convinced the Native Americans that the presence of the priests caused bad weather, draught, epidemics, and other disasters. They decided to condemn them to death. The priests, with admirable courage, invited their judges to a good-bye banquet, according to the custom, and fortunately the massacre was not carried out.

The Jesuits decided then to protect the catechumens from the great power of the sorcerers, isolating them in Christian villages. The first appeared four miles from Quebec. It had a fort, a chapel, houses, a hospital, and a rectory for the priests.

The annual reports of the Jesuits on their missionary activity, widely disseminated, had created a new feeling. At the same time, some volunteers offered to convert the Indians: St. Mary of the Incarnation (1599–1672), an Ursuline of Tours, who had founded with two other nuns a boarding school in Quebec for the instruction of Native American children; Marie-Madeleine de la Peltrie (1603–1671), a French widow, who had created a hospital in Quebec with some nursing sisters from Dieppe; and the members of the Society of Our Lady, which, aided by the Sulpician priest Jean-Jacques Olier (1608–1657) and by the

Company of the Most Holy Sacrament, constructed Ville Marie in 1642, from which Montreal emerged. While this emigration of an apostolic character occurred in Canada, the mission of the Jesuits in Saint-Joseph de Sillery near Quebec was about to become, as the reports of 1656–1657 noted, "the pattern of all Christianity in the New World." The members of the Hurons, after having been instructed and baptized, returned to their villages and carried out a fruitful apostolate in turn.

The Iroquois, on the other hand, showed themselves unshakably hostile. They horribly mutilated Fr. Isaac Jogues (1607–1646) and his assistant René Goupil (1608–1642), pouring over them molten carbon. Fr. Jogues survived and was able to return to Europe. His hands were mutilated and he could no longer celebrate Mass, but he received an exceptional authorization from Pope Urban VIII. When in 1646 he was asked to return to Canada to create a mission in Iroquois territory, he obeyed, knowing what awaited him. He wrote to a confrere, "*Ibo et non redibo*" (I will go but I shall not return). On October 18, 1646, accused of sorcery by the Iroquois, he was decapitated. His scalped head was exhibited on a pike and his body thrown in the Mohawk River. In March 1649, the Iroquois took the villages of St. Ignatius and St. Louis and martyred Fr. Brébeuf and Fr. Gabriele Lallemant (1610–1649). Fr. Brébeuf was pierced with incandescent rods, and the Iroquois flailed him and devoured his flesh before his own eyes. As the martyr continued to praise God, they tore off his lips and his tongue and stuffed his throat with glowing embers. Fr. Lallemant was tortured immediately after with even greater ferocity. Then a savage smashed his skull with a hatchet and pulled out his heart, drinking its blood to assimilate his strength and courage. The village of St. Mary had to be evacuated. Another wave of hatred in the month of December created two more martyrs, Fr. Charles Garnier (1605–1649) and Noel Chabanel (1613–1649). The remaining missionaries took refuge in Quebec. The situation was stabilized only in 1665, following the military intervention of the French. But the Huron population had been decimated, and as for the Iroquois, the defeat of the missionaries was complete. The eight Jesuit missionaries known as the Canadian Martyrs were beatified by Pope Benedict XV in 1925 and canonized by Pope Pius XI in 1930.

The Society of Jesus did not abandon Canada, although it never again had the ardor that had animated it in the mid-seventeenth century.

CHAPTER VII

# The European Crisis of Conscience

## 1. BETWEEN FIDELITY AND APOSTASY

The consequences of the Protestant Revolution were devastating for the Church and for Christian civilization. At the time of the Great Schism in the fourteenth century, Christendom had been split in two for forty years: on one side were those supporting the Roman popes, and on the other, those backing the popes of Avignon. The division did not touch Catholic Faith, however, which remained intact on both sides. The followers of both popes, who even became three for a brief period, all believed in the primacy of the Roman Church. They did not know who the true pope was, but no one placed in doubt that the Church had to be guided by the Roman pontiff.

Protestantism undermined the foundations of this authority, however. The underlying problem of the Reformation was not the state of decadence into which the Roman Curia had fallen, nor was it the theological relationship between faith and works, nor grace and divine will, but rather the concept of the papacy, whose authority over Christians Protestantism denied.

The consequences of this were terrible because entire nations were detached from the unity of the Church: Germany and the Scandinavian countries followed Luther, while much of Switzerland adhered to Calvin, and the British clung to Henry VIII and Elizabeth I.

The apostasy was not only of individuals, but of bishops with their dioceses, parish priests with their parishes, entire convents with their religious brethren, and all in the name of a false concept of obedience. In many of these countries, like England, there were very few who dared challenge the wrath of their sovereigns, sustained by obliging archbishops in Canterbury. Catholics, as has happened so often in history, were offered a dramatic choice: apostasy or the loss of their possessions and freedoms, and then exile and often death.

Among the heroes and martyrs after St. Thomas More and St. John Fisher was St. Edmund Campion (1540–1581). After being ordained a priest and entering the Society of Jesus, he taught in Prague and in 1580 was sent as a missionary to England along with Robert Persons (1546–1610). He was arrested while celebrating Mass clandestinely, accused of sedition against Queen Elizabeth, and finally condemned to death. On the morning of December 1, 1581, he was tied behind a horse and dragged through the city streets to the gallows. There he was hanged, drawn, and quartered. The Catholic Church commemorates him alongside forty other martyrs killed in England and Wales from 1535 to 1679, canonized by Paul VI on October 25, 1970. Catholics were severely discriminated against in England, yet it is estimated that during the reign of Elizabeth I, who took the throne after the Catholic Mary Tudor, a third of the English were still Catholic and only one in twenty Protestant. But the Protestants were ideologized fanatics much more than the Catholics were fervent. This often happens in history: the determined minority imposes itself upon the mass of moderates, tempted by compromise.

What arose to the left of Luther and Calvin was a minority composed of sects and secret assemblies, like the Anabaptists in Germany and Austria who preached a second Baptism for adults baptized as children, and the Socinians in Italy who disseminated the old anti-Trinitarian heresies, denying the dogmas of the Trinity and the divinity of Jesus Christ. The Italian anti-Trinitarians were called Socinians because they followed two heretics from Siena, uncle and nephew Lelio and Fausto Socino and were organized in clandestine groups, the Collegia Vicentina, that practiced esoteric doctrines tending toward atheism.

The Italian heretics were forced to emigrate, especially into Transylvania and Poland, and from there to Holland, disseminating rationalism and religious indifferentism. On his tomb near Krakow, Fausto Socino left the following epitaph: "*Alta ruet Babylon* [the Catholic Church]: *destruxit tecta Lutherus, muros Calvinus, sed fundamenta Socinus.*"

One of the most stunning cases of apostasy in Italy was that of Bernardino Ochino (1487–1564), general of the Capuchins and a famous preacher who abandoned the Faith, married, and fled Italy for Calvin's Geneva, Thomas Cranmer's England, and the Poland of Bona Sforza, taking his message of religious freedom, understood as the right of Christians to profess publicly any religion they choose. This, as the Church sustained in its condemnation of these heretics, is the equivalent of not believing in any religion and wanting to return to Roman paganism.

## 2. THE SAINTS OF THE COUNTER-REFORMATION

After the Council of Trent, the Church closed its ranks. The *Index of Prohibited Books* was instituted, as was the Inquisition, to strike heretics who were nesting in the Church's bosom. The defense of orthodoxy within the Church was entrusted to the Dominicans; to the Jesuits was entrusted the apostolate *ad extra*, which was carried out in two directions: on one hand, the vast missionary work, on the other, the reconquest of lands fallen to heresy, like Germany and England. If St. Francis Xavier was the champion of the missionary apostolate, St. Ignatius entrusted to another one of his first companions, Blessed Peter Faber (1506–1546), the apostolate in Germany, where another great Jesuit saint stood out, Peter Canisius (1521–1597).

Benedict XVI dedicated the general audience of February 9, 2011, to St. Peter Canisius, recalling that he lived in a time in which "the Catholic Faith in Germanic lands seemed to be extinguished in the face of the fascination of the Reformation. Canisius had an almost impossible task, that of revitalizing and renewing the Catholic Faith in German lands." But nourished by Ignatian spirituality, St. Peter Canisius was able to reinforce the Catholic Faith where it had remained in the majority (first in Bavaria, then Vienna, Prague, and Poland, where he became the papal nuncio), as well as sustaining it in the German regions with a Protestant majority. Canisius was also the author of a famous catechism destined to form the Faith of Christians for centuries.

A decisive role was played in the sixteenth and seventeenth centuries by another holy Jesuit who directed the Catholic Counter-Reformation from Rome, St. Robert Bellarmine (1542–1621).

Bellarmine was born in Montepulciano, Tuscany, in 1542. He entered the Society of Jesus, then studied in Padua and at the Roman College. He was in Louvain when he decided to prepare a general refutation of the rampant heretical theses, in order to "provide armor to those whom the Church shall send into combat against the infernal powers," as he put it. In this way, the *Controversie* was born, a voluminous work in which he expounded and confuted with exceptional rigor the doctrines of the heretics, demonstrating the truth of the Catholic Faith. Bellarmine was nominated professor at the Gregorian University in Rome and was then appointed cardinal and archbishop of Capua in 1559. He collaborated with various popes and participated in the trials that led to the condemnation of the apostate friar Giordano Bruno (1548–1600) and that of Galileo Galilei (1564–1642).

Remember that Galileo was not condemned by the Church for his scientific positions, but for having presumed that these positions were to be considered absolute truth and not merely hypotheses to be debated. For the Church, there exists collaboration and harmony between Faith and science, but science must never presume to judge Faith. Galilei wanted to be not just a scientist but also a philosopher and even a theological scientist, stating that in the case of a contradiction between science and Faith, it is science and not Faith that must prevail. It was this philosophical position, not his scientific findings, that were the reason for his condemnation by the Holy Office.

Robert Bellarmine died on September 17, 1621, in Rome. Pope Benedict XV gave him the title "Hammer of Heretics," and his successor Pius XI proclaimed him, in the space of just a few years, blessed, saint, and Doctor of the Church. His body is venerated by the faithful in the Church of St. Ignatius of Loyola in Rome, where the relics of other Jesuit saints are preserved, among them St. Louis Gonzaga (1568–1591), Bellarmine's spiritual son. Some of the faithful devoted to Bellarmine invoke him using the following prayer: "Oh God, who for the spiritual renewal of the Church has given us Bishop St. Robert Bellarmine as a great teacher and model of Christian virtue, we pray that by his intercession we may always preserve the integrity of that faith to which he dedicated his entire life."

As Plinio Corrêa de Oliveira rightly observes:

> St. Robert Bellarmine realized that heresy cannot be defeated only by preaching the truth. It is also necessary to denounce and confute error. Using this method, he converted many heretics, bringing them back to communion with the Church. By canonizing him, the Church sanctioned his methods, and considers them part of her heroic virtues. In fact, the saint practiced the theological virtue of charity and the cardinal

virtues of justice and prudence toward heretics. The Church could not
have canonized him if the method that characterized his entire work
had been contrary to justice, prudence, and charity. It is important to
emphasize this point because, after Vatican II, many have told us that
criticizing heresy and heretics is wrong and contrary to ecumenism and
dialogue. According to what has been presented to us as the "spirit of
Vatican II," the only way to treat heresy consists in finding and applaud-
ing the positive aspects, never in directly combatting its errors. St.
Robert Bellarmine's entire life goes precisely in the opposite direction.

These words should be meditated upon because they help us to understand the
profound relevance in our times of the figure of St. Robert Bellarmine.

Next to Bellarmine, we remember another saint, his friend Cesare Baronio
(1538–1607), the spiritual son, in turn, of St. Phillip Neri. Baronio offered, like
Bellarmine, to confute heretics, but his terrain was that of history. He is the author of an important work, the *Annales Ecclesiastici*, thanks to which he did, on
the historical level, what Bellarmine had done for theology. Baronio's history is
not blindly apologetic. Profoundly honest and objective, he did not hide the
failures and omissions of men of the Church, and sought above all the truth,
ignoring facts that would have fostered the glorification of the Church, but were
not supported by historical sources, while not keeping silent about other regret-
table episodes for the Church, because they were true. The Church, in fact, as
Pope Leo XIII would later recall, does not fear the truth, but is rather its inflexible custodian.

## 3. THE THIRTY YEARS' WAR AND THE PEACE OF WESTPHALIA

In that historical period running from the second half of the 1500s to the first
half of the 1600s, a war of religion began for the conquest of Europe by Protestants
and for the reconquest of Europe by Catholics. Emperor Charles V had seen his
dream of a Christian empire shattered against the rocks of Protestantism. He
abdicated, and his descendants reigned in Spain and Austria, two very different
nations, geographically distant, but under the guidance of the same dynasty, the
Habsburgs, and moved by the same desire to defend the principles of the Catholic
Counter-Reformation.

On the other side, there was Anglican England, France divided by religious
struggles between Catholics and Huguenots, and Lutheran Germany. Italy at
that time was a battlefield among foreign powers. All the wars, peace accords,

and alliances that were born and died in this convulsive epoch were dominated by a religious thrust, and all converge on the war that began in Bohemia in 1618 between the Catholic League, with Emperor Ferdinand II of Austria (1578–1637) and Duke Maximillian of Bavaria (1573–1651) at its head, and the ragged Protestant front which aligned Calvinists, Lutherans, and the enemies of the House of Austria in general. This war, which has come down in history under the name of the Thirty Years' War, after a first religious phase, transformed into a political war. We must remember it as a great Catholic victory.

Everyone has heard of the Battles of Lepanto and Vienna; few know that of White Mountain, in Bohemia, where in 1620 imperial forces vanquished Protestant armies. During that battle, Duke Maximillian of Bavaria, a man of great piety, asked Fr. Domenico Ruzzola (1559–1630), a Spanish Discalced Carmelite living in Rome and already known for his sanctity, to accompany him. Fr. Domenico, though old and sickly, hastened to grant his request and travelled to Prague, the capital of Bohemia, where he found a little painting that portrayed the adoration of the wise men in Bethlehem. Taking this painting, in which Mary, Joseph, and the shepherds had piercing eyes, Fr. Domenico accompanied the Catholic army to White Mountain as their spiritual guide. There, dressed in his Carmelite habit, he mounted a horse, and holding a crucifix in one hand and the painting of the Virgin hung around his neck, he charged into the fray, animating the fight as John of Capistrano had done and Marco d'Aviano would later do. The victors raised the shout, "Mary! Mary!" as the Protestant army was routed. It was November 8, 1620.

Following this victory, attributed to the aid of the Virgin Mary, the beautiful Church of Santa Maria della Vittoria was constructed in Rome and entrusted to the Carmelites. In Prague as well, the Carmelites were entrusted with another church that was rechristened Our Lady of Victories. This place became the center of what today is known as the devotion to the Infant Jesus of Prague. Until the sixteenth century, Jesus was adored as a baby in the crib. From this time on, he was adored as an Infant King. It is important to emphasize this aspect: the regality of Christ is not only that of Christ as an adult, but also as the Infant Jesus, King by right and by conquest of all men in every moment of his life, from the first moments of his conception in the purest womb of Mary to his triumph on Golgotha.

The Battle of White Mountain is listed among the great victories obtained throughout history by Catholics fighting for Christ the King and Mary our

Queen. In recent decades it has often been repeated that Christians are for peace and abhor war. This is only partly true. Christians are certainly in favor of peace because Jesus is the Prince of Peace. But Christ also said he has come not to bring peace, but the sword, and there is no contradiction in these words. There exists but one true Christian peace, that of Christ, and but one just war, that conducted to defend the natural and Christian order.

The Peace of Westphalia, which ended the Thirty Years' War and the period of the Counter-Reformation in 1648, brought about a profound historical shift that witnessed medieval Christian civilization's substitution by modern Europe.

The epoch that was now beginning, that which runs from the Peace of Westphalia (1648) to the French Revolution (1789), is that in which each prince obtained the right to impose upon his subjects the religion he himself professed (*cuius regio, eius et religio*). Christendom, once dominated by two supreme authorities, the pope and the emperor at the service of the one Catholic Faith, was now at an end. The international community formed in Westphalia was an organization of sovereign and independent states, juridically equal. The Peace of Westphalia, affirming the principle of "balance" and "reason of state," ratified in Europe the interests of the sovereign as the supreme law, unfettered from any transcendent reference point.

## 4. JANSENISM

As Europe was entering into this process of anti-Christian secularization, the Church found herself for the first time in history having to fight a new heresy that advanced according to an entirely different strategy from all preceding ones.

This new heresy was Jansenism, a religious current that overturned the Catholic doctrine of grace on the dogmatic level, pushing it toward Calvinism, and on the moral level enclosed Christian life in a brooding and unbearable rigorism. But beyond the theological and moral errors, the worst snare of Jansenism was found in its attempt to reform the Church from within and no longer from the outside, as Protestantism had sought to do.

The movement takes the name of Cornelius Jansen (1585–1638), who proposed an ambitious theological, moral, and disciplinary reform of the Church, summarized in his book *Augustinus*, which appeared in 1640, two years after his death. Jansen was convinced that no one before him had understood St. Augustine, whom he reinterpreted, trying to reconcile the orthodox doctrines of the bishop of Hippo with Calvinist heresy. It was precisely this path of compromise between Calvinism and Catholicism that assured the success of the book. The middle way is always more attractive than the extremes, not only when the extreme paths lead to evil, but also when they express the radicalness of truth and the good.

Jansen maintained that Original Sin has so thoroughly ruined man that, without grace, he can do no good, not even accidentally. God, furthermore, has already decided who must be saved and who condemned, independently of their merits and demerits. This was, in effect, predestination in the Calvinist sense.

Jansen's theories had their great apostle in Abbot Jean du Vergier de Hauranne (1581–1643), and found an effective organizer in the theologian Antoine Arnauld (1612–1694). When in 1653, Pope Innocent X (r. 1644–1655) condemned five propositions on which the theological system of the Jansenists was based, Arnauld suggested that the Jansenists should unite themselves with the papal condemnation, denying however that the condemned propositions were found in the works of Jansen. It was a very clever way out. It was a matter of saying: *I condemn what the Church condemns, but what it condemns is not my doctrine.*

Thus, Jansenism sought to remain inside the Church, without being condemned, while seeking the condemnation of its adversaries who, at that time, were above all the Jesuits, the most faithful defenders of Roman orthodoxy.

Jansenism had a third leader, Pascasio Quesnel (1634–1719), of the Congregation of the Oratory. From Jansen to Quesnel, Jansenism constituted a sort of church within the Church: the Jansenist church, limited to a few holy elect touched by grace. The Jansenists discouraged frequent Communion, or rather surrounded it with many warnings, scruples, and precautions, rendering it de facto impracticable, and more generally they ignored the role of mercy, appealing only to implacable divine justice.

The response of Divine Providence to Jansenism took shape, not through papal interventions and theological writings, but through the diffusion of a new devotion: the worship of the Sacred Heart of Jesus.

## 5. Devotion to the Sacred Heart

This devotion has ancient roots, dating to the patristic and medieval periods. But only in the 1600s, with St. John Eudes (1601–1680), did it enter liturgical worship. In 1643, Eudes founded the Congregation of Jesus and Mary, or Eudists, and composed a work dedicated to the devotion to the admirable Heart of Jesus, which contains a Mass and its own Divine Office. The diffusion of this devotion is due especially to a saint, Margaret Mary Alacoque (1647–1690), a sister in the Order of the Visitation. It was within the Visitation that Providence chose a humble nun, St. Margaret Mary Alacoque, to entrust the great remedy against the new heresy that began in the seventeenth century.

Born in Burgundy in 1647, Margaret had a difficult youth, above all because she had to overcome the resistance of her parents to enter, at twenty-four, the Visitandines, where she offered herself from the very beginning as a "victim to the Heart of Jesus." She was misunderstood by her fellow sisters, judged harshly by her superiors, but comforted by another Jesuit saint, Claude de la Colombière (1641–1682), who remained faithful to her and ordered her to narrate her spiritual experiences in an autobiography. Through the inspiration of the saint, the feast of the Sacred Heart was established, as well as the great promise of the Nine First Fridays of the month, contained in these words of Jesus: "I promise you in the excess of the mercy in My Heart, that My omnipotent Love shall concede to all those who receive Communion on the first Friday of the month, for nine consecutive months, the grace of final perseverance; they shall not die in disgrace, nor without receiving the sacraments, finding in My heart a safe shelter in their extreme hour."

Nothing could be more antithetical to the spirit of Jansenism. The Jansenist conception of God was oppressive and anguished. The Sacred Heart appeared to St. Margaret Mary Alacoque, affirming, to the contrary, that one must surrender to His Love, and indicating in Divine Mercy the remedy to man's sins.

Altogether, there are twelve promises which merit to be known in their entirety:

1) To those devoted to my Sacred Heart I shall give all the grace and help necessary to their state.

2) I shall establish and maintain peace in their families.

3) I shall console them in all their afflictions.

4) I shall be for them a safe refuge in life and above all in the hour of their death.

5) I shall pour abundant blessings on all their labors and undertakings.

6) Sinners shall find in My Heart an endless wellspring of mercy.

7) Tepid souls shall become fervent with
   the practice of this devotion.

8) Fervent souls shall rise rapidly to great perfection.

9) My blessing shall remain in the places where the image
   of the Sacred Heart is exposed and venerated.

10) To all those who work for the salvation of souls, I
    shall give grace to convert hardened hearts.

11) The people who spread this devotion shall have
    their names written forever in My Heart.

12) To all those who receive Communion on the first
    Fridays of nine consecutive months, I shall give the
    grace of final perseverance and eternal salvation.

Jansenists obstinately considered this final perseverance to be reserved to a few
elect, not conditioned by their good works or their merits.

## 6. Louis XIV and the Sacred Heart

Among the celestial messages received by St. Margaret Mary Alacoque, one in
particular had extraordinary importance. On June 12, 1689, she transmitted a
divine message to Mother de Saumaise, in Dijon, with the task of taking it to the
king of France, Louis XIV (1638–1715).

The saint wrote:

> [The Sacred Heart] desires to enter with pomp and magnificence in the
> homes of princes and kings, to be honored as much as it has been of-
> fended, despised, and humiliated in His Passion, and to receive as much
> pleasure in seeing the great of the earth lowered and humbled before
> Him, as He had felt bitterness in being annihilated at their feet. "Behold
> the words I have established for this purpose: Make known to the first-
> born of My Sacred Heart," alluding to our king, "that, as his temporal
> birth was obtained thanks to the devotion to the merits of My Holy
> Infancy, so too shall he obtain his birth in grace and eternal glory by
> means of the consecration he shall make of himself to My adorable
> Heart, which desires to triumph over his, and through him, over the
> hearts of the great of the earth. It longs to reign in his palace, to be
> painted on his banners, and engraved on his armaments to render them
> victorious over his enemies, deposing at his feet those proud and
> haughty heads to render them triumphant over all the enemies of the
> Holy Church."

In 1689, the year of this urgent request, no man in Europe could equal Louis XIV in power and splendor. He was the sun of France, and France the sun of Europe. The egalitarian wave that had crashed over Christian civilization after the Protestant Revolution and the conclusion of the Thirty Years' War seemed to have halted in his kingdom. The most Christian king of France was the symbol of sacred monarchy, and this monarchy represented in Europe the triumph of order, measure, and the classical spirit, in what historians term the *grand-siècle*, the century of many eminent personalities, such as St. Francis de Sales, Bérulle, St. Vincent de Paul, Pascal, Molière, Corneille, Racine, Bossuet, and many other luminaries of spirituality, letters, philosophy, and politics.

From his birth, the miraculous nature of which our Lord himself confirmed, the Sun King seemed called to a great destiny. After the so-called vow of Louis XIII of February 10, 1638, which established Mary as queen of France, on September 5 of the same year, God granted the sovereign's wife, Anna of Austria (1601–1666), a son after twenty-three years of sterility, giving him the name Louis Dieudonné, gift of God, the future Louis XIV.

Louis XIV lacked, however, the humility of St. Louis IX, and did not receive the request of Margaret Mary Alacoque. His successors also refused to heed the message. This failure to correspond to grace had disastrous consequences for the kingdom of France.

Confirmation that matters had gone in this direction comes once more from the Virgin Mary who, appearing in 1930 to Sr. Lucia, lamented of Russia's refusal to consecrate itself to her Immaculate Heart. "Make it known to my ministers," she said, "that having chosen to follow the example of the king of France in delaying the execution of my request, they will follow him in disaster as well. It will never be too late to have recourse to Jesus and Mary." And referring to the pope, the Virgin Mary said, "The Holy Father! Pray constantly for the Holy Father! He will do it, but it will be late! Nevertheless, the Immaculate Heart of Mary shall save Russia. It has been entrusted to her." Sr. Lucia would allude to this decisive revelation in the report of the apparitions of Tuy (Spain), written in 1936 by Fr. Gonçalves, stating that the Lord lamented with her because the consecration of Russia had not been carried out: "They refused to listen to my request! . . . Like the king of France, they too will repent, and they shall perform it, but it will be too late. Russia will already have disseminated its errors throughout the world, provoking wars, and persecutions of the Church: the Holy Father will have to suffer much."

Historians agree upon the last years of the seventeenth century as the twilight of the reign of Louis XIV. According to the historian Paul Hazard, for example, from humanism to the French Revolution, there was no greater crisis than that which upset Europe from 1680 to 1715: France lost its cultural and political hegemony over Europe to Protestant England, where Deism developed and where, in 1717, Freemasonry was born, becoming the driving force of the subversion aimed at destroying the Church and Christian civilization.

A philosophy was created that renounced metaphysics to study the apparent and the tangible. Political life developed without divine right, religion without mysteries, morality without dogmas.

In this horizon the life and mission of St. Louis Marie Grignon de Montfort, the ardent apostle of the Blessed Virgin Mary and untiring propagator of devotion to the Sacred Heart as the heavenly remedy to libertine irreligiosity and Jansenist rigorism, was situated.

Louis Marie Grignon was born in Montfort-la-Canne, in Brittany, on January 31, 1673, and died in Saint-Laurent-sur-Sèvre, in the Vendée, on April 28, 1716. His brief life was lived almost perfectly within the chronological limits (1680–1715) of the "European crisis of conscience" described by the historian Paul Hazard, as a sort of response by Providence to this crisis which is still today the crisis of our time. Political and religious authorities of the age did not realize that French society of the seventeenth and eighteenth centuries was seriously ill due to the revolutionary process, which, in humanism and Protestantism, had undermined the foundations of the edifice of Christianity. So too the religious and political authorities of our time are not aware of the terrible scale of the current crisis, the roots of which lie in the secularist spirit, to which St. Louis Marie helps us to find a remedy.

Raised in an aristocratic family, Louis Marie studied in Paris at the seminary of Saint-Sulpice and was ordained priest in 1700. Although endowed with extraordinary qualities that indicated his inclination for an ecclesiastical career, he chose to dedicate all his energies to the apostolate in those cities and the countryside of France then infected by the poison of Jansenism and the first signs of the Enlightenment. As a pilgrim in Rome, Pope Clement XI (r. 1700–1721) conferred upon him the title "apostolic missionary" and gave him an ivory crucifix with the privilege of a plenary indulgence for whomever should kiss it with devotion. The saint always carried with him this crucifix, which did not assuage the hostility toward him of some bishops who did not want him in their dioceses because of the radicalness of his preaching.

Before he died at just forty-three, worn out by the strain of the apostolate, Louis Marie founded two religious congregations, the Company of Mary and the Daughters of Wisdom, and composed several precious spiritual works, such as the *Treatise on the True Devotion to Mary*, considered one of the highest expressions of Marian devotion of all time. "This little treatise," wrote Fr. Réginald Garrigou-Lagrange, "is a treasure for the Church, as is the summary this blessed man made for a nun titled *The Secret of Mary*." This golden work should be read alongside another little-known, but equally important, work of his, *Fervent Prayer*.

Louis Marie de Montfort was beatified by Leo XIII on January 22, 1888, and proclaimed a saint by Pius XII on July 20, 1947, stating that he was "the greatest apostle of Poitou, Brittany, and the Vendée." The Vendeans who rose up in arms against the impiety of the Revolution were the descendants of the peasants whom the great saint had preserved from the influence of the Revolution through his popular missions, such that Pius XII could affirm without exaggeration that "the Vendée of 1793 was the work of his hands." "If St. Louis Marie Grignion de Montfort had extended his missionary activity to the whole of France," observes Plinio Corrêa de Oliveira, "its history would probably have been different, as would the history of the world as well." If this did not happen, it was because the prophetic words of the saint were not heeded. He appeared as a prophet of doom when he announced the punishment of God on an unrepentant humanity and sought apostles of fire who could renew with their ardor the Church and all society.

## 7.  THE ANNOUNCEMENT OF PUNISHMENTS
## AND THE KINGDOM OF MARY

St. Louis Marie Grignion de Montfort belongs to this category of saints who proclaimed the necessary purification of society through chastisements that are also signs of the depths of divine mercy.

"Through the Blessed Virgin Mary, Jesus Christ came into the world; through her he must reign in the world once more," wrote St. Louis Marie. These words which open the *Treatise on the True Devotion to Mary* immediately clear the field of any ambivalence, perfectly defining the distinction of nature and roles between the Blessed Virgin Mary and Jesus Christ: Mary is the means, Jesus Christ is the only end. The saint establishes a relationship between two different, though closely connected, events: the first is the Incarnation of the Word, the Nativity; the second, shrouded in mystery because it has not yet come about, is the Kingdom of Jesus in the world, a kingdom in history that, as appears clearly from the development of the *Treatise*, is not to be understood as the Parousia, the coming of Jesus at the end of time, but as the triumph of the Mystical Body, the Church, thanks to the miracles produced once more, after the Incarnation, from the union between the Holy Spirit and the Virgin Mary. The saint defines this kingdom as the Kingdom of Mary.

The Kingdom of Mary is the triumph of the Church, founded by Our Lord Jesus Christ, and the apogee of Christian civilization, the fruit of the merits of His Passion. This triumph is necessary in history to allow man, who has a social nature, to render to God in time all the glory that the angels and the blessed shall render Him in eternity. God is always victorious and His triumph must radiate, "on earth as it is in Heaven," in time and in eternity.

St. Louis Marie speaks for this reason of a second coming on earth of Jesus through Mary, but a "glorious and radiant" one, inasmuch as the first was secret and hidden: "but both of them perfect, because both shall be through Mary." The Kingdom of Mary will be a poem of glory, just as the Incarnation of the Word was a poem hidden in humility. In this historical period, St. Louis states, the union of Mary with the souls of her apostles shall reach an intensity without precedent, and she shall lavish the graces she possesses on hearts faithful to her in such an abundant way as to "fashion saints so excellent that their sanctity exceeds that of most other saints, just as the cedars of Lebanon are higher than shrubs."

In *Fervent Prayer*, St. Louis Marie announces, after the inevitable chastisements that await humanity, a great triumph of the Holy Spirit, who, by divine promise, assists the Church throughout history. "The special Kingdom of God the Father lasted until the Flood," writes our saint, "and a flood of water concluded it; the Kingdom of Jesus Christ finished in a deluge of blood, but Your Kingdom, O Spirit of the Father and of the Son, continues still and shall end in a deluge of fire, of love and justice." The Kingdom of the Holy Spirit will be the Kingdom of Mary over souls and over society, by means of the close ties that bind the Blessed Virgin to the Mystical Body of Christ, of which she is the heart, and the third Person of the Most Holy Trinity of whom she is the Bride.

When will this fortunate time come "in which Mary shall reign as mistress and sovereign of hearts to solicit their full submission to the empire of her great and only Jesus?" "This time," writes the saint, "will arrive only when the form of devotion which I teach shall be known and practiced, '*Ut adveniat regnum tuum, adveniat regnum Mariae*' [That your kingdom come, may the Kingdom of Mary come]."

The way in which this special union between Mary and the souls of her apostles shall come about is by the practice of the "true devotion" whose secret he reveals and elaborates in the *Treatise*. The regality of the Virgin Mary must be achieved first of all within souls, and from there will be reflected in the religious and civil life of Christian peoples.

As Plinio Corrêa de Oliveira writes:

> Therefore, the Kingdom of Mary shall be an era in which the union of souls with the Virgin Mary will reach an intensity unprecedented in history, with the exception, clearly, of individual cases. What is the form of this union, in a certain sense the highest of all unions? I do not know of a more perfect means to express and bring about this union than the holy servitude to the Virgin Mary, as St. Louis Marie Grignion de Montfort teaches it in his *Treatise on the True Devotion to Mary*.

The act of consecration to the Virgin Mary of a person or a people is profoundly antithetical to the egalitarian and irreligious spirit. To consecrate is, by definition, to subordinate man and society to God. The expression "Kingdom of Mary" expresses the ideal of the sacralization of the temporal order through the mediation of Mary, which is simply the Christian civilization that the pontiffs have always held up as the goal. Christian civilization, which submits entirely to God and recognizes the supreme regality of Jesus Christ and of Mary, is in this sense sacred and hierarchically ordered.

The triumph of the Immaculate Heart of Mary prophesied by the Virgin Mary in Fátima in 1917 confirms this hope. Pope Pius XII established the feast of Mary Our Queen and ordered the Church to renew every year on that day the consecration of the human race to the Immaculate Heart of Mary, placing in this gesture "great hope that a new age might arise, gladdened by Christian peace and by the triumph of religion," and affirmed that "the invocation of the kingdom of Mary is … the voice of Christian faith and hope," repeating in one of his last discourses, in 1958, the "certainty that the restoration of the Kingdom of Christ through Mary cannot fail to come about."

Beyond the ruins of the modern world, souls inflamed with true faith can see the brilliance of the Kingdom of Mary and find spiritual sustenance in the recitation of the *Fervent Prayer*. This text by St. Louis Marie Grignion de Mont-fort is valid for all times, and especially in periods of crisis like the present, in which we must ask Divine Providence to raise up extraordinary men to face the enemies of the Church "with the radiant and ardent force of the gospel in their mouths and the Rosary in their hands." The Virgin Mary, mediatrix and dis-tributor of graces, is the necessary source of every authentic reaction to the Revolution that threatens the Church and society. Those who trust in her shall obtain her Kingdom.

CHAPTER VIII

# The Church against Internal and External Enemies

## 1. THE HOLY LEAGUES AGAINST THE TURKS

In the same years in which the Spanish and Portuguese were extending the scope of Christianity in Asia and Latin America, the popes were promoting the Holy League to defend Christianity from the Islamic threat. In particular, it was St. Pius V and Blessed Innocent XI who promoted this alliance of Christian princes against the Turks in the sixteenth and seventeenth centuries, obtaining amazing victories. The spirit that animated St. Pius V and Blessed Innocent XI was a crusader spirit, despite the fact that the Holy Leagues cannot properly be termed crusades. The Crusades had an eminently supernatural goal. The Holy Leagues were undertakings in which European Christians defended not only the Catholic Faith but also their own lands, their nations, and their families.

Christian civilization, as so often throughout history, was in danger. The Turks advanced in Europe: the enemy Christianity had to face was not only political but religious. Islam's objective was to extend its empire over all the known lands, to reduce Christians to slavery or dhimmitude, to destroy all that Christendom had created throughout the centuries, and to impose on the religious and social level the law of Muhammad—a law that not only denied the primary dogma of the Trinity but contradicted the fundamental principles of Christian morality, making the law of sexual pleasure not only a supreme earthly aspiration but also the yearned-for heavenly compensation for the followers of the Qur'an, whose paradise is a place of eternal sensual pleasure more than a place of eternal spiritual happiness.

There was, and is, no possible compromise between Islam and Christianity. They are two religions each aimed at the conquest of the world.

On one side, the religion of Jesus Christ, the God-man who by his Resurrection has proved his divinity. On the other side, the religion of Muhammad, the man who demonstrated (and continues to do so today) the falsity of his doctrines by the ferocity and debauchery of his life and that of his followers.

At the dawn of the eighteenth century, the main external enemy of Christian civilization, Islam, seemed to have been defeated. The defense of Christianity against Muslim aggression had lasted a thousand years. In 732, a century after Muhammad's death, Islam's expansion westward was blocked at Poitiers by the Frankish army of Charles Martel. The Crusades represented a new setback for the followers of Muhammad, although in the fifteenth century, Islam renewed its advance, conquering Constantinople in 1453 under Sultan Mehmed II. The ancient capital of the Byzantine Empire changed its name to Istanbul and became the new capital of the Ottoman Empire. From that time, the threatening shadow of the Turks accompanied like a nightmare the history of Europe.

The Ottoman sultans assumed the title of caliph after 1517. They subjugated the Balkans, a land of Orthodox Faith, reaching as far as Belgrade. They conquered Hungary in 1526 and reached the walls of Vienna, first in 1529 and again in 1683. "For nearly a thousand years," recalls the historian Bernard Lewis, "from the first landing of the Moors in Spain to the second Turkish siege of Vienna, Europe remained under constant threat by Islam."

The victory at Lepanto on October 7, 1571, reminds us that Christian civilization has always had its enemies throughout history, and must have its defenders as well. Christians living on the earth are part of a Church called *militant* because it is engaged in combat to defend its Faith and the civilization that has been built upon that Faith. The name Lepanto, in this sense, evokes not only a historical event but has become a symbol that summarizes a theology of history and a conception of the world.

But if, on the symbolic level, Lepanto has this indelible significance, on the historical level the victory of the Christian fleet in 1571 did not have consequences proportionate to the greatness of the endeavor. The expulsion of Islam from Europe was not set into motion, which should have been logical to imagine after the stunning undoing of the Turks. For this to happen—that the expulsion of Muslims from Europe might begin—we must await another event: the liberation of Vienna from the Turks on September 12, 1683.

The liberation of Vienna had as its architect a great pope: Innocent XI, born Benedetto Odescalchi, who reigned from September 21, 1676, to August 12, 1689. In his radio message on October 7, 1956, on the occasion of Innocent XI's beatification, Pius XII recalled that the defense of the Church and of Christian civilization from the threat of Islam was his primary task, together with the spiritual and moral reform of the Church and the defense of the rights of the Church against the France of Louis XIV.

The Turkish defeat under the walls of Vienna was followed by a series of defeats and losses of cities and provinces previously held by the Turks. In 1686, Budapest was liberated; Belgrade followed in 1717. Prince Eugene of Savoy (1663–1736) was the protagonist of these victories and personified, after the death of Innocent XI, the defense of Christianity against Islam. The Austrian Empire imposed on the Turks the humiliating peace treaties of Karlowitz (1699) and Passarowitz (1718), which marked the decline of Ottoman power.

Thanks to Blessed Innocent XI and Prince Eugene of Savoy, Islam was repulsed at the gates of Christendom, while the Peace of Utrecht and of Rastatt in 1713 reconfigured the new political equilibrium in Europe. But in those same years of Christian heroism against Islam, the mutation of culture and mentality that prepared the way for the French Revolution was taking place.

## 2. THE BIRTH OF FREEMASONRY

A century after the liberation of Vienna, Christianity was devastated by an internal enemy worse than the external ones that had threatened it for centuries.

The French Revolution was preceded and prepared for by a vast transformation of spirit and mentality. In the second half of the 1600s and the beginning of the 1700s, as the star of the Sun King was declining, a new culture was forming in Europe whose spirit was profoundly different from that of the Catholic Counter-Reformation. This new culture was born of Protestantism, developing in a rational sense the principle of personal authority using the critical spirit. It flourished first in Holland and England, but found in France the most favorable environment for its development. A true arsenal of new ideas was contained in the *Historical and Critical Dictionary* by Pierre Bayle (1647–1706), who alternated between Protestantism and Catholicism, defining himself finally as a "free thinker." The dictionary, published in 1697, was a mine of doubts, objections, and criticism of Christianity, and offered the first idea of the *Encyclopédie* of the Enlightenment philosophers.

The first form the Enlightenment took was Deistic Naturalism. Naturalism is called Deistic because it recognizes the existence of a supreme being who ordered the universe, but denies every form of revelation, and thus denies all dogma and religious authority. The inspiring principle of Deism is the clear distinction between natural religion and revealed religion. According to Deism, religious problems are to be confronted with reason, and what is incomprehensible, like Original Sin and the eternity of Hell, is to be rejected as irrational. The supernatural is subjected to the judgment of reason, and the only supreme criterion for religious truth is its rationality.

Deism can thus be defined as rational or natural religion. The separation between natural religion, which one can reach through the use of reason, and revealed religion leads to the conflict between Faith and reason, which will come to fruition in the Enlightenment primacy of reason over Faith. Deism rejects, furthermore, the idea of good and evil, and does not posit a life after death. Although it is not militant atheism, it does hold to a substantial philosophical skepticism and moral indifferentism. Today, the position of one who refuses to declare himself a coherent atheist is that of a Deist. Many Catholics today live effectively immersed in Deism, which is very similar to relativism.

The hub from which Deism disseminated was Protestant, Hanoverian England. In London, in 1717, the Grand Lodge of England was founded, to which all modern Freemasonry can be traced.

The origins of Freemasonry are even older, dating to the secret societies of the sixteenth century within the humanist academies and some Protestant sects like the Anabaptists and Socinians. Having migrated from the Italian Socinians to Poland, and from there to Holland and England, Socinianism transformed into Deism, and was then professed as a philosophy by Freemasons.

Deistic Freemasonry reduced God to a generic "Supreme Being" or a "Great Architect of the Universe," depriving religion of its metaphysical basis, reducing it to "natural morality." The idea of "tolerance" is typically Deistic and

Masonic, taken up by the Enlightenment philosophers which they opposed to Catholic "fanaticism."

Fr. Paolo Siano, who dedicated important essays to Freemasonry, affirms three objective and tightly interwoven elements that constitute the "essence" of Freemasonry:

1) a nondogmatic humanism that presumes to overcome all religious and ethical dogmas, but in reality is subjective and relativistic;

2) a rituality that presumes sacred efficacy, placing Freemasons in contact with some "sacred" presence;

3) a Gnostic esotericism that finds in the "esoteric" sciences (alchemy, cabala, hermetism, etc.) the key, the way, the means for the interior search for their divine "Self" or "Ego."

From their foundation, Freemasons have used solemn oaths, promises, and obligations before the Grand Architect of the Universe. It has been documented that in the 1700s, these rituals and oaths obliged Freemasons to secrecy under the threat of death for perjury or betrayal. These Masonic oaths constitute one of the reasons why, in 1738, Pope Clement XII (r. 1730–1740) promulgated the first condemnation against Freemasonry, to be followed by many others.

Freemasonry still exists today and is not simply a club of humanists seeking dialogue, but rather a secretive, esoteric association with degrees of membership and rituals, not always known by the public. In the name of freedom of thought and research, the Freemasons place in doubt Christian dogmas, and yet will not suffer the unwashed to investigate their own initiation structures (rites, rituals, hierarchies, esotericism). Indeed, Freemasons try to reveal their esoteric side as little as possible.

## 3. THE MORAL CRISIS OF THE EIGHTEENTH CENTURY

Besides the intellectual crisis, a profound moral crisis was spreading throughout France, which came to a head during the regency of Duke Phillip of Orléans (r. 1717–1723), the nephew of Louis XIV, and intensified in the second half of the reign of Louis XV (1715–1774). The revolutionary spirit penetrated the court through sensuality, especially following the influence of Madame de Pompadour, protector of the *philosophes*, members of the Enlightenment "Republic of Letters." Worldliness and pagan customs had transformed the medieval noble into a frivolous parlor aristocrat. On the eve of the Revolution, the vast majority of the

French, including the sovereign, were not aware of the abyss in which the nation found itself.

Msgr. Leone Cristiani, in his *Brief History of Heresies*, described the "law of diffusion" of antireligious ideas. It was valid in the eighteenth century, just as it is today. This law is the same as the law of entropy in physics. The diffusion occurs by degree, through which the purity of an idea never stops "degrading."

In the first degree, doctrine remains confined to the higher philosophical spheres, as a discussion of pure ideas.

In the second degree, these ideas drop as oracles into less robust minds, less original, though more daring and cleverer, who hasten to vulgarize them with authoritative statements and simplifications; they then gain a hold over public opinion. A personality like Voltaire, in the eighteenth century, performed this function. Around these vulgarizers, a whole host of disciples, admirers, and fanatical partisans gathers: satirists, journalists, novelists, professors, and politicians. Their doctrines become fashionable and shape public opinion.

Finally, in the third degree, the antireligious theories reach the populace and take on the appearance of primitive, visceral passions. The discussion of ideas mutates into discussions of interests, opposition to people, conflict between groups and parties. Ferocious hate for the enemy is the final stage of this process of the degradation of ideas.

## 4. VOLTAIRE AND THE ENLIGHTENMENT PHILOSOPHERS

Freemasonry was the operative instrument of the Enlightenment, which was not only an intellectual current but a philosophical sect that took hold in Europe in the second half of the eighteenth century. It was founded on the naïve faith according to which the light of reason, recognized as the sole font of truth, would have dissipated forever the darkness of medieval obscurantism, to establish an age of progress and happiness for all humanity.

The essence of the Enlightenment was the extension to all fields, and especially to politics, of the fight against the principle of authority that Protestantism had also waged war upon: the Church.

François-Marie Arouet de Voltaire (1694–1778) was the high priest of the Enlightenment. Returning to Paris after a long journey in England, he began in 1730 his work as a journalist and counselor to the courts and French aristocracy, becoming the main paladin of "free thought" and a diehard enemy of the Church. He presumed to be a poet, a historian, a writer of tragedies, but in all endeavors, he was as superficial as he was sarcastic. Sought out, adulated, lavished with favors by the main sovereigns of Europe, he exercised a downright intellectual dictatorship in the second half of the eighteenth century with his sacrilegious spirit, hostile to all religion and to every absolute principle.

The most formidable anti-Christian war machine was the *Encyclopédie*, a great inventory of the culture of the time, published from 1751 to 1772 in seventeen volumes. Its publication was directed by the philosophers Denis Diderot (1713–1784) and Jean-Baptiste d'Alembert (1717–1783), though all the Enlightenment philosophers of the period collaborated on it: Voltaire, Montesquieu, Condillac, Helvetius, d'Holbach. The *Encyclopédie* was the bible of the new Enlightenment religion.

The guiding word of the Enlightenment is found in the letters of Voltaire to his friends: *"écrasez l'infâme,"* or "crush the infamy." The *infâme* was the Catholic Church.

Those with the patience to plow through his dense correspondence, thousands of letters written to Frederick II, to d'Alembert, and to the other Enlightenment philosophers, run into expressions such as, "If it were possible that five or six worthy men who were in agreement are not able, following the example we have of twelve poor brutes [the apostles], to succeed? It seems to me that success in this matter would honor you immensely," from a letter to d'Alembert on July 24, 1760. From his youth, Voltaire had dedicated his life to "crushing the infamy." This expression returns innumerable times in his letters. "Crush the infamy!" he wrote d'Alembert on June 23, 1760: "How I wish you would crush the infamy. It is the greatest service one can render to the human race."

"In twenty years, you shall see the plan come about," he wrote on February 25, 1758, to d'Alembert. Exactly twenty years later, on February 25, 1778, Voltaire began vomiting blood, which sounded the alarm of his imminent end. He died two months later. There are many famous reports about his death, including one by a famous physician, Tronchin: "Not even the fury of Orestes would be able in the least to give an idea of the enraged and desperate wrath of Voltaire, who reached the point of eating his own excrement at the moment of death."

The entire life of this man, who is portrayed as the champion of ideological tolerance, was conducted in the name of a ferocious hatred. If someone, through his manner of being, his attitude toward others, had ever given proof of a radical, absolute intolerance, it was Voltaire.

The idea of tolerance elaborated by John Locke (1632–1704) in his famous *Letter Concerning Toleration* (1689) and then by Voltaire in his equally famous *Treatise on Tolerance* (1763) is not tolerance understood as a practical, prudential attitude that nevertheless presupposes the truth, but rather a "tolerantism," understood as an ideological dogma, as an absolute value, which thus coincides with absolute indifferentism, the idea that everything must be tolerated because in some way everything is true (and in this sense, one can speak of absolute relativism) or because, to the contrary, everything is false (in this case we find ourselves in the face of absolute skepticism, and absolute incredulity). Everything must be tolerated except that which is opposed to the principle of absolute tolerance.

Voltaire embraced every category, but, like Jean-Jacques Rousseau (1712–1778), he excludes from tolerance those who negate this dogma. Who are those who negate the dogma of tolerance? All who believe in truth, whatever it might be. But among all those who believe in truth, who are the believers par excellence? Naturally, they are Catholics. Rousseau reaches the point, coherent with this thought, of demanding the expulsion of Catholics from the state. According to Rousseau, all opinions and forms of worship can be tolerated, except "intolerance." Because, as he states, "there can no longer be an exclusive national religion, they must tolerate all those who in turn tolerate the other religions.... But whoever dares to say, 'There is no salvation outside the Church' must be expelled from the state." "To merit tolerance, men must start by not being fanatics," Voltaire pontificated in his *Treatise on Tolerance*.

This led to persecution against Catholics: an ideological, intellectual persecution in the age of Deism and of the Enlightenment, but a persecution destined to become physical and bloody in the French Revolution, with the onset of the Terror. If tolerance is an absolute good, there is only one absolute evil, and one absolute error, which is the negation of tolerance: the affirmation of truth. Hence the necessity of the crusade against what today would be termed *fundamentalism*. Fundamentalism in the 1700s, for fanatics of tolerance, was naturally Catholicsm. Tolerance was, according to Condorcet, the "battle cry" of the Enlightenment philosophers.

## 5. JANSENISM AND GALLICANISM IN THE SEVENTEENTH CENTURY

The Enlightenment had unleashed its war machine against Catholicism, but it also had accomplices within the Church. One of these was Jansenism, which after its birth, and despite condemnations, continued its devious work throughout the seventeenth century.

Pope Clement XI (r. 1700–1721) solemnly renewed the condemnation of Jansenism with the bull *Unigenitus,* promulgated in 1713. Among the condemned propositions was the semi-Calvinist attribution of salvation by grace alone, without the contribution of human free will, corrupted by Original Sin. *Unigenitus* unleashed a terrible tempest and was accompanied by publications and controversy. The bull was accepted by all the French bishops except four, who appealed for a general council and were for this reason labeled the Appellants. The archbishop of Paris and the Gallican universities of Paris and Nantes, along with some bishops and many religious, came to the support of the Appellant faction. The pope excommunicated them in 1718, but they renewed their appeal with the support of the Parliament of Paris.

A schismatic Jansenist church was formed in Utrecht, Holland, where it still exists today. Jansenism found followers in Italy as well; the most famous was Scipione de' Ricci (1741–1810), who held in 1786 a synod in Pistoia, his episcopal see. The decisions of this synod were condemned in 1794 in the bull *Auctorum Fidei* by Pius VI (r. 1775–1799).

The historian Émile Appolis (1903–1980), in his work *Entre jansénistes et zelanti. Le "Tiers Parti" catholique au XVIIIe siècle,* defined as a "third party" the Catholics who occupied an intermediate place between the Acceptants, who accepted the bull *Unigenitus* of Clement XI, and the Appellants, who refused to accept it as it was and appealed against it. The members of the "third party" defined themselves as intransigent, mitigated or tolerant, and sought an intermediate path between the zealots or intransigents and the Appellant Jansenists.

Pope Benedict XIV (r. 1740–1758), born Prospero Lambertini, was an affable, simple, jovial character, who inclined to judge men and their actions benevolently, without abandoning the truth. He was the pope of the "third party." According to Appolis, Pope Lambertini was the "perfect incarnation of the third party," because he preferred leading an ordinary life, prudent, without excesses, as far from severe people as from extremely tolerant people.

The question of Gallicanism began to graft itself onto that of Jansenism, the former being the tendency of the Church in France to render itself independent of Rome and to form its own national church, denying the pope any right to intervene in temporal questions. Gallicanism dated back to Phillip the Fair and was resurrected under Louis XIV, against whom Blessed Innocent XI rose up,

vindicating the rights and freedoms of the Church. Political Gallicanism restricted the authority of the Church in favor of the state, while theological
Gallicanism limited the authority of the pope in favor of councils, bishops, and
clergy. Thus, it merged into conciliarism, the heresy that affirmed the primacy
of the council over the pope. From political Gallicanism arose jurisdictionalism
and theological Gallicanism.

In Spain, Gallicanism was called *regalism*; in Italy, *jurisdictionalism*; in Austria, *Josephinism*. The thesis was that of limiting the action of the Church to the
sphere of the consciences of the faithful on the grounds that the public sphere
belongs to the state. Jurisdictionalism seeks to limit the action of the Church to
the sphere of the conscience. The Church would have no authority in society,
only over the consciences of the faithful, and in a limited way in the fields of
Faith and dogma. In Germany, jurisdictionalism was theorized by Febronius,
the pseudonym of a German bishop who became a great disseminator of these
ideas. In German-speaking territories, the Holy Roman Emperor Joseph II
(1741–1790) applied this theory, and for this reason it also came to be known
as Josephinism. The ecclesiastical politics of Joseph II gave him vast control over
the Church. The sovereign nominated bishops and abbots, intervened in the life
of religious orders, and portrayed himself as a reformer of ecclesiastical discipline. In Italy, Ludovico Antonio Muratori (1672–1750) was its theorizer. He
did not reject the Church but wanted to limit its scope to the consciences of the
faithful, excluding all external manifestations of the Church.

With so-called enlightened despotism, natural, absolute, and universal law
does not exist, but rather the state claims the right to decide what is good and
what is evil. Today, on the other hand, the state has retreated and allows everything to be permissible except for the profession of the truth and the practice of
the good. This is the dictatorship of relativism. Its roots date back to the Enlightenment, to the Gallicanism of the eighteenth century.

## 6. FROM THE SUPPRESSION OF THE SOCIETY OF JESUS TO THE FRENCH REVOLUTION

The main enemy in the eighteenth century of the anti-Christian revolution that
threatened the Church and Christian civilization was the Jesuits. The Society of
Jesus had been founded by St. Ignatius of Loyola in 1540. The history of its first
two centuries is marked by prodigious expansion, but also by strong opposition
within and outside of the Catholic world.

This derives from the military character of the Jesuits, born to block the growth of Protestantism. Its polemical and controversial work was accompanied by a great flourishing of sanctity, expressed in figures like Peter Canisius, Louis Gonzaga, Robert Bellarmine, and Peter Claver. The Society of Jesus distinguished itself, furthermore, for its missionary thrust, offering in the figure of St. Francis Xavier the model of the Catholic missionary. The grace of martyrdom was also widely granted to the Jesuits: in Japan, the three holy crucified martyrs of Nagasaki and the many blesseds; in India, Blessed Rudolfo Acquaviva and companions; in England, St. Edmund Campion and Robert Southwell; in Canada, St. John de Brébeuf and companions.

The Jesuits vigorously defended the primacy of the Roman pontiff and were the bulwark against which the attacks of external and internal enemies of the Church crashed. They were hated for their claim to power, but above all for ideological reasons, insofar as they were the most intransigent defenders of the pope and the most determined adversaries of all heretical currents in the seventeenth and eighteenth centuries. Around the mid-1700s, the Jesuits had reached the height of their power, with 22,500 religious in thirty-nine provinces and 1,563 foundations. The Jesuits were the confessors and counselors of sovereigns; they educated youth in their universities and colleges; their work was visible throughout all society. This was the power of which they had to be stripped.

The adversaries of the Jesuits were above all the Enlightenment philosophers, who had engaged them in mortal combat, allied with the heterodox currents that were catching on in the Church, beginning with Jansenism and Gallicanism. The so-called enlightened despots were reigning in Europe, absolute sovereigns who had drunk deeply at the well of Enlightenment ideas. The enemies of the Jesuits convinced them that they represented an obstacle to their royal absolutism.

Some of these sovereigns decided to expel the Jesuits from their kingdoms, accusing them of perverting the social order. The first attack against them was launched in 1759 by the Marquis Sebastiao of Pombal (1699–1782), minister of Joseph I (1714–1777), king of Portugal. After a series of defamatory libels, the Jesuits were accused of involvement in a plot against the king and were expelled from Portugal, Brazil, and India. The height of the persecution was reached in 1761, when the old Fr. Gabriele Malagrida (1689–1761) was burned at the stake in public in Lisbon.

After Portugal's provision for their expulsion, analogous decrees followed on the part of other powers. In France, after the unfortunate bankruptcy of Fr. Antonio Lavalette, superior of the island of Martinique, the Parliament condemned the constitutions and doctrines of the Jesuits and closed their colleges, forcing Louis XV to disband the order. The Jesuits were chased out of Spain in 1767 by King Carlo III (1716–1788), following the counsel of his minister Pedro de Aranda (1719–1798), a friend of Voltaire. In November of the same year, King Ferdinand IV, urged by his minister Bernardo Tanucci (1698–1783), expelled the Jesuits from Naples and Sicily. The duke of Parma, Ferdinand, banished the Jesuits from his lands in February 1768.

This was not enough, however. It was necessary to transform the Society of Jesus from within. But because the general of the Society opposed this, the only option left was to suppress the order, and only the pope could do this.

The occasion presented itself with the death of Clement XIII (1693–1769) on February 2, 1769. The historian Ludwig von Pastor, in the sixteenth volume of his *History of the Popes*, describes with a wealth of documentation the maneuvers carried out before, during, and after the conclave, which, after three months and 179 ballots, witnessed the election of the Franciscan Lorenzo Ganganelli on May 14, who took the name Clement XIV (r. 1769–1774).

Lorenzo Ganganelli, "having reached the cardinalate, like many others, was consumed by the ambition of assuming the tiara." His political line was that of the "third party," an apparent neutrality between the major currents. He belonged to that obsequious class of men who want above all to please others, and thus are obliged to dissemble their own thought and to act with a certain hypocrisy. The new pope was elected on the condition that he abolish the Society of Jesus. Although he had signed no formal promise that would have implicated him in simony, Cardinal Ganganelli took up this task with the ambassadors of the Bourbon court. The Holy Spirit did not fail in assisting the conclave, but the correspondence to Divine Grace on the part of the cardinals was certainly not adequate if their choice was fixed on a prelate whom Pastor calls "a weak and ambitious character who aspired to the tiara."

On July 22, 1769, the new pope received a memo from the ambassadors of the three Bourbon courts of France, Spain, and the two Sicilys, in which the suppression of the Jesuits was insisted upon with force.

On July 21, 1773, with *Dominus ac Redemptor*, Clement XIV suppressed the Society of Jesus. In this document, the pope claimed the right to abolish religious orders and stated his conviction that "it is entirely or almost impossible that, as long as this order exists, the Church can enjoy a true and solid peace." "This brief of July 21, 1773," writes Pastor, "represents the most evident victory of the Enlightenment and royal absolutism over the Church and the pope."

Fr. Lorenzo Ricci, the general of the Society of Jesus, was imprisoned in Castel Sant'Angelo, where he died on November 24, 1775. Pope Clement XIV preceded him to the tomb on September 22, 1774, a year after the dissolution of the order.

A great saint lived through this period, Alphonsus de Liguori, born in Naples in 1696, and bishop of Sant'Agata dei Goti, near Benevento, from 1762 to 1775. The founder of the Redemptorists, his long life came to an end on August 1, 1787. He was proclaimed Doctor of the Church and is considered the patron and most eminent exemplar of Catholic moral theologians.

St. Alphonsus said that the suppression of the Society of Jesus was the fruit of the plotting of the Jansenists and other unbelievers. His biographer Tannoja reports these words:

> If these men bring about the destruction of the Society, they have no more to demand. Having overturned this fortification, in what upheaval with the Church could the state not then be found? Having ruined the Jesuits, in what greater distress could the pope and the Church find themselves?

One day, September 21, 1774, after the celebration of Mass, Alphonsus was seen crestfallen and taciturn. He remained in this state, in silence, for a day and a night, without eating and without taking his rest. When he stirred from this torpor, his companions asked him what had happened to him during those two days in which he had not given any signs of life. He replied, "You say well, but little do you know that I was assisting the pope, who has just died." No one yet knew that on September 22, at one in the afternoon, Clement XIV had passed into the next life. He had received the grace of having St. Alphonsus at his side.

## 7. The Testament of Fr. Lorenzo Ricci

We do well to read the testament of Fr. Lorenzo Ricci:

> The uncertainty of the times in which God might will to call me to himself, and the certainty that that time is near, given my advanced

years and the multitude, long duration, and gravity of the afflictions far beyond my weakness, have warned me to fulfill in a preventive manner my duties, given that the quality of my recent illness might easily prevent me from carrying them out at the point of death.

Thus, considering myself to be on the verge of facing the tribunal of infallible truth and justice, which is the sole divine tribunal, after long and mature consideration and after having prayed humbly to my merciful Redeemer and terrible Judge not to allow that I be carried away by passion especially in one of the last actions of my life, not for any bitterness in my soul, nor for any other emotion or vicious end, but only because I judge that it is my duty to render justice to the truth and to innocence, I make the following two declarations and protests:

1.  I declare and protest that the extinct Society of Jesus has given no reason for its suppression. I declare and protest with the certainty that a superior well-informed of his religion can morally have.

2.  I declare and protest that I have given no reason whatsoever, even the slightest, for being incarcerated. I declare and protest with the highest certainty and evidence, which each one has for his own actions. I make this second protest only because it is necessary for the reputation of the extinct Society of Jesus, of which I was the general accountable.

I do not intend, moreover, that by the force of these protests any of those who have caused harm to the Society of Jesus and to me might judge themselves guilty before God, given that I abstain from such judgment. The thoughts of the mind and the affections of the human heart are known to God alone. He alone sees the errors of the human intellect and discerns if they are able to excuse fault; He alone penetrates the ends that move and work, the spirit with which one acts, the emotions and movements of the heart with which the action is accompanied: and because innocence or guilt depends on the external action, for this reason I leave all judgment to Him who . *interrogabit opera vestra et cogitationes scrutabitur* [shall examine your works and scrutinize your designs] (Wis. 6:4).

And to satisfy Christian duty, I proclaim that I have always, with the divine assistance, forgiven and forgiven sincerely all who have afflicted and harmed me, first by means of the rise of the events against the Society of

Jesus, then with the extinction of the same and the circumstances that accompanied its extinction, and finally with my imprisonment and the harshness added to it, and with the prejudice attached to the reputation — facts that are public and noted throughout the world.

I pray the Lord forgive me first of all of my many sins through His pity and mercy and by the merits of Jesus Christ; and then to forgive the authors and collaborators of the above-mentioned evils and harms: and I intend to die with this sentiment and prayer in my heart.

Finally, I pray and implore whoever shall see these declarations and protests to render them public to the entire world as far as possible; I pray and implore all the titles of humanity, of justice, of Christian charity, that can persuade the fulfillment of this my desire and will.

The Society of Jesus was dispersed, although it did survive in Russia, where Tsarina Catherine II (1729–1796) refused to give the *exequatur* to the brief of suppression. The Jesuits in Russia were accused of disobedience and rebellion against the pope, but ensured the historical continuity of the order, while in other nations ex-Jesuits promoted, in the Ignatian spirit, new religious congregations.

In 1789 the French Revolution broke out, and a dramatic era began for the Church, which witnessed the invasion of the city of Rome and the deportation of Clement XIV's two successors: Pius VI and Pius VII.

Finally, after forty years, Pius VII (r. 1800–1823) revoked the suppression of 1773 on August 7, 1814. This ordered the complete reconstitution of the Society of Jesus throughout the world, "seeming to him a serious fault before God if, in such a calamitous time, he would have withheld from the ship of the Church those valid and expert mariners."

The suppression of the Jesuits was an unjust action, committed by a pope who deceived himself by this gesture of placating European sovereigns. But he sacrificed on the altar of compromise the best defenders of the papacy, the only ones who could have avoided the Revolution. And the French Revolution arrived, overthrowing thrones and altar.

CHAPTER IX

# The French Revolution

## 1. THE ORIGINS OF THE FRENCH REVOLUTION

The age in which we live is the offspring of an event that profoundly defined the history of Europe and the world: the French Revolution. The profound religious, political, and moral crisis we are living through is situated in a process that has its preceding phases in the Revolution of 1789 and, even before that, in humanism and Protestantism. Plinio Corrêa de Oliveira has outlined the itinerary of this centuries-long history that reaches our own time. In his classic work *Revolution and Counter-Revolution*, he writes:

> The political work of the French Revolution was nothing short of a transposition, in the framework of the state, of the Reformation that the most radical Protestant sects had adopted in matters of ecclesiastical organization:
>
> 1. Rebellion against the king, symmetrical to rebellion against the pope;
>
> 2. Rebellion of the peasants against the nobles, symmetrical to the rebellion of the ecclesiastical "peasants," the faithful, against the Church aristocracy, namely the clergy;

3.  The affirmation of popular sovereignty, symmetrical to the gover-
    nance of certain sects, exercised to a greater or lesser degree by
    the faithful.

To understand the crisis of our time, it is necessary therefore to understand the
French Revolution, its origins, its nature, and its consequences.

Every historical event has a concrete factual beginning in time and space. As
regards the French Revolution, everything began, on the factual level, on May 4,
1789, when the king of France, Louis XVI (1754–1793), summoned to Versailles the Estates General of the kingdom, composed of three orders: clergy,
nobility, and the Third Estate. The financial crisis, which was a crisis of the
state's coffers and not an economic crisis in the country, was the spark that set
off the Revolution. Everything precipitated in the space of a few months. But
everything had had an extended period of incubation.

In the manuals of history, one still reads that the French Revolution was the
fruit of oppression and misery. In reality, as the historian Pierre Gaxotte writes,
"Misery can cause uprisings, but cannot sustain revolutions, which have deeper
causes; and anyway, in 1789, the French were not living in misery." On the eve
of the Revolution, France was in fact the richest and most populous country in
Europe. Around 1770, a serious financial crisis struck the French state, though
without damaging the prosperity of the country, such that Gaxotte titled the
second chapter of his celebrated work *La Révolution française* (1928) "The Poor
State in the Rich Country."

The financial crisis on the books of the Crown presented a deficit that was
not insurmountable: an income of 503 million francs against expenditures of
629 million, in other words a difference of a mere 126 million. One has always
read about the unbridled luxury in the court at Versailles. In reality, the expenses
of the court represented only 6 percent of the budget (about 27 million francs)
and included various entries, among which was a considerable part for the pen-
sions of many veterans.

The greater responsibility for the financial crisis lies with the men who directed the French economy in that period, plunging them into debt: the
ministers Robert-Jacques Turgot (1727–1791) and Jacques Necker (1732–
1804). In 1788, for example, half of expenditures went for interest paid on loans.

Before manifesting themselves in the realm of events, revolutions occur on
the level of ideas, and ideas in turn, as Plinio Corrêa de Oliveira explains, have

their origin in a complex matrix of disordered tendencies that constitute the profound soul and impetus of the revolutionary process.

The origin of the French Revolution lies in the revolution of ideas promoted by the faction of Enlightenment philosophers in the second half of the eighteenth century.

Voltaire spoke often of a *"révolution des esprits,"* a revolution of minds, the seeds of which the *philosophes* had been sowing. In 1769, he wrote, "It has been underway already for fifteen years; and in another fifteen, after such a beautiful morning, the full light of day will be here." Centuries of ignorance and obscurantism were, in his mind, destined to be illuminated by the torch of reason, held high by the "philosophical party," the dawn of a new age for humanity under the sign of progress and reason.

Voltaire did not live to see this "full light of day," the radiant sunlight of the "revolution in facts" prepared by the "revolution of ideas" that he had begun. He died, wracked by convulsions, after a terrible agony, tormented by a fire within that was burning his viscera. His merits as the father and initiator of the French Revolution were recognized, nonetheless, by his children. In May 1791, the deputy Michel Regnault requested for Voltaire the honors of the Pantheon, stating that "the Revolution of Voltaire prepared our revolution." The request was immediately converted into a decree by the Assembly. Voltaire's relics, collected in an opulent sarcophagus, were transferred to the Pantheon, the secular temple of the Republic, following a triumphal procession on July 11, 1791. Msgr. Jean-Joseph Gaume (1802–1879), describing the solemn ceremonies of that day, states that never had Paris given such triumphal honors to any saint.

Voltaire died without seeing the Revolution he had prepared: in compensation, his disciple and panegyrist Marquis Nicolas de Condorcet (1743–1794) did live to see it. He was the last of the encyclopedists, those to whom we owe the conclusive formulation of the philosophy of Enlightenment history. In his *Esquisse d'un tableau historique des progrès de l'esprit humain* (1793), Condorcet describes the stages in which the perfection of humanity had occurred in history; in other words, the uninterrupted "forward march" of individuals and peoples "toward truth and happiness."

According to this scheme, which became the reference for all the heirs of the Enlightenment and progressive culture, 1789 was an epochal date: it constitutes man's liberation from misery, ignorance, and oppression.

This date opened for France and for humanity an era of progress, peace, well-being, and happiness. The Revolution of 1789 marks the entrance into the tenth epoch of this triumphal evolution of humanity, the last and definitive one. Not even Condorcet, however, would live to see the proclaimed historical hour of truth and happiness on earth. Imprisoned by his companions of the revolutionary party, he committed suicide in 1794.

The connection between the French Revolution and the ideas of the Enlightenment was well established by Pope Benedict XV in *Anna Jam Exuente* on March 7, 1917:

> After the first three centuries of the beginning of the Church, during which the blood of Christians nourished the entire earth, one can say that the Church had not faced such danger as that which manifested itself at the end of the eighteenth century. At that time, in fact, a philosophy in delirium, the extension of heresy and apostasy of innovators, acquired over spirits a universal power of sedition and provoked such a complete upheaval with the specific purpose of ruining the Christian foundations of society, not only in France, but gradually in all nations. The authority of the Church thus rejected, having ceased to hold religion as guardian and safeguard of law and duty and order in society, they taught that power has its origin in the people and not from God; that all men are equal by nature as by right; that it is licit for each man to do as he pleases, if it is not expressly prohibited by law; that nothing enjoys the force of law if it is not commanded by the multitude; and, worst of all, that one can think and publish in matters of religion whatever one wants, under the pretext that it harms no one.

This relativistic and egalitarian vision of the world was elaborated in the Masonic lodges and carried forward by the "thought societies" that arose before and during the French Revolution.

## 2. THE REVOLUTION OF A MINORITY

There is another myth that must be dispelled: that which says that the French Revolution was a popular revolt against the monarchy.

The Revolution was not the work of the "people," but rather a minority in the revolutionary clubs, which represented the political projection of the Masonic lodges. In 1782, the Masonic Convention of Wilhelmsbad took place in Bavaria. During its secret meetings, the sect of the Bavarian Illuminati, led by

Adam Weishaupt (1748–1830) and by Baron Adolph Knigge (1752–1796), programmed the involvement of various national Masonic lodges in a plan of universal overthrow of monarchies and the establishment of communism and atheism.

To carry out their plan, they promoted the formation of clubs, political groups similar to modern political parties. These clubs had a character that united the extreme revolutionaries.

The structure of the clubs was not democratic, but pyramidal. Admittance required being "coopted," admitted from on high, by the committee of directors, upon the petition of at least two members. Furthermore, the members were subjected to continual "epurations." The meetings were held four times a week, in the evenings from six to ten o'clock; the most important deliberations occurred for the most part quite late into the night, when most of the exhausted members had already left for home.

The historian Augustin Cochin demonstrated the role of these "thought societies" in the preparation of the Revolution: they formed a network dependent on the "mother society," the Jacobin Club. There was no place in France of any importance at the eve of the Revolution that did not have its circle of free thinkers, its patriotic society, its lodge and literary chamber.

What came to be called the "people" was in reality the "popular societies," and the revolutionary government was to be the dictatorship of the societies that instituted the kingdom of the deified populace, establishing the cult of the general will.

With the French Revolution a new morality was born, in which, as has been written, the problem is no longer whether an action is good or bad, but whether it is revolutionary or not, whether it conforms or not to the will of the deified populace.

As in every revolution, the decisive moment occurs in the first days, when it goes afoul of the law. From the opening of the Estates General on May 4, 1789, to the fateful day at the Bastille on July 14 of that same year, two and a half months had passed: time that allowed for leveraging between the king and the Third Estate over the problem of voting. Custom and the logic of the system allowed for the vote to proceed by order of the estates.

In this case, each of the three orders, the clergy, the nobility, and the Third Estate, had the right to one vote. The Third Estate demanded, nevertheless, a meeting of the orders and a head count. In this case, the Third Estate, which had the biggest number of representatives, would have had a majority over the other two orders of a united assembly. The clergy and nobility opposed this, but on June 12, by a unilateral action, the Third Estate met on its own, and on the June 17, its deputies approved a motion according to which "it lies with the Assembly and only the Assembly to interpret and present the general will of the nation." On this day, the Third Estate not only designated itself the National Assembly, but made an act of constitutive power declaring illegal the taxes and duties levied by the state.

This deliberation was the first revolutionary act, which would be sealed three days later on June 20, by the so-called Tennis Court Oath, from the name of the hall where the deputies of the Third Estate were gathered and swore not to adjourn before having given the nation a constitution. The oath of June 20 contains the ideas of Sieyès and Rousseau, according to whom legitimacy derives from the general will of the nation.

Abbot Emmanuel-Joseph Sieyès (1748–1836) was the point of contact between the theories of Rousseau and Jacobin policy, which found its fulfillment in the Terror. His pamphlet *What Is the Third Estate?* appeared in the first days of 1789 and became a foundational document due to the influence it exerted on successive events. According to Sieyès, the sovereignty of France resides infallibly in the nation, which is identified with the Third Estate. "The nation preexists everything, it is the origin of everything. Its will is always in conformity with the law, it is the law itself." Insofar as it is sovereign, the nation is not subject to any law. The will of the nation is absolute and infallible, and constitutes the supreme source of all law.

"From this moment," observed Karl Ludwig von Haller, "the revolution was accomplished, the kingdom of France had changed into a republic."

In the popular imagination, the French Revolution received its birth certificate with its most symbolic episode on July 14, 1789, the day of the storming of the Bastille. The morning of July 14, a crowd of no more than one thousand agitators, for the most part bribed, stormed the Hotel des Invalides and then the Bastille, identified as the symbol of monarchical absolutism. The legend of the Bastille, the dark prison where political prisoners of the ancien régime languished in chains, has been thoroughly debunked. Today we know that, altogether, only seven prisoners were found inside, none of them political prisoners. There were four forgers, two madmen, and one pervert.

Louis XVI could have crushed the revolt, but did not, deluded in thinking he could stop the Revolution without spilling blood. It would be the Revolution that spilled his.

On August 4, the National Assembly abolished the feudal regime that had for centuries constituted the social framework. This too was a historical event. With one stroke, the historical identity of France was erased. On August 26, it approved the Declaration of the Rights of Man and the Citizen, the Magna Carta of the French Revolution and of contemporary pseudo-rights.

## 3. THE ANTI-CHRISTIAN NATURE OF THE REVOLUTION

There have been Christians who would like to "baptize" the French Revolution. But the French Revolution was an anti-Christian revolution, although all anti-Christian revolutions throughout history have needed the betrayal of a part of the Christian community in order to succeed. Then there is a second betrayal, through the omission of their duties. This is the betrayal of those who keep silent for love of their own peace and security. It is the attitude of moderates who hate the defenders of the Faith more than their enemies. It is those who are afraid of the proclamation of truth and prefer the way of negotiation and compromise with error.

The clergy in France numbered about 130,000 men, but they lived tepid lives. They thought about their ecclesiastical careers and leisure. If scandal was rare, observed Gaxotte, so too was zeal:

> Days without conflict, study without faith, religion without an interior flame: this was the life of many clerics. They assisted the poor, but without seeking them. The most active occupied themselves with the complicated management of the foundations of the order; the most erudite wrote memoirs for the academy; the most ambitious advanced in their local assemblies. Among their many earthly concerns, there remained nothing for God.

It was a cleric, the bishop of Autun, Maurice de Talleyrand (1754–1838), who proposed in October 1789 the nationalization (confiscation, in other words) of the goods of the clergy, which was voted upon on November 2. Churches, abbeys, convents, monasteries, parishes, and religious houses assisting the poor, the sick, and orphans, and which tended to the primary and secondary education of society — all were expropriated. These good works arose over the course of centuries thanks to the donations of benefactors as well. The expropriation of these possessions, based on the principle that sees the nation as the owner of these ecclesiastical goods, was a colossal theft.

On February 13, 1790, the National Assembly decreed the prohibition of monastic vows and the suppression of religious orders. On February 23, it was decided that parish priests must read the revolutionary decrees at the start of their homily. The proposal of some members of the clergy to recognize the Catholic religion as the only state religion was rejected. The French Revolution proclaimed the principle of religious freedom and freedom of conscience, placing all religions on the same level, but soon it began to persecute Christianity.

The first stage was emancipation from the Church of Rome. On July 12, 1790, the Civil Constitution of the Clergy was approved, giving new rules for religious life in France. The Constitutional Assembly decided that there should be 1 bishop per department, 83 in all (while before there had been 117) and 10 "metropolitan bishops" (in place of 18 archbishops), since the number of parishes would have to be reduced. Bishops and parish priests were no longer nominated by the pope or ecclesiastical assemblies, but rather by that same electoral body that nominated representatives and administrators: parish priests would be elected by the electors of the district, bishops by those of the department.

All religious were to be paid by the state, thus becoming public functionaries who, like all other civil servants, had to vow fidelity "to the nation, to the law, and to the king." The refusal to do so entailed removal from the appointment and their dismissal. Priests and bishops who refused to swear fidelity to the new Civil Constitution of the Clergy were termed "refractory," banished from the kingdom, imprisoned, and persecuted. From 1793, anyone who hid a priest was considered an accomplice of this crime and thus subject to capital punishment. It was sufficient to have participated in the Mass of a "refractory" priest to be condemned to death.

Once the old Church was knocked down, a new one had to be built. They needed to find a bishop willing to validly consecrate other bishops. The only one who accepted the task was Talleyrand. The two bishops he consecrated went on to consecrate three others, who then consecrated others, until by the end of April, some sixty new bishops had been installed, obedient to the new regime. In his letter of April 13, 1791, Pius VI denounced the constitutional consecrations as criminal and sacrilegious; the consecrators and consecrated were forbidden to celebrate Mass, and priests who had not retracted within forty days were suspended.

## 4. THE REIGN OF TERROR

From November 1789 to September 1792, the first religious persecution was rolled out, culminating in the massacres of September 1792.

One of the scourges of contemporary society is terrorism, which is, on the individual level, what genocide is on the collective level. Yet the practice of terrorism, like that of genocide, dates back to the French Revolution.

Historians usually circumscribe the period of Terror from June or July 1793 to July 28, 1794, the date of Robespierre's death. This was the period when the Jacobin Convention ruled, after the elimination of the Girondins; at this time the Terror was placed at the top of the agenda and propagated by Saint-Just and Robespierre. The Terror did not in fact begin in 1793 or finish in July 1794, but was intrinsic to the French Revolution in all of its phases. The Terror was born with the Revolution and accompanied it until its conclusion, and was directed above all against Christianity.

On April 20, 1792, revolutionary France declared war on Austria and Prussia. As the Prussians were besieging Verdun, the commune of Paris had about six hundred "suspects" arrested, adding to the two thousand already locked within Parisian prisons. The news of the fall of Verdun set off a massacre that led to more than thirteen hundred victims. The American historian Robert Darnton reconstructs the occurrence in the following way:

> In the prison of Abbaye, an impromptu popular tribunal was created. One by one the prisoners were brought out, accused, and summarily condemned based on their behavior. A spirit of fortitude was considered proof of innocence, stuttering a demonstration of guilt. Stanislas Maillard, one of those who had taken part in the storming of the Bastille, assumed the role of public attorney; and the mob, taken from the streets and made to sit on a row of benches, ratified his verdicts with signs of approval and acclamation. If declared innocent, the prisoner was embraced amid tears and taken in triumph through the city streets. If found guilty, he was cut to pieces by a forest of pikes, clubs, and blades. Then his body was stripped and thrown on a pile of cadavers, or quartered and paraded at the top of a pike.

Thus far, we have spoken of the Terror in blood, the murderous Terror, that strikes our sensibilities and imagination. There was, however, another Terror, not bloody, but no less brutal — an intellectual, moral, psychological Terror that accompanied the revolutionary phenomenon even before 1789 and continued even after Napoleon, down to our days. The roots of modern terrorism are found in this ideology. As Augustin Cochin reminds us:

> Before the bloody Terror of 1793, there was in the republic of letters from 1765 to 1780 a bloodless Terror of which the *Encyclopedia* was the Committee of Public Safety and d'Alembert the Robespierre, who severed [opponents] at the guillotine of reputations, later to be substituted by heads. His guillotine was the "infamy," as they said at the time.

The ideological seeds of the Terror can be found in the Enlightenment philosophy of history, theorized by Voltaire and his disciples, who in the French Revolution had their triumph.

According to the new calendar of the revolutionaries, adopted on October 5, 1793, and valid until 1805, the year began on the anniversary of the foundation of the Republic, September 22, 1792. The new "revolutionary" names of the days and months had to be used by law in all public and private documents.

The de-Christianization was manifest also in the change of Christian names and names of localities that contained the word *Saint*. Fourteen hundred streets in Paris received new names because the old ones contained some reference to a king, a queen, or a saint. Louis XV Square, where the executions took place, became Revolution Square, and later the Place de la Concorde. Notre Dame Cathedral became the Temple of Reason; Montmartre became Mont Marat. In the revolutionary liturgy, the "tree of liberty" replaced the cross. In 1792 alone, sixty thousand such trees were planted. They no longer limited themselves to proscribing rebellious priests, but now prohibited Catholic worship. Christianity was outlawed. On October 7, a member of the Convention, the Protestant pastor Philippe Rühl (1737–1795), shattered the Holy Ampoule in the town square in Rheims, which contained the chrism oil with which the kings of France had been crowned from time immemorial.

The Feast of Reason was celebrated in Notre Dame on November 10, 1792, which marked the highpoint of this de-Christianization. The following phase was that of the new revolutionary religion.

Historians distinguish three phases in the revolutionary cult: the Cult of Reason, the Cult of the Supreme Being, and the Theophilanthropy of the Directory. In reality, this was but one religion, whose characteristic was to transfer to humanity the divine character that is due to God alone. "The people is God," as the National Convention explicitly affirmed, "its sovereignty is one, indivisible, indefeasible, immutable, inalienable, immortal, unlimited, uncircumscribed, absolute, and omnipotent."

On July 13, 1793, one of the most intense revolutionary leaders, Jean-Paul Marat (1743–1793), was assassinated by the Girondin, Charlotte Corday (1768–1793), who was guillotined four days later. The relics of Marat were exhibited for public veneration. Marat's heart, enclosed in an urn of agate, was placed on an altar and venerated with the refrain of a litany: *Cor Sacrum Marat, Cor Jesu, Cor Marat.* The public worship of Marat lasted fourteen months. The official ceremony of his apotheosis took place on September 21, 1794, two months after the death of Robespierre.

On March 21, 1793, the Convention instituted the Committee of General Security; every city or district had to have one of these. It was obligatory to compile a list, at first only of foreigners, but later of all "suspect" citizens.

On March 27, the aristocracy was outlawed and citizens were armed with pikes; on the twenty-eighth, emigrants were declared administratively dead and their possessions were confiscated; on March 29, the death penalty was decreed for authors of presumed counterrevolutionary writings. The Convention voted a decree on April 1 that suppressed the inviolability of Convention members "suspected of complicity with the enemy." Again, under the pretext of the war emergency and counterrevolutionary plots, the Committee of Public Safety was constituted on April 6, formed of nine members, concentrating in their hands all executive power.

The Committee of Public Safety governed France from July 1793 until July 27, 1794, organizing the "revolutionary government" — in other words, the Terror. The leader of this committee was Maximilien de Robespierre (1758–1794), a modest provincial attorney who, although he held no office higher than those of his colleagues, had ever greater influence, incarnating the bloodiest phase of the Revolution. In 1789, he was still a monarchist; during the Assembly he was a republican, and during the Convention a socialist. Gaxotte called him "revolutionary doctrine in action."

On August 30, the Jacobins of Paris requested the Terror to be put on the agenda. On September 17, with the Law of Suspects, the Terror began in earnest.

The Committee of General Security was charged with arresting those on the lists of suspects. The wars of revolutionary France against the other European powers were prolonged until the fall of Napoleon.

## 5. THE CLIMAX AND END OF THE REVOLUTION

On December 6, 1792, the Convention had decreed that "Louis Capet shall be brought to court to be interrogated." Upon the proposal of Marat, it was also decided that during the trial, all the voting was to be done by roll call and recorded.

The vote against Louis XVI began in the Convention on January 15, 1793. The sovereign was unanimously declared guilty of conspiring against liberty.

The next day began the nominal appeal on the crucial problem: "What punishment shall be inflicted upon Loius Capet?" Each member rose to the podium and explained his vote. After two ballots, the result was 361 votes for his death and 360 against. By one vote, Louis XVI was condemned to death. Each member who had voted for his condemnation, beginning with the king's cousin, Phillip d'Orléans, could consider his vote to have been decisive.

On January 21, 1793, at ten o'clock, Louis XVI climbed the scaffold. The Irish abbot Henry Edgeworth administered last rites. The sovereign died with great dignity and courage. Pius VI, in a discourse given at the Consistory of June 17, 1793, stated that the death of Louis XVI was voted "in hatred for the Catholic religion" and that it seems difficult to contest "the glory of his martyrdom." The title of martyr can likewise be applied to Marie Antoinette, guilty of nothing except having represented the principle of Christian royalty. Louis XVI was defined by the Portuguese historian João Ameal as an expiatory victim, as "legitimate head of France, anointed king, and the personification of Christian sovereignty."

In the seventeenth century, English revolutionaries tried King Charles I (1600–1649) because they considered him a criminal. Now, however, the French Revolution balked at punishing Louis XVI as a criminal, but rather condemned him as a sovereign: his crime was precisely that of being king. What was on trial was not the man, but the institution of the monarchy as such, and behind this institution, a principle: the traditional conception of sovereignty, expressed in the words of St. Joan of Arc to the Dauphin: "Your majesty is the representative of the King of Heaven."

The idea of the divine legitimacy of royalty was being overturned by the statement of that other Jacobin leader, Louis Antoine de Saint-Just

(1767–1794), to the Convention: "There can be no innocent reign: this absurdity is all too evident. Every king is a rebel and a usurper." "The sole qualification of king," affirmed Robespierre, "attracts the scourges of war upon the stricken nation: neither prison nor exile can render his existence indifferent to public well-being." For the very reason he is called *king*, exclaimed Saint-Just, "this man must either reign or die." In fact, royalty "is an eternal crime against which every man has a right to rebel and to arm himself; it is one of the aggressions that cannot be justified, not even by the blinding of an entire people."

The regicide of Louis XVI can be considered the symbolic fulfillment of the French Revolution. What the Revolution wanted to decapitate was the principle of the *consecratio mundi*, the sacralization of the temporal order.

The Revolution raised a new flag: the source of authority would no longer be God, but the people. There is no divine sovereignty to which an earthly king must submit, nor shall there be a political sovereignty to which the people must be subordinated. Sovereign shall be the people, a society of equals.

This was the ancient dream of medieval heretics, of the Cathars, the Waldensians, the Hussites, the Anabaptists, and then the Deists of the eighteenth century, of Masonic conspirators, the same dream that flourishes in the professional revolutionaries of our day.

The project has not changed: destroy Christian civilization from the root, undo Christian civilization, the fruit of the Most Sacred Blood of our Lord Jesus Christ, regress to barbarism and tribalism. Man does not need the Church, a means of salvation, nor a Creator and Redeemer God: humanity can redeem itself by its own strength, "regenerate" itself, liberate itself from the curse of death and sin, return to the original perfection of Eden, to the original state of the "noble savage," and thus create the perfect revolutionary society, which is the classless society of Marxism, or else the lawless world of the anarchistic society — a pure and immaculate society, paradise on earth, founded on the abolition of all authority and all laws.

## 6. THE VENDÉE

On February 24, 1793, the Convention ordered a draft of three hundred thousand men to reinforce the armies. The inhabitants of three provinces of Western France — the Vendée, Brittany, and Poitou — exasperated by the persecutions against the Church and by the death of the king, instead of responding to the appeal, rose up en masse against the Revolution and took up arms in defense of throne and altar.

A Catholic and royalist militia was formed, composed of many tens of thousands of men, led by those whom the insurgents had chosen from among the nobles of their territories, like Louis-Marie de Lescure, Maurice d'Elbée, and Henri de la Rochejaquelin, but also from among the commoners, such as the game warden Jean-Nicolas Stofflet, or Jacques Cathelinau, a simple peasant who was the initiator of the uprising and was elected first general of the Vendean militia.

Thus began one of the bloodiest civil wars in history, in which victories and defeats alternated, and in which almost every one of the Vendean leaders died in defense of his Faith.

In the face of the military successes of the insurgents, the Convention decided to exterminate the "brigands of the Vendée." In January 1794, punitive military expeditions marched against the Vendée, called "infernal columns," whose aim was to cross from one side of the rebel land to the other and ensure that "nothing escaped national vengeance."

The French historian Reynald Secher documents the authentic genocide carried out from 1793 to 1796 by these republican troops. In the historical documents, we read instructions on how to kill great numbers of women and children: since bullets were expensive, orders were given to smash skulls with the strike of the bayonet, and because bayonets would break, to have recourse to collective drowning.

General Turreau wrote on January 24, 1794, "My columns have already worked wonders, not one rebel has escaped their searches.... If my intentions are carried out, within fifteen days there will no longer exist houses, or supplies, or arms, or inhabitants in the Vendée. All woodlands and tall trees in the Vendée must be felled." Westermann, another republican general, guillotined by his Jacobin companions in 1794, wrote:

> The Vendée no longer exists! It has died under our free sabers, with its women and children. I have crushed children under the hooves of my horses, massacred women who will never again give birth to bandits. I cannot be reprimanded for having taken prisoners. I have exterminated them all.... The roads are covered with cadavers. There are so many in some areas that they form pyramids.

According to Secher, the Vendée lost in all almost 15 percent of its population: 117,257 out of 815,000 people.

The Vendeans resisted until the capture and execution of their last legendary leader, Athanase de Charette, who was shot in 1796. With his death, their heroic struggle ended.

The adventure of the French Revolution came to a close. On June 4, 1794, Robespierre was unanimously elected president of the Convention. On June 8 (Prairial 20 in the revolutionary calendar), while presiding over the Feast of the Supreme Being, Robespierre attempted to inaugurate a new religion, the Cult of the Supreme Being, inspired by Rousseau's theories. But on July 27, 1794 (Thermidor 9), while speaking to the Tribune of the Convention, Robespierre was challenged by the Assembly, which voted immediately afterward to arrest him. The following day, at eight in the morning, Robespierre was guillotined in the Place de la Concorde by the same revolutionaries he had agitated for so long. The excesses of the Jacobins aroused a reaction from among the same revolutionaries. With the Thermidorean reaction, the Revolution took a step backward and assumed a bourgeois character during the reign of the Directory, which lasted from October 1795 until 1799.

Under the Directory, while fighting in the Vendée continued, the Conspiracy of Equals developed, led by François-Noel Babeuf, known as "Gracchus." Babeuf's conspiracy, in which the Italian Filippo Buonarroti participated, represented a communistic moment of the Revolution that left to posterity its Conspiracy of Equals, from which socialism and nineteenth- and twentieth-century communism descend. In the elections of 1797, the monarchists obtained a large majority, and there was talk of a possible restoration of the monarchy. Seeing the Revolution threatened, General Napoleon Bonaparte, in Italy at the time, sent troops to Paris. While the army was still fighting on various fronts, a furious power struggle took place, from which Napoleon emerged victorious through a coup d'etat on November 11, 1799 (Brumaire 18). This put an end to the failed experiment of the Directory.

Napoleon not only stabilized the revolutionary conquests in France but also extended them throughout Europe. In the countries he would conquer, he abolished the old monarchies and imposed the principles of a new civil code that limited the rights of the Church, recognized divorce, and introduced a regime of egalitarianism. The diffusion of the new revolutionary doctrines provoked a great transformation in the political and social structures of the European peoples. One of the great errors of the Revolution was its frontal attack on the Church. Napoleon sought to remedy this with the Concordat of

1801, which restored religious freedom, but did not mark a return to the preceding situation.

The French Revolution exterminated during the Terror and the Vendean genocide more than 186,000 peasants, 168,000 workers, 120,000 merchants, and 90,000 members of the nobility and clergy. In addition to these were the 1.4 million French soldiers who died during the wars of the Revolution and in the Napoleonic Wars. These 2 million deaths are almost equivalent to what the First and Second World Wars of the twentieth century cost France, the deadliest conflicts in history. All this in the name of the "rights of man"!

## 7.  THE ESSENCE OF THE FRENCH REVOLUTION

The French Revolution was the prototype of all revolutions and allows us to speak of Revolution with a capital "R," to indicate the subversion of the religious and metaphysical order, even before the subversion of the political and social orders.

Msgr. Gaume offers us this effective image:

> If, tearing away its mask, you ask him: "Who are you?" he will say, "I am not the one you think I am. Many talk about me, but very few know who I am. I am neither the guerrillas who conspire in the shadows, nor the uprising that thunders in the streets, nor the change from a monarchy into a republic, nor the substitution of one dynasty for another, nor the momentary disruption of public order. I am neither the shouts of the Jacobins, nor the Montagnards, nor the combat on the barricades, nor the looting, nor the burning, nor the agrarian reform, nor the guillotine, nor the Noyades. I am neither Marat, nor Robespierre, nor Babeuf, nor Mazzini, nor Kossuth. These men are my sons, but they are not me. These things are my works, but they are not me. These men and these things are passing matters: but I have been permanent. I am hatred for every religious and social order that man has not established and in which he is neither king nor God. I am the foundation of a religious and social state by the will of man in the place of the will of God. I am God dethroned and man in His place. This is why I am called Revolution, which means overturning."

The goal of the French Revolution and of every revolution is moral and social anarchy: a conception of the world in which humanity can redeem itself, liberate itself from the curse of death and sin, returning to the original perfection, to bring about the perfect revolutionary society, without authority and without laws, a pure and immaculate society founded on the communism of goods and bodies. As Corrêa de Oliveira writes, "It is simultaneously the most liberal and most egalitarian ideal that one can imagine."

The antithesis of Revolution is Christian civilization, which, as St. Pius X states, is the only possible civilization:

> Civilization does not have to be invented, nor does one have to build the new society in the clouds. It has existed before and it still exists: it is Christian civilization, it is Catholic society. It is only a matter of constantly establishing and restoring it upon its natural and divine foundations against the reviving attacks of unhealthy utopia, of rebellion, and of impiety.

There can be no compromise or convergence between Christian civilization and revolutionary utopia, between the ideals of the gospel and the principles of 1789.

To those who propose a "return to 1789" to bring about an unfinished revolution, we respond that two centuries of carrying out revolutions are quite enough: we do not want to return to 1789, but to Christian civilization, and to make of it, not a French Revolution or a Reign of Terror, but our future in this twenty-first century that has just begun.

CHAPTER X

# The Birth of the Counter-Revolution

## 1. Reaction to the French Revolution

The French Revolution was a historical watershed. The society that preceded the Revolution of 1789 was covered in shadow and faults, but in its institutions and its laws it was still a Christian society. In the space of just a few years, this society was uprooted from the ground. "All the laws of nature and of life," writes the historian Augustin Cochin in his masterpiece *Mechanics of the Revolution*, "were violated in this ordeal of a great civilized people, who seemed struck by an impulse of furious insanity." The French Revolution is not, however, merely a historical period of folly and errors; it truly inaugurated a new age for the human race. It marks, in fact, the end of a society that was still structurally Christian, despite all of its errors. The rebellion that, with Protestantism, had swept the ecclesiastical setting, extended to the political and social spheres, as the crowning of a process of centuries-long subversion: it was the end of Christianity as a family of Christian populations, as a civil and social projection of Christianity.

The philosopher Diderot wrote:

> Once men have dared in some way to assault the barrier of religion, that most formidable and most respected barrier that exists, it is impossible to draw to a halt. Once they have raised their eyes threateningly against the majesty of Heaven, the next moment men will not resist directing

their wrathful gaze toward the sovereignty of this earth. The rope that
holds tight and oppresses humanity is formed of two cords: one cannot
break without the other breaking as well.

In France, the Vendeans rebelled against the French Revolution in the name of
"*Dieu et le Roi*," placing the symbol of the Sacred Heart on their banners. The
Vendée was not only a French phenomenon but a European one. When Napoleon
attempted to impose revolutionary ideas in Italy (1796–1799) and then in Switzerland (1797–1798), in the Netherlands (1798), and in Spain (1808), the people
rose up in arms under the symbols of religion and legitimate governments.

The Napoleonic invasion of Italy in 1796 was for Italians what the French
Revolution of 1789 was for France: a devastating hurricane. This was not only a
military invasion but a political and ideological invasion as well, culminating in
the creation of republics in the various regions of Italy modeled on that of the
French Revolution. A minority, mostly of the intellectual and bourgeois classes,
sided with the invaders, acclaiming Bonaparte as a "liberator" and seeing in his
armies the instrument for imposing the revolutionary ideas to which the "reactionary" population expressed profound refusal. This was a movement that, in a
broad sense, has been defined as "Jacobin."

Another part of the population reacted by taking up arms against the Jacobin army, in the name of the religious and civil traditions of the Italian
people. These popular uprisings, manifested spontaneously from 1796 to
1814 throughout the peninsula, from the Alps to Calabria, were called the
"insurgency."

Massimo Viglione and other historians have shed light on these events. The
pattern that emerges justifies the label "Italian Vendée" to explain the scope and
nature of this phenomenon of popular revolts, which was similar to those that
arose in the same period in many other countries.

The first characteristic of this phenomenon of popular rebellions is that
they were a reaction on the military level before becoming a cultural and moral
reality: an *armed reaction* against an invading army.

The second characteristic of fundamental importance is the anti-Jacobin
ideological essence. This ideological dimension has been denied by Marxist
historiography, which has insisted on explaining reactionary insurgency as a
phenomenon produced by the social contradictions of the age. In reality, testi-
monies say that while the French army advanced to "liberate" the populations,

planting trees of liberty, profaning churches, destroying historical coats of arms and insignia, the insurgents raised the cross, planted the flags of their sovereigns, and raised the cry, "Long live Jesus, long live Mary, long live the King, long live the emperor!" Throne and altar, the Church and legitimate sovereigns, were intimately associated in the minds of the insurgents.

There were certainly other reasons for discontent, such as the worsening of the financial situation, military conscription, embezzlement, and ransacking of various sorts that contributed to rendering the situation incendiary, but the final reason for the insurgency was the reaction against the French Revolution.

This is demonstrated by the temporal framework in which this phenomenon unraveled in Italy, which had its climax in the Jacobin Triennial (1796–1799), although it had appeared already in 1792 (before Napoleon, therefore), and concluded with the Bourbon Restoration. Thus, from 1792 to 1814, it was a resistance of a clearly anti-Jacobin character, just as Bonaparte's own forces were driven by a different and opposing ideology.

The third background characteristic of the insurgency demonstrates this as well, namely its presence throughout the peninsula, from the Alps to the Ionian Sea (with the sole exception of Sicily, the only Italian region not invaded by the French). In this sense it was a national insurgency, but this was the case above all because the entire population participated, or rather representatives of all the orders in which Italian society was organized at that time participated: the clergy, the nobility, and the people in general.

The most famous insurgencies occurred in 1797 in Veneto, in Tuscany with the *Viva Maria*, in Tyrol with Andreas Hofer, and above all, in 1799, in the Kingdom of Naples, where Cardinal Fabrizio Ruffo (1744–1827) recruited a Christian royalist army, or army of the Santa Fede (from whence the term *Sanfedismo*), composed of peasants and commoners who sought to restore the Bourbons to the throne. In February 1799, the insurgents of Calabria marched toward Basilicata and Apulia, crushing every obstacle. The victorious army of the Santa Fede entered Naples on June 13, while in the city, the wrath of the populace exploded against the Jacobins. In September, with the aid of the Russian and British armies, the city of Rome, still occupied by the Jacobins, was liberated, but the following year, Napoleon took power in France, reconquered the North, and subsequently marched through southern Italy.

A further characteristic of the insurgency must be highlighted: the ideological aspect is not sufficient to motivate the fury of the anti-Jacobin reaction. It

must be remembered that there was an invading army that insisted on "democ-
ratizing" the peninsula with methods that were closer to banditry than to
democratic methods or ideas. The ransacking of the peninsula was ordered by
the Directory, which, in May 1796, suggested that General Bonaparte abscond
with the most conspicuous of Italy's wealth: its works of art.

From 1796 to 1799, this order was systematically carried out: long caravans
loaded with artistic treasures crossed the peninsula heading toward France to
replenish the exhausted coffers of the Directory. Many of the looted works of art
went to enrich the Louvre. But the plundering of works of art was only one aspect of a policy marked by brutal subjugation, which could only exasperate the
Italian population. The most violent reactions exploded when the most well-
rooted traditions were touched, the sanctuaries dearest to Italians, like Loreto,
which was stripped of all its treasures.

The use of the term "banditry," introduced by the Convention for liquidat-
ing the Vendeans, has been taken up by many historians to disqualify all forms
of counterrevolutionary insurgency, denying their religious and moral inspiration. Obviously, this is a historical falsification that overturns the terms of the
issue. The brutal repression of the insurgents, portrayed as the repression of
banditry, actually manifests the lawless aspect of the Jacobin occupation, which
recalls the Vendean genocide, understood as the will to annihilate a rebellious
population for ideological motives, moved by an anti-Christian animus.

This was confirmed by the Europe-wide dimension of the Napoleonic insurgencies. One of the last occurred in 1809 in Tyrol. A hotel owner in
Passeiertal, Andreas Hofer, led the revolt in the name of the Sacred Heart and of
the Habsburgs, against the annexation of his homeland to Bavaria. Eventually
betrayed, he was handed over to the French. Eugenio di Beauharnais asked his
stepfather to pardon him, but Napoleon insisted on his execution.

## 2. THE CHRISTIAN FRIENDSHIPS

In the darkest period—which ran from 1789 to 1814, the year of Napoleon's fall
and the beginning of the Restoration—besides the popular reaction there was
another profound opposition to the Revolution, this one of a spiritual, moral,
and cultural character, rather than a militaristic one. It was expressed by a dense
network of counterrevolutionary organizations that in those years had spread
throughout the continent.

These associations reported to former members of the Society of Jesus, which, for the most part, had disbanded in 1773, but which remained alive and active and constituted the backbone of the Counter-Revolution that was taking shape.

The most notable and important of these associations was founded by Fr. Nikolaus Albert von Diessbach (1732–1798), between 1779 and 1780, in Turin. From there, it spread rapidly to Milan, Florence, Freiburg, Vienna, Paris, and Warsaw.

Diessbach was a brilliant and courageous Swiss official of Calvinist faith, at the service of the king of Sardinia, but who then converted to Catholicism and entered the Society of Jesus. After just a few years, he lived through the drama of the dissolution of the Jesuits. He then founded an organization by the name of Amicizia Cristiana (Christian friendship), which sought to combat masonic Enlightenment using its own weapons: books and secrecy. This was a battle of ideas that found its privileged instruments in books, newspapers, pamphlets, and leaflets, which the members of Amicizia disseminated well beyond the confines of Piedmont. Secrecy served to guard its members and to keep them humble, but had nothing to do with Masonic secrecy that served to cover the lie by which the higher levels hid the true aims of the sect from the lower levels.

Diessbach's disciple and successor in Turin was the priest Pio Brunone Lanteri (1759–1830), born in Cuneo to a deeply pious family. He wanted to become a Carthusian, but due to his weak health he was not accepted into the order, and instead entered the diocesan seminary. According to witnesses, "He spent all the time he had with Diessbach, going to lunch with him in the pubs, with the aim of fishing for sinners, to impede foul talk, to encourage the reading of good books. For a number of years, he would not go to sleep until well past midnight, using that time to speak with God, and to fortify himself in good doctrine."

Toward the end of February 1782, Diessbach and Lanteri travelled to Vienna, hotbed of Josephinism, to prepare, through preaching, contacts, and the dissemination of pamphlets, the Catholic welcome in Austria of Pius VI (r. 1775–1799), the apostolic pilgrim, who was triumphantly received on March 22. Upon his return to Italy, Lanteri was ordained a priest.

As he wrote on the eve of his ordination:

> My life is a declared battle, even today it has been destined and made a
> spectacle before God, the angels, and men; whatever may happen,
> whether in prosperity or adversity, has been procured for me by God as

an occasion for spoils, may He always be praised in them. I wish to profit from them.... Always openly and freely declared on God's side, I am now formally consecrated to Him, entirely committed to snatch souls from the world and to give them to God. Always think, speak, and act as a saint; this is required of the spirit of a true minister of God, as are the same motivations that the saints had. Speak of God like soldiers speak of war.

In the age in which Diessbach and Lanteri lived, Jansenism, Gallicanism, Josephinism, the Enlightenment, "enlightened Catholicism" — diverse and heterogeneous forces, though sharing a common hatred for the Church of Rome — intertwined and multiplied their efforts, in the shadow of Masonic lodges, to destroy definitively the religious and social order on which Christianity was founded. Diessbach and Lanteri went into battle against this fierce army.

While Diessbach was working in Vienna, where he died in 1798, Lanteri was directing the Turin office of Amicizia, which, under his guidance, passed through the years of persecution extending from the French invasion of 1796 to 1814, maintaining its character as a center for the dissemination of written works and a doctrinal reference point for all of Piedmont. The young priest remained in contact with booksellers and printers around Europe, constantly updating his vast private library and promptly disseminating pamphlets and dissertations of his collaborators and of his own pen, against the errors of the age—above all against Jansenism, which operated as a fifth column within the Church, occupying episcopates, university chairs, parishes, and seminaries.

Lanteri opposed Jansenism with the moral doctrine of St. Alphonsus Liguori, whose work he defined as "a library of all moral theologians," which he spread around all Piedmont. "Attach yourselves to Liguori," he said. "If you want to do good for souls, you need to clothe yourself with His spirit. Oh, blessed the doctrine of this bishop, and blessed the Lord who in these times has given us a man so like unto His heart!" St. Alphonsus Liguori, bishop of Sant'Agata dei Goti and founder of the Congregation of the Redemptorists, was proclaimed a saint by Pope Gregory XVI in 1839 and declared Doctor of the Church in 1871 by Pius IX. He is the highest recognized authority in moral theology, as St. Thomas is in philosophy.

"One can rightly say," wrote the Jesuit Fr. Antonio Bresciani about Lanteri, "he was in Piedmont the support of healthy theology and healthy moral teaching. He was the most powerful hammer against Jansenism."

The natural ally of Jansenism was Gallicanism, which had reemerged in the ecclesiastical policies of Bonaparte. Napoleon had given the order that even in diocesan seminaries, and not only universities, the four Gallican articles were to be taught. Approved by the General Assembly of the French clergy in 1682, these limited papal authority on one hand, sustaining the inferiority of the pope with respect to the council and affirming that the dogmatic definitions of the popes are infallible only after the approval of the Church; on the other hand, they denied the authority of the Church in temporal matters, introducing de facto the principle of secularization of institutions and the separation of Church and state.

Lanteri fought vigorously against Gallicanism as well, not only distinguishing himself for his polemical writings, but also working hard on the practical level, as he did in organizing the material assistance for Pius VII (r. 1800–1823), who had been deported to Savona for having refused to submit the Church to the tight control of the Napoleonic Empire. On June 10, 1809, Pius VII had in fact excommunicated Napoleon. On July 6, his imprisonment began. From Paris to Lyon, to Turin, to Mondovì, to Savona, there was an invisible chain, by means of which the members of the Chevaliers de la Foi, the Congrégation of Lyon, and Amicizia Cristiana — the secret societies that constituted the most active centers of Catholic resistance — were able to obtain the bull of excommunication, penetrating the armor of rigorous Napoleonic control and disseminating the news of the excommunication throughout Paris.

In France, one of the most active collaborators was Duke Mathieu de Montmorency-Laval (1766–1826), who, after having been a follower of the *philosophes*, and having participated in the French Revolution, became an ardent defender of the Church and the monarchy. He died on Good Friday, March 24, 1826, while praying in the Church of St. Thomas Aquinas in Paris.

## 3. Fr. Pierre Picot de Clorivière

Two great men belonged to the ranks of Amicizie Cristiane: Count Joseph de Maistre and Fr. Pierre Picot de Clorivière. Joseph de Maistre is more well known, but Clorivière is extraordinarily relevant to our time.

Pierre Picot de Clorivière was born June 29, 1735, in Saint-Malo, Brittany. He studied law in Paris and entered the Society of Jesus in 1756. He was ordained a priest in 1763 in the province of England, because the Jesuits had been expelled from France in 1762. He was the last French Jesuit to make profession of religious vows in Liege, on August 15, 1773. Clement XIV had signed the suppression of the Society on July 21, but the decree had not yet been promulgated. After the dissolution of the Jesuits, Clorivière lived for some years dedicating himself to prayer and study of things of God, exercising his priestly ministry in the parish of Paramé (diocese of Saint-Malo). Called in 1786 to direct the diocesan seminary in Dinan, the following August he met Adelaide Maria Champion de Cicé (1749–1818), with whom he created a new form of religious life, without the obligation of communal life or habit, so as to live and work in society, despite the decrees of the French Assembly that had prohibited religious life in the entire nation.

Before the Revolution had erupted, in December 1786, Fr. Clorivière had written to Mademoiselle de Cicé: "I foresee nothing good in the conduct of the Estates General; I fear above all for religion, given the disposition of the majority of spirits." In 1790, he refused the Civil Constitution of the Clergy and began a clandestine existence. On February 2, 1791, he founded two new institutes: the Secular Institute of Priests of the Heart of Jesus and the Sisters of the Heart of Mary, inspired by the spirituality of St. Ignatius of Loyola, with the aim of saving souls caught in the revolutionary torment.

The life of the two founders was cruelly tested. Both were sent to prison, and one of Clorivière's brothers was guillotined under the accusation of counterrevolutionary conspiracy. Mother de Cicé died on April 26, 1810. Fr. Clorivière accepted the task of reorganizing the Society of Jesus in France when, on August 7, 1814, Pius VII reestablished it throughout the world. Clorivière died on January 9, 1820, praying before the tabernacle.

Among the priests who witnessed to the Catholic Faith during the years of the Revolution, we also recall Fr. Pierre Coudrin (1768–1837), founder of the Congregation of the Sacred Hearts of Jesus and Mary. Fr. Coudrin secretly exercised his ministry in Poitiers, risking the guillotine. On Christmas Eve 1800, he founded his religious congregation together with Henriette Aymer de la Chevalerie (1767–1834), consecrated to perpetual adoration of the Blessed Sacrament. The congregation was located in a convent near the cemetery of Picpus in Paris, where thirteen hundred people who had been guillotined in the nearby Place du Trône during the Terror were buried.

## 4. THE REVOLUTION WAS SATANIC IN ITS ESSENCE

The first critical witness of the French Revolution seems to be the Irish-born Edmund Burke, author of *Reflections on the French Revolution* (1790), in which he denounced the abstract ideology that produced the Revolution, to which he compared the experience that is born from nature and from history. Seven years later, Joseph de Maistre published his *Considerations on France*, in which, in a more profound way than Burke, he unveiled the metaphysical character of the Revolution and its satanic essence. But Fr. Clorivière was author of a prophetic work of January 27, 1794, which remains very important because it constitutes the first Catholic interpretation of the French Revolution. We shall present some of the more significant pages here:

> The Revolution we have seen unleashed presents three main character-istics, prophesied in Scripture: it was sudden, large, and generalized.
>
> It was sudden in its explosion. We ought to have seen long before the evil that threatened us, and we should have prepared.
>
> The second characteristic of the anti-Christian revolution is that it is great in size: great in the political order, great in the moral order, great above all in the religious order. In its objective it extends to everything; nothing is respected, not even the fundamental princi-ples of natural law; the most universal ideas are not in the least considered, and the most indefeasible rights are violated to forge new ones. These new rights tend toward the suppression of every type of natural, religious, and even divine yoke, like the abolition of every legitimate power.
>
> A third characteristic of the anti-Christian Revolution is that it must be generalized. It was too much for our unfortunate country. The number of those who let themselves be swept into the torrent is immense; those who resisted are relatively few.
>
> It must be feared that this revolution extends to every country or at least to a great number of countries that embraced the Catholic reli-gion. Only three or four years ago, the Catholic religion was the only one recognized in France; its external worship was sumptuous, the clergy capable and respected. France possessed exemplary men,

fervent communities, eloquent preachers, zealous missionaries; disorder was, it seems, neither greater nor less than elsewhere. France, nevertheless, fell, Christianity is now prohibited, and apostasy has taken its place.

From the birth of Christianity, from the creation of the world, one has never seen a revolution in which cruelty showed itself so openly and was taken to such monstruous and extravagant excesses. Nevertheless, it spread with amazing rapidity, through means less proportionate to success, and what should shock and outrage the spirit serves only to give it renewed force. A great people has suddenly changed its principles, customs, laws, and religion. Without reason and against every motive of political interest, of glory, and of happiness, it parades its atheism. It seems intent only on blinding itself, demoralizing itself, gladly soliciting the means to render itself unhappy; it adopts the cruelest petitions, welcomes the most senseless proposals, and applauds the most ridiculous bluster.

All this can be explained only by attributing it to the greatest power left to demons, to this freedom which, according to various passages in Scripture, for a certain time has been given to the powers of darkness. The most extensive permission that the Lord gives to demons to tempt men and to use against them cunning, made possible by their nature, superior to ours, is a chastisement of divine wrath, although God grants them this permission with remorse and begrudgingly, due to the sins of the Muslims.

Those whom the Lord, by a special grace, preserves in certain periods from general evil, must use wise precaution to merit the continuation of a similar assistance. It is important for them to be convinced of the ire with which Hell attacks men in this age, and of the power, more widespread than in any other century, which has been given to Satan. Informed of the power of their enemies, those who have been preserved will better sense the excellence of this favor, will confess that they cannot attribute to themselves the glory, that it demands their awareness and that they must not cease to be vigilant.

The moment has come to make known to the inhabitants of the earth what the enemy of the human race is plotting against them. The call to battle has been sounded, it is no longer time to think of rest.... Pusillanimous fear can only weaken us and give the advantage to our enemies. What is a chastisement for those who are not of God, is only a trial for those who are generously attached to His service. The combat is the more violent, so that the victory might be more glorious, and God increases the strength of his soldiers when he exposes them to greater dangers. He is with us; what should we fear? He will fight for us; what can our enemies do? We can challenge them like the prophet: "Gather together, make your plans, they shall be annihilated."

## 5. Erratic Passions

Plinio Corrêa de Oliveira has proposed that the revolution of ideas and of facts is preceded by a revolution in the field of tendencies, born of erratic passions within the human soul, in particular pride and sensuality. This insight corresponds to what Fr. Clorivière wrote during the years of the French Revolution:

> In general, all the perverse inclinations that adulterate purity of heart likewise adulterate the acuity of the spirit and obfuscate it; it is the privilege of a pure heart to see the light of God in all of its splendor. Two vices, more than all others, have plunged our age into darkness: pride and impurity.
>
> Pride is the extreme opposite of divine light, since it is founded on a lie and can only subsist in darkness. Divine light, which is simply Truth, shows us that greatness, goodness, wisdom, and all perfections reside solely in God; they convince us to remain dependent on God, to return to Him all honor and to prefer none for ourselves. Whoever gratifies himself, esteems himself highly, and wants to be esteemed by others, whoever elevates himself above others — whoever is, in a word, *proud* — distances himself from the light which condemns him, closing his eyes to all humiliating truth; he cannot bear the yoke and so parades his independence. Religion presents him with superiors who represent the authority of God, but he cannot suffer this. Jesus Christ preaches humility to him, and that name becomes odious. The memory of God brings to mind his nothingness, and so he would like to erase it. Eventually he starts to desire the annihilation of God, in some way, with the aim of becoming his own God, and refers all things to himself. This is the path of pride, and in this way, man plunges into every error.
>
> Pride is the peculiar character of the sects that have upended the edifice of religion and the form of government that had flourished for fourteen hundred years. Only the one who has abandoned himself to

impiety has experienced the phrase, "they refuse with disdain every domination and blaspheme all that bears even the least stamp of the divine Majesty."

Like pride, the vice of the flesh intercepts the celestial light, but not in the same way. Pride does so by fixing man's gaze on his own greatness and nobility. If some odd ray from above filters through the thick crust wrapping his soul, it is an inopportune light, of which he seeks to be liberated by immersing himself in dissipation and vice.

If faith awakens his fears, the sensual man treats them as prejudices from his infancy and, finding in systems of impiety the justification for his chains, he hurls himself into these systems, and thinks in this way that he can silence his remorse. An age in which good customs reign is not an age of incredulity. Dissolute conduct has opened the way to its reign.

The agents of destructive revolution, presenting to the people the infernal doctrine of their liberty, have loosened the bridle of their passions, aided and encouraged their weakness for vice, broken inhibitions, and dissipated all shame with which modesty opposed the lower inclinations. All this time they were nourished by pride, showing them clearly the phantom of equality and destroying all subordination. Thus, it was no longer difficult to substitute deceit for truth, and the most monstrous superstition for the pure religion of Jesus Christ. People need to be brought back to their consciences, therefore, the interior judgment that the High Teacher has established in the heart of each man. If reason and customs retake their sphere of influence, it will not be without the help of the religion of Jesus Christ, and the powerful means which it offers to overcome the passions so as to be enamored of virtue, in particular the use of the sacraments.

## 6. INTELLECTUALS OF THE RESTORATION

The age of the French Revolution closed, at least provisionally, after the military defeat of Napoleon and the fall of the political system he had extended throughout Europe. The Congress of Vienna, held from September 22, 1814, to June 10, 1815, sanctioned a new period of European history known as the Restoration. The great architect of the Congress of Vienna was Prince Clemens Lothar von Metternich (1773–1859), who fought with all his power the liberal revolution that was threatening the thrones of Europe. In this period, the counterrevolutionary school of thought developed, which counted among its first authors in France Joseph de Maistre and Louis de Bonald; in Spain, Juan Donoso Cortés and Jaime Balmes; in Switzerland, Karl Ludwig von Haller; in Austria, Karl von Vogelsang; and in Italy, Monaldo Leopardi and Clemente Solaro della Margarita.

In Piedmont, on May 21, 1814, an edict abolished the Napoleonic Code, establishing the return to the laws and constitutions of 1770. Civil marriage and divorce, introduced by Napoleon, were suppressed; religious congregations were reestablished, with pride of place given to the Jesuits. Amicizia Cristiana was transformed in 1817 to Amicizia Cattolica (Catholic friendship). The aims were identical, as was the means of its apostolate (the printed word), but the number of members was enlarged, the lay character was accentuated, and above all, secrecy was abolished, necessary in times of persecution but no longer justifiable in the new climate.

Meetings were held in the palace of Marquis Cesare Taparelli d'Azeglio, father of the more famous Massimo and the Jesuit Fr. Luigi Taparelli d'Azeglio. In these years, de Maistre's works *St. Petersburg Dialogues*, *L'Eglise gallicane*, and *On the Pope* were published and disseminated by Amicizia.

The free distribution of books, preferably "of reduced volume but strong in reasoning and unction," remained its primary activity. "In the eight years of Amicizia's activity," the Marquis d'Azeglio wrote in 1825, "we have disseminated hundreds of thousands of volumes, ten thousand alone sent to America." "Our aim," wrote Joseph de Maistre, "is precisely the counterpart of the pernicious propaganda of the previous century, and ... we are absolutely certain we are not deceived, doing in favor of the good precisely what it did with such deplorable success for evil."

In Austria, the inheritance of Amicizia was received and renewed by St. Clemente Maria Hofbauer, who gathered around himself a group of famous converts such as Friedrich Schlegel and his wife, Dorothea Veit, and Adam Müller. This circle exercised notable influence over the Catholic Restoration in Austria, especially after the Congress of Vienna. They cultivated the ideal of a monarchy that would be free of any residue of the Enlightenment and of Josephinism, returning to the purity of medieval and Counter-Reformation sources.

These intellectuals and others who followed them in the nineteenth century charted the development and metaphysical underpinnings of the French Revolution.

## 7. THE POPES AND THE COUNTER-REVOLUTION

The French Revolution was denounced by all successive popes, beginning with Pius VI in his address on June 17, 1793, on the martyrdom of the king of France, Louis XVI:

> After the continuous series of blasphemies which began in France, who will continue to doubt that the first plots of these conspirators that unsettle and subvert all Europe must be imputed to hatred of religion? No one can deny that the same cause led to the tragic death of Louis XVI.

*Annum Ingressi* can also be considered a counterrevolutionary manifesto, published by Pope Leo XIII (r. 1878–1903) on March 19, 1902, in the twenty-fifth year of his pontificate. Leo XIII summarized in it the history of the struggles and triumphs of the Church, with the intention of "considering in its genesis, in its causes, in its various forms, the war that is being waged to the harm of the Church, to highlight its baleful consequences, and to point out remedies."

The pontiff identified the phases of the anti-Christian revolution in the rebellion of the "so-called Reformation of the sixteenth century." In fact, "The baleful and deleterious systems of rationalism and pantheism came out of this system, as well as naturalism and materialism, which established ancient errors under new appearances, already refuted victoriously by the Fathers and apologists of Christian ages."

The French Revolution was a consequence of Protestantism, which in turn produced communist egalitarianism. From practical atheism there necessarily follows, according to Leo XIII, an overthrow of the moral and social order, which has its logical and coherent outcome in political and social anarchy. Every phase of this revolutionary process is connected. The return to Christianity, actualized and identified with the Catholic Church, is the only solution to the evils that afflict society, and which can only get worse. As the pope states:

> The main documents of our pontificate were directed precisely toward the aim of denouncing these evils and indicating in the doctrine of the Church the only wholesome remedy, the encyclicals on Christian philosophy, on human freedom, on Christian matrimony, on the sect of the Freemasons, on public powers, on the Christian constitution of states, on socialism, on the principle obligations of Christian citizens, on the worker question, and on related issues.

The logical (rather than chronological) order that the pope established among his encyclicals confirms that *Aeterni Patris* constituted the cornerstone of his thought, and that the other encyclicals were developments of this.

The letter concludes with words of faith in the final victory of the persecuted Church:

> Nineteen centuries of life, lived out amid the ebb and flow of human events, teach us that the tempests do not sink the ship, but rather pass. Final success is reserved to the One who lovingly and masterfully watches over His immaculate Bride, and of whom it is written: "Jesus Christ is the same yesterday, today, and forever!" (Heb. 13:8).

With this faith, the Church Militant struggles and lives on in the storms of history.

# About the Author

ROBERTO DE MATTEI IS a historian who has taught at the University of Rome, "La Sapienza," the University of Cassino, and the European University of Rome. From 2003 to 2011, he served two terms as vice president of the National Research Council of Italy. He is the president of the Lepanto Foundation and the director of the periodical *Radici Cristiane* and of the information agency *Corrispondenza Romana*. He has collaborated with numerous newspapers and periodicals, such as *L'Osservatore Romano, Libero, Il Giornale d'Italia, Il Tempo*, and *Il Foglio*, and is the author of more than thirty books translated into multiple languages, among which are *The Second Vatican Council: A History Never Written*, which received the Acqui Storia Prize in 2011; *The Rally of Leo XIII: The Failure of a Pastoral Project; Criticism of Revolution in the Thought of Augusto Del Noce; Pius V: The History of a Holy Pope; Turkey in Europe: Beneficial or Catastrophe?*; and *The Church in the Storms*, taken from conversations broadcast on Radio Maria.

# Sophia Institute

Sophia Institute is a nonprofit institution that seeks to nurture the spiritual, moral, and cultural life of souls and to spread the Gospel of Christ in conformity with the authentic teachings of the Roman Catholic Church.

Sophia Institute Press fulfills this mission by offering translations, reprints, and new publications that afford readers a rich source of the enduring wisdom of mankind.

Sophia Institute also operates the popular online resource CatholicExchange.com. *Catholic Exchange* provides world news from a Catholic perspective as well as daily devotionals and articles that will help readers to grow in holiness and live a life consistent with the teachings of the Church.

In 2013, Sophia Institute launched Sophia Institute for Teachers to renew and rebuild Catholic culture through service to Catholic education. With the goal of nurturing the spiritual, moral, and cultural life of souls, and an abiding respect for the role and work of teachers, we strive to provide materials and programs that are at once enlightening to the mind and ennobling to the heart; faithful and complete, as well as useful and practical.

Sophia Institute gratefully recognizes the Solidarity Association for preserving and encouraging the growth of our apostolate over the course of many years. Without their generous and timely support, this book would not be in your hands.

www.SophiaInstitute.com
www.CatholicExchange.com
www.SophiaTeachers.org

Sophia Institute Press® is a registered trademark of Sophia Institute.
Sophia Institute is a tax-exempt institution as defined by the
Internal Revenue Code, Section 501(c)(3). Tax ID 22-2548708.